`OleRevertServerDoc`	Notifies library of a server document reverted to saved state	`DdeCmpStringHandles`	Compares two string handles
`OleRevokeClientDoc`	Notifies library of closed client document	`DdeConnect`	Establishes a conversation
`OleRevokeServerDoc`	Notifies library of closed server document	`DdeConnectList`	Establishes multiple conversations
`OleRevokeObject`	Revokes access to an object	`DdeCreateDataHandle`	Creates a data handle
		`DdeCreateStringHandle`	Creates a string handle
`OleRevokeServer`	Revokes a registered server	`DdeDisconnect`	Terminates a conversation
`OleSavedClientDoc`	Notifies library that a client document has been saved	`DdeDisconnectList`	Destroys a conversation list
`OleSavedServerDoc`	Notifies library that a server document has been saved	`DdeEnableCallback`	Enables or disables one or more conversations
`OleSaveToStream`	Saves an object to a stream	`DdeFreeDataHandle`	Frees a global memory object
`OleSetBounds`	Sets an object's bounding rectangle	`DdeFreeStringHandle`	Frees a string handle
`OleSetColorScheme`	Specifies the client's preferred palette	`DdeGetData`	Copies a global memory object to a buffer
`OleSetData`	Sends an object's data to the server	`DdeGetLastError`	Returns the last DDEML error
`OleSetHostNames`	Sets client and object names	`DdeInitialize`	Registers an application with the DDEML
`OleSetLinkUpdateOptions`	Sets link update options for an object	`DdeKeepStringHandle`	Increments the reference count for a string handle
`OleSetTargetDevice`	Specifies the target output device for an object	`DdeNameService`	Registers or unregisters a service name
`OleUnblockServer`	Processes a request from the queue created by `OleBlockServer`	`DdePostAdvise`	Prompts a server to send advise data
		`DdeQueryConvInfo`	Gets information about a conversation
`OleUnlockServer`	Releases a locked server	`DdeQueryNextServer`	Gets the next handle in a conversation list
`OleUpdate`	Updates an object	`DdeQueryString`	Copies string-handle text to a buffer

DDEML API

		`DdeReconnect`	Reconnects a conversation with a server
`DdeAbandonTransaction`	Abandons an asynchronous transaction	`DdeSetUserHandle`	Attaches a user-defined handle with a transaction
`DdeAccessData`	Accesses a global memory object	`DdeUnaccessData`	Frees a global memory object
`DdeAddData`	Adds data to a global memory object	`DdeUninitialize`	Frees DDEML resources
`DdeClientTransaction`	Begins a transaction		

Windows Programmer's Guide to

OLE/DDE

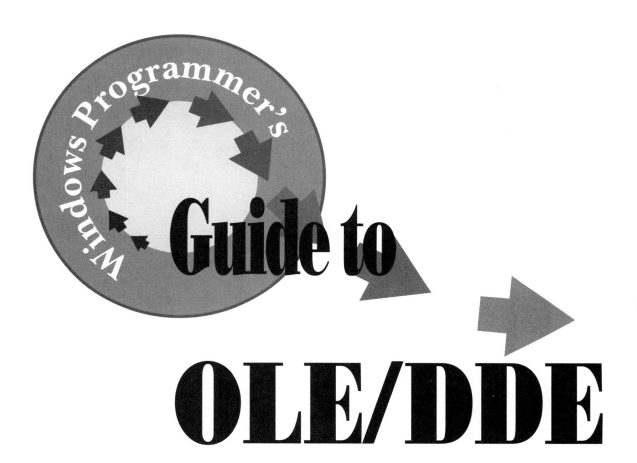

Windows Programmer's Guide to OLE/DDE

Guide to

OLE/DDE

Jeffrey Clark

SAMS

A Division of Prentice Hall Computer Publishing

11711 North College, Carmel, Indiana 46032 USA

To my wife, Wendy, who was understanding and supportive beyond my expectations while I wrote my first book.

Composed in New Baskerville and MCPdigital by
Prentice Hall Computer Publishing

Printed in the United States of America

Screen reproductions in this book were created by means of the program Collage Plus from Inner Media, Inc., Hollis, NH.

Publisher
Richard K. Swadley

Publishing Manager
Joseph Wikert

Managing Editor
Neweleen A. Trebnik

Acquisitions Editor
Greg Croy

Development Editor
Stacy Hiquet

Production Editors
Lori Cates
Cheri Clark

Editorial Coordinator
Becky Freeman

Editorial Assistant
Rosemarie Graham

Project Coordinator
San Dee Phillips

Technical Editors
Greg Guntle
Mike Sax

Cover Designer
Jean Bisesi

Production Director
Jeff Valler

Production Manager
Corinne Walls

Book Designer
Michele Laseau

Production Analyst
Mary Beth Wakefield

Page Layout Coordinator
Matthew Morrill

Proofreading/Indexing Coordinator
Joelynn Gifford

Graphics Image Specialist
Dennis Sheehan

Production
Phil Worthington, Dennis Clay
Hager, Michelle Cleary, Carrie
Keesling, Phil Kitchel, Laurie Lee,
Cindy L. Phipps, Caroline Roop,
Kelli Widdifield

Indexer
Jeanne Clark

Overview

Contents

Acknowledgments

I never thought writing a book would be such a large and complicated task. It was through the support and the help of others that this book became a reality. I would like to thank the following people and organizations:

To Prentice Hall Computer Publishing for giving me a chance to write this book and also for helping me make key decisions about the format and the content of the book. In particular, I would like to thank Joseph Wikert, Stacy Hiquet, Lori Cates, Cheri Clark, Mike Sax, and Greg Guntle for their guidance and help.

To Microsoft Corporation for their great technical support during the beta testing of the Windows 3.1 SDK.

To the many people who participated in the CompuServe WINBTDEV forum. Your questions and your advice made this book possible.

To my friends Mike and Steph Watson for providing moral support through their confidence in me.

Trademarks

All terms mentioned in this book that are known to be trademarks or service marks are listed below. In addition, terms suspected of being trademarks or service marks have been appropriately capitalized. Sams cannot attest to the accuracy of this information. Use of a term in this book should not be regarded as affecting the validity of any trademark or service mark.

Gateway 2000 is a trademark of Gateway 2000, Inc.

IBM is a registered trademark of International Business Machines Corporation.

CodeView, Microsoft Mouse, Microsoft Windows, Microsoft Word, and Microsoft Word for Windows are registered trademarks of Microsoft Corporation.

NEC MultiSync is a registered trademark of NEC Home Electronics (USA) Inc.

Introduction

Microsoft Windows is one of the fastest-growing application development platforms. Since the release of Windows 3.0 in May 1990, software development companies have introduced thousands of Windows applications. At the same time, Microsoft Corporation has expanded the Windows platform by making it more robust and adding extensions to the Windows programming API.

Windows 3.1 represents the largest advance to date in the Windows product line. This book covers two of the areas of expansion in the Windows API: the Dynamic Data Exchange Management Library (DDEML) and Object Linking and Embedding (OLE). Table I.1 shows the evolution of the Windows API.

Table I.1. The evolution of the Windows API.

Version	Release Date	Number of Function Calls
Windows 1.0	11/85	379
Windows 2.0	11/87	458
Windows 3.0	5/90	578
Windows 3.1	4/92	771

The preceding table represents only part of the Windows API, because there are Multimedia and Pen Extensions comprising another 275 functions. Developers of Windows 3.1 applications have the large task of understanding some 468 new functions, for a total of 1,046 functions. This book can help developers who need to understand the DDEML and OLE APIs.

Overview

This book is for intermediate to advanced Windows programmers who want to learn about the DDEML and OLE APIs. This book was written with the assumption that the reader understands the programming principles covered in beginning-level programming books. The chapters with example programs in this book focus on OLE or DDEML and do not explain basic Windows programming.

The book is presented in two parts, each containing four chapters. Part I covers the DDEML API. Chapter 1 is a conceptual chapter that reviews the DDE protocol in terms of message-based DDE. Chapters 2 through 4 cover the DDEML API in detail through the use of example applications. Chapter 2 uses an example DDEML server application as the focal point of discussion. Chapter 3 completes the client/server loop of a DDEML program by presenting a DDEML client application. Chapter 4 explains an extension to the DDEML API for monitor applications.

Part II discusses OLE. Chapter 5 is a conceptual chapter that introduces the basic structures and procedures of developing an OLE application. Chapter 6 implements an example OLE server application. An example OLE client application is covered in Chapter 7. The last chapter of the book is an introduction to developing an OLE object handler.

The most difficult aspect of writing this book was providing example programs that demonstrate complete DDEML and OLE applications. The result of this endeavor is large applications that consume many pages in the book. This is particularly true with the OLE applications. From a personal standpoint, I prefer to read code in conjunction with supporting text. From a practical standpoint, I had to keep the book to a manageable size. Thus, there is significantly more code than text. The combination of the two should provide you with the details required to write OLE and DDEML applications.

I use the medium memory model for the example programs in the book because I view these programs as starting points to real applications. Because I have no idea how large a real application will become, the medium memory model is more appropriate because it is easier to write very large applications using the medium memory model than it is to write them using the small memory model.

Required Programming Tools

You need Windows 3.1 and a C or C++ compiler that includes the libraries and header files required to develop Windows 3.1 applications, or the Microsoft Windows 3.1 Software Development Kit (SDK). I used the following development tools to write the example programs in this book:

Windows 3.1

Microsoft C 6.0a

Microsoft Windows 3.1 Software Development Kit

The minimum hardware requirements for developing Windows 3.1 applications are the same as for running Windows 3.1. They are an 80286 (or higher) PC with 640K of conventional memory, plus 256K of extended memory, a display adapter supported by Windows, a mouse, and a hard disk that can hold Windows 3.1 (at least 6M) and your development tools.

My hardware configuration is

Gateway 2000 486/33

16M memory

200M hard disk

1024K Diamond SpeedStar VGA Adapter

NEC Multisync 3D monitor

Monochrome adapter and monitor

Microsoft Mouse

I use the monochrome monitor for debugging. This came from a need for dual screen debugging under Windows 3.0 with the CodeView debugger. I have found, however, that using two monitors is more productive, although the 3.1 SDK includes CodeView for a single monitor.

Conventions Used in This Book

I use a few of the new `typedefs` from the Windows 3.1 header files. For example, `CALLBACK` replaces `FAR PASCAL`, and `HINSTANCE` replaces `HANDLE` for instance variable types. I believe that these types are better at documenting Windows programs. These types were added to the Windows 3.1 SDK for the `STRICT` programming option. I do not use the `STRICT` programming option, however, because that would introduce another level of detail to the book.

I use a **`bold monospace`** typeface for Windows functions and a normal `monospace` typeface for application-specific functions. For example,

SendMessage() is a Windows function and `ProcessClientMessage()` is an application-specific function. All program listings are printed in a `monospace` typeface. Placeholders within code lines are set in *monospace italic* type. When I introduce a new term in the text, I use an *italic* typeface. Hot keys for menu items are shown in **boldface** text.

Some program lines in the book were too long for one line; however, these lines must not be broken when you type them in your program. Such lines are marked with the code continuation icon, as in the following example:

```
IDS_QUERYLINKS,      "The file contains links to\nother
     documents.\nUpdate links now?"
```

Example Programs

The example programs in this book were compiled using Microsoft C 6.0a. To use the Microsoft C/C++ 7.0 compiler, you need to make a few changes to the source files. These changes are outlined in the README.NOW file on the companion diskette.

Dynamic Data
Exchange

PART

I

Dynamic Data Exchange Concepts

Dynamic data exchange (DDE) is a method of interprocess communication. *Interprocess communication* (IPC) consists of passing data between processes and synchronizing events. DDE uses shared memory to exchange data between applications and a protocol to synchronize the passing of data. Windows also uses the clipboard, dynamic link libraries (DLLs), and object linking and embedding (OLE) for interprocess communication.

The clipboard consists of functions that use global memory to transfer data between applications. This global memory is not the same as the clipboard program, which is an application that displays data from the global memory. The clipboard typically transfers data between applications on a one-time basis. An example of this is copying a range of cells from a spreadsheet and pasting the cells to a word processing document. The next access to the clipboard most likely will cut or copy different data to the clipboard rather than paste the same data.

A DLL is a module that contains code, data, and Windows resources that multiple Windows programs can access. Multiple programs can share one instance of a DLL. Only one instance of a DLL can exist at time, however. A DLL and an application use a global memory block to share data. To accomplish this, an application calls a function in a DLL that allocates a global memory block. Then the application and the DLL use the global memory block to exchange data. When the application calling the function in the DLL terminates, the global memory block is deallocated. The life span of the global memory block can be only as long as the life of the application calling the DLL. Thus, two applications cannot access the same global memory block allocated by a DLL.

OLE is a protocol that uses the DDE protocol. The OLE protocol, on an elementary basis, is a set of DDE Execute commands. This relationship is one of the reasons I discuss DDE before OLE in this book. Thus, when you read about DDE, remember that DDE is an integral part of OLE. The following topics start the discussion of DDE:

- The DDE protocol

- DDE messages

- The Dynamic Data Exchange Management Library

The DDE Protocol

The DDE protocol is a set of rules that all DDE applications should follow. It is possible to ignore the DDE protocol when you write your applications; however, the results may be unpredictable if you do. This is especially true when you are writing a set of DDE applications that work in a closed environment without interaction with other DDE applications. When it comes time to update a nonprotocol compliant application to allow it to communicate with someone else's DDE application, the update can be difficult because the other application expects a standard method of communication. Additionally, if a user accesses a DDE application that does not follow the DDE protocol via an application that does, the application may not perform correctly, or even may hang the system. In other words, to save time and headaches later, write DDE applications that adhere to the DDE protocol.

The DDE protocol is applicable to the two types of DDE applications. The first type is message-based DDE applications, whereas the second is Dynamic Data Exchange Management Library (DDEML) applications. DDEML applications use a Dynamic Link Library (DLL) that comes with Windows 3.1. I will describe the DDE protocol using message-based DDE. This is more complex than using the DDEML; however, it shows what DDEML does under the hood. Additionally, understanding message-based DDE provides a good base to understanding OLE, because OLE uses message-based DDE in its internals.

> **Note:** Because message-based DDE and DDEML applications use the DDE protocol, both of these types of applications can communicate with each other. If either of these types of applications does not follow the DDE protocol, however, communications between applications may fail.

Conversation Synchronization

DDE applications fall into four categories: *client, server, client/server,* and *monitor.* A DDE conversation occurs between a client application and a server application. A client application requests data or services from a server application. A server responds to a client application's request for data or services. A client/server application is both a client application and a server application, thus requesting and providing information. A monitor application can intercept DDE messages from all other DDE applications but cannot act on them. Monitor applications are useful for debugging purposes.

DDE applications can have multiple concurrent conversations. The DDE protocol specifies that messages within a conversation must be handled synchronously. An application can, however, switch between conversations asynchronously. An example of this would be an application with two conversations that receives four messages. Messages one, two, and four are for the first conversation, whereas message three is for the second conversation. Messages one, two, and four must be processed in sequence. The application could process the third message before or after any of the other messages, however, assuming the application has received the third message.

DDE applications must uniquely define all conversations. The client and server applications window handles define a conversation. Thus, a client can have conversations with multiple servers and manage the conversations with the window handle pairs. What if, however, a client application wants to have multiple conversations with a single server? If there is only one client/server window handle pair, managing the conversations would be impossible. You can eliminate this situation by creating a new window in your DDE applications for each conversation. Don't rely on a third-party application to create a new window for each conversation. You can ensure that you have a unique pair of window handles for each conversation, if your program creates a new window for each conversation.

Application Names, Topic Names, and Item Names

DDE applications use a three-tiered identification system to distinguish themselves from other DDE applications. An *application name* is at the top of the hierarchy. The application name refers to a server application. A *topic name* further defines a server application. Server applications can support one or more topics. Each topic can have one or more *item names*, which identify the details within a topic name.

An example of a three-tiered identification system is a server application that retrieves quotations from stock markets. The executable name for the server application is QUOTES.EXE. The server application, however, uses the application name *StockQuotes*. The server supports multiple stock markets and multiple stocks within each stock market. The topic names the server uses are

NYSE, AMEX, and *NASDAQ*. Within each of these topic names are item names. The item names identify the stocks, such as IBM and Intel. A client application wanting to get the value of Intel's stock would use the application name *StockQuotes*, the topic name *NASDAQ*, and the item name *Intel* in its DDE communications.

Conversation Initialization

Besides processing messages in the correct order, it is important for applications to send or post messages at an appropriate time. A DDE conversation begins when a client application initiates a conversation by sending a `WM_DDE_INITIATE` message with an application and a topic name. For a conversation to begin, there also must be a server application to respond to the `WM_DDE_INITIATE` message. For this to work, however, the client application should provide a little more information about itself and which server it wants. So when the client application sends the `WM_DDE_INITIATE` message, it passes its window handle and specifies the application and topic for the conversation.

You can think of starting a DDE conversation as being similar to starting a conversation with a group of people standing in a dark room. If you knew the names of the people, you could say, "George, this is Joe. How would you like to talk about programming Windows in assembly language?" A number of things could occur at this point. George may have left the room just before the lights went out. Thus, you wouldn't get a reply from George. Or George might think that you were insane and just ignore you, because he wouldn't waste his time programming Windows in assembly language, let alone talk about it. Or the group of people could be total bit-heads, and three of them could have George for a name. In this case, you would get a response from all three. Then there is the last situation: Just one George is in the room, and he wants to talk to you.

This is fine when you know the people in the room and have some idea of what to talk about. But what if you didn't know any of the people or their interests? The polite thing to do would be to say, "My name is Joe. Is there anyone who wants to talk about anything?" Then everyone who was willing to talk would reply by stating their names and the things they would like to talk about. You can achieve similar results in a DDE application by sending the `WM_DDE_INITIATE` message and specifying `NULL` for the application name and topic name.

A well-behaved DDE application should resolve all potential results of sending an initiate message. The most probable situation to arise is that the initiate message gets no response. At this point, the client application should prompt the user to start the server application; otherwise, the client application won't be able to continue. The second situation is when multiple servers respond to the initiate message. The client application will have to terminate all unwanted conversations by using the WM_DDE_TERMINATE message.

Exchanges in a Conversation

After establishing a DDE conversation, the client and server applications begin their real work: exchanging data and performing services. Exchanging data seems appropriate for a dynamic data exchange application, but server applications can also perform services. A service might be to open a file or connect to another computer and download a file. The WM_DDE_EXECUTE message specifies that a client application wants a server application to perform a service. The WM_DDE_EXECUTE message is passed with a string that contains a command for the server application. DDE protocol defines the format for the string; however, it does not define the contents of the string.

Data exchanging can occur in three ways. First, a client application can request data on a one-time basis from a server application. In this case, the client application sends a WM_DDE_REQUEST message. Then the server application acknowledges the request with the WM_DDE_ACK or WM_DDE_DATA message. If the server application responds with a WM_DDE_DATA message, the client application can access the data. If the server application cannot respond to the request, it sends a negative reply with the WM_DDE_ACK message.

The second method of exchanging data is when a client application sends data to a server application. When this occurs, the client application *pokes* data to the server application using the WM_DDE_POKE message. When the server application receives this message, it responds to the client application with a WM_DDE_ACK message specifying whether it accepted the data.

The third way data exchange takes place is when the server application advises the client application that an item has changed value. This request can take two forms. In the first form, the server application sends notification that the data item has changed, but the server application does not send data. In the second form, the server sends the data every time the data changes. The client application requests this by sending a WM_DDE_ADVISE message to the server application. The server application responds to this message with a WM_DDE_ACK message. Then each time the data changes, the server application sends a WM_DDE_DATA message. If the client application wants only notification, the WM_DDE_DATA message does not include data. The latter method is useful when

a data item, such as a bitmap, is time-consuming to render. When the client application no longer wants to receive data or notification from the server, it sends a `WM_DDE_UNADVISE` message.

The methods for exchanging data are often associated with the term *link*. A link denotes how data is exchanged. If a client application requests data and the server application immediately sends the data to the client application, this is a *cold link*. A *warm link* is when a server application advises a client application that a data item has changed values, but does not send the value to the client application. A *hot link* occurs when the server application sends the new value for a data item to the client application every time the value has changed.

Conversation Termination

Either a client or a server application can terminate a conversation. An application sends a `WM_DDE_TERMINATE` message when it wants to terminate a conversation. When the partner in the conversation receives this message, it should also post a `WM_DDE_TERMINATE` message. This must occur before an application calls the **PostQuitMessage()** function and leaves its main message loop. It can occur at any time during a conversation, however.

DDE Messages

The heart of DDE protocol is the DDE message. The DDE protocol defines the when, how, and where of DDE message use. The format for DDE messages specifies that wParam contains the handle to the sender's window. The lParam parameter contains low-order and high-order words that specify DDE message-specific information. You should use **SendMessage()** to issue the `WM_DDE_INITIATE` message and the `WM_DDE_ACK` message in reply to a `WM_DDE_INITIATE` message. Otherwise, use **PostMessage()** for all other DDE messages. The handle for the **SendMessage()** or **PostMessage()** function is either the handle to the server or client application after a DDE conversation exists, or –1 when the client application attempts to initiate a conversation. A handle of –1 in the **SendMessage()** function broadcasts the message to all nonchild windows on a system.

When you send DDE messages, the lParam parameter contains two 16-bit words: a low-order word and a high-order word. The MAKELONG macro combines these two words to form one 32-bit value.

```
SendMessage(hwnd, msg, wParam, MAKELONG(loworder,highorder));
```

The lParam parameter for DDE messages contains a combination of handles to global memory blocks and *atoms*. Atoms are integers—16-bit words—that identify a character string. DDE messages pass atoms rather than strings because that is a more compact method of specifying an array of characters.

Windows supports two types of atoms. The first type is a local atom. This is not a concern in programming DDE applications, because local atoms cannot be shared between two applications. The second type of atom is a global atom. DDE applications store global atoms in Windows' *global atom table* that exists in a shared data segment within a Windows DLL. This allows all Windows programs to access atoms.

Four atom functions are commonly used in DDE applications: **GlobalAddAtom()**, **GlobalDeleteAtom()**, **GlobalFindAtom()**, and **GlobalGetAtomName()**. As you might suspect, **GlobalAddAtom()** adds an atom to the global atom table. The first call to **GlobalAddAtom()** inserts a string in the global atom table and returns a unique value—the atom—that identifies the string. **GlobalAddAtom()** also maintains a *reference count* for each atom. The reference count is initially set to 1. Calling **GlobalAddAtom()** multiple times for an identical string increments the reference count on each call. **GlobalDeleteAtom()** decrements the reference count. When the reference count reaches 0, the string is deleted from the global atom table.

```
ATOM aAtom;

// string is added to table, reference count = 1,
// aAtom contains a unique value

aAtom = GlobalAddAtom(lpsz);

// reference count = 0, string is removed from table

GlobalDeleteAtom(aAtom);
```

GlobalFindAtom() returns an atom for an existing string in the global atom table. If the string is not found, **GlobalFindAtom()** returns 0. A call to **GlobalFindAtom()** does not change the reference count of an atom. **GlobalGetAtomName()** retrieves the character string associated with an atom. It returns the number of bytes of the string copied, or 0 if the string does not exist.

```
ATOM aAtom;

aAtom = GlobalFindAtom(lpsz);
nLen = GlobalGetAtomName(aAtom, lpBuf, sizeof lpBuf);
```

Here's a typical example of two DDE applications using atoms to initiate a conversation:

```
// Client Application

ATOM aApplication, aTopic;

aApplication = GlobalAddAtom("GeorgeServer");
aTopic = GlobalAddAtom("WinMASM");
SendMessage(-1,WM_DDE_INITIATE,hwndClient,
                    MAKELONG(aApplication, aTopic);
GlobalDeleteAtom(aApplication);
GlobalDeleteAtom(aTopic);


// Server Application

case WM_DDE_INITIATE:
    aApplication = GlobalAddAtom("GeorgeServer");
    aTopic = GlobalAddAtom("WinMASM");
    if ((LOWORD(lParam) == aApplication ¦¦ !LOWORD(lParam)) &&
        (HIWORD(lParam) == aTopic ¦¦ !HIWORD(lParam)))
         if(!SendMessage(wParam, WM_DDE_ACK, hwndServer,
                            MAKELONG(aApplication,aTopic))

            {
            GlobalDeleteAtom(aApplication);
            GlobalDeleteAtom(aTopic);
            }
    return FALSE;
```

Besides atoms, DDE applications pass handles to global memory blocks in DDE messages. The global memory blocks contain DDE structures, or data. Definitions for the DDE structures are in dde.h, and they correspond to DDE messages. To allocate global memory for a DDE application, use **GlobalAlloc()** with the GMEM_DDESHARE parameter.

```
hData = GlobalAlloc(GHND ¦ GMEM_DDESHARE, sizeof(datablock));
```

With these preliminaries out of the way, we can forge on and discuss DDE messages in detail. Table 1.1 summarizes information pertaining to DDE messages.

Table 1.1. DDE messages.

DDE Messages	hwnd	wParam	Low-order Word in lParam	High-order Word in lParam	DDE Structure
WM_DDE_ACK					
Reply to INITIATE[1]	hwndClient	hwndServer	aApplication	aTopic	
Reply to EXECUTE[2]	hwndClient	hwndServer	wStatus	hCommands	DDEACK
Other[2]	hwndServer or hwndClient	hwndServer or hwndClient	wStatus	aItem	DDEACK
WM_DDE_ADVISE[2] DDEADVISE	hwndServer	hwndClient	hOptions	aItem	
WM_DDE_DATA[2]	hwndClient	hwndServer	hData	aItem	DDEDATA
WM_DDE_EXECUTE[2]	hwndServer	hwndClient	(Reserved)	hCommands	
WM_DDE_INITIATE[1]	−1	hwndClient	aApplication	aTopic	
WM_DDE_POKE[2]	hwndServer	hwndClient	hData	aItem	DDEPOKE
WM_DDE_REQUEST[2]	hwndServer	hwndClient	cfFormat	aItem	
WM_DDE_TERMINATE[2]	hwndServer or hwndClient	hwndServer or hwndClient	(Reserved)	(Reserved)	
WM_DDE_UNADVISE[2]	hwndServer	hwndClient	(Reserved)	aItem	

[1]*Use* **SendMessage**
[2]*Use* **PostMessage**

WM_DDE_ACK

The WM_DDE_ACK message notifies an application that its conversation partner has received its message. The exception to this is the WM_DDE_TERMINATE message and sometimes the WM_DDE_REQUEST message. The WM_DDE_ACK message has three formats, one to respond to a WM_DDE_INITIATE message, another for WM_DDE_EXECUTE, and a third for all other DDE messages.

When responding to a WM_DDE_INITIATE message, a server application sends a WM_DDE_ACK message with an lParam that contains atoms which identify the application and topic names. The other two formats of the WM_DDE_ACK message use the DDEACK data structure.

```
typedef struct {
        unsigned bAppReturnCode:8,
                reserved:6,
                fBusy:1,
        fAck:1;
} DDEACK;
```

The member fAck is set to 0 or 1, in which 1 is a positive acknowledgment and 0 is negative. If an application is busy and cannot respond to a DDE request, it sets the member fBusy to 1. fBusy can be set only when fAck is 0. The bAppReturnCode member can contain application-specific return codes.

When a server application responds to a WM_DDE_EXECUTE message, it uses the DDEACK data structure in the low-order word of lParam and a handle to a global memory block that contains a command string in the high-order word of lParam. Because the DDEACK structure is the same size as a WORD value, it can be passed as a value. Other structures used in DDE messages are allocated as global memory blocks and sent as handles in the low-order word of lParam. The last format for WM_DDE_ACK also uses the DDEACK data structure in the low-order word of lParam; however, the high-order word of lParam contains an atom for the item name for which the response is sent.

WM_DDE_INITIATE and *WM_DDE_TERMINATE*

The WM_DDE_INITIATE and WM_DDE_TERMINATE messages mark the beginning and the end of a conversation. When a client application wants to start a conversation, it sends a WM_DDE_INITIATE message. The lParam of the WM_DDE_INITIATE command contains atoms that specify the application name in the low-order word and the topic name in the high-order word. If a client application wants to query all servers and topics, the application and topic name should be NULL.

A client application must use the **SendMessage()** function—not **PostMessage()**— to send a WM_DDE_INITIATE message. The **SendMessage()** function does not return until the processing of a message is complete, whereas the **PostMessage()** function returns immediately. This difference is important to the WM_DDE_INITIATE message, because the client application calls **GlobalDeleteAtom()** to delete the application and topic name after **SendMessage()** returns. The use of **SendMessage()** ensures that application and topic atoms and their reference counts are valid. The use of **PostMessage()** potentially would allow the client application to delete the atoms before the server processes the WM_DDE_INITIATE message.

The handle parameter in the **SendMessage()** function can contain a handle to the server's window if the client application had a previous conversation with the server. Otherwise, the handle should be –1, which broadcasts the WM_DDE_INITIATE message to all nonchild windows on the system.

When the server application receives a WM_DDE_INITIATE message, it should first create atoms for the application name and topic names it supports. If the atoms have the same values as those in the lParam of the WM_DDE_INITIATE message, the server should respond with a WM_DDE_ACK message with the atoms the server application created for its application and topic names in the lParam. If the lParam of the WM_DDE_INITIATE message contains a NULL for either the application name or the topic name atom, the server should respond with the correct number of WM_DDE_ACK messages. The server should use **SendMessage()** for the WM_DDE_ACK message. If **SendMessage()** fails, the server should delete the atoms created before sending the WM_DDE_ACK message. Table 1.2 outlines how the server application should respond to a WM_DDE_INITIATE message.

Table 1.2. Responding to WM_DDE_INITIATE.

lParam	*Server Response*
low-order word = NULL high-order word = NULL	Create atoms for application name and topic names; send WM_DDE_ACK messages for each topic name the server supports.
low-order word = NULL high-order word = aTopic	Create atoms for application name and topic names; if aTopic matches one of the server's topics, send *one* WM_DDE_ACK message for that topic.
low-order word = aApplication high-order word = NULL	Create atoms for application name and topic names; if aApplication matches the server's application name, send WM_DDE_ACK messages for each topic name the server supports.
low-order word = aApplication high-order word = aTopic	Create atoms for application name and topics; if aApplication matches the server's application name and aTopic matches one of the server's topic names, send *one* WM_DDE_ACK message for that application/topic name pair.

When the server successfully sends a WM_DDE_ACK message, the conversation begins. This introduces several complexities to the client application if the server sends a WM_DDE_ACK message for multiple topics or if multiple servers respond. The client application is responsible for saving the handles for each server window. The client application then must determine which conversations to keep and which to terminate, which takes us to the WM_DDE_TERMINATE message. The WM_DDE_TERMINATE message ends a conversation. The protocol for this message is simple. The sending application posts the WM_DDE_TERMINATE message, and then the receiving application posts another WM_DDE_TERMINATE message to the sending application. Only the handle and wParam change in this message.

WM_DDE_POKE

A client application can update data in a server application with the WM_DDE_POKE message. This message uses the DDEPOKE structure and an atom that specifies the item name that the server application should update. The low-order word of lParam contains a handle to the DDEPOKE structure. The high-order word of lParam contains the atom for the item name. The definition for DDEPOKE is as follows:

```
typedef struct {
        unsigned unused:13,
            fRelease:1,
            fReserved:2;
        int cfFormat;
        BYTE Value[1];
} DDEPOKE;
```

The client application allocates a global memory block for the size DDEPOKE structure and the poked data. The poked data size is the size of the data rendered in the chosen clipboard format. The client application copies the data starting at the Value member of the DDEPOKE structure. The value of the structure member cfFormat is the clipboard format of the data, in other words, CF_TEXT or CF_BITMAP. The fRelease member contains 0 or 1. If fRelease is set to 0, the server application should not free the global memory block; otherwise, the server should free the global memory block. If the server application does not free the global memory block, the deletion is the responsibility of the client application when it receives the WM_DDE_ACK message from the server application.

> **Note:** In versions of Windows before SDK 3.0, DDEPOKE was incorrectly
> defined. Subsequent versions of the SDK contain the following
> structure to allow for programming around applications that use the
> incorrectly defined structure:
>
> ```
> typedef struc{
>     unsigned unused:12,
>             fAck:1,
>             fRelease:1,
>             fReserved:1,
>             fAckReq:1,
>     int cfFormat;
>     BYTE rgb[1];
> } DDEUP;
> ```

When the server application receives the WM_DDE_POKE message, it should
attempt to set the item specified by the atom in the message. If the server is
successful, it posts a WM_DDE_ACK message with the DDEACK structure member
fAck set to TRUE. If the server is unsuccessful or does not recognize the atom,
it posts a WM_DDE_ACK message with fAck set to FALSE.

Here's a code fragment of a client posting a WM_DDE_POKE message:

```
ATOM aItem;
HANDLE hData;
char ach[STRINGSIZE];
LPDDEPOKE lpPokeData;

hData = GlobalAlloc(GHND | GMEM_DDESHARE,
                    sizeof(DDEPOKE) + STRINGSIZE);
if(!hData)
    return FALSE;

lpPokeData = (DDEPOKE FAR *) GlobalLock(hData);
if(!lpPokeData)
    {
    GlobalFree(hData);
```

```
     return FALSE;
     }

lstrcpy((LSPTR)&lpPokeData->Value[0], ach);
lpPokeData->cfFormat = CF_TEXT;
lpPokeData->fRelease = FALSE;
GlobalUnlock(hData);
aItem = GlobalAddAtom("Poked Data");

if(!PostMessage(hwndServer, WM_DDE_POKE, hwndClient,
              MAKELONG(hData, aItem)))

    {
    GlobalFree(hData);
    GlobalDeleteAtom(aItem);
    return FALSE;
    }
```

On the server side of things, the window message loop would look something like this:

```
case WM_DDE_POKE:
     hData = LOWORD(lParam);
     aItem = HIWORD(lParam);

     lpPokeData = (DDEPOKE FAR *)GlobalLock(hData);
     if(!lpPokeData)
         { /* Negative ack */
         PostMessage(hwndClient, WM_DDE_ACK,hwndServer,
                   MAKELONG(0, aItem));
         return FALSE;
         }
      else
         {
         if(lpPokeData->cfFormat == CF_TEXT)
             strcpy(szItem, lpPokeData->Value);
         else
             { /* negative ack */
             PostMessage(hwndClient, hwndServer, WM_DDE_ACK,
                       MAKELONG(0,aItem);
             return FALSE;
             }

         GlobalUnlock(hData);
```

```
                    /* positive ack */

                    PostMessage(hwndClient,WM_DDE_ACK, hwndServer,
                              MAKELONG(0x8000, aItem));
                    }
```

WM_DDE_EXECUTE

The WM_DDE_EXECUTE message allows a client application to post a command to a server application. The client application stores a command string in a global memory block and passes the handle to the global memory block in the high-order word of lParam. The command string must be null-terminated and follow a strict syntax. The command string consists of one or more opcode strings delimited by brackets. Each opcode string can optionally have parameters. Parameters for an opcode are delimited by parentheses. Multiple parameters are separated by commas. Here are a few examples:

[*command1*]

[*command2(parameter1)*]

[*command3(parameter1, parameter2, parameter3)*]

[*command1*][*command3(parameter1, parameter2, parameter3)*]

When the server application receives the WM_DDE_EXECUTE message, it should respond with a WM_DDE_ACK message. If the server successfully executes the command, the DDEACK structure member fAck is set to TRUE. If the command is not successfully executed or the server does not recognize the command, the server posts a WM_DDE_ACK message with fAck set to FALSE. The server also sends the handle to the command back to the client application in the high-order word of lParam. When the client receives the WM_DDE_ACK message from the server, it deletes the command string from global memory.

The following section of code shows the client side of the WM_DDE_EXECUTE message:

```
char * szExecute;
HANDLE hExecute;
LPSTR lpExecute;

if(!hExecute = GlobalAlloc(GMEM_MOVEABLE ¦ GMEM_DDESHARE,
                           (DWORD)lstrlen(szExecute) + 1)))
     return FALSE;
```

```
if(!(lpExecute = GlobalLock(hExecute)))
    {
    GlobalFree(hExecute);
    return FALSE;
    }

lstrcpy(lpExecute, szExecute);
GlobalUnlock(hExecute);

if!PostMessage(hwndServer, WM_DDE_EXECUTE, hwndClient,
            MAKELONG(NULL, hExecute)))
    GlobalFree(hExecute);
```

The following code is for the server side of the WM_DDE_EXECUTE message:

```
HANDLE  hCommand;
LPSTR   lpCommand;
char    achExecute[MAX_EXECUTE_STRING_SIZE + 1];

case WM_DDE_EXECUTE:
    hCommand = HIWORD(lParam);

    if(!(lpCommand = GlobalLock(hCommand)))
        { /* negative ack */
        PostMessage(hwndClient, WM_DDE_ACK, hwndServer,
                MAKELONG(0, hCommand));
        return FALSE;
        }

    if (lstrlen(lpCommand) > MAX_EXECUTE_STRING_SIZE)
        lpCommand[EXECUTE_STRING_MAX_SIZE] = 0;
    lstrcpy(achExecute, lpstrCommand);

    GlobalUnlock(hCommand);

    /* positive acknowledgment */

    PostMessage(hwndClient, WM_DDE_ACK, hwndServer,
            MAKELONG(0x8000, hCommand));
```

WM_DDE_DATA

A server application posts the WM_DDE_DATA message to notify a client application that a data item's value has changed. The lParam parameter contains a handle to the DDEDATA structure in its low-order word and an atom that identifies the data item in the high-order word. When the conversation is a hot or cold link, the server application appends data to the DDEDATA structure. When there is a warm link, the server application posts notification only to the client application. The DDEDATA structure is defined as:

```
typedef struct {
    unsigned unused:12,
             fResponse:1,
             fRelease:1,
             reserved:1,
             fAckReq:1;
      int cfFormat;
      BYTE Value[1];
} DDEDATA;
```

The server sets the fResponse member of DDEDATA to 1 if the WM_DDE_DATA message is a response to a WM_DDE_REQUEST message; otherwise, the server sets it to zero, implying that the response is to a WM_DDE_ADVISE message. The fRelease member of DDEDATA specifies whether the client application is to free the global memory block associated with the data. If the fRelease member is 1, the client application frees the memory; otherwise, the server application frees the memory when it receives a WM_DDE_ACK message from the client application. If the server application wants the client application to acknowledge the WM_DDE_DATA message, the server application sets the fAckReq member of DDEDATA. Obviously, fRelease and fAckReq cannot both be zero.

When the server application sends data to the client application, it should copy the data to the global memory block starting at the Value member of DDEDATA. The size of the global memory block is the size of the DDEDATA structure plus the size of the data in its rendered clipboard format. DDEDATA structure member cfFormat contains the clipboard format. When the server application notifies the client application that a data value has changed but does not provide the data value, the Value member of DDEDATA is NULL.

WM_DDE_REQUEST

A client application requests data from a server application with the WM_DDE_REQUEST message. If the server application can satisfy the request, it posts a WM_DDE_DATA message. If the server application cannot render the data for the client application, it sends a negative WM_DDE_ACK message. When the client application receives a negative WM_DDE_ACK message, it should delete the atom. The client application posts the WM_DDE_REQUEST message with a lParam containing the clipboard format of the data and an atom that specifies the data item. The clipboard format is in the low-order word of lParam. The atom is in the high-order word of lParam.

The following code shows how a client application might post a WM_DDE_REQUEST message.

```
char * szItem;
ATOM   aItem;


aItem = GlobalAddAtom((LPSTR)szItem);


if(!PostMessage(hwndServer,WM_DDE_REQUEST, hwndClient,
                MAKELONG(CF_TEXT,atomItem)))
     GlobalDeleteAtom(atomItem);
```

The server application would respond with:

```
case WM_DDE_REQUEST:
     cfFormat = LOWORD(lParam);
     aItem = HIWORD(lParam);

     if(cfFormat == CF_TEXT)
         {
         hData = GlobalAlloc(GNHD | GMEM_DDESHARE,
                     sizeof(DDEDATA) + lstrlen(&DataItem[0]));
         if(!hData)
             return FALSE;
         lpData = (DDEDATA FAR *) GlobalLock(hData);
         if(!lpData)
             return FALSE;
         lstrcpy(&lpData->Value[0], &DataItem[0]);
         lpData->fAckReq = TRUE;
         lpData->fRelease = TRUE;
         lpData->fResponse = TRUE;
         lpData->cfFormat = CF_TEXT;
```

```
            GlobalUnlock(hData);
            if(!PostMessage(wParam, WM_DDE_DATA, hwndServer,
                        MAKELONG(hData, aItem)))
                {
                GlobalFree(hData);
                GlobalDeleteAtom(aItem);
                }
            return FALSE;
            }
    else
        { /* Negative Ack */
        if(!PostMessage(wParam, WM_DDE_ACK, hwndServer,
                    MAKELONG(0, aItem)))
                GlobalDeleteAtom(aItem);
        }
    return FALSE;
```

Then the client application could process the WM_DDE_DATA message with the
following code:

```
case WM_DDE_DATA:
    hData = LOWORD(lParam);
    aItem = HIWORD(lParam);
    if(!hData)
        {
        GlobalDeleteAtom(aItem);
        return FALSE;
        }
    lpData = (LPDDEDATA) GlobalLock(hData);
    if(!lpData)
        {
        if(!PostMessage(wParam, WM_DDE_ACK, hwndClient,
                    MAKELONG(0, aItem)))
            {
            GlobalDeleteAtom(aItem);
            GlobalFree(hData);
            }
        return FALSE;
        }
    if(lpData->cfFormat == CF_TEXT)
        {
        lstrcpy(achClientsDataNow, &lpData->Value[0]);
        if(lpData->fAckReq)
```

```
        {
        if(!PostMessage(wParam, WM_DDE_ACK, hwndClient,
                        MAKELONG(0x8000,aItem)))
            GlobalDeleteAtom(aItem);
        }
    fRelease = lpData->fRelease;
    GlobalUnlock(hData);
    if(fRelease)
        GlobalFree(hData);
    }
else
    {
    if(!PostMessage(wParam, WM_DDE_ACK, hwndClient,
                MAKELONG(0, aItem)))
        {
        GlobalDeleteAtom(aItem);
        GlobalFree(hData);
        }
    return FALSE;
    }
```

WM_DDE_ADVISE and WM_DDE_UNADVISE

The WM_DDE_ADVISE message requests a server application to send notification to a client application whenever the specified data item changes values. The low-order word of lParam for WM_DDE_ADVISE contains a global memory handle to the DDEADVISE structure. The high-order word contains an atom that specifies a data item. The server application posts a WM_DDE_ACK message in response to a WM_DDE_ADVISE message. If the acknowledgment is positive, the server application deletes the global memory block associated with DDEADVISE; otherwise, the client application must free the global memory block.

The DDEADVISE structure is as follows:

```
typedef struct {
    unsigned reserved:14,
        fDeferUpd:1,
        fAckReq:1;
    int  cfFormat;
} DDEADVISE;
```

The cfFormat member of the DDEADVISE structure specifies the clipboard format that the server application uses to render the data. If the client application requires data in multiple clipboard formats, it should send one WM_DDE_ADVISE message for each format. If the client application wants the server application to send WM_DDE_DATA messages with the fAckReq member of DDEDATA, the client application assigns 1 to the fAckReq member of DDEADVISE. This ensures that the client application can send a WM_DDE_ACK message in response to WM_DDE_DATA messages, thus allowing the client application to control the flow of data from the server application.

If the client application sets the fDeferUpd member of the DDEADVISE structure, the server application sends WM_DDE_DATA messages with no data, thereby creating a warm link. If the server wants the value of the data, it posts a WM_DDE_REQUEST message. When fDeferUpd is FALSE, the server application posts WM_DDE_DATA messages with a handle to the DDEDATA structure containing the new value of the item. This creates a hot link.

When a client application no longer requires a data item or a clipboard format for a data item, the client application posts a WM_DDE_UNADVISE message. The low-order word in lParam contains the clipboard format of the data item. The high-order word in lParam contains an atom to the data item. If the client application specifies NULL for the clipboard format, the server application should terminate all WM_DDE_ADVISE links for the data item. If a client application specifies NULL for the data item, the server application should terminate WM_DDE_ADVISE links for all data items. After the server application receives the WM_DDE_ADVISE message, it should respond positively or negatively by posting a WM_DDE_ACK message.

Here's an example of the code from the client application's point of view:

```
ATOM            aItem;
HANDLE          hOptions;
DDEADVISE FAR * lpOptions;

if(!(hOptions = GlobalAlloc(GMEM_MOVEABLE ¦ GMEM_DDESHARE,
                        (LONG)sizeof(DDEADVISE))))
    return FALSE;

if(!(lpOptions = (DDEADVISE FAR *)GlobalLock(hOptions)))
    {
    GlobalFree(hOptions);
    return FALSE;
    }

lpOptions->cfFormat = CF_TEXT;
lpOptions->fAckReq = TRUE;
```

```
lpOptions->fDeferUpd = FALSE; /* Hot Link ! */
GlobalUnlock(hOptions);

aItem = GlobalAddAtom((LPSTR)szItem);

if(!PostMessage(hwndServer, WM_DDE_ADVISE, hwndClient,
                MAKELONG(hOptions, aItem)))

    {
    GlobalDeleteAtom(aItem);
    GlobalFree(hOptions);
    }
```

The server application would then check to see whether it supported the item.
If it did, it would send a WM_DDE_DATA message every time the item changed:

```
hData = GlobalAlloc(GNHD | GMEM_DDESHARE,
                    sizeof(DDEDATA) + lstrlen(&DataItem[0]));
if(!hData)
    return FALSE;
lpData = (DDEDATA FAR *) GlobalLock(hData);
if(!lpData)
    return FALSE;
lstrcpy(&lpData->Value[0], &DataItem[0]);
lpData->fAckReq = TRUE;
lpData->fRelease = TRUE;
lpData->fResponse = TRUE;
lpData->cfFormat = CF_TEXT;
GlobalUnlock(hData);
if(!PostMessage(hwndClient, WM_DDE_DATA, hwndServer,
                MAKELONG(hData, aItem)))

    {
    GlobalFree(hData);
    GlobalDeleteAtom(aItem);
    }
```

Then the client application could process the WM_DDE_DATA message with the
following code:

```
case WM_DDE_DATA:
    hData = LOWORD(lParam);
    aItem = HIWORD(lParam);
    if(!hData)
        {
        GlobalDeleteAtom(aItem);
```

26

```
            return FALSE;
            }
        lpData = (LPDDEDATA) GlobalLock(hData);
        if(!lpData)
            {
            if(!PostMessage(wParam, WM_DDE_ACK, hwndClient,
                        MAKELONG(0, aItem)))
                {
                GlobalDeleteAtom(aItem);
                GlobalFree(hData);
                }
            return FALSE;
            }
        if(lpData->cfFormat == CF_TEXT)
            {
            lstrcpy(achClientsDataNow, &lpData->Value[0]);
            if(lpData->fAckReq)
                {
                if(!PostMessage(wParam, WM_DDE_ACK, hwndClient,
                            MAKELONG(0x8000,aItem)))
                    GlobalDeleteAtom(aItem);
                }
            fRelease = lpData->fRelease;
            GlobalUnlock(hData);
            if(fRelease)
                GlobalFree(hData);
            }
        else
            {
            if(!PostMessage(wParam, WM_DDE_ACK, hwndClient,
                        MAKELONG(0, aItem)))
                {
                GlobalDeleteAtom(aItem);
                GlobalFree(hData);
                }
            return FALSE;
            }
```

When the client no longer requires the data item, it sends a WM_DDE_UNADVISE message to the server:

```
ATOM aItem;
aItem = GlobalAddAtom(&szItem[0]);
```

```
if(!PostMessage(hwndServer, WM_DDE_UNADVISE, hwndClient,
             MAKELONG(CF_TEXT,aItem)))
    GlobalDeleteAtom(aItem);
```

The Dynamic Data Exchange Management Library—DDEML

The *Dynamic Data Exchange Management Library* (DDEML) is a dynamic-link library that provides an API for DDE. The DDEML is new for Windows 3.1. It provides a consistent method to implement the DDE protocol in applications. The functions in the DDEML simplify sending, posting, and receiving DDE messages. Additionally, the DDEML provides services to handle strings and data exchanged between DDE applications. DDEML is easier to use than message-based DDE and can eliminate problems that lead to inconsistencies in the DDE protocol. In short, DDEML does much of the dirty work for you and simultaneously enforces the DDE protocol.

Message-based DDE applications are compatible with DDEML applications—sometimes. If a message-based DDE application follows the DDE protocol, it will work with DDEML applications. Message-based DDE applications that do not follow the DDE protocol may or may not correctly communicate with DDEML applications. A message-based DDE application designed to communicate with only one other application can lead to inconsistencies in the DDE protocol because the application may contain only the code that it and the partner application require to communicate.

The correct way to design a DDE application is to assume that it is independent of all other DDE applications. This means that any DDE application should be able to access the data or services any other DDE application provides. The DDEML provides the framework to create such applications.

To use DDEML services, the DDEML.DLL file must be in the Windows system directory or in the system path. DDEML runs under Windows 3.0; however, Microsoft provides the DDEML.DLL only with Windows 3.1. Additionally, DDEML runs only in protected mode. This isn't a problem with Windows 3.1, because Windows 3.1 does not run in real mode. Because the DDEML runs under Windows 3.0, it is a good idea to have your applications call **GetWinFlags()** to see whether Windows is running in protected mode.

Programming a DDEML application is similar to programming a message-based DDE application; in some ways, however, it is very different. To start, the DDEML is a manager of DDE conversations. In message-based DDE, conversation management is the programmer's responsibility. Because DDEML manages conversations, it requires applications that use the DDEML to follow certain conventions. These conventions help enforce the underlying DDE protocol.

Callback Functions

One of the programming conventions DDEML requires is a *callback function*. All conversations in message-based DDE applications are unique because each conversation has a client/server window handle pair. In message-based DDE applications, each window has its own callback function that receives DDE messages and other messages to manage the window. DDEML applications differ from message-based DDE applications by using a DDE-only callback function. This callback function receives only messages pertaining to DDE.

When an application requires the use of the DDEML, it must register a DDE callback function with the DDEML. It does this through the **DdeInitialize()** function. The **DdeInitialize()** function is different from sending a WM_DDE_INITIATE message because it only registers an application with the DDEML. It does not request a conversation with a server.

The DDE callback function has different parameters than a callback function for a window. It has the following prototype:

```
HDDEDATA EXPENTRY DdeCallback(wType, wFmt, hConv, hsz1, hsz2,
                     hData, dwData1,dwData2)

WORD wType;          /* transaction type                 */
WORD wFmt;           /* clipboard data format            */
HCONV hConv;         /* handle of the conversation       */
HSZ hsz1;            /* handle of a string               */
HSZ hsz2;            /* handle of a string               */
HDDEDATA hData;      /* handle of a global memory object */
DWORD dwData1;       /* transaction-specific data        */
DWORD dwData2;       /* transaction-specific data        */
```

Note: Because the name `DdeCallback` is a placeholder, you can name the callback function any valid application-defined function name.

DDEML Applications

DDEML applications are of three types: *client, server,* and *monitor.* Client applications and server applications are the most commonly developed of the three. (Chapter 4 discusses DDEML monitor applications.) DDE client applications request data or services from DDE server applications. Notice that a client application can request a service from a server. A service might be something as simple as opening a file, or as complex as performing a quarterly consolidation of database tables and generating a report and graphics based on the consolidated tables. Data exchanged from a server to a client application can take the form of a text string or something vastly larger, such as a bitmap.

Client and server applications use a standard format to communicate with each other. First, the client application always initiates a conversation with a server application. To initiate the conversation, the client application calls the DDEML function `DdeConnect()`. A successful call to `DdeConnect()` returns a handle to a conversation. This differs from message-based DDE applications, because the DDEML generates the handle that identifies a conversation. In message-based DDE, the pair of handles from the client and server windows identifies a conversation. DDEML applications use the conversation handle in subsequent DDE *transactions.* DDE transactions are the elements, or function calls and messages, that make up a conversation.

A client application may want to terminate a conversation when it has received the data or services it required. The client application uses the `DdeDisconnect()` function to terminate a conversation. When any DDE application wants to terminate all DDE interaction, it calls the `DdeUninitialize()` function. When this occurs, the DDEML will not send transactions to the application's DDE callback function. In essence, the application is without DDE services until it registers itself with the DDEML again.

It is a good practice to disconnect and uninitialize when you complete client-side DDE activities. This reduces overhead for DDEML and increases system performance. Idle DDE applications can still consume system resources, which can be noticeable on machines with slow microprocessors or little memory.

Service Names, Topic Names, and Item Names

A DDE server application can identify the data and services that client applications request by using *service names, topic names,* and *item names.* A service name is a string that a client application uses to establish a conversation with a server application. A service name is equivalent to an application name used in message-based DDE. It is possible to have multiple servers that accept the same service name. To eliminate this ambiguity, topic names and item names further define the service name. Topic names and item names are also strings. The combination of topic names and item names allows a client application to exchange data and services with a server application.

You know from message-based DDE that client applications establish conversations by broadcasting a WM_DDE_INITIATE message to all nonchild windows. The DDEML can control some of this activity with the help of the server application. Using the **DdeNameServe()** function, the server application can specify to the DDEML the service names it will accept. When the DDEML knows the service names a server application supports, it avoids posting unnecessary transactions to that server. This decreases message traffic on the system, and thus increases system performance.

Client applications use service names and topic names in the **DdeConnect()** function. This is similar to sending a WM_DDE_INITIATE message to a server. If the server supports the service and topic names, **DdeConnect()** returns a handle to a conversation. You can establish multiple conversations by calling the **DdeConnectList()** function. (The details for conversation initiation are in Chapter 2, "DDEML Conversation Management.")

DDEML Transactions

After establishing conversations, client applications issue transactions by calling the **DdeClientTransaction()** function. The **DdeClientTransaction()** function has the following prototype:

```
HDDEDATA DdeClientTransaction(lpbData, cbDataLen, hConv, hszItem,
                              wFmt, wType, dwTimeout, lpdwResult)

LPBYTE lpbData;      /* pointer to data to pass to server */
DWORD cbDataLen;     /* length of the data               */
HCONV hConv;         /* handle of the conversation       */
```

```
HSZ hszItem;            /* handle of the item-name string   */
WORD wFmt;              /* clipboard data format            */
WORD wType;             /* transaction type                 */
DWORD dwTimeout;        /* timeout duration                 */
LPDWORD lpdwResult;     /* points to transaction result     */
```

The hConv parameter is a handle to a conversation that the DDEML creates. The DDEML uses this to route a transaction to the appropriate server application DDE callback function. The wType parameter is the transaction type. The transaction type corresponds to the DDE messages discussed earlier in this chapter. The major transaction types are XTYP_REQUEST, XTYP_POKE, XTYP_ADVSTART, XTYP_ADVSTOP, and XTYP_EXECUTE.

The lpbData and cbDataLen parameters specify a data handle and the length of the data in XTYP_EXECUTE and XTYP_POKE transactions. The hszItem parameter is the item name for the transaction. The wFmt parameter is the clipboard format of the data item. The client application uses the lpdwResult parameter to determine the status of the transaction after the **DdeClientTransaction()** function returns.

The dwTimeout parameter specifies the maximum time to wait for the server application to process the transaction. When a client application specifies a value other than TIMEOUT_ASYNC in the parameter, the transaction is synchronous. For synchronous transactions, the **DdeClientTransaction()** function does not return until the server application processes the transaction or the transaction times out.

Specifying TIMEOUT_ASYNC in dwTimeout generates an *asynchronous transaction*. Asynchronous transactions allow a client application to issue multiple transactions without waiting for the server to process the transaction. When a client application issues a synchronous transaction, it enters a modal loop where it can process user input, but it cannot issue another synchronous transaction until **DdeClientTransaction()** returns. When a client application issues an asynchronous transaction, the **DdeClientTransaction()** function returns a transaction identifier when the transaction starts. The client application uses the transaction identifier to distinguish XTYP_XACT_COMPLETE transactions posted by the DDEML to the client application DDE callback function.

Many DDEML transactions require strings and data. Because DDEML is similar to message-based DDE, it isn't surprising that the DDEML uses atoms and global memory objects. DDEML, however, provides a more organized method of creating atoms and handles to global memory objects. There are two primary functions for accomplishing these tasks: **DdeCreateStringHandle()** and **DdeCreateDataHandle()**.

DdeCreateStringHandle() is an atom-management function, although it returns a string handle rather than an atom. DDEML applications use this function to create string handles that are in most DDEML functions. Its function prototype follows:

```
HSZ  EXPENTRY DdeCreateStringHandle(DWORD idInst, LPSTR psz,
                                    int iCodePage);
```

The `idInst` parameter is an instance identifier for the last call to **DdeInitialize()**. The `psz` parameter is the string, and `iCodePage` is the code page in which the string is rendered. This is usually `CP_WINANSI`. If you are not using the Windows default keyboard driver, you should call `GetKBCodePage` to get `iCodePage`.

Here is an example of creating a server name:

```
DWORD idInst;
HSZ hszServerName;

hszServerName = DdeCreateStringHandle(idInst, "GeorgeServer",
                                      CP_WINANSI);
```

The **DdeCreateDataHandle()** function is similar to **DdeCreateStringHandle()**, except it creates a handle to a global memory object. It has the following function prototype:

```
HDDEDATA EXPENTRY DdeCreateDataHandle(DWORD idInst, LPBYTE pScr,
                                      DWORD cb,  DWORD cbOff, HSZ
                                      hszItem,WORD wFmt, WORD
                                      afCmd);
```

The `idInst` parameter is the application instance parameter for the last call to **DdeInitialize()**. The `pScr` parameter is the data object that has a size of `cb`. The `cbOff` parameter specifies the offset to where the data object starts. The `hszItem` parameter specifies the handle to the item name. The `wFmt` parameter is the clipboard format used to render the data. Finally, the `afCmd` parameter specifies whether the system or application owns the data object. To specify application ownership, use the `HDATA_APPWONED` flag in `afCmd`.

Here's an example of a data handle being returned for a DDE callback function:

```
DWORD idInst;
char ach[1000];

return(DdeCreateDataHandle(idInst, (LPBYTE) &ach, sizeof(ach),
       0L, (HSZ) NULL, CF_TEXT, 0));
```

The *XTYP_POKE* Transaction

A client application can poke data to a server application by specifying the transaction type XTYP_POKE in the **DdeClientTransaction()** function. The **DdeCreateDataHandle()** function creates a global memory object for the poked data and returns a handle to the data that the client application uses in the **DdeClientTransaction()**. Additionally, the client application passes an item name and clipboard format for the data.

Then the DDEML passes the XTYP_POKE transaction to the server's DDE callback function. The server should return DDE_FACK to the DDEML if it successfully processes the transaction. If the server is busy, it should return DDE_FBUSY. Otherwise, the server should return DDE_FNOTPROCESSED. The client application should check the status flag, lpdwResult, when the **DdeClientTransaction()** function returns, to be sure the transaction was successful. If the lpdwResult flag is DDE_FBUSY, the client can issue the transaction later in the conversation.

The *XTYP_EXECUTE* Transaction

The XTYP_EXECUTE transaction requests a server application to execute a command string. The format of the command string follows the same definition described earlier in this chapter, in the section about the WM_DDE_EXECUTE message. The client application creates a data handle for the string using the **DdeCreateDataHandle()** function. Then the client application can pass the data handle, clipboard format, conversation handle, topic name, and item name to the **DdeClientTransaction()** function.

The DDEML sends the XTYP_EXECUTE transaction to the server application's callback function. The server can access the data through the **DdeAccessData()** function. If the server can execute the command string, it should return DDE_FACK. If the server is busy, it should return DDE_FBUSY. Otherwise, the server should return DDE_FNOTPROCESSED. The client application should check the lpdwResult status flag when the **DdeClientTransaction()** function returns, to be sure that the transaction was successful. If the lpdwResult flag is DDE_FBUSY, the client can issue the transaction later in the conversation.

The *XTYP_REQUEST* Transaction

When a client application calls the **DdeClientTransaction()** function with the transaction type of XTYP_REQUEST, the DDEML requests data from the specified server application for the client application. If the server application can render the data item, it should return a handle to the data item. The DDEML passes the data handle as the return value from the **DdeClientTransaction()**. If the server cannot render the data item, it should return NULL to the DDEML, and the DDEML will return NULL to the client application. In this case, the client application can check the lpdwResult flag to see whether the server was busy. If the server application was not busy, the client application can assume that the server cannot render the data item.

The *XTYP_ADVSTART* and *XTYP_ADVSTOP* Transactions

Client applications can establish links to a server application by using the XTYP_ADVSTART transaction. To create a warm link, the client application should combine XTYP_ADVSTART with the XTYPF_NODATA flag using a bitwise or. XTYP_ADVSTART establishes a hot link when it is used alone.

When the server receives the advise request, it should determine whether it can render the data item. If it can, it should return TRUE from its DDE callback function. This starts an *advise loop*. If the server returns FALSE, an advise loop is not created. When an advise loop exists, the server should call the **DdePostAdvise()** function each time the data item changes values. This sends an XTYP_ADVREQ transaction to the server's callback function. After the server processes the XTYP_ADVREQ transaction, it returns the data handle to the DDEML. If the advise loop is a hot link, the DDEML then uses the data handle when sending an XTYP_ADVDATA transaction to the client's callback function. If the advise loop is a warm link, the client application can post an XTYP_REQUEST transaction to receive the data handle.

When the client application wishes to end an advise loop, it posts an XTYP_ADVSTOP transaction using the **DdeClientTransaction()** function.

Summary

As you have probably guessed by now, DDE programming involves a few rules. The DDEML makes some DDE programming easier, but try to remember the underlying DDE protocol presented in the sections on message-based DDE applications. The DDEML API is slicker than **PostMessage()** and **GlobalAddAtom()**, but this is what DDEML does under the hood. A better understanding of the DDE protocol will lead to better applications.

This doesn't mean that DDEML is a walk in the park. You will encounter a myriad of potential errors to trap when writing DDEML applications. As your programs grow in complexity, it can become virtually impossible to program for all error conditions, especially if you communicate with third-party DDE applications whose code you have no control over. My only words of advice are to test your application as thoroughly as possible to make it easier for the next person who has to write a DDE program to communicate with yours.

DDEML
Conversation
Management

This chapter covers DDEML application initialization and conversation management. Applications are required to register with the DDEML before they can perform any other DDEML-related task. This is the initialization process. After applications register with the DDEML, they can start conversations. Conversations consist of transactions between client and server applications. *Conversation management* is the process that creates, suspends, and terminates conversations. *Transaction management,* the process of exchanging data between applications, is covered in Chapter 3, "Transaction Management."

The initialization process involves many intricacies. Determining the methods for initialization is perhaps the most critical part of developing a DDEML application. The options that you specify during initialization can impact how your application processes transactions and can affect application performance. This chapter should give you a thorough understanding of

☐ The DDEML initialization process

☐ DDEML conversation management

The DDEML Initialization Process

The initialization process is required for applications to communicate with the DDEML. In a sense, initialization is a handshake between the DDEML and an application. The initialization process is the first time an application meets with the DDEML. Until an application shakes hands with the DDEML, it is unable to access any other DDEML function. I see many parallels between dynamic data exchange and human interaction. Sometimes it seems that good DDE programs border on being polite. The converse of this is also true. Poorly written DDE programs tend to be rude, as if a program said, "Give me that data," and then didn't acknowledge receiving the data. The application supplying the data has no idea whether the receiving program has the data. It should have received at least a thank-you.

From a development point of view, the initialization process is more than just getting the rights to access DDEML services. This process determines how the

DDEML interacts with an application. If an application gives the DDEML a weak handshake, the DDEML will walk all over the application during conversations. If an application gives a strong, firm, and commanding handshake, however, the DDEML will cooperate with the application and make the development process much easier. This is because an application can partially dictate how a conversation flows by specifying *flags*, the terms that a conversation will follow.

The DDEML uses flags from the initialization process as the ground rules for a conversation. If an application says it does not want to receive a certain type of transaction, the DDEML will not send that type of transaction to the application. On the other hand, if an application does not bother to tell the DDEML which transactions it does not want, the DDEML will send transactions to the application without knowing what the application really wants or doesn't want. You should keep one idea in mind at all times when developing DDEML applications: The more precisely you communicate, the more effective your communications will be.

Initializing Applications—
DdeInitialize()

DDEML applications must register with the DDEML before calling any other DDEML functions. The **DdeInitialize()** function accomplishes this. You can call **DdeInitialize()** at any point in your program, but you must call it before any other DDEML function.

The prototypes and definitions for the DDEML are in ddeml.h. You should include ddeml.h in every source file that contains a reference to DDEML functions or definitions. The **DdeInitialize()** function has the following prototype:

```
WORD EXPENTRY DdeInitialize(LPDWORD idInst,
                            PFNCALLBACK pfnCallback,
                            DWORD afCmd,
                            DWORD dwRes);
```

The first thing you may notice about this prototype is the return value: WORD EXPENTRY. The definition for EXPENTRY is _export far pascal. All DDEML functions have EXPENTRY in their prototype because they are functions within a dynamic-link library, DDEML.DLL. **DdeInitialize()** returns a WORD that specifies an error code. The possible error codes for **DdeInitialize()** are the following:

DMLERR_NO_ERROR	Specifies that the call was successful.
DMLERR_DDL_USAGE	Specifies that an application is using the DDEML incorrectly, e.g., a client application performing server functions.
DMLERR_INVALIDPARAMETER	Specifies that DdeInitialize has an invalid parameter.
DMLERR_SYS_ERROR	Indicates an internal DDEML problem.

The idInst parameter must be zero for the first call to **DdeInitialize()**. On returning, the idInst parameter contains an instance identifier. Calls to other DDEML functions will require the instance identifier, so it should be accessible from all program modules that call DDEML functions. The pfnCallback parameter is an instance thunk for the DDE callback function. The **MakeProcInstance()** function creates the value for this parameter. Make sure you add the callback function to the export section in the module definition file. dwRes is a reserved parameter, and it should always be zero.

The afCmd parameter specifies flags that the DDEML uses to route transactions to callback functions. Transactions are the details that make up a conversation and are the results of DDEML function calls. Transactions are identified by constants that begin with XTYP_.

The transaction process goes something like this: An application calls a DDEML function. The DDEML function then determines where the request goes and sends an XTYP_ transaction to the appropriate DDE callback function. Then the DDE callback function uses a switch or an if-else type programming structure to determine which transaction it has received. Then the callback function takes appropriate action and returns a value to the DDEML. The DDEML uses the return value from the callback function to create the return value to the function call that originated the sequence.

Specifying the correct flags in afCmd will dictate how the communication process flows. Using the correct combination of flags enables the DDEML to send—or not send—transactions to an application's callback function. When you use a combination of flags that instructs the DDEML not to send transactions, the overall effect is less message traffic on the system, which creates better system performance. Specifying an incorrect combination of flags may leave your application without the transactions it requires to operate correctly. Knowing what transactions an application requires is very important in the initialization process. Thus, it is a good idea to have an overall design for an application before writing the initialization code for an application.

Here are the flags for the `afCmd`. You can combine the flags using a bitwise-`or` operator: `¦`.

APPCLASS_STANDARD   This flag registers an application with the DDEML as a standard application, which means it can receive both client and server transactions. This is the most general flag used in **DdeInitialize()**.

APPCMD_CLIENTONLY   Specifies that the DDEML should send client transactions only to the application's callback function, thus preventing the application from becoming a server. The APPCMD_CLIENTONLY flag includes the CBF_FAIL_ALLSVRACTIONS flag in its definition.

CBF_FAIL_ALLSVRXACTIONS   This flag is a combination of all CBF_FAIL_ flags. CBF_FAIL_ flags specify to the DDEML that it should not send transactions to a server application's callback function.

The following list shows the CBF_FAIL_ flags and the transactions not sent to a server application's callback function:

CBF_FAIL_ADVISES—XTYP_ADVSTART and XTYP_ADVSTOP

CBF_FAIL_CONNECTIONS—XTYP_CONNECT and XTYP_WILDCONNECT

CBF_FAIL_EXECUTES—XTYP_EXECUTE

CBF_FAIL_POKES—XTYP_POKE

CBF_FAIL_REQUESTS—XTYP_REQUEST

CBF_FAIL_SELFCONNECTS—XTYP_CONNECT. This prevents a server from connecting with the same instance of itself. However, it allows a server to connect with other instances of itself.

Usually, an application uses a combination of the CBF_FAIL_ flags to ignore transactions it does not support. For example, if a server application did not support poked data from a client application, it could specify CBF_FAIL_POKES. When a client attempts to poke data to the server, DDEML returns DDE_FNOTPROCESSED to the client. In fact, if an application attempts to send any of the previously mentioned transactions, the DDEML returns DDE_FNOTPROCESSED.

APPCMD_FILTERINITS — When an application specifies this flag, the DDEML sends only the XTYP_CONNECT and XTYP_WILDCONNECT transactions to the server's DDE callback function after the server has registered its service names. See the next section in this chapter for more information about service names. APPCMD_FILTERINITS is a default for all first calls to **DdeInitialize()**.

CBF_SKIP_ALLNOTIFICATIONS — This flag prevents the DDEML from sending notification transactions. The CBF_SKIP_ALLNOTIFICATIONS flag is a combination of CBF_SKIP_ flags.

The following list shows the CBF_SKIP_ flags and the associated transactions that they block:

CBF_SKIP_CONNECT_CONFIRMS—XTYP_CONNECT_CONFIRM

CBF_SKIP_DISCONNECTS—XTYP_DISCONNECT

CBF_SKIP_REGISTRATIONS—XTYP_REGISTER

CBF_SKIP_UNREGISTRATIONS—XTYP_UNREGISTER

APPCLASS_MONITOR. This flag is for a special class of DDEML applications. It registers the application as a monitor application, which allows it to spy on all DDE messages and transactions. (Chapter 4, "DDEML Monitor Applications," covers monitor applications in detail.)

The APPCMD_CLIENTONLY and APPCMD_FILTERINITS flags are of particular interest to us in this chapter because the example programs for this chapter use these flags. The client application specifies the APPCMD_CLIENTONLY flag. This indicates to the DDEML that the client application should not receive any transactions intended for server applications. The server application uses the APPCMD_FILTERINITS flag. The purpose of the APPCMD_FILTERINITS is to prevent connect transactions from reaching the server's DDE callback function until the server has registered its service names.

The DDEML sends XTYP_CONNECT and XTYP_WILDCONNECT transactions in reply to the **DdeConnect()** and **DdeConnectList()** functions. The **DdeConnect()** and **DdeConnectList()** functions create conversations. When an application's callback function receives an XTYP_CONNECT or XTYP_WILDCONNECT transaction,

it also receives a service name and a topic name. You may recall from Chapter 1 that service names are part of the three-tiered identification hierarchy that DDEML applications use. Below service names in the hierarchy are topic names and item names. If the server specifies the APPCMD_FILTERINITS flag in the **DdeInitialize()** function, it will not receive XTYP_CONNECT or XTYP_WILDCONNECT transactions until after the server registers a service name.

Registering Service Names

A server application can use the **DdeNameService()** function to identify the service that it supports to the DDEML. When the DDEML knows the service names of an application, the DDEML will send only XTYP_CONNECT transactions to an application for the supported service name. The **DdeNameService()** function has another purpose: When a server application calls **DdeNameService()**, the DDEML sends XTYP_REGISTER transactions to all client applications on the system. A client application can use the XTYP_REGISTER transactions to create a list of servers available on the system. There is an exception to this: If the client application specified a CBF_SKIP_REGISTRATIONS flag in its **DdeInitialize()** function, the DDEML will not send an XTYP_REGISTER transaction to that client application.

Here is the prototype for the **DdeNameService()** function:

```
HDDEDATA EXPENTRY DdeNameService(DWORD idInst, HSZ hsz1,
                                 HSZ hsz2, WORD afCmd);
```

The first parameter, idInst, should be familiar. Its value came from a call to **DdeInitialize()**. The second and third parameters are handles to strings; however, the third parameter is a reserved parameter and should be NULL. The hsz1 parameter is a handle to a string that identifies the service name. The last parameter, afCmd, specifies flags. The most typically used flag is DNS_REGISTER. This registers a service name with the DDEML. If a server application wants to unregister a service name, it can specify DNS_UNREGISTER. Another flag, DNS_FILTERON, specifies to the DDEML that the server application does not want to receive XTYP_CONNECT transactions for service names that the server has not registered. This is a default flag that does not need to be specified unless a prior call to **DdeNameService()** specified DNS_FILTEROFF. DNS_FILTEROFF notifies the DDEML to send XTYP_CONNECT transactions to the server's callback function.

The hsz1 parameter comes from a call to **DdeCreateStringHandle()**. This is one of the string-management functions provided by the DDEML. **DdeCreateStringHandle()** replaces the use of atom functions found in message-based DDE applications. In actuality, **DdeCreateStringHandle()** uses the global atom table but hides this from the programmer. The prototype for **DdeCreateStringHandle()** follows:

```
HSZ  EXPENTRY DdeCreateStringHandle(DWORD idInst, LPSTR psz,
                                    int iCodePage);
```

In short, the **DdeCreateStringHandle()** function uses three parameters. The idInst parameter comes from the last call of **DdeInitialize()**. The psz parameter is the string for which the handle is created. The iCodePage parameter specifies the code page used to render the string. This is usually set to CP_WINANSI. Now I can show you a call to **DdeInitialize()** for a server application that uses service name registration. An example follows:

```
lpDdeProc = MakeProcInstance((FARPROC)DdeCallBack, hInst);
idInst = 0L;
if(lpDdeProc)
    {
    if(DMLERR_NO_ERROR == DdeInitialize((LPDWORD) &idInst,
                                        (PFNCALLBACK) lpDdeProc,
                                        APPCMD_FILTERINITS,
                                        0L))
        {
        hszName = DdeCreateStringHandle(idInst, "DDEServe",
                                        CP_WINANSI);
        DdeNameService(idInst, hszName, NULL, DNS_REGISTER);
        }
    else
        FreeProcInstance((FARPROC)lpDdeProc);
    }
```

In the preceding code, **MakeProcInstance()** creates an instance thunk for the server application's DDE callback function. If the call to **MakeProcInstance()** was successful, the server calls **DdeInitialize()**. The idInst parameter has the value of zero. The second parameter contains the return value of **MakeProcInstance()**. The third parameter specifies to the DDEML to withhold XTYP_CONNECT and XTYP_WILDCONNECT transactions until the server registers its service name.

DdeCreateStringHandle() creates a handle for the server's service name, DDEServe. The return value, hszName, is the second parameter in **DdeNameService()**. The first parameter in **DdeCreateStringHandle()** and **DdeNameService()** is the updated value of idInst. Your program should clean up after itself by calling **FreeProcInstance()** if the call to **DdeInitialize()**

failed. If everything is successful, you won't have to call **FreeProcInstance()** until you no longer need the DDE callback function.

Error Trapping—*DdeGetLastError()*

The **DdeGetLastError()** function is a handy function. An application can call **DdeGetLastError()** at any time to retrieve the last DDEML error. **DdeGetLastError()** returns an error code, or DMLERR_NO_ERROR. It has only one parameter: idInst. idInst is the instance identifier gotten from a call to the **DdeInitialize()** function. After an application calls **DdeGetLastError()**, the DDEML resets the last error to DMLERR_NO_ERROR.

It is easy to set up an error handler for DDEML. You can use the debug terminal that comes with the SDK to display your error messages. The debug terminal is a Windows application, DBWIN.EXE, that displays output strings from the debug version of Windows. Applications can display messages to the debug terminal by using the **OutputDebugString()** function. This is similar to a DISPLAY statement in COBOL. (I can't believe I wrote that.) You do not need the debug version of Windows to send messages to the debug terminal. Here's a debug handler you can include in your applications while you develop:

```
WORD PASCAL DdeErrorHandler(WORD TheError)
    {
    switch(TheError)
        {
        case DMLERR_ADVACKTIMEOUT:
            OutputDebugString("DMLERR_ADVACKTIMEOUT");
            break;
        case DMLERR_BUSY:
            OutputDebugString("DMLERR_BUSY");
            break;
        case DMLERR_DATAACKTIMEOUT:
            OutputDebugString("DMLERR_DATAACKTIMEOUT");
            break;
        case DMLERR_DLL_NOT_INITIALIZED:
            OutputDebugString("DMLERR_DLL_NOT_INITIALIZED");
            break;
        case DMLERR_DLL_USAGE:
            OutputDebugString("DMLERR_DLL_USAGE");
            break;
```

```
            case DMLERR_EXECACKTIMEOUT:
                OutputDebugString("DMLERR_EXECACKTIMEOUT");
                break;
            case DMLERR_INVALIDPARAMETER:
                OutputDebugString("DMLERR_INVALIDPARAMETER");
                break;
            case DMLERR_LOW_MEMORY:
                OutputDebugString("DMLERR_LOW_MEMORY");
                break;
            case DMLERR_MEMORY_ERROR:
                OutputDebugString("DMLERR_MEMORY_ERROR");
                break;
            case DMLERR_NOTPROCESSED:
                OutputDebugString("DMLERR_NOTPROCESSED");
                break;
            case DMLERR_NO_CONV_ESTABLISHED:
                OutputDebugString("DMLERR_NO_CONV_ESTABLISHED");
                break;
            case DMLERR_POKEACKTIMEOUT:
                OutputDebugString("DMLERR_POKEACKTIMEOUT");
                break;
            case DMLERR_POSTMSG_FAILED:
                OutputDebugString("DMLERR_POSTMSG_FAILED");
                break;
            case DMLERR_REENTRANCY:
                OutputDebugString("DMLERR_REENTRANCY");
                break;
            case DMLERR_SERVER_DIED:
                OutputDebugString("DMLERR_SERVER_DIED");
                break;
            case DMLERR_SYS_ERROR:
                OutputDebugString("DMLERR_SYS_ERROR");
                break;
            case DMLERR_UNADVACKTIMEOUT:
                OutputDebugString("DMLERR_UNADVACKTIMEOUT");
                break;
            case DMLERR_UNFOUND_QUEUE_ID:
                OutputDebugString("DMLERR_UNFOUND_QUEUE_ID");
                break;
        }
    return TheError;
    }
```

The call to the error handler would look like this:

```
DdeFunction(...);
if(DMLERR_NO_ERROR == DdeErrorHandler(DdeGetLastError(idInst))
     ok to process;
else
     have a problem here, better do something about it;
```

You can be more sophisticated with this error handler, such as by adding a line number and source file to the output message by passing the line number and source file name. You can get line numbers and source file names by using the `__LINE__` and `__FILE__` global identifiers. This solution, however, offers only an approximation of where an error occurred. The call to the `DdeGetLastError()` function is not where the error occurred, but where you decided to detect it. If you know the logic of your program, however, the debug messages generated by this method should be sufficient to help you track down the errors in your program.

Freeing DDEML Resources— *DdeUninitialize()*

An application can end all interaction with the DDEML by calling the **DdeUninitialize()** function. The **DdeUninitialize()** function frees all DDEML resources and terminates all conversations. If the DDEML is unable to terminate a conversation, the application that called **DdeUninitialize()** will enter a modal loop. The DDEML supplies a message box that enables the user to abort, retry, or ignore a time-out period that the DDEML waits for an application to terminate a conversation.

The **DdeUninitialize()** function has the following form:

```
DdeUninitialize(idInst);
```

in which idInst is the instance identifier from a call to **DdeInitialize()**.

Conversation Management

After DDEML applications register with the **DdeInitialize()** function, a conversation can begin. A client application always initiates a conversation. There are two methods for initiating a conversation: **DdeConnect()** and

DdeConnectList(). **DdeConnect()** is similar to sending a WM_DDE_INITIATE message in message-based DDE. **DdeConnectList()** allows a client application to connect to several server applications simultaneously.

When an application wants to terminate a conversation, it uses the **DdeDisconnect()** or **DdeDisconnectList()** functions. Additionally, if a server application terminates a conversation, a client application may try to reestablish the conversation using the **DdeReconnect()** function.

Using Topic Names

For a client application to establish a conversation, it needs to specify a service name and a topic name in the **DdeConnect()** function. A topic name further defines a service name. Typically, server applications support one service name that has multiple topic names. All servers should support at least two topic names. The first topic name is the *system topic*. This allows client applications to inquire about system-related items that aid in transaction processing. The other topics are related to the services the server provides.

The definition for the system topic is SZDDESYS_TOPIC, which has a value of "System". A server can support a number of system items under the system topic. The SZDDESYS_ITEM_SYSITEMS item contains a list of items supported under the system topic. Thus, if a client application wants to know the system items that a server supports under the system topic, it can request the SZDDESYS_ITEM_SYSITEMS item. A server can support six other system items, which is discussed in Chapter 3.

Establishing a Conversation— *DdeConnect()*

A client application initiates single conversations with the **DdeConnect()** function. The **DdeConnect()** function returns a handle to a conversation. In message-based DDE, a conversation is defined by a pair of window handles: one from a server and one from a client. In DDEML-based DDE, the DDEML generates a handle to a conversation. Internally, the DDEML manages a table of conversations. When an application uses a handle to a conversation in a DDEML function call, the DDEML immediately knows where to send the transaction by accessing its table of conversations.

The **DdeConnect()** function has the following prototype:

```
HCONV EXPENTRY DdeConnect(DWORD idInst, HSZ hszService,
                          HSZ hszTopic, PCONVCONTEXT pCC);
```

The `idInst` parameter is the instance identifier gotten from a call to **DdeInitialize()**. The `hszService` and `hszTopic` parameters are handles to strings that contain service and topic names. These handles come from calls to **DdeCreateStringHandle()**. The `pCC` parameter points to the `CONVCONTEXT` structure. The `CONVCONTEXT` structure has the following `typedef`:

```
typedef struct _CONVCONTEXT {
    WORD    cb;
    WORD    wFlags;
    WORD    wCountryID;
    int     iCodePage;
    DWORD   dwLangID;
    DWORD   dwSecurity;
} CONVCONTEXT;
```

Applications typically specify `NULL` for the `pCC` parameter in **DdeConnect()**, because the `CONVCONTEXT` structure allows applications to exchange data in multiple languages, and the DDEML sends a default `CONVCONTEXT` when specifying `NULL`. However, the `dwSecurity` member can specify an application-defined security code. Use your imagination on this one. For instance, you could sell the security code for your applications to allow other applications to communicate with **DdeConnect()**. The other members in the `CONVCONTEXT` structure are of interest only to those who are programming for multiple languages.

Here's an example call to **DdeConnect()**:

```
hConv = DdeConnect(idInst, hszService, hszTopic, (LPVOID)NULL);
```

The `hszService` and `hszTopic` parameters can contain values or be `NULL`. When a client application calls **DdeConnect()** with a non-`NULL` `hszService` parameter, the DDEML sends `XTYP_CONNECT` transactions to the callback function of all server applications that have a registered service name matching `hszService`. If a server application does not specify `APPCMD_FILTERINITS` in the **DdeInitialize()** function, the DDEML will also send `XTYP_CONNECT` transactions to that server. Note that `APPCMD_FILTERINITS` is a default for the first call to **DdeInitialize()** in an application. On subsequent calls to **DdeInitialize()**, however, the `APPCMD_FILTERINITS` flag must be explicitly specified. Another way for the `XTYP_CONNECT` transaction to reach a server is by calling **DdeNameService()** with the `DNS_FILTEROFF` flag to turn off service-name filtering.

If the `hszService` or `hszTopic` parameter is `NULL`, the DDEML will send an `XTYP_WILDCONNECT` transaction to all servers not filtering connect transactions. This requires more overhead than when a client specifies a value for `hszService`, and the results are not very predictable. Many servers could respond to the `XTYP_WILDCONNECT` transaction, but the DDEML chooses which server will be a partner in a conversation.

When the server's DDE callback function receives an `XTYP_CONNECT` transaction, it can compare the service and topic names to its own and return `TRUE` if there is a match and `FALSE` if there isn't a match. If the server returns `TRUE`, the DDEML generates a conversation handle and returns the handle to the client application through the **DdeConnect()** function. If more than one server responds positively to the `XTYP_CONNECT` transaction, the DDEML picks only one server for the conversation. Then the DDEML sends an `XTYP_CONNECT_CONFIRM` transaction to the lucky server that is a partner in the conversation.

When a server's DDE callback function receives an `XTYP_WILDCONNECT` transaction, the server should create an array of `HSZPAIR` structures. Each element of the array contains two members that specify a service name and topic name combination. The array of `HSZPAIR` structures should be null-terminated. After the server creates the array, it returns a data handle to the DDEML using the **DdeCreateDataHandle()** function. The DDEML picks only one service name and topic name combination from all responding servers and then returns a conversation handle to the client application. Then the DDEML sends an `XTYP_CONNECT_CONFIRM` transaction to the server selected for the conversation.

The server side of the DdeConnect() message is similar to this:

```
HDDEDATA EXPENTRY DdeCallBack(WORD wType, WORD wFmt,
        HCONV hConv, HSZ hsz1, HSZ hsz2, HDDEDATA hData,
        DWORD lData1,DWORD lData2)
    {
    if(wType == XTYP_CONNECT)
        {
        if(hszName == hsz2)
            for(i = 0; i < CTOPICS; i++)
                if(hsz1 == ahszTopics[i])
                    return (HDDEDATA)TRUE;
        }
    if(wType == XTYP_WILDCONNECT)
        {
        if(hsz2 != hszName && hsz2 != NULL)
            return FALSE;
```

```
        j = 0;
        for(i = 0; i < CTOPICS; i++)
            {
            if(hsz1 == NULL || hsz1 == ahszTopics[i])
                {
                hszPair[j].hszSvc = hszName;
                hszPair[j].hszTopic = ahszTopics[i];
                j++;
                }
            }
        hszPair[j].hszSvc = (HSZ)NULL;
        hszPair[j].hszTopic = (HSZ)NULL;
        return (HDDEDATA)DdeCreateDataHandle(idInst,
                (LPBYTE)&hszPair[0],sizeof(hszPair),0L,0,CF_TEXT,0);
        }
```

```
return (HDDEDATA)FALSE;
```

In the preceding code, the service-name handle specified in the **DdeConnect()** function is the hsz2 parameter in the DdeCallBack() function. The topic-name handle specified in the **DdeConnect()** function is the hsz1 parameter. If either hsz1 or hsz2 is NULL, the DDEML will generate an XTYP_WILDCONNECT transaction, which is the value in wType. For an XTYP_CONNECT transaction, the callback function determines whether the hsz2 parameter matches any of its supported service names, and the hsz1 parameter for a supported topic name. If there is a match, the server returns TRUE to the DDEML. Note that the preceding example has only one service name: hszName.

If the server receives an XTYP_WILDCONNECT transaction, it generates a null-terminated array of HSZPAIR structures that contains all the valid service-name and topic-name combinations. The server returns a handle to the array using the **DdeCreateDataHandle()** function.

Establishing Multiple Conversations—*DdeConnectList()* **and** *DdeQueryNextServer()*

The **DdeConnectList()** function returns a handle to a conversation list. The **DdeConnectList()** function also initiates conversations with all servers with service names and topic names that match those the client application specified in the **DdeConnectList()** function. A client application can use the conversation list handle to retrieve individual conversation handles by using the **DdeQueryNextServer()** function. Here is the prototype for **DdeConnectList()**:

```
HCONVLIST EXPENTRY DdeConnectList(DWORD idInst, HSZ hszService,
      HSZ hszTopic,  HCONVLIST hConvList, PCONVCONTEXT pCC);
```

The **DdeConnectList()** function is similar to the **DdeConnect()** function. The idInst, hszService, hszTopic, and pCC parameters are the same as the **DdeConnect()** function. The hConvList parameter is a handle to a conversation list. It must be NULL on the first call to **DdeConnectList()**. On subsequent calls, the hConvList parameter identifies an existing conversation list handle. When the DDEML receives an hConvList parameter with a valid conversation list handle, it enumerates the conversation list; in other words, it removes terminated conversations from the conversation list.

When a client application calls the **DdeConnectList()** function, it causes the DDEML to send an XTYP_WILDCONNECT message to all servers that respond to the specified service name. The server applications respond by returning a handle to an array of HSZPAIR structures. The DDEML then sends an XTYP_CONNECT_CONFIRM transaction to each responding server for each service and topic name combination in the array of HSZPAIR structures. At this point, the DDEML generates a handle to a conversation list that the client receives as the return value from **DdeConnectList()**.

After a client has a conversation list handle, it can retrieve individual conversation handles by using the **DdeQueryNextServer()** function. The **DdeQueryNextServer()** function has the following prototype:

```
HCONV EXPENTRY DdeQueryNextServer(HCONVLIST hConvList,
                                  HCONV hConvPrev);
```

The **DdeQueryNextServer()** function has two parameters. The first parameter, hConvList, contains a conversation list handle gotten from the **DdeConnectList()** function. The second parameter is NULL on the first call to **DdeQueryNextServer()**. This tells the DDEML to return the first conversation handle in the conversation list. On subsequent calls to **DdeQueryNextServer()**, you should specify the last conversation handle gotten from **DdeQueryNextServer()** in the hConvPrev parameter. This allows the DDEML to index the list of conversation handles. The **DdeQueryNextServer()** function returns NULL if it passed the last conversation in the list. When the client gets a conversation handle from **DdeQueryNextServer()**, it is often useful to retrieve additional information about the conversation. The **DdeQueryConvInfo()** function provides this information.

Getting Conversation Information—*DdeQueryConvInfo()*

Whenever you need more information about a conversation, you can call **DdeQueryConvInfo()**. The **DdeQueryConvInfo()** function provides a wealth of information through the CONVINFO structure. The **DdeQueryConvInfo()** function has the following prototype:

```
WORD EXPENTRY DdeQueryConvInfo(HCONV hConv,
                    DWORD idTransaction, PCONVINFO pConvInfo);
```

The first parameter, hConv, is a conversation handle. The second parameter, idTransaction, is a transaction identification number. This isn't a concern to you right now. You will revisit **DdeQueryConvInfo()** in a later chapter to discuss items not covered here. The last parameter is a pointer to the CONVINFO structure. This is where the DDEML provides conversation information. The CONVINFO structure has the following typedef:

```
typedef struct _CONVINFO {
    DWORD       cb;
    DWORD       hUser;
    HCONV       hConvPartner;
    HSZ         hszSvcPartner;
    HSZ         hszServiceReq;
    HSZ         hszTopic;
    HSZ         hszItem;
    WORD        wFmt;
    WORD        wType;
    WORD        wStatus;
    WORD        wConvst;
    WORD        wLastError;
    HCONVLIST   hConvList;
    CONVCONTEXT ConvCtxt;
} CONVINFO;
```

As you can see, there's much information in the CONVINFO structure; however, the only items of interest to you now are the cb, hszSvcPartner, and hszTopic members. The cb member is the size of the CONVINFO structure. The hszSvcPartner and hszTopic members contain the string handles for a conversation's service and topic names. The example client application at the end of this chapter uses the **DdeQueryConvInfo()** function to get service and topic-name handles for a conversation. After the application has the handles, it can use the **DdeQueryString()** function to acquire the string values for the service and topic names. The code to do this looks something like the following code:

```
CONVINFO ci;

ci.cb = sizeof(CONVINFO);
DdeQueryConvInfo(hConv, QID_SYNC, &ci);

cbService = (WORD)DdeQueryString(idInst, ci.hszSvcPartner,
                                  NULL, 0, 0);
cbTopic = (WORD)DdeQueryString(idInst, ci.hszTopic, NULL, 0, 0);

DdeQueryString(idInst, ci,hszSvcPartner, &achName[0],
               cbService+1, 0);
DdeQueryString(idInst, ci.hszTopic, &achTopic[0], cbTopic+1, 0);
```

The idTransaction parameter in **DdeQueryConvInfo()** is QID_SYNC, which specifies a synchronous transaction. This replaces the asynchronous transaction id, because this application has yet to submit a transaction. The first two calls to **DdeQueryString()** get the length of service and topic name strings. The second call gets the strings. The length returned by **DdeQueryString()** is the length of the string minus the NULL terminating character. Thus, if you add 1 to the length, **DdeQueryString()** will return the string plus the NULL terminating character.

Terminating a Conversation—
DdeDisconnect() **and** *DdeDisconnectList()*

An application can terminate a conversation with the **DdeDisconnect()** function. Applications should terminate a conversation when they no longer need the services provided by the topic of the conversation. This reduces the amount of tracking the DDEML has to do. Additionally, when an application calls **DdeConnectList()**, it may get a number of unwanted conversations. **DdeDisconnect()** can terminate individual conversations from a conversation list. The **DdeDisconnect()** function takes one parameter: a conversation handle. It returns TRUE if it successfully terminated the conversation and FALSE if it was unsuccessful. Here's an example of **DdeDisconnect()**:

```
if(DdeDisconnect(hConv))
    MessageBox(hwnd, "Conversation Terminated", "Client", MB_OK);
```

```
else
    MessageBox(hwnd, "Error in DdeDisconnect", "Client", MB_OK);
```

The DdeDisconnectList() function destroys a conversation list and terminates all active conversations within the list. The DdeDisconnectList() function has one parameter: a conversation list handle. It returns TRUE if the call was successful and FALSE if it was unsuccessful.

Reestablishing a Terminated Conversation—*DdeReconnect()*

Occasionally, a server application may use the **DdeDisconnect()** function to terminate a conversation that a client application wants to remain active. The disconnection may happen due to the design of the server application. If a client application still requires a conversation that a server application terminated, it can attempt to reconnect with the server using the **DdeReconnect()** function.

The **DdeReconnect()** function has one parameter, which is a handle to a terminated conversation. If the **DdeReconnect()** function is successful, it returns a handle to the reconnected conversation. If the reconnection is unsuccessful, the function returns NULL. When an application calls the **DdeReconnect()** function, the DDEML attempts to reestablish any advise loops that were active before the server terminated the conversation. I discuss advise loops in Chapter 3, "DDEML Transaction Management."

Example DDEML Client and Server Applications

When you write DDEML applications, keep a couple of requirements in mind. DDEML applications must execute in a protected-mode Windows environment. This means Windows must run in either 386 enhanced mode or standard mode. This is not a problem under Windows 3.1, because Windows 3.1 does not support real mode. Windows 3.0 supports real mode, however, and can also run DDEML applications despite the fact that DDEML.DLL did not ship with Windows 3.0. You can distribute the DDEML.DLL with your applications to enable them to run under Windows 3.0.

It is a friendly practice to ensure that your program can execute under the environment the user has running. Windows can do some of this work for you. If the DDEML.DLL file is not in the system path, Windows will prompt the user to place a diskette containing DDEML.DLL into drive A. This is not the most friendly approach, at least from my personal experience. Almost every time this happens to me, I don't have the diskette containing the file, or I don't know anything about the file.

You can go to extremes in programming for the existence of DDEML.DLL; however, I think a good trade-off is an install program for your applications that copies DDEML.DLL into the system directory if it does not exist. Testing for a protected-mode Windows environment is much easier. This requires only a few lines of code. I include this code in all my applications, although it is unlikely that someone will be running Windows in real mode. To test for the use of a protected-mode environment, you can use the **GetWinFlags()** function.

GetWinFlags() returns a 32-bit value that specifies the configuration of the current Windows environment. It has flags for CPUs, math coprocessors, EMS frame size, and system modes. You can use the WF_PMODE flag to determine whether Windows is running in protected mode. I use the following code to test for protected mode when the main window receives the WM_CREATE message:

```
dwWinFlags = GetWinFlags();
      if(dwWinFlags & WF_PMODE)
```

If this condition is TRUE, I continue with the main window initialization; otherwise, I display a message box that informs the user to get a "real machine" to run Windows.

The Example DDEML Server Application

The server application uses the **DdeNameService()** function to register its service names. When the server receives an XTYP_CONNECT_CONFIRM transaction, it increments a counter for the number of current conversations. When the server receives an XTYP_DISCONNECT transaction, the server decrements the counter. The counter is displayed in the client area of the server's window. Each time the counter changes, the server invalidates the rectangle for the window, thus producing a WM_PAINT message. At this point, the server paints a message specifying the number of current conversations.

Listing 2.1. The server.h header file.

```
#define NOCOMM
#define DDEMLDB
#include <windows.h>
#include <ddeml.h>
#include "resource.h"
#include "dialogs.h"

#ifndef MAIN
#define EXTERN extern
#else
#define EXTERN
#endif

#define SZCLASSNAME 40
#define SZWINDOWTITLE 40
#define SZMESSAGE 128
#define CTOPICS 3

EXTERN DWORD idInst;
EXTERN HINSTANCE hInst;
EXTERN HWND hwnd;
EXTERN FARPROC lpDdeProc;
EXTERN WORD cServers;
EXTERN WORD cyText;
EXTERN RECT rcConnCount;
EXTERN HSZ hszName;
EXTERN HSZ ahszTopics[CTOPICS];

int PASCAL WinMain (HINSTANCE, HINSTANCE, LPSTR, int);
BOOL InitApplication(HINSTANCE);
BOOL InitInstance(HINSTANCE, int);
BOOL PASCAL CreateDlgBox(HWND, LPCSTR, FARPROC);
LRESULT CALLBACK MainWndProc(HWND, WORD, WPARAM, LPARAM);
LRESULT CALLBACK AboutDlgProc(HWND, WORD, WPARAM, LPARAM);
HDDEDATA EXPENTRY DdeCallBack(WORD, WORD, HCONV, HSZ, HSZ,
                             HDDEDATA, DWORD, DWORD);
```

Listing 2.2. The dialogs.h header file.

```
#define IDD_ABOUT 100
```

Listing 2.3. The resource.h header file.

```
#define IDM_DDECLIENTMENU    10
#define IDM_ABOUT            11
#define IDM_CONNECTIONS      12
#define IDS_CLASSNAME        1
#define IDS_WINDOWTITLE      2
#define IDS_INITSUCCESS      3
#define IDS_INITFAIL         4
#define IDS_NOTPMODE         5
```

Listing 2.4. The server.c source file.

```c
#include "server.h"

BOOL PASCAL InitializeDDEML(HWND);
BOOL PASCAL CleanUpDDEML(HWND);
VOID PASCAL MsgBox(HWND, WORD, WORD);
VOID PASCAL DrawLine(HDC, RECT*, RECT*, PSTR);
/***********************************************************/
/* Function: MainWndProc                                 */
/* Purpose: Processes messages for main window.          */
/***********************************************************/
LRESULT CALLBACK MainWndProc(HWND hWnd, WORD message,
                             WPARAM wParam, LPARAM lParam)

    {
    DWORD dwWinFlags;
    PAINTSTRUCT ps;
    RECT rc;
    char szT[80];

    switch(message)
        {
        case WM_CREATE:
```

continues

Listing 2.4. continued

```c
            dwWinFlags = GetWinFlags();
            if(dwWinFlags & WF_PMODE)
                {
                if(!InitializeDDEML(hWnd))
                    {
                    MsgBox(hWnd, IDS_INITFAIL, MB_OK | MB_ICONSTOP);
                    return -1;
                    }
                }
            else
                {
                MsgBox(hWnd, IDS_NOTPMODE, MB_OK | MB_ICONSTOP);
                return -1;
                }
            return FALSE;
        case WM_COMMAND:
            switch((WORD)wParam)
                {
                /* User selected About ... from menu */
                case IDM_ABOUT:
                    CreateDlgBox(hWnd,
                                 (LPCSTR)MAKEINTRESOURCE(IDD_ABOUT),
                                 (FARPROC)AboutDlgProc);

                    break;
                }
            break;

        case WM_PAINT:
            BeginPaint(hwnd, &ps);
            SetBkMode(ps.hdc, TRANSPARENT);
            GetClientRect(hwnd, &rc);
            rc.bottom = rc.top + cyText;

            wsprintf(szT, "# of connections:%d", cServers);
            rcConnCount = rc;
            DrawLine(ps.hdc, &ps.rcPaint, &rc, szT);

            EndPaint(hwnd, &ps);
            break;
```

```
        case WM_DESTROY:
            /* Application is ending--post a WM_QUIT message */
            CleanUpDDEML(hWnd);
            PostQuitMessage(0);
            break;
        default:
            return DefWindowProc(hWnd, message, wParam, lParam);
        }
    return FALSE;
    }

/*****************************************************************/
/* Function: InitializeDDEML                                     */
/* Purpose: Register application and callback func with DDEML.   */
/* Returns: TRUE/FALSE                                           */
/*****************************************************************/
BOOL PASCAL InitializeDDEML(HWND hWnd)
    {
    BOOL bResult;

    lpDdeProc = MakeProcInstance((FARPROC)DdeCallBack, hInst);
    idInst = 0L;
    bResult = FALSE;
    if(lpDdeProc)
        {
        if(DMLERR_NO_ERROR == DdeInitialize((LPDWORD) &idInst,
                                    (PFNCALLBACK) lpDdeProc,
                                    APPCMD_FILTERINITS,
                                    0L))
            {
            hszName = DdeCreateStringHandle(idInst, "DDEServe",
                                    CP_WINANSI);
            ahszTopics[0] = DdeCreateStringHandle(idInst,
                                    "System", CP_WINANSI);
            ahszTopics[1] = DdeCreateStringHandle(idInst,
                                    "AMEX", CP_WINANSI);
            ahszTopics[2] = DdeCreateStringHandle(idInst,
                                    "NYSE", CP_WINANSI);
            DdeNameService(idInst, hszName, NULL, DNS_REGISTER);
            bResult = TRUE;
            }
```

continues

Listing 2.4. continued

```
        else
            FreeProcInstance((FARPROC)lpDdeProc);
        }
    return bResult;
    }


/**********************************************************************/
/* Function: CleanUpDDEML                                           */
/* Purpose: Uninitialize application and free resources.            */
/* Returns: TRUE                                                    */
/**********************************************************************/
BOOL PASCAL CleanUpDDEML(HWND hWnd)
    {
    if(lpDdeProc)
        {
        DdeUninitialize(idInst);
        FreeProcInstance((FARPROC)lpDdeProc);
        }
    return TRUE;
    }


/**********************************************************************/
/* Function: MsgBox                                                 */
/* Purpose: Creates a message box.                                  */
/**********************************************************************/
VOID PASCAL MsgBox(HWND hWnd, WORD wMsg, WORD wType)
    {
    char szWindowTitle[SZWINDOWTITLE];
    char szMessage[SZMESSAGE];

    LoadString(hInst, IDS_WINDOWTITLE,
                szWindowTitle, sizeof szWindowTitle);
    LoadString(hInst, wMsg,
                szMessage, sizeof szMessage);
    MessageBox(hWnd, szMessage, szWindowTitle, wType);
    }


/**********************************************************************/
/* Function: DrawLine                                               */
/* Purpose: Draws text line.                                        */
/**********************************************************************/
```

```
VOID PASCAL DrawLine(HDC hdc, RECT *prcClip,
                     RECT *prcText, PSTR psz)
    {
    RECT rc;

    if (IntersectRect(&rc, prcText, prcClip))
        {
        DrawText(hdc, psz, -1, prcText,
                 DT_LEFT ¦ DT_EXTERNALLEADING ¦
                 DT_SINGLELINE ¦ DT_EXPANDTABS ¦
                 DT_NOCLIP ¦ DT_NOPREFIX);
        }
    OffsetRect(prcText, 0, cyText);
    }
```

Listing 2.5. The dialogs.c source file.

```
#include "server.h"

/******************************************************************/
/* Function: CreateDlgBox                                         */
/* Purpose: Generic function to create dialog boxes.              */
/* Returns: TRUE/FALSE                                            */
/******************************************************************/
BOOL PASCAL CreateDlgBox(HWND hWnd, LPCSTR lpTemplateName,
                         FARPROC lpDlgProc)
    {
    BOOL    bResult;

    lpDlgProc = MakeProcInstance(lpDlgProc, hInst);
    if(lpDlgProc)
        {
        DialogBox(hInst, lpTemplateName, hWnd, (DLGPROC)lpDlgProc);
        FreeProcInstance(lpDlgProc);
        bResult = TRUE;
        }
    else
        bResult = FALSE;
```

continues

Listing 2.5. continued

```
    return bResult;
    }

/**********************************************************************/
/* Function: AboutDlgProc                                          */
/* Purpose: Handles messages for the About dialog box.             */
/* Returns: TRUE/FALSE                                             */
/**********************************************************************/
LRESULT CALLBACK AboutDlgProc(HWND hDlg, WORD message,
                              WPARAM wParam, LPARAM lParam)

    {

    switch(message)
        {
        case WM_INITDIALOG:
            return (LRESULT)TRUE;
        case WM_COMMAND:
            switch((WORD)wParam)
                {
                case IDOK:
                case IDCANCEL:
                    EndDialog(hDlg, TRUE);
                    return (LRESULT)TRUE;
                }
            break;
        }
    return (LRESULT)FALSE;
    }
```

Listing 2.6. The dde.c source file.

```
#include "server.h"

/**********************************************************************/
/* Function: DdeCallBack                                           */
/* Purpose: This function handles callbacks from the DDEML.        */
/* Parameters:                                                     */
/*            WORD wType       - transaction type                  */
/*            WORD wFmt        - clipboard data format             */
```

```
/*              HCONV hConv     - handle of the conversation    */
/*              HSZ hsz1        - handle of a string            */
/*              HSZ hsz2        - handle of a string            */
/*              HDDEDATA hData  - handle of a global memory object */
/*              DWORD dwData1   - transaction-specific data     */
/*              DWORD dwData2   - transaction-specific data     */
/* Returns: Results vary depending on transaction type.         */
/*****************************************************************/
HDDEDATA EXPENTRY DdeCallBack(WORD wType, WORD wFmt, HCONV hConv,
                             HSZ hsz1, HSZ hsz2, HDDEDATA hData,
                             DWORD lData1,DWORD lData2)
    {
    WORD i, j;
    HSZPAIR hszPair[CTOPICS+1];

    if (wType == XTYP_CONNECT_CONFIRM) {
        cServers++;
        InvalidateRect(hwnd, &rcConnCount, TRUE);
        return(0);
    }
    if (wType == XTYP_DISCONNECT) {
        cServers--;
        InvalidateRect(hwnd, &rcConnCount, TRUE);
        return(0);
    }


    if(wType == XTYP_CONNECT)
        {
        if(hszName == hsz2)
            for(i = 0; i < CTOPICS; i++)
                if(hsz1 == ahszTopics[i])
                    return (HDDEDATA)TRUE;
        }
    if(wType == XTYP_WILDCONNECT)
        {
        if(hsz2 != hszName && hsz2 != NULL)
            return FALSE;

        j = 0;
        for(i = 0; i < CTOPICS; i++)
            {
```

continues

Listing 2.6. continued

```
            if(hsz1 == NULL || hsz1 == ahszTopics[i])
                {
                hszPair[j].hszSvc = hszName;
                hszPair[j].hszTopic = ahszTopics[i];
                j++;
                }
            }
        hszPair[j].hszSvc = (HSZ)NULL;
        hszPair[j].hszTopic = (HSZ)NULL;
        return (HDDEDATA)DdeCreateDataHandle(idInst,
                (LPBYTE)&hszPair[0],sizeof(hszPair),0L,0,CF_TEXT,0);
        }
    return NULL;
    }
```

Listing 2.7. The winmain.c source file.

```
#define MAIN
#include "server.h"

/*********************************************************************/
/* Function: WinMain                                                 */
/* Purpose: Main function for windows app. Initializes all           */
/*          instances of app, translates and dispatches messages.    */
/* Returns: Value of PostQuitMessage                                 */
/*********************************************************************/
int PASCAL WinMain(HINSTANCE hInstance, HINSTANCE hPrevInstance,
                LPSTR lpszCmdLine, int nCmdShow)

    {
    MSG msg;

    /* If there isn't a previous instance of app, then  */
    /* initialize the first instance of app.            */
    if(!hPrevInstance)
        if(!InitApplication(hInstance))
            return FALSE;

    /* Perform initialization for all instances of application */
    if(!InitInstance(hInstance, nCmdShow))
```

```
        return FALSE;

    /* Get messages for this application until WM_QUIT is received*/
    while(GetMessage(&msg, 0, 0, 0))
        {
        TranslateMessage(&msg);
        DispatchMessage(&msg);
        }
    return (int)msg.wParam;
}
```

Listing 2.8. The init.c source file.

```
#include "server.h"

/******************************************************************/
/* Function: InitApplication                                      */
/* Purpose: Performs all initialization for first instance of app.*/
/* Returns: TRUE if successful, FALSE if failure                  */
/******************************************************************/
BOOL InitApplication(HINSTANCE hInstance)
    {
    BOOL bResult;
    char szClassName[SZCLASSNAME];
    WNDCLASS wc;

    /* Load the window class name from resource string table */

    if(!LoadString(hInstance, IDS_CLASSNAME,
                   szClassName, sizeof szClassName))
        return FALSE;

    /* Class styles */
    wc.style        = 0;
    /* Name of message loop function for windows of this class */
    wc.lpfnWndProc  = MainWndProc;
    /* Not using Class Extra data */
    wc.cbClsExtra   = 0;
    /* Not using Window Extra data */
    wc.cbWndExtra   = 0;
```

continues

Listing 2.8. continued

```
    /* Instance that owns this class */
    wc.hInstance      = hInstance;
    /* Use default application icon */
    wc.hIcon          = LoadIcon(NULL, IDI_APPLICATION);
    /* Use arrow cursor */
    wc.hCursor        = LoadCursor(NULL, IDC_ARROW);
    /* Use system background color */
    wc.hbrBackground = GetStockObject(WHITE_BRUSH);
    /* Resource name for menu */
    wc.lpszMenuName  = MAKEINTRESOURCE(IDM_DDESERVERMENU);
    /* Name given to this class */
    wc.lpszClassName = szClassName;

    /* Register the window class */
    bResult = RegisterClass(&wc);

    /* return result based on registration */
    return bResult;
    }

/**********************************************************************/
/* Function: InitInstance                                           */
/* Purpose: Performs all initialization for all instances of app. */
/* Returns: TRUE if successful, FALSE if failure                   */
/**********************************************************************/
BOOL InitInstance (HINSTANCE hInstance, int nCmdShow)
    {
    RECT Rect;
    TEXTMETRIC metrics;
    HDC hdc;

    char szClassName[SZCLASSNAME];
    char szWindowTitle[SZWINDOWTITLE];

    hInst = hInstance;

    /* Load the window class name from resource string table */
    if(!LoadString(hInst, IDS_CLASSNAME,
                   szClassName, sizeof szClassName))
        return FALSE;
```

```
    /* Load the window title from resource string table */
    if(!LoadString(hInst, IDS_WINDOWTITLE,
                   szWindowTitle, sizeof szWindowTitle))
        return FALSE;

    hwnd = CreateWindow(szClassName,          /* Window class */
                        szWindowTitle,        /* Text for title bar */
                        WS_OVERLAPPEDWINDOW,  /* Style(s)*/
                        CW_USEDEFAULT,        /* Default x  pos */
                        CW_USEDEFAULT,        /* Default y  pos */
                        CW_USEDEFAULT,        /* Default cx pos */
                        CW_USEDEFAULT,        /* Default cy pos */
                        0,                    /* Parent window  */
                        0,                    /* Menu           */
                        hInstance,            /* Owning instance */
                        NULL);                /* User-defined params*/

    /* If CreateWindow wasn't successful, return FALSE */
    if(!hwnd)
        return FALSE;

    GetClientRect(hwnd, (LPRECT) &Rect);

    hdc = GetDC(hwnd);
    GetTextMetrics(hdc, &metrics);
    cyText = metrics.tmHeight + metrics.tmExternalLeading;
    ReleaseDC(hwnd, hdc);

    /* Show and paint window */
    ShowWindow(hwnd, nCmdShow);
    UpdateWindow(hwnd);

    return TRUE;
    }
```

Listing 2.9. The server.rc resource file.

```
#include <windows.h>
#include "resource.h"
#include "dialogs.h"
```

continues

Listing 2.9. continued

```
IDM_DDESERVERMENU MENU
    BEGIN
        POPUP "&Help"
        BEGIN
            MENUITEM "&About Server ...",IDM_ABOUT
        END
    END

STRINGTABLE
    BEGIN
        IDS_CLASSNAME     "DDEServerClass"
        IDS_WINDOWTITLE   "DDE Server"
        IDS_INITSUCCESS   "DDEML Initialization Successful."
        IDS_INITFAIL      "DDEML Initialization Failed."
        IDS_NOTPMODE      "Windows must run in protected\n
            mode to run this program."
    END

#include "server.dlg"
```

Listing 2.10. The server.dlg dialog file.

```
DLGINCLUDE RCDATA DISCARDABLE
BEGIN
    "DIALOGS.H\0"
END

IDD_ABOUT DIALOG 130, 47, 140, 94
STYLE DS_MODALFRAME ¦ WS_POPUP ¦ WS_VISIBLE ¦ WS_CAPTION ¦ WS_SYSMENU
CAPTION "About DDE Server"
FONT 10, "System"
BEGIN
    CTEXT      "Microsoft Windows", -1, 22, 10, 92, 8
    CTEXT      "DDEML Server Application", -1, 13, 28, 111, 8
    LTEXT      "Copyright Jeffrey Clark 1991", -1, 20, 49, 105, 8
    PUSHBUTTON "OK", IDOK, 49, 70, 40, 14
END
```

Listing 2.11. The server.def module definition file.

```
NAME Server

DESCRIPTION 'DDE Example Server, Copyright Jeffrey Clark, 1991'

EXETYPE WINDOWS

STUB 'WINSTUB.EXE'

CODE PRELOAD MOVEABLE DISCARDABLE
DATA PRELOAD MOVEABLE MULTIPLE

HEAPSIZE 1024
STACKSIZE 8192

SEGMENTS
    WINMAIN_TEXT    MOVEABLE                 PRELOAD
    SERVER_TEXT     MOVEABLE                 PRELOAD
    INIT_TEXT       MOVEABLE DISCARDABLE PRELOAD
    DDE_TEXT        MOVEABLE DISCARDABLE LOADONCALL
    DIALOGS_TEXT    MOVEABLE DISCARDABLE LOADONCALL

EXPORTS
    MainWndProc @1
    AboutDlgProc @2
    DdeCallBack @3
```

Listing 2.12. The SERVER make file.

```
CC = cl -c -AM -Gsw -Od -W3 -Zpi -Fo$@

all: server.exe

server.h: dialogs.h resource.h

server.res: server.rc server.dlg dialogs.h resource.h
  rc -r server

dialogs.obj: dialogs.c server.h
  $(CC) $*.c
```

continues

71

Listing 2.12. continued

```
init.obj: init.c server.h
  $(CC) $*.c

winmain.obj: winmain.c server.h
  $(CC) $*.c

server.obj: server.c server.h
  $(CC) $*.c

dde.obj: dde.c server.h
  $(CC) $*.c

server.exe::  dialogs.obj init.obj winmain.obj server.obj dde.obj \
              server.res server.def
    link /CO /MAP /NOD @<<
dialogs+
init+
winmain+
server+
dde
$@

libw mlibcew ddeml
server.def
<<
    mapsym server
    rc server.res
```

The Example DDEML Client Application

The client program, shown in Figure 2.1, is a little more complicated than the server program. It has a dialog box that enables the user to connect and disconnect to servers. It also enables the user to do a wildcard connect that uses the **DdeConnectList()** function. After the client creates a conversation, the program places the service and topic names in a list box. The user can then select an individual conversation to disconnect. When the user leaves the dialog box, all conversations and conversation lists are disconnected. This eliminates a lot of tracking code that would take too much space for this example. Additionally, the client application enables the user to connect to only one server at a time, because connecting to more than one server at a time would require additional tracking code.

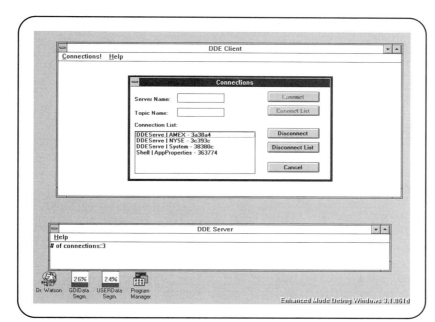

Figure 2.1.
Example client application.

Listing 2.13. The client.h header file.

```
#define NOCOMM
#define DDEMLDB
#include <windows.h>
#include <ddeml.h>
#include "resource.h"
#include "dialogs.h"

#ifndef MAIN
#define EXTERN extern
#else
#define EXTERN
#endif
```

continues

Listing 2.13. continued

```c
#define SZCLASSNAME 40
#define SZWINDOWTITLE 40
#define SZMESSAGE 128

#define MAX_NAME_SIZE 100

EXTERN DWORD idInst;
EXTERN HINSTANCE hInst;
EXTERN HWND hwnd;
EXTERN FARPROC lpDdeProc;

#define MAX_CONNECTS 100

typedef struct tagconnects {
    char achServiceName[20];
    char achTopicName[20];
    HCONV hConv;
    } MYCONNECTS;

int PASCAL WinMain (HINSTANCE, HINSTANCE, LPSTR, int);
BOOL InitApplication(HINSTANCE);
BOOL InitInstance(HINSTANCE, int);
BOOL PASCAL CreateDlgBox(HWND, LPCSTR, FARPROC);
LRESULT CALLBACK MainWndProc(HWND, WORD, WPARAM, LPARAM);
LRESULT CALLBACK AboutDlgProc(HWND, WORD, WPARAM, LPARAM);
LRESULT CALLBACK ConnectDlgProc(HWND, WORD, WPARAM, LPARAM);
HDDEDATA EXPENTRY DdeCallBack(WORD, WORD, HCONV, HSZ, HSZ,
                             HDDEDATA, DWORD, DWORD);
```

Listing 2.14. The dialogs.h header file.

```c
#define IDD_ABOUT                100
#define IDC_SERVERNAME           201
#define IDC_TOPICNAME            202
#define IDC_CONNECTLIST          203
#define IDD_CONNECTIONS          200
#define IDC_DISCONNECT           204
#define IDC_CONNECT              205
#define IDC_CONNECTLISTCHECK     206
```

```
#define IDC_DISCONNECTLIST        207
#define IDC_LIST                  208
```

Listing 2.15. The resource.h header file.

```
#define IDM_DDECLIENTMENU    10
#define IDM_ABOUT            11
#define IDM_CONNECTIONS      12

#define IDS_CLASSNAME        1
#define IDS_WINDOWTITLE      2
#define IDS_INITSUCCESS      3
#define IDS_INITFAIL         4
#define IDS_NOTPMODE         5
```

Listing 2.16. The client.c source file.

```
#include "client.h"

BOOL PASCAL InitializeDDEML(HWND);
BOOL PASCAL CleanUpDDEML(HWND);
VOID PASCAL MsgBox(HWND, WORD, WORD);

/*******************************************************************/
/* Function: MainWndProc                                          */
/* Purpose: Processes messages for main window.                   */
/* Returns: Varies                                                */
/*******************************************************************/
LRESULT CALLBACK MainWndProc(HWND hWnd, WORD message,
                        WPARAM wParam, LPARAM lParam)
    {
    DWORD dwWinFlags;

    switch(message)
        {
        case WM_CREATE:
            dwWinFlags = GetWinFlags();
            if(dwWinFlags & WF_PMODE)
```

continues

Listing 2.16. continued

```
                {
                if(!InitializeDDEML(hWnd))
                    {
                    MsgBox(hWnd, IDS_INITFAIL, MB_OK | MB_ICONSTOP);
                    return -1;
                    }
                }
            else
                {
                MsgBox(hWnd, IDS_NOTPMODE, MB_OK | MB_ICONSTOP);
                return -1;
                }
            return FALSE;

        case WM_COMMAND:
            switch((WORD)wParam)
                {
                /* User selected About... from menu */
                 case IDM_ABOUT:
                    CreateDlgBox(hWnd,
                             (LPCSTR)MAKEINTRESOURCE(IDD_ABOUT),
                             (FARPROC)AboutDlgProc);
                    break;
                 case IDM_CONNECTIONS:
                    CreateDlgBox(hWnd,
                             (LPCSTR)MAKEINTRESOURCE(IDD_CONNECTIONS),
                             (FARPROC)ConnectDlgProc);
                    break;
                }
            break;
        case WM_DESTROY:
            CleanUpDDEML(hWnd);
            /* Application is ending--post a WM_QUIT message */
            PostQuitMessage(0);
            break;
        default:
            return DefWindowProc(hWnd, message, wParam, lParam);
        }
    return FALSE;
    }
```

```
/**********************************************************************/
/* Function: InitializeDDEML                                          */
/* Purpose: Registers application and callback function with DDEML.  */
/* Returns: TRUE/FALSE                                                */
/**********************************************************************/
BOOL PASCAL InitializeDDEML(HWND hWnd)
    {
    BOOL bResult;

    lpDdeProc = MakeProcInstance((FARPROC)DdeCallBack, hInst);
    idInst = 0L;
    bResult = FALSE;

    if(lpDdeProc)
        {
        if(DMLERR_NO_ERROR == DdeInitialize((LPDWORD) &idInst,
                                            (PFNCALLBACK) lpDdeProc,
                                            APPCMD_CLIENTONLY,
                                            0L))
            bResult = TRUE;
        else
            FreeProcInstance((FARPROC)lpDdeProc);
        }
    return bResult;
    }


/**********************************************************************/
/* Function: CleanUpDDEML                                             */
/* Purpose: Uninitializes applications and frees callback.           */
/* Returns: TRUE                                                      */
/**********************************************************************/
BOOL PASCAL CleanUpDDEML(HWND hWnd)
    {
    if(lpDdeProc)
        {
        DdeUninitialize(idInst);
        FreeProcInstance((FARPROC)lpDdeProc);
        }
    return TRUE;
    }
```

continues

Listing 2.16. continued

```c
/******************************************************************/
/* Function: MsgBox                                              */
/* Purpose: Creates a message box.                               */
/******************************************************************/
VOID PASCAL MsgBox(HWND hWnd, WORD wMsg, WORD wType)
    {
    char szWindowTitle[SZWINDOWTITLE];
    char szMessage[SZMESSAGE];

    LoadString(hInst, IDS_WINDOWTITLE,
                szWindowTitle, sizeof szWindowTitle);
    LoadString(hInst, wMsg,
                szMessage, sizeof szMessage);
    MessageBox(hWnd, szMessage, szWindowTitle, wType);
    }
```

Listing 2.17. The dialogs.c source file.

```c
#include "client.h"

HCONV hConv, hConvList;
HCONV ahConv[100];
WORD cConnects;

VOID PASCAL AddConversation(HWND, HSZ, HSZ, HCONV, BOOL);
VOID PASCAL AddConvItemToList(HWND, HSZ, HSZ, HCONV);
/******************************************************************/
/* Function: CreateDlgBox                                        */
/* Purpose: Generic function to create dialog boxes.             */
/* Returns: TRUE/FALSE                                           */
/******************************************************************/
BOOL PASCAL CreateDlgBox(HWND hWnd, LPCSTR lpTemplateName,
                        FARPROC lpDlgProc)
    {
    BOOL    bResult;

    lpDlgProc = MakeProcInstance(lpDlgProc, hInst);
    if(lpDlgProc)
```

```
        {
        DialogBox(hInst, lpTemplateName, hWnd, (DLGPROC)lpDlgProc);
        FreeProcInstance(lpDlgProc);
        bResult = TRUE;
        }
    else
        bResult = FALSE;

    return bResult;
    }

/*******************************************************************/
/* Function: ConnectDlgProc                                        */
/* Purpose: Handles messages for the Connections dialog box.       */
/* Returns: TRUE/FALSE                                             */
/*******************************************************************/
LRESULT CALLBACK ConnectDlgProc(HWND hDlg, WORD message,
                                WPARAM wParam, LPARAM lParam)
    {
    char ach[MAX_NAME_SIZE];
    HSZ hszService, hszTopic;
    WORD  i, dwIndex, dwRemaining;
    CONVINFO ci;

    switch(message)
        {
        case WM_INITDIALOG:
            EnableWindow(GetDlgItem(hDlg, IDC_DISCONNECT),FALSE);
            EnableWindow(GetDlgItem(hDlg, IDC_DISCONNECTLIST),FALSE);
            hConv = hConvList = cConnects = 0;
            return (LRESULT)TRUE;

        case WM_COMMAND:
            switch((WORD)wParam)
                {
                case IDOK:
                case IDCANCEL:
                    if(hConvList)
                        DdeDisconnectList(hConvList);
                    else
                        if(hConv)
```

continues

79

Listing 2.17. continued

```
                        DdeDisconnect(ahConv[0]);
                EndDialog(hDlg, TRUE);
                return (LRESULT)TRUE;
                break;
            case IDC_CONNECT:
                GetDlgItemText(hDlg, IDC_SERVERNAME,
                                ach, MAX_NAME_SIZE);
                hszService = DdeCreateStringHandle(idInst,
                                                ach, 0);

                GetDlgItemText(hDlg, IDC_TOPICNAME,
                                ach, MAX_NAME_SIZE);
                hszTopic = DdeCreateStringHandle(idInst,
                                                ach, 0);

                hConv = DdeConnect(idInst, hszService,
                                hszTopic, (LPVOID)NULL);
                if (hConv)
                    {
                    PostMessage(hDlg,WM_NEXTDLGCTL,
                        (WPARAM)GetDlgItem(hDlg,IDC_LIST),TRUE);
                    EnableWindow(GetDlgItem(hDlg,IDC_DISCONNECT),
                                        TRUE);
                    EnableWindow(GetDlgItem(hDlg,IDC_CONNECT),
                                        FALSE);
                    EnableWindow(GetDlgItem(hDlg,IDC_CONNECTLIST),
                                        FALSE);
                    ci.cb = sizeof(CONVINFO);
                    DdeQueryConvInfo(hConv, QID_SYNC, &ci);
                    AddConvItemToList(hDlg, ci.hszSvcPartner,
                                        ci.hszTopic, hConv);
                    }
                else
                    {
                    DdeFreeStringHandle(idInst, hszService);
                    DdeFreeStringHandle(idInst, hszTopic);
                    }
                return (LRESULT)TRUE;
                break;
```

```
case IDC_CONNECTLIST:
    GetDlgItemText(hDlg, IDC_SERVERNAME,
                    ach, MAX_NAME_SIZE);
    hszService = DdeCreateStringHandle(idInst,
                                        ach, 0);

    GetDlgItemText(hDlg, IDC_TOPICNAME,
                    ach, MAX_NAME_SIZE);
    hszTopic = DdeCreateStringHandle(idInst,
                                        ach, 0);

    hConvList = (HCONV)DdeConnectList(idInst,
                        hszService,
                        hszTopic,
                        NULL,
                        (LPVOID)NULL);
    if (hConvList)
        {
        PostMessage(hDlg,WM_NEXTDLGCTL,
            (WPARAM)GetDlgItem(hDlg,IDC_LIST),TRUE);
        EnableWindow(GetDlgItem(hDlg,IDC_CONNECT),
                            FALSE);
        EnableWindow(GetDlgItem(hDlg,IDC_CONNECTLIST),
                            FALSE);
        EnableWindow(GetDlgItem(hDlg,IDC_DISCONNECT),
                            TRUE);
        EnableWindow(GetDlgItem(hDlg,
                    IDC_DISCONNECTLIST),TRUE);
        ci.hszSvcPartner = hszService;
        ci.hszTopic = hszTopic;
        AddConversation(hDlg, ci.hszSvcPartner,
                        ci.hszTopic, hConvList, TRUE);
        }
    else
        {
        DdeFreeStringHandle(idInst, hszService);
        DdeFreeStringHandle(idInst, hszTopic);
        }
    return (LRESULT)TRUE;
    break;
```

continues

Listing 2.17. continued

```
                case IDC_DISCONNECT:
                    dwIndex = (WORD)SendDlgItemMessage(hDlg,
                                                    IDC_LIST),
                                                    LB_GETCURSEL,
                                                    0,0);
                    if(dwIndex != LB_ERR)
                        {
                        DdeDisconnect(ahConv[(WORD)dwIndex]);
                        dwRemaining = (WORD)SendDlgItemMessage(hDlg,
                                    IDC_LIST), LB_DELETESTRING,
                                    (WPARAM)dwIndex,0L);
                        for(i = dwIndex; i < dwRemaining+1; i++)
                            ahConv[i] = ahConv[i+1];
                        if(!dwRemaining)
                            {
                            cConnects = 0;
                            EnableWindow(GetDlgItem(hDlg,IDC_CONNECT),
                                                    TRUE);
                            PostMessage(hDlg,WM_NEXTDLGCTL,
                                        (WPARAM)GetDlgItem(hDlg,
                                        IDC_CONNECT),TRUE);
                            EnableWindow(GetDlgItem(hDlg,
                                        IDC_DISCONNECT),FALSE);
                            EnableWindow(GetDlgItem(hDlg,
                                        IDC_CONNECTLIST),TRUE);
                            hConv = 0;
                            if(hConvList)
                                {
                                DdeDisconnectList(hConvList);
                                EnableWindow(GetDlgItem(hDlg,
                                            IDC_DISCONNECTLIST),
                                            FALSE);
                                hConvList = 0;
                                }
                            }
                        }
                    return (LRESULT)TRUE;
                    break;
                case IDC_DISCONNECTLIST:
                    if(hConvList)
                        {
```

82

```
                        DdeDisconnectList(hConvList);
                        SendDlgItemMessage(hDlg,IDC_LIST),
                                        LB_RESETCONTENT,0,0L);
                        EnableWindow(GetDlgItem(hDlg,IDC_CONNECT),
                                                TRUE);
                        PostMessage(hDlg,WM_NEXTDLGCTL,
                            (WPARAM)GetDlgItem(hDlg,IDC_CONNECT),
                                                TRUE);
                        EnableWindow(GetDlgItem(hDlg,IDC_DISCONNECT),
                                                FALSE);
                        EnableWindow(GetDlgItem(hDlg,
                                    IDC_DISCONNECTLIST),FALSE);
                        EnableWindow(GetDlgItem(hDlg,
                                    IDC_CONNECTLIST),TRUE);
                        hConvList = 0;
                        cConnects = 0;
                        break;
                        }
                    return (LRESULT)TRUE;
                    break;
                }
            }
        return (LRESULT)FALSE;
        }

VOID FAR PASCAL AddConversation(HWND hDlg, HSZ hszService,
                    HSZ hszTopic, HCONV hConv, BOOL fList)
    {
    if (fList)
        {
        CONVINFO ci;
        HCONV hConvChild = 0;

        ci.cb = sizeof(CONVINFO);
        while (hConvChild = DdeQueryNextServer((HCONVLIST)hConv,
            hConvChild))
            {
            if (DdeQueryConvInfo(hConvChild, QID_SYNC, &ci))
                AddConversation(hDlg, ci.hszSvcPartner, ci.hszTopic,
                    hConvChild, FALSE);
            }
        }
```

continues

Listing 2.17. continued

```
    else
        AddConvItemToList(hDlg, hszService, hszTopic, hConv);
    }

VOID PASCAL AddConvItemToList(HWND hDlg, HSZ hszService,
                             HSZ hszTopic, HCONV hConv)

    {
    char achListLine[64];
    char achName[20];
    char achTopic[20];
    WORD cb, cbService, cbTopic, ErrMsg;

    cbService = (WORD)DdeQueryString(idInst, hszService, NULL, 0, 0);
    cbTopic = (WORD)DdeQueryString(idInst, hszTopic, NULL, 0, 0);
    cb = cbService + cbTopic + 20;
    DdeQueryString(idInst, hszService, achName, cb, 0);

    DdeQueryString(idInst, hszTopic, achTopic,
                   cb, 0);

    ErrMsg = DdeGetLastError(idInst);
    wsprintf(achListLine, "%ls ¦ %ls - %lx",
                                (LPSTR)achName,
                                (LPSTR)achTopic,
                                hConv);
    ahConv[cConnects] = hConv;
    cConnects++;
    SendDlgItemMessage(hDlg,IDC_LIST),LB_ADDSTRING,
                            NULL,(LONG)(LPSTR)achListLine);
    }


/********************************************************************/
/* Function: AboutDlgProc                                           */
/* Purpose: Handles messages for the About dialog box.              */
/* Returns: TRUE/FALSE                                              */
/********************************************************************/
LRESULT CALLBACK AboutDlgProc(HWND hDlg, WORD message,
                             WPARAM wParam, LPARAM lParam)

    {
```

```
switch(message)
    {
    case WM_INITDIALOG:
        return (LRESULT)TRUE;
    case WM_COMMAND:
        switch((WORD)wParam)
            {
            case IDOK:
            case IDCANCEL:
                EndDialog(hDlg, TRUE);
                return (LRESULT)TRUE;
            }
        break;
    }
return (LRESULT)FALSE;
}
```

Listing 2.18. The dde.c source file.

```
#include "client.h"
/*******************************************************************/
/* Function: DdeCallBack                                           */
/* Purpose: This function handles callbacks from the DDEML.        */
/* Parameters:                                                     */
/*              WORD wType      - transaction type                 */
/*              WORD wFmt       - clipboard data format            */
/*              HCONV hConv     - handle of the conversation       */
/*              HSZ hsz1        - handle of a string               */
/*              HSZ hsz2        - handle of a string               */
/*              HDDEDATA hData  - handle of a global memory object */
/*              DWORD dwData1   - transaction-specific data        */
/*              DWORD dwData2   - transaction-specific data        */
/* Returns: Results vary depending on transaction type            */
/*******************************************************************/
HDDEDATA EXPENTRY DdeCallBack(WORD wType, WORD wFmt, HCONV hConv,
                             HSZ hsz1, HSZ hsz2, HDDEDATA hData,
                             DWORD lData1,DWORD lData2)
    {
    return NULL;
    }
```

Listing 2.19. The winmain.c source file.

```c
#define MAIN
#include "client.h"

/********************************************************************/
/* Function: WinMain                                               */
/* Purpose: Main function for windows app. Initializes all         */
/*          instances of app, translates and dispatches messages.*/
/* Returns: Value of PostQuitMessage                               */
/********************************************************************/
int PASCAL WinMain(HINSTANCE hInstance, HINSTANCE hPrevInstance,
                LPSTR lpszCmdLine, int nCmdShow)

    {
    MSG msg;

    /* If there isn't a previous instance of app, then */
    /* initialize the first instance of app.           */
    if(!hPrevInstance)
        if(!InitApplication(hInstance))
            return FALSE;

    /* Perform initialization for all instances of application */
    if(!InitInstance(hInstance, nCmdShow))
        return FALSE;

    /* Get messages for this application until WM_QUIT is received */
    while(GetMessage(&msg, 0, 0, 0))
        {
        TranslateMessage(&msg);
        DispatchMessage(&msg);
        }
    return (int)msg.wParam;
    }
```

Listing 2.20. The init.c source file.

```c
#include "client.h"
```

```
/*********************************************************************/
/* Function: InitApplication                                        */
/* Purpose: Performs all initialization for first instance of app.*/
/* Returns: TRUE if successful, FALSE if failure.                   */
/*********************************************************************/
BOOL InitApplication(HINSTANCE hInstance)
    {
    BOOL bResult;
    char szClassName[SZCLASSNAME];
    WNDCLASS wc;

    /* Load the window class name from resource string table */

    if(!LoadString(hInstance, IDS_CLASSNAME,
                   szClassName, sizeof szClassName))
        return FALSE;

    /* Class styles */
    wc.style          = 0;
    /* Name of message loop function for windows of this class */
    wc.lpfnWndProc    = MainWndProc;
    /* Not using Class Extra data */
    wc.cbClsExtra     = 0;
    /* Not using Window Extra data */
    wc.cbWndExtra     = 0;
    /* Instance that owns this class */
    wc.hInstance      = hInstance;
    /* Use default application icon */
    wc.hIcon          = LoadIcon(NULL, IDI_APPLICATION);
    /* Use arrow cursor */
    wc.hCursor        = LoadCursor(NULL, IDC_ARROW);
    /* Use system background color */
    wc.hbrBackground  = GetStockObject(WHITE_BRUSH);
    /* Resource name for menu */
    wc.lpszMenuName   = MAKEINTRESOURCE(IDM_DDECLIENTMENU);
    /* Name given to this class */
    wc.lpszClassName  = szClassName;

    /* Register the window class */
    bResult = RegisterClass(&wc);
```

continues

Listing 2.20. continued

```c
    /* return result based on registration */
    return bResult;
    }

/*********************************************************************/
/* Function: InitInstance                                        */
/* Purpose: Performs all initialization for all instances of app.*/
/* Returns: TRUE if successful, FALSE if failure                 */
/*********************************************************************/
BOOL InitInstance (HINSTANCE hInstance, int nCmdShow)
    {
    char szClassName[SZCLASSNAME];
    char szWindowTitle[SZWINDOWTITLE];

    hInst = hInstance;

    /* Load the window class name from resource string table */
    if(!LoadString(hInst, IDS_CLASSNAME,
                   szClassName, sizeof szClassName))
        return FALSE;

    /* Load the window title from resource string table */
    if(!LoadString(hInst, IDS_WINDOWTITLE,
                   szWindowTitle, sizeof szWindowTitle))
        return FALSE;

    hwnd = CreateWindow(szClassName,          /* Window class */
                        szWindowTitle,        /* Text for title bar */
                        WS_OVERLAPPEDWINDOW,  /* Style(s) */
                        CW_USEDEFAULT,        /* Default x  pos */
                        CW_USEDEFAULT,        /* Default y  pos */
                        CW_USEDEFAULT,        /* Default cx pos */
                        CW_USEDEFAULT,        /* Default cy pos */
                        0,                    /* Parent window  */
                        0,                    /* Menu           */
                        hInstance,            /* Owning instance */
                        NULL);                /* User-defined params*/

    /* If CreateWindow wasn't successful, return FALSE */
    if(!hwnd)
        return FALSE;
```

88

```
/* Show and paint window */
ShowWindow(hwnd, nCmdShow);
UpdateWindow(hwnd);

return TRUE;
}
```

Listing 2.21. The client.rc resource file.

```
#include <windows.h>
#include "resource.h"
#include "dialogs.h"

IDM_DDECLIENTMENU MENU
    BEGIN
        MENUITEM "&Connections!", IDM_CONNECTIONS
        POPUP "&Help"
        BEGIN
            MENUITEM "&About Client ...",IDM_ABOUT
        END
    END

STRINGTABLE
    BEGIN
        IDS_CLASSNAME     "DDEClientClass"
        IDS_WINDOWTITLE   "DDE Client"
        IDS_INITSUCCESS   "DDEML Initialization Successful."
        IDS_INITFAIL      "DDEML Initialization Failed."
        IDS_NOTPMODE      "Windows must run in protected\n mode to
        run this program."

    END
#include "client.dlg"
```

Listing 2.22. The client.dlg dialog file.

```
DLGINCLUDE RCDATA DISCARDABLE
BEGIN
```

continues

Listing 2.22. continued

```
    "DIALOGS.H\0"
END

IDD_ABOUT DIALOG 112, 39, 152, 86
STYLE DS_MODALFRAME | WS_POPUP | WS_VISIBLE | WS_CAPTION | WS_SYSMENU
CAPTION "About Client"
FONT 10, "System"
BEGIN
    PUSHBUTTON "OK", IDOK, 52, 64, 40, 14
    CTEXT      "Microsoft Windows", -1, 40, 13, 67, 8
    CTEXT      "DDEML Client Application", -1, 31, 31, 88, 8
    CTEXT      "Copyright Jeffrey Clark, 1991", -1, 19, 47, 117, 8
END

IDD_CONNECTIONS DIALOG 86, 50, 243, 127
STYLE DS_MODALFRAME | WS_POPUP | WS_VISIBLE | WS_CAPTION | WS_SYSMENU
CAPTION "Connections"
FONT 8, "Helv"
BEGIN
    LTEXT      "Server Name:", -1, 5, 13, 48, 8
    EDITTEXT   IDC_SERVERNAME, 57, 9, 57, 12, ES_AUTOHSCROLL
    LTEXT      "Topic Name:", -1, 5, 32, 43, 8
    EDITTEXT   IDC_TOPICNAME, 57, 29, 57, 12, ES_AUTOHSCROLL
    PUSHBUTTON "Connect", IDC_CONNECT, 167, 6, 63, 14
    PUSHBUTTON "Connect List", IDC_CONNECTLIST, 167, 25, 63, 14
    LTEXT      "Connection List:", -1, 5, 49, 55, 8
    LISTBOX    IDC_LIST, 6, 63, 145, 64, LBS_SORT | WS_VSCROLL |
                    WS_TABSTOP
    PUSHBUTTON "Disconnect", IDC_DISCONNECT, 167, 57, 63, 14
    PUSHBUTTON "Disconnect List", IDC_DISCONNECTLIST, 167, 76, 63, 14
    PUSHBUTTON "Cancel", IDCANCEL, 167, 103, 63, 14
END
```

Listing 2.23. The client.def module definition file.

```
NAME Client

DESCRIPTION 'DDE Example Client, Copyright Jeffrey Clark, 1991'

EXETYPE WINDOWS

STUB 'WINSTUB.EXE'

CODE PRELOAD MOVEABLE DISCARDABLE
DATA PRELOAD MOVEABLE MULTIPLE

HEAPSIZE 1024
STACKSIZE 8192

SEGMENTS
    WINMAIN_TEXT    MOVEABLE                 PRELOAD
    CLIENT_TEXT     MOVEABLE                 PRELOAD
    INIT_TEXT       MOVEABLE DISCARDABLE PRELOAD
    DDE_TEXT        MOVEABLE DISCARDABLE LOADONCALL
    DIALOGS_TEXT    MOVEABLE DISCARDABLE LOADONCALL

EXPORTS
    MainWndProc @1
    AboutDlgProc @2
    DdeCallBack @3
    ConnectDlgProc @4
```

Listing 2.24. The CLIENT make file.

```
CC = cl -c -AM -Gsw -Od -W3 -Zpi -Fo$@

all: client.exe

client.h: dialogs.h resource.h

client.res: client.rc client.dlg dialogs.h resource.h
  rc -r client
```

continues

Listing 2.24. continued

```
dialogs.obj: dialogs.c client.h
  $(CC) $*.c

init.obj: init.c client.h
  $(CC) $*.c

winmain.obj: winmain.c client.h
  $(CC) $*.c
client.obj: client.c client.h
  $(CC) $*.c

dde.obj: dde.c client.h
  $(CC) $*.c

client.exe:: dialogs.obj init.obj winmain.obj client.obj dde.obj \
             client.res client.def
    link /CO /MAP /NOD @<<
dialogs+
init+
winmain+
client+
dde
$@

libw mlibcew ddeml
client.def
<<
    mapsym client
    rc client.res
```

Summary

This chapter contains much information about the DDEML initialization and conversation management. Although initialization and conversation management are fairly straightforward topics, I cannot overstate their importance. They are the foundation that supports DDEML transaction processing. A strong foundation is obviously easier to build on than a weak foundation. This is very true in DDEML application programming, and Windows programming in general.

Thus, you should use the example applications in this chapter to thoroughly understand the initialization and connection process. I encourage you to experiment with these applications. You can add several features, such as conversation tracking and conversation reconnection. After you read the next chapter, you should reread the section about the **DdeInitialize()** function. This will give you a clearer understanding of how the flags in the **DdeInitialize()** function relate to how the DDEML manages transactions.

DDEML
Transaction
Management

This chapter covers the details of a DDEML conversation. The details consist of *strings, data,* and *transactions.* Strings and data are part of what makes transactions unique. Chapter 2 covered some DDEML string functions required for creating string handles for service and topic names. It also covered how to create a data handle to an array of service name and topic name pairs. In addition to the previously mentioned concepts, this chapter describes all the DDEML string and data functions, giving you the tools you need to write transactions in a DDEML program. This chapter presents its topics in the following order:

- DDEML string management

- DDEML data management

- DDEML transaction functions

- Example DDEML client and server applications

DDEML String Management

Because the DDEML allows message-based DDE applications to communicate with DDEML applications, the underlying facilities that the DDEML uses for strings must be the same. Thus, DDEML string-management functions use the global atom table to handle strings. In some ways, the DDEML string-management functions are more complex than calling normal atom functions. For example, calling **GlobalAddAtom()** requires only one parameter, whereas its DDEML counterpart **DdeCreateStringHandle()** requires three parameters. However, there is a trade-off here.

The DDEML does more work than just providing a string handle when you call **DdeCreateStringHandle()**. The additional work it does enforces the DDE protocol. A good example of this is a problem I encountered when programming one of the example programs. The example client application for this chapter pokes a value to the example server program. I copied some code from where the client application sends an execute transaction to the server application. The code is very similar. Both the execute code and the poke code require a data handle. The client application uses the **DdeCreateDataHandle()**

function to create a data handle. After the client application obtains the data handle to the poke or execute value, it sends the transaction to the server.

There is one major difference in the poke and execute code that wasn't obvious when I copied the execute code. A poke transaction requires a string handle for the item name; however, an execute transaction doesn't have an item name. I made that change right away when I looked at the format for the poke transaction. I thought I had saved a lot of time by copying this code and having to make only a few minor changes—very productive. Actually, my problem was very informative. The code did not work. I must have looked at the code in CodeView for 30 minutes, making a change here and a change there. Then I got smart and looked at the function prototype for the **DdeCreateDataHandle()** function. The **DdeCreateDataHandle()** function has a parameter that takes a string handle to an item name associated with the data value. Although I felt rather stupid at the time, this is what made me realize what the DDEML does with string handles.

The DDEML does more than make a call to **GlobalAddAtom()** when an application calls **DdeCreateStringHandle()**. It uses the string handles in other DDEML functions to enforce the DDE protocol. Transactions will not work correctly unless all the supporting data and string handles exist in the way the DDEML expects them.

Because the DDEML string-management functions use the global atom table, you can expect them to behave in a manner similar to atom functions. When an application calls the **DdeCreateStringHandle()** function, the DDEML adds a string to the global atom table. Each call to **DdeCreateStringHandle()** that has the same string increments the reference count for the string. An example of this is when a client connects to a server application. The server application creates a string handle for its service name. The client application also creates a string handle for the server's service name. Say the server makes the first call to **DdeCreateStringHandle()**. This adds the string to the global atom table. When the client calls **DdeCreateStringHandle()** for the server's service name— the second call—the reference count is incremented for that string.

The reference count decrements when an application calls the **DdeFreeStringHandle()** function. When the reference count reaches zero, the atom manager removes the string from the global atom table. When an application receives a string handle through the DdeCallBack() function and wants to use the string handle in later processing, it can increment the reference count by calling the **DdeKeepStringHandle()** function. An application that does not increment the reference count by calling **DdeKeepStringHandle()** cannot rely on a valid string handle after the DdeCallBack() function returns. The application that created the string handle can call **DdeFreeStringHandle()** later, thus setting the reference count to zero and removing the string from the global atom table.

Creating String Handles

The **DdeCreateStringHandle()** function creates string handles. This function is fairly straightforward and has the following prototype:

```
HSZ  EXPENTRY DdeCreateStringHandle(DWORD idInst,
                                    LPSTR psz, int iCodePage);
```

The idInst parameter comes from a call to **DdeInitialize()**. The DDEML uses this parameter to associate the string handle to an instance of an application. The psz parameter is the string that the DDEML adds to the global atom table. The iCodePage parameter specifies the code page used to render the string. Most applications set iCodePage to CP_WINANSI. A 0 value defaults to CP_WINANSI. If your application runs in more than one language, use the value returned by the **GetKBCodePage()** function.

Incrementing and Decrementing the Reference Count

The reference count for a string increments when an application calls **DdeCreateStringHandle()**. Two applications can call **DdeCreateStringHandle()** for the same string, each incrementing the reference count; however, an application cannot call **DdeCreateStringHandle()** to increment the reference count of an instance-specific string handle. For example, an application cannot generate a string value using an instance-specific string handle with the **DdeQueryString()** function and then call **DdeCreateStringHandle()** using the string value. This creates a second string handle in addition to the instance-specific string handle.

When an application receives a string handle through the DdeCallBack() function, the application may need to access the string handle after its calls return in the DdeCallBack() function. The application can increment the reference count of the string by calling the **DdeKeepStringHandle()** function. The string handle will be accessible to the application until it decrements the reference count.

The **DdeKeepStringHandle()** function has the following prototype:

```
BOOL EXPENTRY DdeKeepStringHandle(DWORD idInst, HSZ hsz);
```

DdeKeepStringHandle() has two parameters: idInst and hsz. idInst comes from a previous call to **DdeInitialize()**, whereas hsz is a string handle. The **DdeKeepStringHandle()** function returns TRUE if the call is successful and FALSE if the call fails.

When an application no longer requires the use of a string handle, it should free the resources associated with the string handle. To do this, an application can call **DdeFreeStringHandle()**. **DdeFreeStringHandle()** decrements the reference count for a string. When the reference count reaches zero, the atom manager removes the string from the global atom table.

Programs call the **DdeFreeStringHandle()** function the same way they call **DdeKeepStringHandle()**. **DdeFreeStringHandle()** has the following prototype:

```
BOOL EXPENTRY DdeFreeStringHandle(DWORD idInst, HSZ hsz);
```

Getting and Comparing Strings

When an application receives a string handle in its DdeCallBack() function, most likely it will need one of two things: the association of the string value with a string handle or a comparison of the string value to another string. The **DdeQueryString()** function allows an application to retrieve the string value for a given string handle. The **DdeCmpStringHandles()** function allows an application to compare the string values of two string handles.

The **DdeQueryString()** function can be a little tricky. Here's its prototype:

```
DWORD EXPENTRY DdeQueryString(DWORD idInst, HSZ hsz,
                    LPSTR psz, DWORD cchMax, int iCodePage);
```

The third parameter, psz, points to a buffer that receives the string value for the string handle, hsz. The string value is always null-terminated. The fourth parameter, cchMax, is the length of the psz buffer. The buffer must be large enough to hold the string and the NULL terminating character. If the buffer is not long enough, the string will be truncated but still will have a NULL terminating character. This doesn't sound like a problem, but applications typically call **DdeQueryString()** twice to get a string. The first call uses a NULL buffer and returns the length of the string. The application can allocate a buffer by calling **LocalAlloc()** with the return length from the first call to **DdeQueryString()**. The length that **DdeQueryString()** returns, however, does not include the NULL terminating character. Thus, when an application allocates memory for the string buffer, and when it calls **DdeQueryString()** for the second time, it must add 1 to the return length from the first call. I guess this is tricky only when you forget to add 1 to the length.

Here's an example call to **DdeQueryString()**:

```
DWORD cd;
HSZ hszItem;
PSTR pszItem;
HLOCAL hMem;


cd = DdeQueryString(idInst, hszItem, (LPSTR) NULL, 0L, 0) + 1;
hMem = LocalAlloc(LPTR, (WORD) cd);
if(hMem)
     {
     pszItem = LocalLock(hMem);
     DdeQueryString(idInst, hszItem, pszItem, cd, 0);
     . . .
     }
```

An application can use the **DdeCmpStringHandles()** function to compare the value to two string values that have string handles. This function is much easier to use than copying two string values to local variables using the **DdeQueryString()** function and then using **lstrcmp()** to compare the strings. The call

```
if(!DdeCmpStringHandles(hsz1, hsz2))
    MessageBox(hwnd, "Strings are Equal","Message",MB_OK);
```

is equivalent to

```
DdeQueryString(idInst, hsz1, psz1, cd1, 0);
DdeQueryString(idInst, hsz2, psz2, cd2, 0);
if(!lstrcmp(psz1, psz2))
    MessageBox(hwnd, "Strings are Equal", "Message", MB_OK);
```

The **DdeCmpStringHandles()** function returns 0 if the values are equal, −1 if hsz1 is less than hsz2, or 1 if hsz1 is greater than hsz2.

DDEML Data Management

DDE applications use global memory to pass data between applications. The DDEML provides several data-management functions to create, manipulate, and free global memory objects. The data-management functions are similar to string-management functions. Applications get a handle to a global memory object by calling the **DdeCreateDataHandle()** function. An application can pass a data handle to the DDEML, and then the DDEML passes the data handle to the partner in the conversation. When an application receives the data handle, it can access the global memory object associated with the data handle by using another DDEML data-management function.

The data-management functions differ from the string-management functions because no reference count is associated with a data handle. When an application creates a data handle, it typically returns the data to the DDEML. At that point, the DDEML invalidates the data handle so that the application that created the data handle can no longer use the handle. As an exception to this invalidation, an application can create a global memory object that it owns. Usually the DDEML controls and maintains global memory objects; however, when an application owns the global memory object, it is responsible to its management. This means that the application must clean up after itself.

Creating Global Memory Objects

The **DdeCreateDataHandle()** function copies a data object into global memory and returns a handle to the data object. The returned data handle is typically used in one of two ways. First, a server application returns the data handle to the DDEML from the DdeCallBack() function. Second, client applications use it in poke and execute transactions. The **DdeCreateDataHandle()** function has the following prototype:

```
HDDEDATA EXPENTRY DdeCreateDataHandle(DWORD idInst, LPBYTE pSrc,
        DWORD cb, DWORD cbOff, HSZ hszItem, WORD wFmt, WORD afCmd);
```

The first parameter specifies the instance identifier from the last call to **DdeInitialize()**. The second parameter is a pointer to a buffer that contains the data. An application can specify NULL for this parameter if it wants just to allocate space for a global memory object. The application can later add data to the global memory. The third parameter, cb, specifies the amount of memory to allocate. If cb is zero, the DDEML will ignore the second parameter. The cbOff parameter specifies an offset within the second parameter for the DDEML to start copying the data. The hszItem parameter is a handle to an item name associated with data. The application must specify this parameter, except when creating a data handle for a command string to be used in an execute transaction. The wFmt parameter provides the clipboard format of the data item. This does not affect how the DDEML stores a data item. The last parameter, afCmd, can have one of two values. If an application wants to own the data item, it should specify HDATA_APPOWNED for afCmd. Otherwise, it should specify NULL.

When an application specifies HDATA_APPOWNED for the afCmd parameter, the DDEML will not invalidate the data handle after the application returns the data handle to the DDEML. In this case, the application that called **DdeCreateDataHandle()** is responsible for freeing the resources associated with the data handle. The **DdeFreeDataHandle()** function can free these resources.

Accessing Global Memory Objects

An application can access a global memory object in several ways. First, an application can add data to a global memory object by calling the **DdeAddData()** function. Second, an application can call **DdeAccessData()** or **DdeGetData()**. An application must call the **DdeAddData()** function with a valid data handle. The DDEML invalidates a data handle after an application returns the data handle to the DDEML, unless the application specified HDATA_APPOWNED when it called **DdeCreateDataHandle()**. The prototype for **DdeAddData()** follows:

```
HDDEDATA EXPENTRY DdeAddData(HDDEDATA hData, LPBYTE pSrc,
                            DWORD cb, DWORD cbOff);
```

The first parameter is the data handle gotten from **DdeCreateDataHandle()**. The second parameter, pSrc, is a pointer to a data buffer. The third parameter, cb, specifies the length of the data object to be added to global memory. The last parameter is the offset to the global memory object, which is the starting point for the data in pSrc to be copied. If the new data overlaps the existing data, the **DdeAddData()** function overwrites the existing data. **DdeAddData()** returns a handle to a global memory object. This handle replaces all other data handles to the global memory object. Here's an example of **DdeAddData()**:

```
hData = DdeCreateDataHandle(idInst, (LPBYTE) NULL, 0L, 0L,
                            hszItem, CF_TEXT, 0);

    < Generate the data here >

/* Add data to the global memory object. */
hData = DdeAddData(hData,(LPBYTE)&szBuf,
                (DWORD)strlen(szBuf) + 1, 0),
return hData;
```

The **DdeAccessData()** function enables an application to read and write a global memory object associated with a data handle. An application can use **DdeAccessData()** to write to a global memory object if the data handle has been passed to another DDEML function. Typically, applications use **DdeAccessData()** to view data. After an application completes its actions with data, it must call **DdeUnaccessData()**. The following are prototypes for **DdeAccessData()** and **DdeUnaccessData()**:

```
LPBYTE EXPENTRY DdeAccessData(HDDEDATA hData,
                                LPDWORD pcbDataSize);
BOOL EXPENTRY DdeUnaccessData(HDDEDATA hData);
```

The **DdeAccessData()** function returns a pointer to the first byte of the global memory object. The first parameter is a handle to the data item. The second parameter receives the length of the data item. The following example counts the number of *a*'s in a global memory object that is a character string:

```
lpsz = DdeAccessData(hData, &cb);
cba = 0;
for(i = 0; i < (int) cb; i++)
     if(*lpsz++ == 'a')
          cba++;
DdeUnaccessData(hData);
```

The last method to access data is through the **DdeGetData()** function. **DdeGetData()** allows an application to copy the global memory object to a buffer. The prototype of **DdeGetData()** is

```
DWORD EXPENTRY DdeGetData(HDDEDATA hData, LPBYTE pDst,
                           DWORD cbMax, DWORD cbOff);
```

The first parameter is the handle to the data object. The second parameter, pDst, is the buffer that receives the data object. The third parameter, cbMax, specifies the maximum amount of data to be copied, which must be less than or equal to the size of the destination buffer. The last parameter is an offset within the global memory object. This is the starting point of the copy.

Freeing Global Memory Objects

In three instances, an application must free a global memory object allocated by **DdeCreateDataHandle()**. The first situation is if an application creates a data handle but does not use the data handle in a DDEML function. The reason for this is that the DDEML does not know when to invalidate the data handle and free the global memory because the data handle was never used by a

DDEML function. The second instance in which an application must free global memory is when it specifies HDATA_APPOWNED when it calls **DdeCreateDataHandle()**. This specification causes the application to own the global memory object. The application can do what it wants with the memory object, and the DDEML will not interfere. This is useful when an application serves multiple client applications that request the same data item. The data item may be difficult to render and time-consuming to allocate to global memory. If the application owns the memory, it can allocate the memory once and then service all client applications requesting the data item.

The last case in which an application is responsible for freeing a global memory object is when a client application receives a data handle from the return of **DdeClientTransaction()**. The DDEML cannot know when the client application completes its processing of the global memory object; thus the client application has to free the global memory object.

The **DdeFreeDataHandle()** function provides the facility to free a global memory object. Its format is very simple. It has one parameter: a data handle. **DdeFreeDataHandle()** returns TRUE if the call was successful and FALSE if it failed.

Transaction Management

Transactions are the messages that the DDEML passes to DdeCallBack() functions. DDEML client applications request data and services from server applications by calling the **DdeClientTransaction()** function with a transaction identifier. When the client application calls **DdeClientTransaction()**, the DDEML deciphers the parameters and passes the appropriate information to the server's DdeCallBack() function. The point to be made here is that the client application does not directly interact with the server application. It goes through the DDEML for everything.

There are two transaction categories: *synchronous* and *asynchronous*. Synchronous transactions are the easiest to use, but they do have drawbacks. A synchronous transaction specifies a timeout value in the **DdeClientTransaction()** function. When a client calls the **DdeClientTransaction()** function for a synchronous transaction, the **DdeClientTransaction()** function does not return until the transaction is complete or until the timeout value expires. While the client application waits for **DdeClientTransaction()** to return, it enters a modal loop, where the client application can process user input but cannot call **DdeClientTransaction()** again. This is one of the disadvantages of synchronous transactions. Client applications can process only one transaction at a time.

Asynchronous transactions are more flexible than synchronous transactions, but they are a little more complex. Applications sending asynchronous transactions specify TIMEOUT_ASYNC in the **DdeClientTransaction()** function, causing the **DdeClientApplication()** function to return immediately. Thus, a client application can send many asynchronous transactions without waiting. When an asynchronous transaction completes, the DDEML sends an XTYP_XACT_COMPLETE transaction to the client. The client application has to track the transactions it has sent, which makes asynchronous transactions more complex than synchronous transactions.

Applications can control transaction flow by using the **DdeEnableCallback()** function, or by returning CBR_BLOCK from the DdeCallBack() function. CBR_BLOCK suspends transactions for a conversation handle. An example of this would be a server application that receives a request transaction for a data item that takes a long time to be rendered. When it receives the request transaction, it can return CBR_BLOCK. Then the server can render the data item and store it for quick access later. The server can turn on transactions for the blocked conversation by calling **DdeEnableCallback()**. At this point, the server receives the transaction it originally returned: CBR_BLOCK. Because the data item has been rendered, the server can quickly process the request without rendering the data item again. The **DdeEnableCallback()** function can also block one transaction, all transactions for a conversation handle, or all transactions for all conversations.

DDEML Transactions—
DdeClientTransaction()

The DDEML client applications submit transactions with the **DdeClientTransaction()** function. The **DdeClientTransaction()** function has the following prototype:

```
HDDEDATA EXPENTRY DdeClientTransaction(LPBYTE pData,
          DWORD cbData, HCONV hConv, HSZ hszItem,
          WORD wFmt, WORD wType, DWORD dwTimeout,
          LPDWORD pdwResult);
```

When a client application calls **DdeClientTransaction()**, it must specify a conversation handle in the hConv parameter. The DDEML uses the hConv parameter to route the transaction to the correct server application.

The dwTimeout parameter specifies the timeout period for a transaction. A client application specifies a timeout period in milliseconds, or TIMEOUT_ASYNC. A typical timeout period for a synchronous transaction is 1,000 milliseconds, which translates to one second. For an application to submit an asynchronous transaction, the timeout period must be TIMEOUT_ASYNC.

The wType parameter specifies the transaction. The client application can send the following transactions:

XTYP_ADVSTART	Starts an advise link with a server application.
XTYP_ADVSTOP	Terminates an advise link with a server application.
XTYP_EXECUTE	Sends a command string to be processed by a server application.
XTYP_POKE	Sends a data item to a server application.
XTYP_REQUEST	Sends a request for data to a server application.

The pdwResult parameter identifies a variable that receives the results of a transaction. pdwResult is optional. Applications can specify NULL for this parameter if they do not check the results of transactions. If an application submitting a synchronous transaction specifies a variable for this parameter, the low-order word of pdwResult contains DDE_ status flags. Microsoft recommends that new applications not use DDE_ status flags because the company may eliminate support for them in future versions of the DDEML. Asynchronous transactions receive a transaction identifier in pdwResult. If a server application does not respond in a reasonable time frame, a client application can abandon the transaction by using the transaction identifier in the **DdeAbandonTransaction()** function.

The other parameters in **DdeClientTransaction()** are dependent on the transaction specified by the client application. Following are discussions on transactions that describe the use of the other parameters for **DdeClientTransaction()**.

Using Advise Loops

A client application initiates an advise loop by specifying XTYP_ADVSTART in the wType parameter of the **DdeClientTransaction()** function. There are two types of advise loops: a *warm link* and a *hot link*. In a warm link, the server application sends a notification to the client application that a data item in an advise loop has changed. It does not, however, send the value of the data item to the client application. The client application must specifically request the data item to receive the data item's value. To create a warm link, the client application

combines the XTYPF_NODATA flag with the XTYP_ADVSTART transaction by using a bitwise OR. In a hot link, the server application sends data to the client application every time a data item in an advise loop changes.

A client can control the timing of the data it receives by combining the XTYPF_ACKREQ flag with the XTYP_ADVSTART transaction. When a client application specifies the XTYPF_ACKREQ flag, the server application will not send the next update for a data item until the client application has acknowledged that it has received and processed the previous update of a data item. This acknowledgment is DDE_FACK, and the client application returns this from the DdeCallBack() function to the DDEML after processing an XTYP_ADVDATA transaction. The DDEML generates the XTYP_ADVDATA transaction when a server responds to an XTYP_ADVREQ transaction.

The DDEML generates the XTYP_ADVREQ transaction when the server calls the **DdePostAdvise()** function. The server calls the **DdePostAdvise()** function when a data item changes value. The server continues to call the **DdePostAdvise()** function each time the advised data item changes value until the client application sends an XTYP_ADVSTOP transaction. Here's an outline of the general flow of a hot link:

Client Application:

```
if(DdeClientTransaction(NULL, NULL, hConv, hszItem,
                        CF_TEXT, XTYP_ADVSTART, 1000, NULL))
    <Advise loop started>
else
    <Advise loop failed>
```

Server Application:

```
HDDEDATA EXPENTRY DdeCallBack(WORD wType, WORD wFmt,
                 HCONV hConv, HSZ hsz1, HSZ hsz2,
                 HDDEDATA hData, DWORD lData1,DWORD lData2)
    {
    if(wType == XTYP_ADVSTART)
        {
        if< support the clipboard format (wFmt),
          topic (hsz1) and item (hsz2) then>
            {
            bAdviseItem = TRUE;
            return (HDDEDATA) TRUE;
        else
            return (HDDEDATA) FALSE;
```

106

Client Application:

```
< return from DdeClientTransaction() is TRUE -
hurry up and wait for data item to change>
```

Server Application:

```
<data item changes>
lstrcpy(achItem,"A NEW VALUE");
if(bAdviseItem)
    DdePostAdvise(idInst, hszTopic, hszItem);
```

Server Application:

```
HDDEDATA EXPENTRY DdeCallBack(WORD wType, WORD wFmt,
                  HCONV hConv, HSZ hsz1, HSZ hsz2,
                  HDDEDATA hData, DWORD lData1,DWORD lData2)
    {
    if(wType == XTYP_ADVREQ)
        if< the correct wFmt and hsz1 and hsz2>
        return DdeCreateDataHandle(idInst,
                (LPBYTE)&achItem[0],lstrlen(achItem)+1,
                0L,hsz2,CF_TEXT,0);
```

Client Application:

```
HDDEDATA EXPENTRY DdeCallBack(WORD wType, WORD wFmt,
                  HCONV hConv, HSZ hsz1, HSZ hsz2,
                  HDDEDATA hData, DWORD lData1,DWORD lData2)
    {
    if(wType == XTYP_ADVDATA)
        {
        if(hsz2 == hszItem)
            {
            DdeGetData(hData,(LPBYTE)achItem,10,0L);
            return DDE_FACK;
            }
        }
```

The server application continues to update the data item until:

Client Application:

```
DdeClientTransaction(NULL, NULL, hConv, hszItem,
                  CF_TEXT, XTYP_ADVSTOP, 1000, NULL);
```

Server Application:

```
HDDEDATA EXPENTRY DdeCallBack(WORD wType, WORD wFmt,
                   HCONV hConv, HSZ hsz1, HSZ hsz2,
                   HDDEDATA hData, DWORD lData1,DWORD lData2)
    {
    if(wType == XTYP_ADVSTOP)
        if(hsz2 == hszItem)
            bAdviseItem = FALSE;
```

The preceding outline is very basic. Any number of advise loops can be active concurrently. In fact, there can be multiple advise loops for one data item; however, each advise loop must be for a different clipboard format. The wFmt parameter in the **DdeClientTransaction()** specifies the clipboard format of the data item. Thus, a client application can call **DdeClientTransaction()** to submit an XTYP_ADVSTART transaction for a data item multiple times, each with a different clipboard format. The client application can terminate individual advise loops for a data item by specifying the clipboard format and the item name in an XTYP_ADVSTOP transaction.

When the client application specifies the XTYPF_ACKREQ flag with the XTYP_ADVSTART transaction in **DdeClientTransaction()**, the DDEML will hold XTYP_ADVREQ messages to the server's DdeCallBack() function until the client transaction returns DDE_FACK upon receiving data from the server. If a number of XTYP_ADVREQ transactions are in the queue because the client application takes a long time to return DDE_FACK, the DDEML will send additional information along with the XTYP_ADVREQ transaction in the lData1 parameter of the server's DdeCallBack() function. In this situation, the low-order word of lData1 contains the CADV_LATEACK flag. This will inform the server application that it is sending data to the client application faster than the client application can process it.

If the server application has outstanding advise loops for multiple client applications requesting the same data item, this may cause the DDEML to hold XTYP_ADVREQ transactions in a queue. If the server's outstanding advise loops are unrelated to the client application's ability to process XTYP_ADVDATA transactions quickly, the DDEML places a count of outstanding XTYP_ADVREQ transactions for the data item in the lData1 parameter of the server's DdeCallBack() function. The server can use the value of lData1 to determine whether it should create the data handle returned for XTYP_ADVREQ transactions with the HDATA_APPOWNED flag. This will allow the server to use the same data handle for each XTYP_ADVREQ transaction until the lData1 parameter is zero. This will save processing time because the server does not have to call **DdeCreateDataHandle()** for each XTYP_ADVREQ transaction.

Requesting Data

A client application that infrequently needs to update a data item from a server can use the XTYP_REQUEST transaction type in the **DdeClientTransaction()** function. This need may occur during normal processing or while the client is in a warm link with a server. When a client application has a warm link with a server, it will receive XTYP_ADVDATA transactions in its DdeCallBack() function. The hData parameter in the DdeCallBack() function will be NULL for a warm link. If this is the case and the client application wants to receive the data value, the client application can call **DdeClientTransaction()** with the wType parameter set to XTYP_REQUEST.

The client application will receive the data handle for the data item as the return value from **DdeClientTransaction()** if the transaction is synchronous. If the transaction is asynchronous, the client application will receive an XTYP_XACT_COMPLETE transaction in its DdeCallBack() function. If the server cannot process the XTYP_REQUEST transaction, the **DdeClientTransaction()** function returns NULL. The client application can determine why the server could not process the XTYP_REQUEST transaction by examining the pdwResult parameter in the **DdeClientTransaction()** function. The pdwResult parameter points to DDE_FNOTPROCESSED or DDE_FBUSY if the **DdeClientTransaction()** function failed.

Here's an example of a synchronous request transaction:

Client Application:

```
hData = DdeClientTransaction(NULL, NULL, hConv, hszItem,
                CF_TEXT, XTYP_REQUEST, 1000, &pdwResult);
```

Server Application:

```
HDDEDATA EXPENTRY DdeCallBack(WORD wType, WORD wFmt,
                HCONV hConv, HSZ hsz1, HSZ hsz2,
                HDDEDATA hData, DWORD lData1,DWORD lData2)
    {
    if(wType == XTYP_REQUEST)
        if< the correct wFmt and hsz1 and hsz2>
        return DdeCreateDataHandle(idInst,
                (LPBYTE)&achItem[0],lstrlen(achItem)+1,
                0L,hsz2,CF_TEXT,0);
```

Client Application:

```
if(hData)
    {
```

```
            DdeGetData(hData,(LPBYTE)achItem,10,0L);
            DdeFreeDataHandle(hData);
            }
    else
            {
            if(pdwResult == DDE_FBUSY)
                MessageBox(hwnd, "Server is Busy", "Client", MB_OK);
            else
                if(pdwResult == DDE_FNOTPROCESSED)
                    MessageBox(hwnd, "Server did not process",
                               "Client", MB_OK);

            }
```

Here's an example of an asynchronous request transaction:

Client Application:

```
DdeClientTransaction(NULL, NULL, hConv, hszItem,
                     CF_TEXT, XTYP_REQUEST, TIMEOUT_ASYNC,
                     &pdwResult);
```

Server Application:

```
HDDEDATA EXPENTRY DdeCallBack(WORD wType, WORD wFmt,
                  HCONV hConv, HSZ hsz1, HSZ hsz2,
                  HDDEDATA hData, DWORD lData1,DWORD lData2)

    {
    if(wType == XTYP_REQUEST)
        if< the correct wFmt and hsz1 and hsz2>
        return DdeCreateDataHandle(idInst,
                (LPBYTE)&achItem[0],lstrlen(achItem)+1,
                0L,hsz2,CF_TEXT,0);
```

Client Application:

```
HDDEDATA EXPENTRY DdeCallBack(WORD wType, WORD wFmt,
                  HCONV hConv, HSZ hsz1, HSZ hsz2,
                  HDDEDATA hData, DWORD lData1,DWORD lData2)

    {
    if(wType == XTYP_XACT_COMPLETE &&
       lData1 == XTYP_REQUEST)
        {
        if< the wFmt, hsz1, and hsz2 is correct >
            if(hData)
                DdeGetData(hData,(LPBYTE)achItem,10,0L);
```

```
            else
                <transaction not successful>
        }
    }
```

Note that when the client application receives an XTYP_XACT_COMPLETE trans-action in its DdeCallBack() function, the lData1 parameter contains the transaction type of the completed transaction.

Poking Data

A client application can send data to a server application by calling the **DdeClientTransaction()** function with a transaction type of XTYP_POKE. A client application can use the **DdeCreateDataHandle()** function to create a data handle to the data item that the client pokes to the server, or it can use a pointer to a buffer containing the data item. The client application specifies the data handle or pointer to a buffer in the first parameter of **DdeClientTransaction()**. If the client specifies a data handle in **DdeClientTransaction()**, the cbData parameter of **DdeClientTransaction()** should be −1. If the client application passes a pointer to a data buffer, the cbData parameter should be the length of the data buffer.

If the XTYP_POKE transaction is synchronous, the pdwResult parameter in the **DdeClientTransaction()** function contains the result of the transaction after the **DdeClientTransaction()** function returns. If the XTYP_POKE transaction is asynchronous, the pdwResult parameter contains a transaction identifier that can be used to abandon the transaction if the server does not respond in a timely manner.

When a server application receives the XTYP_POKE transaction in the DdeCallBack() function, the server application can use the **DdeGetData()** function to get the poked data. If the server successfully processes the data, it should return DDE_FACK. If the server is too busy to process the transaction, it should return DDE_FBUSY. If the server cannot process the data, it should return DDE_FNOTPROCESSED.

Here's an example of an XTYP_POKE transaction:

Client Application:

```
hData = DdeCreateDataHandle(idInst,
            (LPBYTE)&achUpdate[0],lstrlen(achUpdate),
            0L,hszItem,CF_TEXT,0);
```

111

```
DdeClientTransaction((LPBYTE)hData,-1,
          hConv, hszItem, CF_TEXT, XTYP_POKE,
          1000, NULL);
```

Server Application:

```
HDDEDATA EXPENTRY DdeCallBack(WORD wType, WORD wFmt,
                  HCONV hConv, HSZ hsz1, HSZ hsz2,
                  HDDEDATA hData, DWORD lData1, DWORD lData2)

  {
  if(wType == XTYP_POKE)
      {
      if< wfmt, hsz1 and hsz2 are correct>
          {
          DdeGetData(hData,(LPBYTE)achUpdate,20,0L);
          return (HDDEDATA)DDE_FACK;
          }
      else
          return (HDDEDATA)DDE_FNOTPROCESSED;
      }
  }
```

Sending Commands

A client application can send a command to a server application by using the XTYP_EXECUTE transaction. This transaction is very similar to the XTYP_POKE transaction; however, the commands sent to the server must follow a strict syntax. You can find this syntax in Chapter 1, in the section about the WM_DDE_EXECUTE message.

The main difference between the XTYP_EXECUTE and XTYP_POKE transactions is that an item name handle is not specified in the **DdeClientTransaction()** for the XTYP_EXECUTE transaction. Otherwise, DDEML applications handle the XTYP_EXECUTE transaction the same way as they do an XTYP_POKE transaction.

Here's an example of an XTYP_EXECUTE transaction:

Client Application:

```
lstrcpy(achCommand,"[OpenFile](NETINC.XLS)");
hData = DdeCreateDataHandle(idInst,
          (LPBYTE)&achCommand[0],lstrlen(achCommand),
          0L,NULL,CF_TEXT,0);
```

```
DdeClientTransaction((LPBYTE)hData,-1,
            hConv, hszItem, CF_TEXT, XTYP_EXECUTE,
            1000, NULL);
```

Server Application:

```
HDDEDATA EXPENTRY DdeCallBack(WORD wType, WORD wFmt,
                    HCONV hConv, HSZ hsz1, HSZ hsz2,
                    HDDEDATA hData, DWORD lData1, DWORD lData2)
    {
    if(wType == XTYP_EXECUTE)
        {
        if< wfmt and hsz1 are correct>
            {
            DdeGetData(hData,(LPBYTE)achCommand,30,0L);
            return (HDDEDATA)DDE_FACK;
            }
        else
            return (HDDEDATA)DDE_FNOTPROCESSED;
        }
    }
```

Transaction Control

Asynchronous transactions offer more flexibility than synchronous transactions, but with that flexibility comes complexity. The DDEML offers
two functions that can help manage asynchronous transactions:
DdeAbandonTransaction() and **DdeSetUserHandle()**. If a client application
submits a transaction to a server application using the **DdeClientTransaction()**
function with a timeout period of TIMEOUT_ASYNC, the DDEML generates an
asynchronous transaction. The client application can use the pdwResult
parameter to later abandon the transaction. This is useful if the client
application needs the data quickly and the data is not useful after a specified
time. By abandoning the transaction, the client application can avoid
unwanted transactions reaching its DdeCallBack() function. The client application can use the **DdeAbandonTransaction()** function to abandon the transaction. Here's the function prototype for **DdeAbandonTransaction()**:

```
BOOL EXPENTRY DdeAbandonTransaction(DWORD idInst, HCONV hConv,
                                    DWORD idTransaction);
```

The idInst parameter specifies the return value from **DdeInitialize()**. The
hConv parameter is the handle to the conversation and the idTransaction is

the value of the `pdwResult` parameter to **DdeClientTransaction()** after the **DdeClientTransaction()** function has returned.

The **DdeSetUserHandle()** function is helpful in identifying where the results of an asynchronous transaction should go. Imagine a client application that submits many asynchronous transactions continuously for many different items. If the client application displays the results of many items, most likely it will use a number of windows. The client application may even be an MDI application. The **DdeSetUserHandle()** function is perfect for assigning a window handle to a transaction. When the client application receives the `XTYP_XACT_COMPLETE` transaction, it can easily determine where the data item should be displayed.

The **DdeSetUserHandle()** function has the following prototype:

```
BOOL EXPENTRY DdeSetUserHandle(HCONV hConv, DWORD id,
                               DWORD hUser);
```

If the call to **DdeSetUserHandle()** is successful, it returns `TRUE`; otherwise, it returns `FALSE`. The first parameter is a handle to the conversation. The second parameter contains the transaction identifier returned by the **DdeClientTransaction()** in the `pdwResult` parameter. If the client application wants to associate the user handle with just a conversation and not a particular asynchronous transaction, the second parameter should be `QID_SYNC`. The last parameter is the user handle. This can be anything as long as it is a `DWORD`.

When the client application wants to access the user handle, it can call the **DdeQueryConvInfo()** function. The `CONVINFO` structure will contain the user handle in the `hUser` member. Additionally, the `CONVINFO` structure has a wealth of information about the current status of a conversation and a transaction. Here's the `typedef` for the `CONVINFO` structure:

```
typedef struct _CONVINFO {
    DWORD    cb;
    DWORD    hUser;
    HCONV    hConvPartner;
    HSZ      hszSvcPartner;
    HSZ      hszServiceReq;
    HSZ      hszTopic;
    HSZ      hszItem;
    WORD     wFmt;
    WORD     wType;
    WORD     wStatus;
    WORD     wConvst;
    WORD     wLastError;
```

```
    HCONVLIST hConvList;
    CONVCONTEXT ConvCtxt;
} CONVINFO;
```

The cb, hConvPartner, hszSvcPartner, hszServiceReq, hszTopic, hConvList, and ConvCtxt members were discussed in Chapter 2, so this discussion focuses on the remaining members. The hszItem member is a transaction-related member that changes throughout a conversation as the item name changes with transactions. The wFmt is also a transaction-related member. The wFmt is the clipboard format for the data item associated with the item name hszItem. The wType member specifies the current transaction in a conversation. The wStatus member is a little more interesting. This member gives the current status of a conversation. It can be a combination of the values in Table 3.1.

Table 3.1. Conversation status.

ST_CONNECTED	The conversation is connected.
ST_ADVISE	The conversation is in an advise loop.
ST_ISLOCAL	Both sides of the conversation use the DDEML.
ST_BLOCKED	The conversation is blocked.
ST_CLIENT	The conversation is a client-side conversation.
ST_TERMINATED	The conversation is terminated.
ST_INLIST	The conversation is in a connected list.
ST_BLOCKNEXT	The conversation is blocked after the next callback.
ST_ISSELF	The application is connected to itself.

The wConvst member identifies the state of a conversation. It can be one of the values in Table 3.2.

Table 3.2. Conversation states.

XST_NULL	Quiescent state—no state.
XST_INCOMPLETE	Quiescent state—incomplete.
XST_CONNECTED	Quiescent state—connected.
XST_INIT1	Initializing.

continues

Table 3.2. continued

XST_INIT2	Initializing.
XST_REQSENT	XTYP_RESQUEST sent by client.
XST_DATARCVD	Data received by client.
XST_POKESENT	XTYP_POKE sent by client.
XST_POKEACKRCVD	XTYP_POKE acknowledgment by server.
XST_EXECSENT	XTYP_EXECUTE sent by client.
XST_EXECACKRCVD	XTYP_EXECUTE acknowledged by server.
XST_ADVSENT	XTYP_ADVSTART sent by client.
XST_UNADVSENT	XTYP_ADVSTOP sent by client.
XST_ADVACKRCVD	XTYP_ADVSTART acknowledged by server.
XST_UNADVACKRCVD	XTYP_ADVSTOP acknowledged by server.
XST_ADVDATASENT	XTYP_ADVDATA sent by server.
XST_ADVDATAACKRCVD	XTYP_ADVDATA acknowledged by server.

Example Programs— TICKER and QUOTE

This chapter includes two example programs: TICKER.EXE and QUOTE.EXE. TICKER is a DDEML client application, whereas QUOTE is a server application. I thought of these programs when I was watching stock quotes on the Financial News Network. The primary requirement for the applications is to include the following transactions: XTYP_REQUEST, XTYP_ADVSTART, XTYP_ADVSTOP, XTYP_POKE, and XTYP_EXECUTE.

The TICKER application requests stock prices from QUOTE. When QUOTE receives a request, it generates a random value within a range for the stock price. TICKER displays the value in one of two ways. If TICKER requests a one-time stock quote, it will display the stock price in the dialog box. When TICKER tracks a stock, the value of the stock is placed on a scrolling ticker. QUOTE updates the values of tracked stocks based on a time interval. The TICKER application can set the update interval.

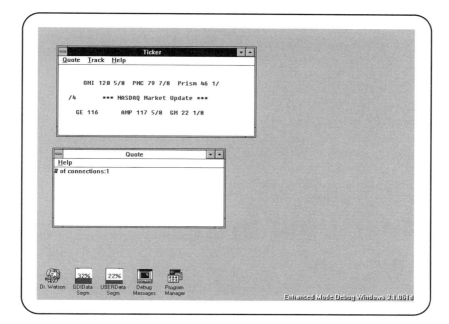

Figure 3.1.
TICKER and
QUOTE.

Application Design

You must overcome a couple of design problems in the example programs. The first problem is how to simulate a live stock market. Obviously, you cannot tap into a real stock market to get the quotes, so you must devise a random method to generate stock values. This isn't very realistic, but it will have to suffice. Stock prices are first generated by a random-number generator. The range for the random-number generator is between 10 and 160. The srand() and rand() functions provide the random numbers. This means that simulated quotes will not reflect the true value of a real stock.

As stock prices change on the real stock market, their value rarely goes up or down a great deal. Thus, the QUOTE application should allow only minor changes to the price of a stock. QUOTE does this by subtracting or adding an eighth of a point to a stock's price. To determine the direction of the price change, QUOTE calls the random-number generator. If the number returned is greater than the current stock price, QUOTE adds an eighth of a point to the price. If the number returned is less than the current stock price, QUOTE subtracts an eighth of a point from the price.

Another design problem for the example applications is the number of real stocks. You could spend a week typing a table of stock names and values. By the

time you finished, there would be new stocks on the market, and the prices would have changed. The solution to this is to dynamically build a table of stocks. Both example programs have an array of structures for tracking stocks. This array has a default size of 100. When users of the TICKER program want a stock price, they enter the name of the stock. The TICKER program adds the stock to the array. Then it sends a command to QUOTE to track the stock.

If you think of QUOTE as a program that simulates a communications program connected to a stock market service, it makes sense for the client application—TICKER—to send a command. TICKER is requesting a service from QUOTE. Thus, when QUOTE receives the command, it can add the stock name to an array. The stock name is a parameter in the command.

TICKER, a DDEML Client Application

TICKER has four major dialog boxes. Each dialog box corresponds to a least one DDEML transaction. The Quote dialog box enables a user to request a stock price. There is a combo box for the stock exchange, an edit control for the stock name, a Cancel button, and a Get Quote button. When the user selects an exchange, enters a stock name, and presses the Get Quote button, the TICKER program adds the stock to the array of stocks if the stock doesn't already exist in the array. After adding the stock to the array, TICKER sends an XTYP_EXECUTE transaction to QUOTE. The command has the following format:

```
[trackstock](stockname)
```

After the QUOTE program receives the stock name, TICKER sends an XTYP_REQUEST transaction for the stock price. TICKER displays the stock price in the dialog box.

The TICKER application establishes only one conversation with the QUOTE application. This keeps the program size down because TICKER doesn't have to track multiple conversations. TICKER can establish a conversation with any request to QUOTE. The service name is Quotes. The topic name is Stocks. Logically, the name of the stock exchange should be the topic name; however, space is limited and having multiple topic names would include more tracking logic in QUOTE. TICKER does use the stock exchange for the tickers, but the stock and the exchange are only loosely related. The item name is the stock name for the request.

The Track dialog box is similar to the Quote dialog box; however, the Track dialog box procedure sends an XTYP_ADVSTART transaction to QUOTE rather than an XTYP_REQUEST transaction. The UnTrack dialog box maintains a list of tracked stocks. When you select a stock and press the UnTrack button, TICKER sends an XTYP_ADVSTOP transaction for the stock (item name) to QUOTE. The Market Updates dialog box enables you to change the rate at which stocks change prices. QUOTE uses WM_TIMER messages to change tracked stock values. The Market Updates dialog box gives a selection of times between 5 and 30 seconds. The SetTimer() function takes an integer value for a parameter. Because this parameter must be an integer value, the market update intervals are limited. When you select a market update interval and press the OK button in the Market Updates dialog box, TICKER sends an XTYP_POKE transaction with the market update interval.

The TICKER application maintains three tickers in its main window's client area. TICKER updates the tickers when it receives XTYP_ADVDATA transactions. There are three character arrays—one for each ticker. Each time TICKER receives an XTYP_ADVDATA transaction, it updates the ticker associated with the advised stock's exchange. The TICKER scrolls the tickers across the window based on timer messages. Each ticker has an output buffer. When TICKER receives a WM_TIMER message, it scrolls each ticker by one character. To do this, TICKER copies characters for the length of the ticker from a character array to the output buffer. Each WM_TIMER message increments the starting position of the copy in the character array. This gives the illusion that the ticker scrolls across the screen.

Listing 3.1. The ticker.h header file.

```
#define NOCOMM
#define DDEMLDB
#include <windows.h>
#include <ddeml.h>
#include "resource.h"
#include "dialogs.h"

#ifndef MAIN
#define EXTERN extern
#else
#define EXTERN
#endif
```

continues

119

Listing 3.1. continued

```c
#define SZCLASSNAME 40
#define SZWINDOWTITLE 40
#define SZMESSAGE 128
#define MAX_NAME_SIZE 100
#define MAX_CONNECTS 100

#define AMEX 0
#define NASDAQ 1
#define NYSE 2
#define FIVESECONDS 5000

EXTERN DWORD idInst;
EXTERN HINSTANCE hInst;
EXTERN HWND hWnd;
EXTERN FARPROC lpDdeProc;
EXTERN int cbStockCount;
EXTERN HCONV hConv;

typedef struct tagStocks {
    WORD wExchange;
    HSZ  hszStock;
    BOOL bAdvise;
    char achValue[10];
    } STOCKS;

EXTERN STOCKS Stocks[100];
EXTERN char achExLoop[3][1200];
EXTERN WORD wMarketUpdate;
EXTERN WORD acbExchange[3];

int PASCAL WinMain (HINSTANCE, HINSTANCE, LPSTR, int);
BOOL InitApplication(HINSTANCE);
BOOL InitInstance(HINSTANCE, int);
VOID PASCAL MsgBox(HWND, WORD, WORD);
BOOL PASCAL CreateDlgBox(HWND, LPCSTR, FARPROC);
LRESULT CALLBACK MainWndProc(HWND, WORD, WPARAM, LPARAM);
LRESULT CALLBACK AboutDlgProc(HWND, WORD, WPARAM, LPARAM);
LRESULT CALLBACK QuoteDlgProc(HWND, WORD, WPARAM, LPARAM);
LRESULT CALLBACK TrackDlgProc(HWND, WORD, WPARAM, LPARAM);
LRESULT CALLBACK UnTrackDlgProc(HWND, WORD, WPARAM, LPARAM);
```

```
LRESULT CALLBACK MarketDlgProc(HWND, WORD, WPARAM, LPARAM);
HDDEDATA EXPENTRY DdeCallBack(WORD, WORD, HCONV, HSZ, HSZ,
                             HDDEDATA, DWORD, DWORD);
```

Listing 3.2. The dialogs.h header file.

```
#define IDD_EXCHANGE          201
#define IDD_STOCK             202
#define IDD_PRICE             203
#define IDD_GETQUOTE          204
#define IDD_TRACKBOX          300
#define IDD_ABOUTBOX          100
#define IDD_QUOTEBOX          200
#define IDD_UNTRACKBOX        400
#define IDD_STOCKLIST         401
#define IDD_UNTRACK           402
#define IDD_MARKETUPDATEBOX   500
#define IDD_UPDATE15          503
#define IDD_UPDATE30          506
#define IDD_UPDATE5           501
#define IDD_UPDATE10          502
#define IDD_UPDATE20          504
#define IDD_UPDATE25          505
```

Listing 3.3. The resource.h header file.

```
#define IDM_DDETICKERMENU   10
#define IDM_ABOUT           11
#define IDM_QUOTE           12
#define IDM_TRACK           13
#define IDM_UNTRACK         14
#define IDM_MARKETUPDATES   15

#define IDS_CLASSNAME        1
#define IDS_WINDOWTITLE      2
#define IDS_INITSUCCESS      3
#define IDS_INITFAIL         4
#define IDS_NOTPMODE         5
```

continues

Listing 3.3. continued

```
#define IDS_SERVICE         6
#define IDS_TOPIC           7
#define IDS_NOEXCHANGE      8
#define IDS_NOSTOCK         9
#define IDS_NOCONNECT      10
#define IDS_TIMEITEM       11
#define IDS_EXCHANGESTART  12
#define IDS_EXCHANGE2      13
#define IDS_EXCHANGEEND    14
#define IDS_AMEX           15
#define IDS_NASDAQ         16
#define IDS_NYSE           17
#define IDS_DISCONNECT     18
```

Listing 3.4. The ticker.c source file.

```
#include "ticker.h"
#include <string.h>

#define TICKLEN 40
char ach[3][TICKLEN+1];
WORD wStartChar[3] = {0,0,0};
WORD wLoopLen[3] = {0,0,0};
WORD wOldLoopLen[3] = {0,0,0};
WORD wDelay = 250;
int cyText;
int cxText;
BOOL PASCAL InitializeDDEML(HWND);
BOOL PASCAL CleanUpDDEML(HWND);
/*********************************************************************/
/* Function: MainWndProc                                             */
/* Purpose: Processes messages for main window.                      */
/* Returns: Varies                                                   */
/*********************************************************************/
LRESULT CALLBACK MainWndProc(HWND hwnd, WORD message,
            WPARAM wParam, LPARAM lParam)
    {
    int i, j;
    DWORD dwWinFlags;
```

```
HDC             hdc;

switch(message)
    {
    case WM_CREATE:
        dwWinFlags = GetWinFlags();
        if(dwWinFlags & WF_PMODE)
            {
            if(!InitializeDDEML(hwnd))
                {
                MsgBox(hwnd, IDS_INITFAIL, MB_OK | MB_ICONSTOP);
                return -1;
                }
            }
        else
            {
            MsgBox(hwnd, IDS_NOTPMODE, MB_OK | MB_ICONSTOP);
            return -1;
            }
        return FALSE;

    case WM_COMMAND:
        switch((WORD)wParam)
            {
            /* User selected About ... from menu */
            case IDM_ABOUT:
                CreateDlgBox(hwnd,
                        (LPCSTR)MAKEINTRESOURCE(IDD_ABOUTBOX),
                        (FARPROC)AboutDlgProc);
                break;
            case IDM_QUOTE:
                KillTimer(hwnd, 1);
                CreateDlgBox(hwnd,
                        (LPCSTR)MAKEINTRESOURCE(IDD_QUOTEBOX),
                        (FARPROC)QuoteDlgProc);
                SetTimer(hwnd, 1, wDelay, NULL);
                break;
            case IDM_TRACK:
                KillTimer(hwnd, 1);
                CreateDlgBox(hwnd,
                        (LPCSTR)MAKEINTRESOURCE(IDD_TRACKBOX),
```

continues

Listing 3.4. continued

```
                            (FARPROC)TrackDlgProc);
            SetTimer(hwnd, 1, wDelay, NULL);
            break;
        case IDM_UNTRACK:
            KillTimer(hwnd, 1);
            CreateDlgBox(hwnd,
                    (LPCSTR)MAKEINTRESOURCE(IDD_UNTRACKBOX),
                     (FARPROC)UnTrackDlgProc);
            SetTimer(hwnd, 1, wDelay, NULL);
            break;
        case IDM_MARKETUPDATES:
            KillTimer(hwnd, 1);
            CreateDlgBox(hwnd,
                    (LPCSTR)MAKEINTRESOURCE(IDD_MARKETUPDATEBOX),
                     (FARPROC)MarketDlgProc);
            SetTimer(hwnd, 1, wDelay, NULL);
            break;
        }
    break;
case WM_TIMER:
    for(i = 0; i <= 2; i++)
        {
        wLoopLen[i] = lstrlen((LPCSTR)&achExLoop[i]);
        if(wLoopLen[i] != wOldLoopLen[i])
            {
            wOldLoopLen[i] = wLoopLen[i];
            wStartChar[i] = 0;
            }
        if(wStartChar[i] > wLoopLen[i]-TICKLEN)
            {
            if(wStartChar[i] == wLoopLen[i])
                wStartChar[i] = 0;
            else
                {
                strncpy(ach[i], &achExLoop[i][wStartChar[i]],
                        TICKLEN);
                strncat(ach[i],&achExLoop[i][0],
                        wStartChar[i]-(wLoopLen[i]-TICKLEN));
                }
            }
```

```
                        else
                            strncpy(ach[i], &achExLoop[i][wStartChar[i]],
                                    TICKLEN);
                        wStartChar[i]++;
                        }

                hdc = GetDC(hwnd);

                SelectObject(hdc, GetStockObject(SYSTEM_FIXED_FONT));

                j = 1;
                for(i = 0; i <= 2; i++)
                    {
                    TextOut(hdc, cxText*3, cyText*2*j,
                            (LPSTR)&ach[i],
                            lstrlen((LPCSTR)&ach[i]));
                    j++;
                    }

                ReleaseDC(hwnd, hdc);
                break;

            case WM_DESTROY:
                KillTimer(hwnd, 1);
                CleanUpDDEML(hwnd);
                PostQuitMessage(0);
                break;
            default:
                return DefWindowProc(hwnd, message, wParam, lParam);
            }
        return FALSE;
        }

/**********************************************************************/
/* Function: InitializeDDEML                                          */
/* Purpose: Registers application and callback function with DDEML.*/
/* Returns: TRUE/FALSE                                                */
/**********************************************************************/
BOOL PASCAL InitializeDDEML(HWND hwnd)
    {
    BOOL bResult;
```

continues

Listing 3.4. continued

```c
    HDC hdc;
    TEXTMETRIC tm;

    lpDdeProc = MakeProcInstance((FARPROC)DdeCallBack, hInst);
    idInst = 0L;
    bResult = FALSE;

    if(lpDdeProc)
        {
        if(DMLERR_NO_ERROR == DdeInitialize((LPDWORD) &idInst,
                                            (PFNCALLBACK) lpDdeProc,
                                            APPCMD_CLIENTONLY,
                                            0L))

            {
            SetTimer(hwnd, 1, wDelay, NULL);
            hdc = GetDC(hwnd);
            GetTextMetrics(hdc, &tm);
            cyText = tm.tmHeight + tm.tmExternalLeading;
            cxText = tm.tmAveCharWidth;
            ReleaseDC(hwnd, hdc);
            bResult = TRUE;
            }
        else
            FreeProcInstance((FARPROC)lpDdeProc);
        }
    return bResult;
    }

/***********************************************************************/
/* Function: CleanUpDDEML                                              */
/* Purpose: Uninitializes applications and frees callback resources.*/
/* Returns: TRUE                                                       */
/***********************************************************************/
BOOL PASCAL CleanUpDDEML(HWND hwnd)
    {
    if(hConv)
        DdeDisconnect(hConv);
    if(lpDdeProc)
        {
        DdeUninitialize(idInst);
        FreeProcInstance((FARPROC)lpDdeProc);
```

```
        }
    return TRUE;
    }

/***********************************************************************/
/* Function: MsgBox                                                    */
/* Purpose: Creates a message box.                                     */
/***********************************************************************/
VOID PASCAL MsgBox(HWND hwnd, WORD wMsg, WORD wType)
    {
    char szWindowTitle[SZWINDOWTITLE];
    char szMessage[SZMESSAGE];

    LoadString(hInst, IDS_WINDOWTITLE,
               szWindowTitle, sizeof szWindowTitle);
    LoadString(hInst, wMsg,
               szMessage, sizeof szMessage);
    MessageBox(hwnd, szMessage, szWindowTitle, wType);
    }
```

Listing 3.5. The dde.c source file.

```
#include "ticker.h"
#include <stdio.h>

/***********************************************************************/
/*   Function: DdeCallBack                                             */
/*   Purpose: This function handles callbacks from the DDEML.          */
/*   Parameters:                                                       */
/*               WORD wType      - transaction type                    */
/*               WORD wFmt       - clipboard data format               */
/*               HCONV hConv     - handle of the conversation          */
/*               HSZ hsz1        - handle of a string                  */
/*               HSZ hsz2        - handle of a string                  */
/*               HDDEDATA hData  - handle of a global memory object    */
/*               DWORD dwData1   - transaction-specific data           */
/*               DWORD dwData2   - transaction-specific data           */
/*   Returns: Results vary depending on transaction type.              */
/***********************************************************************/
```

continues

127

Listing 3.5. continued

```
HDDEDATA EXPENTRY DdeCallBack(WORD wType, WORD wFmt, HCONV hConv,
                             HSZ hsz1, HSZ hsz2, HDDEDATA hData,
                             DWORD lData1, DWORD lData2)
    {
    WORD cb;
    int i, j;
    char achValue[10];
    char achStock[10];
    char ach[20];
    BOOL bFound;

    if(wType == XTYP_DISCONNECT)
        {
        MsgBox(hWnd,IDS_DISCONNECT,MB_OK | MB_ICONINFORMATION);
        }
    if(wType == XTYP_ADVDATA)
        {
        DdeGetData(hData,(LPBYTE)achValue,10,0L);
        bFound = FALSE;
        for(i = 0; i <= cbStockCount; i++)
            {
            if(Stocks[i].hszStock == hsz2)
                {
                lstrcpy(Stocks[i].achValue, achValue);
                LoadString(hInst, Stocks[i].wExchange+IDS_AMEX,
                        &achExLoop[Stocks[i].wExchange][0],
                        sizeof(achExLoop[i]));

                for(j = 0; j <= cbStockCount; j++)
                    {
                    if(Stocks[j].wExchange == Stocks[i].wExchange &&
                       Stocks[j].bAdvise)
                        {
                        cb = (WORD)DdeQueryString(idInst,
                                Stocks[j].hszStock, NULL, 0, 0);
                        DdeQueryString(idInst, Stocks[j].hszStock,
                                &achStock[0],  cb+2, 0);
                        sprintf(ach," %s %s",
                                achStock,Stocks[j].achValue);
                        lstrcat(achExLoop[Stocks[j].wExchange],ach);
                        }
```

```
                    }
                bFound = TRUE;
                break;
                }
            }
        if(bFound)
            return DDE_FACK;
        else
            return DDE_FNOTPROCESSED;
        }
    return NULL;
    }
```

Listing 3.6. The dialogs.c source file.

```c
#include "ticker.h"
#include <stdlib.h>
#include <string.h>


HSZ ahsz[100];

int PASCAL ProcessDialog(HWND, BOOL);
BOOL PASCAL Connect(HWND);
VOID PASCAL LoadExchange(HWND);
/*********************************************************************/
/* Function: CreateDlgBox                                          */
/* Purpose: Generic function to create dialog boxes.               */
/* Returns: TRUE/FALSE                                             */
/*********************************************************************/
BOOL PASCAL CreateDlgBox(HWND hWnd, LPCSTR lpTemplateName,
                    FARPROC lpDlgProc)
    {
    BOOL    bResult;

    lpDlgProc = MakeProcInstance(lpDlgProc, hInst);
    if(lpDlgProc)
        {
        DialogBox(hInst, lpTemplateName, hWnd, (DLGPROC)lpDlgProc);
        FreeProcInstance(lpDlgProc);
```

continues

Listing 3.6. continued

```
        bResult = TRUE;
        }
    else
        bResult = FALSE;

    return bResult;
    }

/**********************************************************************/
/* Function: QuoteDlgProc                                           */
/* Purpose: Handles messages for the Quotes dialog box.             */
/* Returns: TRUE/FALSE                                              */
/**********************************************************************/
LRESULT CALLBACK QuoteDlgProc(HWND hDlg, WORD message,
                            WPARAM wParam, LPARAM lParam)

    {
    int RequestItem;
    char achValue[10];
    HDDEDATA hData;

    switch(message)
        {
        case WM_INITDIALOG:
            LoadExchange(hDlg);
            return (LRESULT)TRUE;

        case WM_COMMAND:
            switch((WORD)wParam)
                {
                case IDD_GETQUOTE:
                    RequestItem = ProcessDialog(hDlg, FALSE);
                    if(RequestItem == -1)
                        return TRUE;
                    hData = DdeClientTransaction(NULL,NULL,hConv,
                                (HSZ)Stocks[RequestItem].hszStock,
                                CF_TEXT,XTYP_REQUEST,1000,NULL);
                    DdeGetData(hData,(LPBYTE)achValue,10,0L);
                    DdeFreeDataHandle(hData);
                    SendDlgItemMessage(hDlg,IDD_PRICE,WM_SETTEXT,
                                0,(LONG)(LPSTR)achValue);
```

```
                            return (LRESULT)TRUE;
                            break;
                    case IDCANCEL:
                            EndDialog(hDlg, TRUE);
                            return (LRESULT)TRUE;
                            break;
                }
        }
    return (LRESULT)FALSE;
    }

/************************************************************************/
/* Function: TrackDlgProc                                             */
/* Purpose: Handles messages for the Track dialog box.               */
/* Returns: TRUE/FALSE                                                */
/************************************************************************/
LRESULT CALLBACK TrackDlgProc(HWND hDlg, WORD message,
                              WPARAM wParam, LPARAM lParam)

    {
    int RequestItem, i;
    WORD cb;
    char achStock[10];
    HDDEDATA hData;

    switch(message)
        {
        case WM_INITDIALOG:
            LoadExchange(hDlg);
            for(i = 0; i <= cbStockCount; i++)
                {
                if(!Stocks[i].bAdvise)
                    {
                    cb = (WORD)DdeQueryString(idInst,
                            Stocks[i].hszStock, NULL, 0, 0);
                    DdeQueryString(idInst, Stocks[i].hszStock,
                            achStock,  cb+2, 0);
                    SendDlgItemMessage(hDlg, IDD_STOCK,
                            CB_ADDSTRING,0,(LONG)(LPSTR)achStock);
                    }
                }
            return (LRESULT)TRUE;
```

continues

131

Listing 3.6. continued

```
            case WM_COMMAND:
                switch((WORD)wParam)
                    {
                    case IDOK:
                        RequestItem = ProcessDialog(hDlg, TRUE);
                        if(RequestItem == -1)
                            return TRUE;
                        hData = DdeClientTransaction(NULL,NULL,hConv,
                                    (HSZ)Stocks[RequestItem].hszStock,
                                    CF_TEXT,XTYP_ADVSTART,1000,NULL);
                        /* fall through */
                    case IDCANCEL:
                        EndDialog(hDlg, TRUE);
                        return (LRESULT)TRUE;
                        break;
                    }
            }
        return (LRESULT)FALSE;
        }
/**********************************************************************/
/* Function: UnTrackDlgProc                                         */
/* Purpose: Handles messages for the UnTrack dialog box.            */
/* Returns: TRUE/FALSE                                              */
/**********************************************************************/
LRESULT CALLBACK UnTrackDlgProc(HWND hDlg, WORD message,
                                WPARAM wParam, LPARAM lParam)

    {
    int i, j, cb, wIndex;
    char achStock[10];

    switch(message)
        {
        case WM_INITDIALOG:
            j = 0;
            for(i = 0; i <= cbStockCount; i++)
                {
                if(Stocks[i].bAdvise)
                    {
                    ahsz[j++] = Stocks[i].hszStock;
                    cb = (WORD)DdeQueryString(idInst,
                            Stocks[i].hszStock, NULL, 0, 0);
```

```
                  DdeQueryString(idInst, Stocks[i].hszStock,
                              achStock,  cb+2, 0);
                  SendDlgItemMessage(hDlg,IDD_STOCKLIST,
                          LB_ADDSTRING,0,(LONG)(LPSTR)achStock);
                  }
              }
          return (LRESULT)TRUE;

      case WM_COMMAND:
          switch((WORD)wParam)
              {
              case IDD_UNTRACK:
                  wIndex = (WORD)SendDlgItemMessage(hDlg,
                      IDD_STOCKLIST,
                      LB_GETCURSEL,0,0);
                  if(wIndex != LB_ERR)
                      {
                      DdeClientTransaction(NULL,NULL,hConv,
                          ahsz[wIndex], CF_TEXT, XTYP_ADVSTOP,
                          1000,NULL);
                      for(i = 0; i <= cbStockCount; i++)
                          {
                          if(Stocks[i].hszStock == ahsz[wIndex])
                              {
                              Stocks[i].bAdvise = FALSE;
                              break;
                              }
                          }
                      acbExchange[Stocks[i].wExchange]--;
                      if(!acbExchange[Stocks[i].wExchange])
                          LoadString(hInst, Stocks[i].wExchange +
                              IDS_AMEX,
                              &achExLoop[Stocks[i].wExchange][0],
                          sizeof(achExLoop[Stocks[i].wExchange]));

                      SendDlgItemMessage(hDlg,IDD_STOCKLIST,
                          LB_RESETCONTENT, 0, 0L);
                      j = 0;
                      for(i = 0; i <= cbStockCount; i++)
                          {
                          if(Stocks[i].bAdvise)
```

continues

133

Listing 3.6. continued

```
                                   {
                                   ahsz[j++] = Stocks[i].hszStock;
                                   cb = (WORD)DdeQueryString(idInst,
                                        Stocks[i].hszStock, NULL, 0, 0);
                                   DdeQueryString(idInst,
                                        Stocks[i].hszStock,
                                        achStock,  cb+2, 0);
                                   SendDlgItemMessage(hDlg,IDD_STOCKLIST,
                                        LB_ADDSTRING,0,
                                        (LONG)(LPSTR)achStock);
                                   }
                            }
                    }
                return TRUE;
            case IDCANCEL:
                EndDialog(hDlg, TRUE);
                return (LRESULT)TRUE;
            }
        break;
    }
    return (LRESULT)FALSE;
    }


/***********************************************************************/
/* Function: MarketDlgProc                                             */
/* Purpose: Handles messages for the Market Updates dialog box.        */
/* Returns: TRUE/FALSE                                                 */
/***********************************************************************/
LRESULT CALLBACK MarketDlgProc(HWND hDlg, WORD message,
                               WPARAM wParam, LPARAM lParam)

    {
    int i;
    char achUpdate[20], achItem[20];
    HSZ hszItem;
    HDDEDATA hData;

    switch(message)
        {
        case WM_INITDIALOG:
            SendDlgItemMessage(hDlg,IDD_MARKETUPDATEBOX +
```

```
                    wMarketUpdate, BM_SETCHECK, 1, 0L);
              return (LRESULT)TRUE;
         case WM_COMMAND:
              switch((WORD)wParam)
                  {
                  case IDOK:
                      for(i = 1+IDD_MARKETUPDATEBOX;
                          i <= 6+IDD_MARKETUPDATEBOX; i++)
                          if(IsDlgButtonChecked(hDlg,i))
                              break;
                      wMarketUpdate = i-IDD_MARKETUPDATEBOX;
                      _itoa((wMarketUpdate*FIVESECONDS),achUpdate,10);

                      if(!Connect(hDlg))
                          return TRUE;

                      LoadString(hInst, IDS_TIMEITEM,
                                  achItem, sizeof(achItem));
                      hszItem = DdeCreateStringHandle(idInst,
                                      achItem, 0);

                      hData = DdeCreateDataHandle(idInst,
                              (LPBYTE)achUpdate,lstrlen(achUpdate),
                              0L,hszItem,CF_TEXT,0);

                      if(hData)
                          {
                          DdeClientTransaction((LPBYTE)hData,-1,
                                  hConv, hszItem, CF_TEXT, XTYP_POKE,
                                  1000, NULL);
                          }
                      /* fall through */
                  case IDCANCEL:
                      EndDialog(hDlg, TRUE);
                      return (LRESULT)TRUE;
                  }
              break;
         }
    return (LRESULT)FALSE;
    }
```

continues

135

Listing 3.6. continued

```
/**********************************************************************/
/* Function: AboutDlgProc                                             */
/* Purpose: Handles messages for the About dialog box.                */
/* Returns: TRUE/FALSE                                                */
/**********************************************************************/
LRESULT CALLBACK AboutDlgProc(HWND hDlg, WORD message,
                              WPARAM wParam, LPARAM lParam)

    {
    switch(message)
        {
        case WM_INITDIALOG:
            return (LRESULT)TRUE;
        case WM_COMMAND:
            switch((WORD)wParam)
                {
                case IDOK:
                case IDCANCEL:
                    EndDialog(hDlg, TRUE);
                    return (LRESULT)TRUE;
                }
            break;
        }
    return (LRESULT)FALSE;
    }


/**********************************************************************/
/* Function: LoadExchange                                             */
/* Purpose: Loads Exchange combo box control.                         */
/* Returns: TRUE/FALSE                                                */
/**********************************************************************/
VOID PASCAL LoadExchange(HWND hDlg)
    {
    int i;
    char ach[10];

    for(i = IDS_EXCHANGESTART; i <= IDS_EXCHANGEEND; i++)
        {
        LoadString(hInst, i,
                   ach, sizeof(ach));
        SendDlgItemMessage(hDlg, IDD_EXCHANGE,
```

CHAPTER 3

```
                                    CB_ADDSTRING,0,(LONG)(LPSTR)ach);
        }
    }

/**********************************************************************/
/* Function: ProcessDialog                                           */
/* Purpose: Handles common processing for Track and Quote dialogs. */
/* Returns: TRUE/FALSE                                               */
/**********************************************************************/
int PASCAL ProcessDialog(HWND hDlg, BOOL bAdvise)
    {
    int i, RequestItem;
    WORD wIndex;
    BOOL bFound;
    char achStock[7], achCommand[64];
    HSZ  hszStock;
    HDDEDATA hCommand;

    wIndex = (WORD)SendDlgItemMessage(hDlg,IDD_EXCHANGE,
                                      CB_GETCURSEL,0,0L);
    if(wIndex == CB_ERR)
        {
        MsgBox(hDlg,IDS_NOEXCHANGE, MB_OK | MB_ICONINFORMATION);
        return -1;
        }

    SendDlgItemMessage(hDlg,IDD_STOCK,
                       WM_GETTEXT,10,(LONG)(LPSTR)achStock);
    if(achStock[0] == '\0')
        {
        MsgBox(hDlg, IDS_NOSTOCK, MB_OK | MB_ICONINFORMATION);
        return -1;
        }

    if(!Connect(hDlg))
        return -1;

    hszStock = DdeCreateStringHandle(idInst, achStock, 0);
    bFound = FALSE;
    for(i = 0; i <= cbStockCount; i++)
        if(Stocks[i].hszStock == hszStock)
```

continues

137

Listing 3.6. continued

```
                {
            Stocks[i].wExchange = wIndex;
            if(bAdvise && !Stocks[i].bAdvise)
                acbExchange[Stocks[i].wExchange]++;
            Stocks[i].bAdvise = bAdvise;
            bFound = TRUE;
            RequestItem = i;
            break;
            }
    if(!bFound)
        {
        cbStockCount++;
        Stocks[cbStockCount].hszStock = hszStock;
        Stocks[cbStockCount].wExchange = wIndex;
        Stocks[cbStockCount].bAdvise = bAdvise;
        RequestItem = cbStockCount;
        acbExchange[Stocks[RequestItem].wExchange]++;
        lstrcpy(achCommand,"[trackstock](");
        lstrcat(achCommand,achStock);
        lstrcat(achCommand,")");
        hCommand = DdeCreateDataHandle(idInst,
                        (LPBYTE)achCommand,sizeof(achCommand),
                        0L,0,CF_TEXT,0);
        DdeClientTransaction((LPBYTE)hCommand, -1, hConv, NULL,
                            NULL, XTYP_EXECUTE, 1000, NULL);
        }
    return RequestItem;
    }


/*********************************************************************/
/* Function: Connect                                                 */
/* Purpose: Connects to quote application.                           */
/* Returns: TRUE/FALSE                                               */
/*********************************************************************/
BOOL PASCAL Connect(HWND hDlg)
    {
    char achService[20], achTopic[20];
    HSZ hszService, hszTopic;

    if(hConv)
        return TRUE;
```

```
LoadString(hInst, IDS_SERVICE,
            achService, sizeof(achService));
hszService = DdeCreateStringHandle(idInst, achService, 0);

LoadString(hInst, IDS_TOPIC,
            achTopic, sizeof(achTopic));
hszTopic = DdeCreateStringHandle(idInst, achTopic, 0);

hConv = DdeConnect(idInst, hszService, hszTopic,
                    (LPVOID)NULL);
if(!hConv)
    {
    MsgBox(hDlg, IDS_NOCONNECT, MB_OK ¦ MB_ICONEXCLAMATION);
    return FALSE;
    }
return TRUE;
}
```

Listing 3.7. The winmain.c source file.

```
#define MAIN
#include "ticker.h"

/**********************************************************************/
/* Function: WinMain                                                  */
/* Purpose: Main function for windows app. Initializes all            */
/*          instances of app, translates and dispatches messages.     */
/* Returns: Value of PostQuitMessage                                  */
/**********************************************************************/
int PASCAL WinMain(HINSTANCE hInstance, HINSTANCE hPrevInstance,
                LPSTR lpszCmdLine, int nCmdShow)
    {
    MSG msg;

    /* If there isn't a previous instance of app, then initialize  */
    /* the first instance of app.                                  */
    if(!hPrevInstance)
        if(!InitApplication(hInstance))
            return FALSE;
```

continues

Listing 3.7. continued

```c
    /* Perform initialization for all instances of application    */
    if(!InitInstance(hInstance, nCmdShow))
        return FALSE;

    /* Get messages for this application until WM_QUIT is received */
    while(GetMessage(&msg, 0, 0, 0))
        {
        TranslateMessage(&msg);
        DispatchMessage(&msg);
        }
    return (int)msg.wParam;
    }
```

Listing 3.8. The init.c source file.

```c
#include "server.h"

/**********************************************************************/
/* Function: InitApplication                                        */
/* Purpose: Performs all initialization for first instance of app.  */
/* Returns: TRUE if successful, FALSE if failure                    */
/**********************************************************************/
BOOL InitApplication(HINSTANCE hInstance)
    {
    BOOL bResult;
    char szClassName[SZCLASSNAME];
    WNDCLASS wc;

    /* Load the window class name from resource string table */

    if(!LoadString(hInstance, IDS_CLASSNAME,
        szClassName, sizeof szClassName))
        return FALSE;

    /* Class styles */
    wc.style        = 0;
    /* Name of message loop function for windows of this class */
    wc.lpfnWndProc  = MainWndProc;
    /* Not using Class Extra data */
```

```
          wc.cbClsExtra    = 0;
          /* Not using Window Extra data */
          wc.cbWndExtra    = 0;
          /* Instance that owns this class */
          wc.hInstance     = hInstance;
          /* Use default application icon */
          wc.hIcon         = LoadIcon(NULL, IDI_APPLICATION);
          /* Use arrow cursor */
          wc.hCursor       = LoadCursor(NULL, IDC_ARROW);
          /* Use system background color */
          wc.hbrBackground = GetStockObject(WHITE_BRUSH);
          /* Resource name for menu */
          wc.lpszMenuName  = MAKEINTRESOURCE(IDM_DDETICKERMENU);
          /* Name given to this class */
          wc.lpszClassName = szClassName;

          /* Register the window class */
          bResult = RegisterClass(&wc);

          /* return result based on registration */
          return bResult;
          }

/**********************************************************************/
/* Function: InitInstance                                             */
/* Purpose: Performs all initialization for all instances of app.     */
/* Returns: TRUE if successful, FALSE if failure                      */
/**********************************************************************/
BOOL InitInstance (HINSTANCE hInstance, int nCmdShow)
     {
     int i;
     char szClassName[SZCLASSNAME];
     char szWindowTitle[SZWINDOWTITLE];

     hInst = hInstance;

     /* Load the window class name from resource string table */
     if(!LoadString(hInst, IDS_CLASSNAME,
                    szClassName, sizeof szClassName))
         return FALSE;
```

continues

141

Listing 3.8. continued

```c
/* Load the window title from resource string table */
if(!LoadString(hInst, IDS_WINDOWTITLE,
                szWindowTitle, sizeof szWindowTitle))
    return FALSE;

hWnd = CreateWindow(szClassName,          /* Window class        */
                    szWindowTitle,        /* Text for title bar  */
                    WS_OVERLAPPEDWINDOW,
                    CW_USEDEFAULT,        /* Default x  pos       */
                    CW_USEDEFAULT,        /* Default y  pos       */
                    CW_USEDEFAULT,        /* Default cx pos       */
                    CW_USEDEFAULT,        /* Default cy pos       */
                    0,                    /* Parent window        */
                    0,                    /* Menu                 */
                    hInstance,            /* Owning instance      */
                    NULL);                /* User-defined params  */

/* If CreateWindow wasn't successful, return FALSE */
if(!hWnd)
    return FALSE;

cbStockCount = -1;

for(i = 0; i <= 2; i++)
    LoadString(hInst, i+IDS_AMEX, &achExLoop[i][0],
                sizeof(achExLoop[i]));

wMarketUpdate = 3;

/* Show and paint window */
ShowWindow(hWnd, nCmdShow);
UpdateWindow(hWnd);

return TRUE;
}
```

Listing 3.9. The ticker.rc resource file.

```
#include <windows.h>
#include "resource.h"
#include "dialogs.h"

IDM_DDETICKERMENU MENU
    BEGIN
        MENUITEM "&Quote", IDM_QUOTE

        POPUP "&Track"
        BEGIN
            MENUITEM "&Track ...",           IDM_TRACK
            MENUITEM "&UnTrack ...",         IDM_UNTRACK
            MENUITEM SEPARATOR
            MENUITEM "&Market Updates ...", IDM_MARKETUPDATES
        END

        POPUP "&Help"
        BEGIN
            MENUITEM "&About Ticker ...",   IDM_ABOUT
        END
    END

STRINGTABLE
    BEGIN
        IDS_CLASSNAME      "DDETickerClass"
        IDS_WINDOWTITLE    "Ticker"
        IDS_INITSUCCESS    "DDEML Initialization Successful."
        IDS_INITFAIL       "DDEML Initialization Failed."
        IDS_NOTPMODE       "Windows must run in protected\n  mode to
          run this program."
        IDS_SERVICE        "Quote"
        IDS_TOPIC          "Stocks"
        IDS_NOEXCHANGE     "Select an exchange."
        IDS_NOSTOCK        "Enter a stock name."
        IDS_NOCONNECT      "Conversation not established."
        IDS_TIMEITEM       "Time"
        IDS_EXCHANGESTART  "AMEX"
        IDS_EXCHANGE2      "NASDAQ"
        IDS_EXCHANGEEND    "NYSE"
```

continues

Listing 3.9. The ticker.rc resource file.

```
        IDS_AMEX            "        *** AMEX Market Update ***      "
        IDS_NASDAQ          "        *** NASDAQ Market Update ***    "
        IDS_NYSE            "        *** NYSE Market Update ***      "
        IDS_DISCONNECT      "Server Disconnected."
    END


#include "ticker.dlg"
```

Listing 3.10. The ticker.dlg dialog definition file.

```
DLGINCLUDE RCDATA DISCARDABLE
BEGIN
    "DIALOGS.H\0"
END


IDD_ABOUTBOX DIALOG 115, 48, 152, 86
STYLE DS_MODALFRAME ¦ WS_POPUP ¦ WS_VISIBLE ¦ WS_CAPTION ¦ WS_SYSMENU
CAPTION "About Ticker"
FONT 8, "Helv"
BEGIN
    PUSHBUTTON       "OK", IDOK, 55, 66, 40, 14
    CTEXT            "Microsoft Windows", -1, 42, 12, 67, 8
    CTEXT            "Ticker Application", -1, 33, 30, 88, 8
    CTEXT            "Copyright _ Jeffrey Clark, 1991", -1, 20, 48,
                     117, 8
END


IDD_QUOTEBOX DIALOG 116, 60, 160, 69
STYLE DS_MODALFRAME ¦ WS_POPUP ¦ WS_VISIBLE ¦ WS_CAPTION ¦ WS_SYSMENU
CAPTION "Quote"
FONT 8, "Helv"
BEGIN
    LTEXT            "Exchange:", -1, 6, 12, 37, 8
    COMBOBOX         IDD_EXCHANGE, 43, 11, 48, 43, CBS_DROPDOWN ¦
                     CBS_SORT ¦
                     WS_VSCROLL ¦ WS_TABSTOP
    LTEXT            "Stock:", -1, 20, 33, 20, 8
    EDITTEXT         IDD_STOCK, 43, 31, 32, 12, ES_AUTOHSCROLL
    LTEXT            "Price:", -1, 5, 53, 20, 8
```

```
        LTEXT              " ", IDD_PRICE, 29, 53, 60, 8
        PUSHBUTTON         "Get Quote", IDD_GETQUOTE, 109, 9, 46, 14
        PUSHBUTTON         "Cancel", IDCANCEL, 109, 30, 46, 14
    END


    IDD_TRACKBOX DIALOG 125, 54, 160, 72
    STYLE DS_MODALFRAME ¦ WS_POPUP ¦ WS_VISIBLE ¦ WS_CAPTION ¦ WS_SYSMENU
    CAPTION "Track"
    FONT 8, "Helv"
    BEGIN
        LTEXT              "Exchange:", -1, 5, 11, 35, 8
        COMBOBOX           IDD_EXCHANGE, 41, 9, 48, 46, CBS_DROPDOWN ¦
                           CBS_SORT ¦
                           WS_VSCROLL ¦ WS_TABSTOP
        LTEXT              "Stock:", -1, 17, 32, 20, 8
        COMBOBOX           IDD_STOCK, 40, 30, 48, 41, CBS_DROPDOWN ¦
                           CBS_SORT ¦
                           WS_VSCROLL ¦ WS_TABSTOP
        PUSHBUTTON         "OK", IDOK, 111, 8, 40, 14
        PUSHBUTTON         "Cancel", IDCANCEL, 111, 29, 40, 14
    END


    IDD_UNTRACKBOX DIALOG 106, 35, 108, 100
    STYLE DS_MODALFRAME ¦ WS_POPUP ¦ WS_VISIBLE ¦ WS_CAPTION ¦ WS_SYSMENU
    CAPTION "UnTrack"
    FONT 8, "Helv"
    BEGIN
        LTEXT              "Stock:", -1, 5, 4, 20, 8
        LISTBOX            IDD_STOCKLIST, 4, 15, 48, 85, WS_VSCROLL ¦
                           WS_TABSTOP
        PUSHBUTTON         "UnTrack", IDD_UNTRACK, 59, 14, 40, 14
        PUSHBUTTON         "Cancel", IDCANCEL, 59, 34, 40, 14
    END


    IDD_MARKETUPDATEBOX DIALOG 106, 31, 160, 79
    STYLE DS_MODALFRAME ¦ WS_POPUP ¦ WS_VISIBLE ¦ WS_CAPTION ¦ WS_SYSMENU
    CAPTION "Market Updates"
    FONT 8, "Helv"
    BEGIN
        GROUPBOX           "Update Market Every", -1, 3, 4, 96, 71, WS_GROUP
        CONTROL            "5 sec.", IDD_UPDATE5, "Button",
```

continues

145

Listing 3.10. continued

```
                          BS_AUTORADIOBUTTON ¦
                          WS_GROUP, 11, 20, 39, 10
        CONTROL           "10 sec.", IDD_UPDATE10, "Button",
                          BS_AUTORADIOBUTTON,
                          11, 38, 39, 10
        CONTROL           "15 sec.", IDD_UPDATE15, "Button",
                          BS_AUTORADIOBUTTON,
                          11, 56, 39, 10
        CONTROL           "20 sec.", IDD_UPDATE20, "Button",
                          BS_AUTORADIOBUTTON,
                          58, 20, 39, 10
        CONTROL           "25 sec.", IDD_UPDATE25, "Button",
                          BS_AUTORADIOBUTTON,
                          58, 38, 39, 10
        CONTROL           "30 sec.", IDD_UPDATE30, "Button",
                          BS_AUTORADIOBUTTON,
                          58, 56, 39, 10
        PUSHBUTTON        "OK", IDOK, 108, 10, 40, 14
        PUSHBUTTON        "Cancel", IDCANCEL, 108, 31, 40, 14
END
```

Listing 3.11. The ticker.def module definition file.

```
NAME Ticker

DESCRIPTION 'Ticker Copyright Jeffrey Clark, 1991'

EXETYPE WINDOWS

STUB 'WINSTUB.EXE'

CODE PRELOAD MOVEABLE DISCARDABLE
DATA PRELOAD MOVEABLE MULTIPLE

HEAPSIZE 1024
STACKSIZE 8192

SEGMENTS
    WINMAIN_TEXT      MOVEABLE              PRELOAD
```

```
    TICKER_TEXT      MOVEABLE                 PRELOAD
    INIT_TEXT        MOVEABLE  DISCARDABLE  PRELOAD
    DDE_TEXT         MOVEABLE  DISCARDABLE  LOADONCALL
    DIALOGS_TEXT     MOVEABLE  DISCARDABLE  LOADONCALL

EXPORTS
    MainWndProc @1
    AboutDlgProc @2
    DdeCallBack @3
    QuoteDlgProc @4
    TrackDlgProc @5
    UnTrackDlgProc @6
    MarketDlgProc @7
```

Listing 3.12. The TICKER make file.

```
CC = cl -c -AM -Gsw -Od -W3 -Zpi -Fo$@

all: ticker.exe

ticker.h: dialogs.h resource.h

ticker.res: ticker.rc ticker.dlg dialogs.h resource.h
  rc -r ticker

dialogs.obj: dialogs.c ticker.h
  $(CC) $*.c

init.obj: init.c ticker.h
  $(CC) $*.c

winmain.obj: winmain.c ticker.h
  $(CC) $*.c

ticker.obj: ticker.c ticker.h
  $(CC) $*.c

dde.obj: dde.c ticker.h
  $(CC) $*.c
```

continues

Listing 3.12. continued

```
ticker.exe::  dialogs.obj init.obj winmain.obj ticker.obj dde.obj \
              ticker.res ticker.def
    link /CO /MAP /NOD @<<
dialogs+
init+
winmain+
ticker+
dde
$@

libw mlibcew ddeml
ticker.def
<<
    mapsym ticker
    rc ticker.res
```

QUOTE, a DDEML Server Application

The QUOTE application is fairly simple. It processes transactions in its DdeCallBack() function and displays the number of current conversations. QUOTE maintains an array of structures. Each element in the array contains a stock, a price, and an indicator for an advise loop. QUOTE updates stocks based on WM_TIMER messages. It updates a stock only if the advise indicator is set.

QUOTE supports the system topic so that other DDE applications can query QUOTE for information. Under the system topic are a number of system item names that applications should support. Although this support is not necessary, it is very informative to people trying to access applications from their own DDE applications or a software package that supports DDE. The DDEML header file has several defined system topic items. QUOTE supports most of these items.

The SZDDESYS_ITEM_SYSITEMS definition has a value of SysItems. QUOTE supports this item through XTYP_REQUEST transactions. If another DDE application requests this item, QUOTE will return a data handle to a tab-delimited string containing system items. QUOTE supports a number of system items.

The DDEML defines the SZDDESYS_ITEM_TOPICS system item as Topics. QUOTE responds to XTYP_REQUEST transactions for this item by returning a data handle to a tab-delimited string that contains System(tab)Stocks. QUOTE supports XTYP_REQUEST transactions for all system items. If the system item is a list, the string is tab-delimited.

Other system items supported by QUOTE are SZDDESYS_ITEM_STATUS, SZDDESYS_ITEM_FORMATS, SZDDESYS_ITEM_HELP, and SZDDE_ITEM_ITEMLIST. The DDEML defines these items as Status, Formats, Help, and TopicItemList, respectively. The status system item gives an indication to the status of QUOTE. This is always Ready. QUOTE supports only one clipboard format: CF_TEXT. When responding to SZDDESYS_ITEM_FORMATS requests, the CF_ is dropped from the string as a matter of convention. It would be nice if all applications supported SZDDESYS_ITEM_HELP. This item gives a description of how to use a DDEML server. Applications that respond to SZDDE_ITEM_ITEMLIST should list the nonsystem topic items currently available. In QUOTE, this changes as TICKER requests QUOTE to track stocks.

That about wraps it up for the server side of DDEML. Listings 3.13 through 3.24 are for the QUOTE DDEML server application.

Listing 3.13. The quote.h header file.

```
#define NOCOMM
#define DDEMLDB
#include <windows.h>
#include <dde.h>
#include <ddeml.h>
#include "resource.h"
#include "dialogs.h"

#ifndef MAIN
#define EXTERN extern
#else
#define EXTERN
#endif

#define SZCLASSNAME 40
#define SZWINDOWTITLE 40
#define SZMESSAGE 128
#define CTOPICS 2
#define CITEMS 100
```

continues

Listing 3.13. continued

```
#define getrandom(min, max)((rand() % (int)(((max)+1)-(min)))+(min))
#define PM_UPDATETIMER WM_USER+99

typedef struct tagStocks {
    HSZ hszStock;
    BOOL bAdvise;
    double dPrice;
    } STOCKS;

EXTERN DWORD idInst;
EXTERN HINSTANCE hInst;
EXTERN HWND hwnd;
EXTERN FARPROC lpDdeProc;
EXTERN WORD cConn;
EXTERN WORD cyText;
EXTERN WORD cxText;
EXTERN RECT rect;
EXTERN HSZ hszName;
EXTERN HSZ hszSystem;
EXTERN HSZ hszTime;
EXTERN HSZ hszTopics;
EXTERN HSZ hszSysItems;
EXTERN HSZ hszStatus;
EXTERN HSZ hszFormats;
EXTERN HSZ hszHelp;
EXTERN HSZ hszTopicItemList;
EXTERN HSZ ahszTopics[CTOPICS];
EXTERN HSZ ahszItems[CITEMS];
EXTERN double dItems[CITEMS];
EXTERN int cbItems;
EXTERN STOCKS Stocks[CITEMS];

int PASCAL WinMain (HINSTANCE, HINSTANCE, LPSTR, int);
BOOL InitApplication(HINSTANCE);
BOOL InitInstance(HINSTANCE, int);
BOOL PASCAL CreateDlgBox(HWND, LPCSTR, FARPROC);
LRESULT CALLBACK MainWndProc(HWND, WORD, WPARAM, LPARAM);
LRESULT CALLBACK AboutDlgProc(HWND, WORD, WPARAM, LPARAM);
HDDEDATA EXPENTRY DdeCallBack(WORD, WORD, HCONV, HSZ, HSZ,
                             HDDEDATA, DWORD, DWORD);
```

Listing 3.14. The dialogs.h header file.

```
#define IDD_ABOUT 100
```

Listing 3.15. The resource.h header file.

```
#define IDM_DDEQUOTEMENU    10
#define IDM_ABOUT           11

#define IDS_CLASSNAME       1
#define IDS_WINDOWTITLE     2
#define IDS_INITSUCCESS     3
#define IDS_INITFAIL        4
#define IDS_NOTPMODE        5
#define IDS_NOTIMER         6
#define IDS_SERVICENAME     7
#define IDS_TOPICSTART      8
#define IDS_TOPICSEND       9
#define IDS_TIMEITEM        10
#define IDS_TOPICS          11
#define IDS_SYSITEMS        12
#define IDS_STATUS          13
#define IDS_FORMATS         14
```

Listing 3.16. The quote.c source file.

```
#include "quote.h"
#include <stdlib.h>
#include <time.h>

BOOL PASCAL InitializeDDEML(HWND);
BOOL PASCAL CleanUpDDEML(HWND);
VOID PASCAL MsgBox(HWND, WORD, WORD);
VOID PASCAL DrawLine(HDC, RECT* , RECT*, PSTR);
/*******************************************************************/
/* Function: MainWndProc                                         */
/* Purpose: Processes messages for main window.                  */
/*******************************************************************/
```

continues

Listing 3.16. continued

```c
LRESULT CALLBACK MainWndProc(HWND hWnd, WORD message,
            WPARAM wParam, LPARAM lParam)
    {
    int i;
    DWORD dwWinFlags;
    PAINTSTRUCT ps;
    RECT rc;
    char ach[80];

    switch(message)
        {
        case WM_CREATE:
            hwnd = hWnd;
            dwWinFlags = GetWinFlags();
            if(dwWinFlags & WF_PMODE)
                {
                if(!InitializeDDEML(hWnd))
                    {
                    MsgBox(hWnd, IDS_INITFAIL, MB_OK | MB_ICONSTOP);
                    return -1;
                    }
                }
            else
                {
                MsgBox(hWnd, IDS_NOTPMODE, MB_OK | MB_ICONSTOP);
                return -1;
                }
            return FALSE;

        case PM_UPDATETIMER:
            KillTimer(hWnd,1);
            if(SetTimer(hWnd, 1, wParam, NULL) == NULL)
                MsgBox(hWnd, IDS_NOTIMER, MB_OK | MB_ICONINFORMATION);
            return FALSE;

        case WM_COMMAND:
            switch((WORD)wParam)
                {
                /* User selected About ... from menu */
                case IDM_ABOUT:
```

```
                    CreateDlgBox(hWnd, (LPCSTR)MAKEINTRESOURCE
                                (IDD_ABOUT),
                                (FARPROC)AboutDlgProc);
                break;
            }
        break;
    case WM_TIMER:
        for(i = 0; i <= cbItems; i++)
            {
            if(Stocks[i].bAdvise)
                {
                DdePostAdvise(idInst,
                            ahszTopics[1],
                            Stocks[i].hszStock);
                }
            }
        break;
    case WM_PAINT:
        BeginPaint(hwnd, &ps);
        SetBkMode(ps.hdc, TRANSPARENT);
        GetClientRect(hwnd, &rc);
        rc.bottom = rc.top + cyText;

        wsprintf(ach, "# of connections:%d", cConn);
        rect = rc;
        DrawLine(ps.hdc, &ps.rcPaint, &rc, ach);
        EndPaint(hwnd, &ps);
        break;
    case WM_DESTROY:
        /* Application is ending--post a WM_QUIT message */
        CleanUpDDEML(hWnd);
        PostQuitMessage(0);
        break;
    default:
        return DefWindowProc(hWnd, message, wParam, lParam);
    }
return FALSE;
}
```

continues

Listing 3.16. continued

```c
/***********************************************************************/
/* Function: InitializeDDEML                                           */
/* Purpose: Register application and callback func with DDEML.         */
/* Returns: TRUE/FALSE                                                 */
/***********************************************************************/
BOOL PASCAL InitializeDDEML(HWND hWnd)
    {
    BOOL bResult;
    char ach[20];

    lpDdeProc = MakeProcInstance((FARPROC)DdeCallBack, hInst);
    idInst = 0L;
    bResult = FALSE;
    if(lpDdeProc)
        {
        if(DMLERR_NO_ERROR == DdeInitialize((LPDWORD) &idInst,
                                            (PFNCALLBACK) lpDdeProc,
                                            APPCMD_FILTERINITS,
                                            0L))
            {
            LoadString(hInst, IDS_SERVICENAME,
                       &ach[0], sizeof(ach));
            hszName = DdeCreateStringHandle(idInst, &ach[0], 0);

            LoadString(hInst, IDS_TOPICSTART,
                       &ach[0], sizeof(ach));
            ahszTopics[0] = DdeCreateStringHandle(idInst,
                                                  &ach[0], 0);

            LoadString(hInst, IDS_TOPICSEND,
                       &ach[0], sizeof(ach));
            ahszTopics[1] = DdeCreateStringHandle(idInst,
                                                  &ach[0], 0);

            DdeNameService(idInst, hszName, NULL, DNS_REGISTER);

            LoadString(hInst, IDS_TIMEITEM,
                       &ach[0], sizeof(ach));

            hszTime = DdeCreateStringHandle(idInst,&ach[0],0);
```

```
                hszSystem = DdeCreateStringHandle(idInst,
                            SZDDESYS_TOPIC,0);
                hszTopics = DdeCreateStringHandle(idInst,
                            SZDDESYS_ITEM_TOPICS,0);
                hszSysItems = DdeCreateStringHandle(idInst,
                            SZDDESYS_ITEM_SYSITEMS,0);
                hszStatus = DdeCreateStringHandle(idInst,
                            SZDDESYS_ITEM_STATUS,0);
                hszFormats = DdeCreateStringHandle(idInst,
                            SZDDESYS_ITEM_FORMATS,0);
                hszHelp = DdeCreateStringHandle(idInst,
                            SZDDESYS_ITEM_HELP,0);
                hszTopicItemList = DdeCreateStringHandle(idInst,
                            SZDDE_ITEM_ITEMLIST, 0);

                if(SetTimer(hWnd, 1, 15000, NULL) == NULL)
                    MsgBox(hWnd, IDS_NOTIMER, MB_OK ¦ MB_ICONINFORMATION);

                srand((unsigned)time(NULL));
                bResult = TRUE;
                }
            else
                FreeProcInstance((FARPROC)lpDdeProc);
            }
        return bResult;
        }

/**********************************************************************/
/* Function: CleanUpDDEML                                             */
/* Purpose: Uninitialize application and free resources of callback.  */
/* Returns: TRUE                                                      */
/**********************************************************************/
BOOL PASCAL CleanUpDDEML(HWND hWnd)
    {
    DdeNameService(idInst, hszName, NULL, DNS_UNREGISTER);
    if(lpDdeProc)
        {
        DdeUninitialize(idInst);
        FreeProcInstance((FARPROC)lpDdeProc);
        }
    return TRUE;
    }
```

continues

Listing 3.16. continued

```c
/**********************************************************************/
/* Function: MsgBox                                                   */
/* Purpose: Creates a message box.                                    */
/**********************************************************************/
VOID PASCAL MsgBox(HWND hWnd, WORD wMsg, WORD wType)
    {
    char szWindowTitle[SZWINDOWTITLE];
    char szMessage[SZMESSAGE];

    LoadString(hInst, IDS_WINDOWTITLE,
                &szWindowTitle[0], sizeof szWindowTitle);
    LoadString(hInst, wMsg,
                &szMessage[0], sizeof szMessage);
    MessageBox(hWnd, szMessage, szWindowTitle, wType);
    }


/**********************************************************************/
/* Function: DrawLine                                                 */
/* Purpose: Draws text line.                                          */
/**********************************************************************/
VOID PASCAL DrawLine(HDC hdc, RECT *prcClip, RECT *prcText, PSTR psz)
    {
    RECT rc;

    if(IntersectRect(&rc, prcText, prcClip))
        {
        DrawText(hdc, psz, -1, prcText,
                DT_LEFT | DT_EXTERNALLEADING | DT_SINGLELINE |
                DT_EXPANDTABS | DT_NOCLIP | DT_NOPREFIX);
        }
    OffsetRect(prcText, 0, cyText);
    }
```

Listing 3.17. The dde.c source file.

```c
#include "quote.h"
#include <stdio.h>
#include <stdlib.h>
#include <string.h>
```

```
#include <math.h>

#define START TRUE
#define STOP  FALSE

char achHelp[] = "Quote Help:\r\n\n"\
    "Topics Supported: System Quote.\r\n\n"\
    "Items supported under the 'Quote' topic:\r\n"\
    "\tTime:\tMarket update item interval - can be poked.\r\n"\
    "\tstock names:\twhere stocks names are added using\r\n"\
    "\t\tan EXECUTE for a command format of:\r\n"\
    "\t\t[trackstock](stockname)\r\n";

BOOL PASCAL GetDataHandleData(HDDEDATA);
HDDEDATA PASCAL GetStockPrice(HSZ);
HDDEDATA PASCAL SupportedTopics(HSZ);
HDDEDATA PASCAL SupportedSysItems(HSZ);
HDDEDATA PASCAL CurrentStatus(HSZ);
HDDEDATA PASCAL SupportedFormats(HSZ);
HDDEDATA PASCAL HelpText(HSZ);
HDDEDATA PASCAL CurrentTopicItemList(HSZ);
HDDEDATA PASCAL SetMarketTime(HSZ, HDDEDATA);
HDDEDATA PASCAL ProcessAdvise(HSZ, BOOL);
/**********************************************************************/
/*   Function: DdeCallBack                                         */
/*   Purpose: This function handles callbacks from the DDEML.      */
/*   Parameters:                                                    */
/*              WORD wType      - transaction type                 */
/*              WORD wFmt       - clipboard data format            */
/*              HCONV hConv     - handle of the conversation       */
/*              HSZ hsz1        - handle of a string               */
/*              HSZ hsz2        - handle of a string               */
/*              HDDEDATA hData  - handle of a global memory object */
/*              DWORD dwData1   - transaction-specific data        */
/*              DWORD dwData2   - transaction-specific data        */
/*   Returns: Results vary depending on transaction type.          */
/**********************************************************************/
HDDEDATA EXPENTRY DdeCallBack(WORD wType, WORD wFmt, HCONV hConv,
                             HSZ hsz1,  HSZ hsz2, HDDEDATA hData,
                             DWORD lData1, DWORD lData2)
```

continues

Listing 3.17. continued

```
{
int i, j;
HSZPAIR hszPair[CTOPICS+1];

switch(wType)
    {
    case XTYP_CONNECT_CONFIRM:
        cConn++;
        InvalidateRect(hwnd, &rect, TRUE);
        return (HDDEDATA)FALSE;
        break;

    case XTYP_DISCONNECT:
        cConn--;
        InvalidateRect(hwnd, &rect, TRUE);
        return (HDDEDATA)FALSE;
        break;

    case XTYP_CONNECT:
        if(hszName == hsz2)
            for(i = 0; i <= CTOPICS; i++)
                if(hsz1 == ahszTopics[i])
                    return (HDDEDATA)TRUE;
        break;

    case XTYP_WILDCONNECT:
        if(hsz2 != hszName && hsz2 != NULL)
            return (HDDEDATA)FALSE;

        j = 0;
        for(i = 0; i < CTOPICS; i++)
            {
            if(hsz1 == NULL || hsz1 == ahszTopics[i])
                {
                hszPair[j].hszSvc = hszName;
                hszPair[j].hszTopic = ahszTopics[i];
                j++;
                }
            }
        hszPair[j].hszSvc = (HSZ)NULL;
        hszPair[j].hszTopic = (HSZ)NULL;
```

```
                return (HDDEDATA)DdeCreateDataHandle(idInst,
                        (LPBYTE)hszPair,sizeof(hszPair),0L,0,CF_TEXT,0);
            break;

        case XTYP_EXECUTE:
            if(hsz1 != ahszTopics[1])
                return (HDDEDATA)DDE_FNOTPROCESSED;
            if(GetDataHandleData(hData))
                return (HDDEDATA)DDE_FACK;
            else
                return (HDDEDATA)DDE_FNOTPROCESSED;
            break;
        }

    /* This server supports only one format--CF_TEXT */
    if(wFmt != CF_TEXT)
        return (HDDEDATA)DDE_FNOTPROCESSED;

    if(wType == XTYP_REQUEST)
        {
        if(!DdeCmpStringHandles(hsz1, hszSystem))
            {
            if(!DdeCmpStringHandles(hsz2,hszTopics))
                return SupportedTopics(hsz2);
            else if(!DdeCmpStringHandles(hsz2,hszSysItems))
                return SupportedSysItems(hsz2);
            else if(!DdeCmpStringHandles(hsz2,hszStatus))
                return CurrentStatus(hsz2);
            else if(!DdeCmpStringHandles(hsz2,hszFormats))
                return SupportedFormats(hsz2);
            else if(!DdeCmpStringHandles(hsz2,hszHelp))
                return HelpText(hsz2);
            else if(!DdeCmpStringHandles(hsz2,hszTopicItemList))
                return CurrentTopicItemList(hsz2);
            }
        else
            return GetStockPrice(hsz2);
        }


    /* The following transactions must be on the Stocks Topic */
```

continues

Listing 3.17. continued

```
        if(hsz1 != ahszTopics[1])
            return (HDDEDATA)DDE_FNOTPROCESSED;

        /* Format sensitive transactions */
        switch(wType)
            {
            case XTYP_ADVREQ:
                return GetStockPrice(hsz2);
                break;

            case XTYP_ADVSTART:
                return ProcessAdvise(hsz2, START);
                break;

            case XTYP_ADVSTOP:
                return ProcessAdvise(hsz2, STOP);
                break;

            case XTYP_POKE:
                return SetMarketTime(hsz2, hData);
                break;
            }
        return (HDDEDATA)NULL;
        }

/***********************************************************************/
/*  Function: GetDataHandleData                                        */
/*  Purpose: This function gets a data handle's value                  */
/*           and concatenates the string value to achBuf.              */
/***********************************************************************/
BOOL PASCAL GetDataHandleData(HDDEDATA hData)
    {
    char achItem[20];
    char achCommand[64];
    BOOL retval;
    int i;

    retval = TRUE;
    DdeGetData(hData,(LPBYTE)achCommand,64,0L);
    if(!strncmp(achCommand,"[trackstock]",12))
```

```
    {
    lstrcpy(achItem,achCommand[13]);
    achItem[lstrlen(achItem)-1] = '\0';
    cbItems++;
    Stocks[cbItems].hszStock = DdeCreateStringHandle(idInst,
                                   achItem,CP_WINANSI);
    Stocks[cbItems].bAdvise = FALSE;

    Stocks[cbItems].dPrice = getrandom(10,160);
    i = 0;
    while(i == 0)
        {
        i = getrandom(1,8);
        if(i == 4)
            i = 0;
        }
    switch(i)
        {
        case 1:
            Stocks[cbItems].dPrice += .125;
            break;
        case 2:
            Stocks[cbItems].dPrice += .25;
            break;
        case 3:
            Stocks[cbItems].dPrice += .375;
            break;
        case 5:
            Stocks[cbItems].dPrice += .5;
            break;
        case 6:
            Stocks[cbItems].dPrice += .625;
            break;
        case 7:
            Stocks[cbItems].dPrice += .75;
            break;
        case 8:
            Stocks[cbItems].dPrice += .875;
            break;
        }
    }
```

continues

161

Listing 3.17. continued

```
    else
        retval = FALSE;
    return retval;
    }


/***********************************************************************/
/*   Function: GetStockPrice                                           */
/*   Purpose: This function gets text representation of a              */
/*            stock price for a string handle.                         */
/***********************************************************************/
HDDEDATA PASCAL GetStockPrice(HSZ hsz2)
    {
    int i;
    BOOL bItemFound;
    char achItem[10];
    char achFraction[6];
    double dtmp, dint;

    bItemFound = FALSE;
    for(i = 0; i <= cbItems; i++)
        {
        if(hsz2 == Stocks[i].hszStock)
            {
            bItemFound = TRUE;
            break;
            }
        }
    if(bItemFound)
        {
        dtmp = getrandom(12,160);
        if(dtmp > Stocks[i].dPrice)
            Stocks[i].dPrice += .125;
        else
            if(dtmp < Stocks[i].dPrice)
                Stocks[i].dPrice -= .125;

        dtmp = modf(Stocks[i].dPrice, &dint);
        if(dtmp == .000)
            lstrcpy(achFraction, "      ");
```

```
        else if(dtmp == .125)
            lstrcpy(achFraction, " 1/8 ");
        else if(dtmp == .250)
            lstrcpy(achFraction, " 1/4 ");
        else if(dtmp == .375)
            lstrcpy(achFraction, " 3/8 ");
        else if(dtmp == .500)
            lstrcpy(achFraction, " 1/2 ");
        else if(dtmp == .625)
            lstrcpy(achFraction, " 5/8 ");
        else if(dtmp == .750)
            lstrcpy(achFraction, " 3/4 ");
        else if(dtmp == .875)
            lstrcpy(achFraction, " 7/8 ");

        sprintf(achItem,"%.0lf%s", dint, achFraction);
        return DdeCreateDataHandle(idInst,
                (LPBYTE)achItem,lstrlen(achItem)+1,
                    0L,hsz2,CF_TEXT,0);
        }
    else
        return (HDDEDATA)NULL;
    }

/*********************************************************************/
/*  Function: SetMarketTime                                        */
/*  Purpose: This function sends a private message to the main     */
/*           window to set the market time.                        */
/*********************************************************************/
HDDEDATA PASCAL SetMarketTime(HSZ hsz2, HDDEDATA hData)
    {
    char achUpdate[20];
    WORD wMarketUpdate;

    if(hsz2 == hszTime)
        {
        DdeGetData(hData, (LPBYTE)achUpdate, 20, 0L);
        wMarketUpdate = atoi(achUpdate);
        PostMessage(hwnd, PM_UPDATETIMER, wMarketUpdate, 0L);
        return (HDDEDATA)DDE_FACK;
        }
```

continues

163

Listing 3.17. continued

```
    else
        return (HDDEDATA)DDE_FNOTPROCESSED;
    }

/***********************************************************************/
/*  Function: ProcessAdvise                                         */
/*  Purpose: This function sets the advise indicator for a stock.   */
/***********************************************************************/
HDDEDATA PASCAL ProcessAdvise(HSZ hsz2, BOOL bAdvise)
    {
    BOOL bItemFound;
    int i;

    bItemFound = FALSE;
    for(i = 0; i <= cbItems; i++)
        {
        if(hsz2 == Stocks[i].hszStock)
            {
            bItemFound = TRUE;
            break;
            }
        }
    if(bItemFound)
        {
        Stocks[i].bAdvise = bAdvise;
        return (HDDEDATA)TRUE;
        }
    return (HDDEDATA)FALSE;
    }

HDDEDATA PASCAL SupportedTopics(HSZ hsz2)
    {
    char achTopics[80];

    LoadString(hInst, IDS_TOPICS,
                achTopics, sizeof(achTopics));
    return DdeCreateDataHandle(idInst,(LPBYTE)achTopics,
                lstrlen(achTopics)+1, 0L, hsz2, CF_TEXT, 0);
    }
```

```
HDDEDATA PASCAL SupportedSysItems(HSZ hsz2)
    {
    char achSysItems[80];

    LoadString(hInst, IDS_SYSITEMS,
               achSysItems, sizeof(achSysItems));
    return DdeCreateDataHandle(idInst, (LPBYTE)achSysItems,
               lstrlen(achSysItems)+1, 0L, hsz2, CF_TEXT, 0);
    }

HDDEDATA PASCAL CurrentStatus(HSZ hsz2)
    {
    char achStatus[10];

    LoadString(hInst, IDS_STATUS,
               achStatus, sizeof(achStatus));
    return DdeCreateDataHandle(idInst, (LPBYTE)achStatus,
               lstrlen(achStatus)+1, 0L, hsz2, CF_TEXT, 0);
    }

HDDEDATA PASCAL SupportedFormats(HSZ hsz2)
    {
    char achFormats[80];

    LoadString(hInst, IDS_FORMATS,
               achFormats, sizeof(achFormats));
    return DdeCreateDataHandle(idInst, (LPBYTE)achFormats[0],
               lstrlen(achFormats)+1, 0L,hsz2,CF_TEXT,0);
    }

HDDEDATA PASCAL HelpText(HSZ hsz2)
    {
    return DdeCreateDataHandle(idInst, (LPBYTE)achHelp,
               lstrlen(achHelp)+1, 0L, hsz2, CF_TEXT, 0);
    }

HDDEDATA PASCAL CurrentTopicItemList(HSZ hsz2)
    {
    int i, cb;
    char achT[20];
    char ach[1000];
```

continues

Listing 3.17. continued

```
        /* This item is always supported under Stocks */

        LoadString(hInst, IDS_TIMEITEM,
                   ach, sizeof(ach));

        /* These items vary */
        for(i = 0; i <= cbItems; i++)
            {
            cb = (WORD)DdeQueryString(idInst,
                        Stocks[i].hszStock, NULL, 0, 0);
            DdeQueryString(idInst, Stocks[i].hszStock,
                           achT,  cb+1, 0);
            lstrcat(ach,"\t");
            lstrcat(ach,achT);
            }
        return DdeCreateDataHandle(idInst, (LPBYTE)ach,
                   lstrlen(ach)+1, 0L, hsz2, CF_TEXT, 0);
    }
```

Listing 3.18. The dialogs.c source file.

```
#include "quote.h"

/**********************************************************************/
/* Function: CreateDlgBox                                             */
/* Purpose: Generic function to create dialog boxes.                  */
/* Returns: TRUE/FALSE                                                */
/**********************************************************************/
BOOL PASCAL CreateDlgBox(HWND hWnd, LPCSTR lpTemplateName,
                         FARPROC lpDlgProc)

    {
    BOOL    bResult;

    lpDlgProc = MakeProcInstance(lpDlgProc, hInst);
    if(lpDlgProc)
        {
        DialogBox(hInst, lpTemplateName, hWnd, (DLGPROC)lpDlgProc);
        FreeProcInstance(lpDlgProc);
        bResult = TRUE;
```

```
        }
    else
        bResult = FALSE;

    return bResult;
    }

/***********************************************************************/
/* Function: AboutDlgProc                                           */
/* Purpose: Handles messages for the About dialog box.              */
/* Returns: TRUE/FALSE                                              */
/***********************************************************************/
LRESULT CALLBACK AboutDlgProc(HWND hDlg, WORD message,
                              WPARAM wParam, LPARAM lParam)
    {
    switch(message)
        {
        case WM_INITDIALOG:
            return (LRESULT)TRUE;
        case WM_COMMAND:
            switch((WORD)wParam)
                {
                case IDOK:
                case IDCANCEL:
                    EndDialog(hDlg, TRUE);
                    return (LRESULT)TRUE;
                }
            break;
        }
    return (LRESULT)FALSE;
    }
```

Listing 3.19. The winmain.c source file.

```
#define MAIN
#include "quote.h"

/***********************************************************************/
/* Function: WinMain                                                */
/* Purpose: Main function for windows app. Initializes all          */
```

continues

Listing 3.19. continued

```
/*         instances of app, translates and dispatches messages.  */
/* Returns: Value of PostQuitMessage                              */
/*****************************************************************/
int PASCAL WinMain(HINSTANCE hInstance, HINSTANCE hPrevInstance,
                LPSTR lpszCmdLine, int nCmdShow)

    {
    MSG msg;

    /* If there isn't a previous instance of app, then initialize  */
    /* the first instance of app.                                  */
    if(!hPrevInstance)
        if(!InitApplication(hInstance))
            return FALSE;

    /* Perform initialization for all instances of application     */
    if(!InitInstance(hInstance, nCmdShow))
        return FALSE;

    /* Get messages for this application until WM_QUIT is received */
    while(GetMessage(&msg, 0, 0, 0))
        {
        TranslateMessage(&msg);
        DispatchMessage(&msg);
        }
    return (int)msg.wParam;
}
```

Listing 3.20. The init.c source file.

```
#include "quote.h"

/*****************************************************************/
/* Function: InitApplication                                     */
/* Purpose: Performs all initialization for first instance of app. */
/* Returns: TRUE if successful, FALSE if failure                 */
/*****************************************************************/
BOOL InitApplication(HINSTANCE hInstance)
    {
    BOOL bResult;
```

```
        char szClassName[SZCLASSNAME];
        WNDCLASS wc;

        /* Load the window class name from resource string table */

        if(!LoadString(hInstance, IDS_CLASSNAME,
           szClassName, sizeof szClassName))
           return FALSE;

        /* Class styles */
        wc.style         = 0;
        /* Name of message loop function for windows of this class */
        wc.lpfnWndProc   = MainWndProc;
        /* Not using Class Extra data */
        wc.cbClsExtra    = 0;
        /* Not using Window Extra data */
        wc.cbWndExtra    = 0;
        /* Instance that owns this class */
        wc.hInstance     = hInstance;
        /* Use default application icon */
        wc.hIcon         = LoadIcon(NULL, IDI_APPLICATION);
        /* Use arrow cursor */
        wc.hCursor       = LoadCursor(NULL, IDC_ARROW);
        /* Use system background color */
        wc.hbrBackground = GetStockObject(WHITE_BRUSH);
        /* Resource name for menu */
        wc.lpszMenuName  = MAKEINTRESOURCE(IDM_DDEQUOTEMENU);
        /* Name given to this class */
        wc.lpszClassName = szClassName;

        /* Register the window class */
        bResult = RegisterClass(&wc);

        /* return result based on registration */
        return bResult;
        }

/**********************************************************************/
/* Function: InitInstance                                           */
/* Purpose: Performs all initialization for all instances of app.   */
```

continues

Listing 3.20. continued

```
/* Returns: TRUE if successful, FALSE if failure                    */
/*******************************************************************/
BOOL InitInstance (HINSTANCE hInstance, int nCmdShow)
    {
    RECT Rect;
    TEXTMETRIC tm;
    HDC hdc;

    char szClassName[SZCLASSNAME];
    char szWindowTitle[SZWINDOWTITLE];

    hInst = hInstance;

    /* Load the window class name from resource string table */
    if(!LoadString(hInst, IDS_CLASSNAME,
        szClassName, sizeof szClassName))
        return FALSE;

    /* Load the window title from resource string table */
    if(!LoadString(hInst, IDS_WINDOWTITLE,
        szWindowTitle, sizeof szWindowTitle))
        return FALSE;

    hwnd = CreateWindow(szClassName,      /* Window class to create */
                        szWindowTitle,    /* Text for title bar     */
                        WS_OVERLAPPEDWINDOW,
                        CW_USEDEFAULT,    /* Default x  position     */
                        CW_USEDEFAULT,    /* Default y  position     */
                        CW_USEDEFAULT,    /* Default cx position     */
                        CW_USEDEFAULT,    /* Default cy position     */
                        0,                /* Parent window           */
                        0,                /* Menu                    */
                        hInstance,        /* Owning instance         */
                        NULL);            /* User-defined params     */

    /* If CreateWindow wasn't successful--return FALSE */
    if(!hwnd)
        return FALSE;
```

```
GetClientRect(hwnd, (LPRECT) &Rect);

hdc = GetDC(hwnd);
GetTextMetrics(hdc, &tm);
cyText = tm.tmHeight + tm.tmExternalLeading;
cxText = tm.tmAveCharWidth;
ReleaseDC(hwnd, hdc);

cbItems = -1;
/* Show and paint window */
ShowWindow(hwnd, nCmdShow);
UpdateWindow(hwnd);

return TRUE;
}
```

Listing 3.21. The quote.rc resource file.

```
#include <windows.h>
#include "resource.h"
#include "dialogs.h"


IDM_DDEQUOTEMENU MENU
    BEGIN
        POPUP "&Help"
        BEGIN
            MENUITEM "&About Quote ...",IDM_ABOUT
        END
    END


STRINGTABLE
    BEGIN
        IDS_CLASSNAME    "DDEQuoteClass"
        IDS_WINDOWTITLE  "Quote"
        IDS_INITSUCCESS  "DDEML Initialization Successful."
        IDS_INITFAIL     "DDEML Initialization Failed."
        IDS_NOTPMODE     "Windows must run in protected\n  mode to
          run this program."
```

continues

171

Listing 3.21. continued

```
        IDS_NOTIMER      "Cannot create timer."
        IDS_SERVICENAME  "Quote"
        IDS_TOPICSTART   "System"
        IDS_TOPICSEND    "Stocks"
        IDS_TIMEITEM     "Time"
        IDS_TOPICS       "System\tStocks"
      ↳ IDS_SYSITEMS     "SysItems\tTopics\tStatus\tFormats\tHelp\
          tTopicItemList"
        IDS_STATUS       "Ready"
        IDS_FORMATS      "TEXT"
    END


#include "quote.dlg"
```

Listing 3.22. The quote.dlg dialog definition file.

```
DLGINCLUDE RCDATA DISCARDABLE
BEGIN
    "DIALOGS.H\0"
END


IDD_ABOUT DIALOG 130, 57, 140, 81
STYLE DS_MODALFRAME ¦ WS_POPUP ¦ WS_VISIBLE ¦ WS_CAPTION ¦ WS_SYSMENU
CAPTION "About Quote"
FONT 8, "Helv"
BEGIN
    CTEXT           "Microsoft Windows", -1, 23, 8, 92, 8
    CTEXT           "Quote Application", -1, 15, 23, 111, 8
    LTEXT           "Copyright _ Jeffrey Clark 1991", -1, 20, 39,
                    105, 8
    PUSHBUTTON      "OK", IDOK, 49, 57, 40, 14
END
```

Listing 3.23. The quote.def module definition file.

```
NAME Quote

DESCRIPTION 'Quote, Copyright Jeffrey Clark, 1991'

EXETYPE WINDOWS

STUB 'WINSTUB.EXE'

CODE PRELOAD MOVEABLE DISCARDABLE
DATA PRELOAD MOVEABLE MULTIPLE

HEAPSIZE 1024
STACKSIZE 8192

SEGMENTS
    WINMAIN_TEXT    MOVEABLE                  PRELOAD
    QUOTE_TEXT      MOVEABLE                  PRELOAD
    INIT_TEXT       MOVEABLE DISCARDABLE PRELOAD
    DDE_TEXT        MOVEABLE DISCARDABLE LOADONCALL
    DIALOGS_TEXT    MOVEABLE DISCARDABLE LOADONCALL

EXPORTS
    MainWndProc @1
    AboutDlgProc @2
    DdeCallBack @3
```

Listing 3.24. The QUOTE make file.

```
CC = cl -c -AM -Gsw -Od -W3 -Zpi -Fo$@

all: quote.exe

quote.h: dialogs.h resource.h

quote.res: quote.rc quote.dlg dialogs.h resource.h
  rc -r quote
```

continues

173

Listing 3.24. continued

```
dialogs.obj: dialogs.c quote.h
  $(CC) $*.c

init.obj: init.c quote.h
  $(CC) $*.c

winmain.obj: winmain.c quote.h
  $(CC) $*.c

quote.obj: quote.c quote.h
  $(CC) $*.c

dde.obj: dde.c quote.h
  $(CC) $*.c

quote.exe::  dialogs.obj init.obj winmain.obj quote.obj dde.obj \
             quote.res quote.def
    link /CO /MAP /NOD @<<
dialogs+
init+
winmain+
quote+
dde
$@

libw mlibcew ddeml
quote.def
<<
    mapsym quote
    rc quote.res
```

Summary

This chapter covers much ground in DDEML transaction management. Transaction management can be very complex in larger applications, especially if multiple servers and clients are communicating with each other. Demands on system resources can significantly affect the processing of

DDEML applications. The example programs presented in this chapter do not suggest methods of how to handle transaction processing delays because this topic is best treated on an application-by-application basis. The tools in this chapter should provide the building blocks for more complex applications. When you develop DDEML applications, be sure to stress-test your applications. Use the stress-testing tools that come with the Windows 3.1 SDK. This can give you some indication of how your application will perform when system resources are scarce.

DDEML Monitor
Applications

This chapter explains how to create a DDEML *monitor application*. A monitor application is a debugging tool that enables you to see DDE activity. The SDK comes with a DDEML monitor application called *DDE Spy*. The example program for this chapter resembles DDE Spy in functionality; however, the example program provides a slightly different user interface. You should be able to easily adapt the example program to fit the way you debug. The example program in this chapter had to be rather generic because I couldn't assume that the reader has the same third-party interface libraries that I use for making custom programs.

Writing a DDEML monitor application is fairly straightforward. If you have looked at Microsoft's DDE Spy application, it may seem like smoke and magic. This is far from the truth. A DDEML monitor application has a DdeCallBack() function like all DDEML applications. In the DdeCallBack() function, the monitor application receives XTYP_MONITOR transactions. The monitor transactions provide the necessary information to display data to the user for debugging purposes.

Monitor Application Initialization

Like all DDEML applications, the DDEML requires monitor applications to register with the DDEML. The **DdeInitialize()** function performs the initialization. Unlike other DDEML applications, monitor applications do not need to connect to server or client applications. The DDEML uses the activity from client and server applications to generate the XTYP_MONITOR transactions it sends to the monitor application. The **DdeInitialize()** function provides the DDEML with all the information it needs to send XTYP_MONITOR transactions to a monitor application.

Monitor applications can specify several flags in the **DdeInitialize()** function to control the number and type of XTYP_MONITOR transactions it receives. These flags are combined with the application class flag, APPCLASS_MONITOR. Table 4.1 contains monitor application flags.

Table 4.1. Monitor application flags.

Flag	Description
MF_CALLBACKS	DDEML sends XTYP_MONITOR transactions whenever a DdeCallBack() function receives a transaction.
MF_CONV	DDEML sends XTYP_MONITOR transactions whenever a conversation is established or terminated.
MF_ERRORS	DDEML sends XTYP_MONITOR transactions whenever a DDEML-related error occurs.
MF_HSZ_INFO	DDEML sends XTYP_MONITOR transactions whenever a change to the global atom table occurs.
MF_LINKS	DDEML sends XTYP_MONITOR transactions whenever an advise loop is started or ended.
MF_POSTMSGS	DDEML sends XTYP_MONITOR transactions whenever a DDE application posts a transaction or WM_DDE_ message.
MF_SENDMSGS	DDEML sends XTYP_MONITOR transactions whenever a DDE application sends a transaction or WM_DDE_ message.

Here's an example of a **DdeInitialize()** function for a monitor application:

```
lpDdeProc = MakeProcInstance((FARPROC)DdeCallBack, hInst);
idInst = 0L;
if(DMLERR_NO_ERROR == DdeInitialize((LPDWORD) &idInst,
                                    (PFNCALLBACK) lpDdeProc,
                                    APPCLASS_MONITOR |
                                    MF_CALLBACKS   |
                                    MF_CONV        |
                                    MF_ERRORS      |
                                    MF_HSZ_INFO    |
                                    MF_LINKS       |
                                    MF_POSTMSGS    |
                                    MF_SENDMSGS,
                                    0L))

        return TRUE;
```

Using the preceding flags, an application can track different DDE events. The example program for this chapter uses all the monitor flags. The example program uses configuration dialogs to control the debug output. The configuration dialogs specify which XTYP_MONITOR transactions to ignore and which XTYP_MONITOR transactions to report. Each of the monitor flags has an associated structure that is passed with the XTYP_MONITOR message to the monitor application's DdeCallBack() function. The next section explores the monitor structures.

Monitor Application Structures

The keys to getting debug information are structures the DDEML provides for monitor applications. They directly relate to monitor flags. Monitor applications can access the structures through the dwData2 parameter in the DdeCallBack() function. The **DdeAccessData()** function retrieves a pointer to the structure. Table 4.2 contains monitor structures.

Table 4.2. Monitor structures.

Structure	Monitor Flag	Description
MONCBSTRUCT	MF_CALLBACKS	Information on transactions passed to DdeCallBack() functions.
MONCONVSTRUCT	MF_CONV	Information whenever a conversation is established or terminated.
MONERRSTRUCT	MF_ERRORS	Information on DDEML-related errors.
MONHSZSTRUCT	MF_HSZ_INFO	Information about changes to the global atom table.
MONLINKSTRUCT	MF_LINKS	Information about advise loops.
MONMSGSTRUCT	MF_POSTMSGS	Information about WM_DDE_MF_SENDMSGS messages and XTYP_transactions.

A closer look at the monitor structures reveals specific information about DDE events. The MONCBSTRUCT has the following typedef:

```
typedef struct {
    WORD    cb;
    WORD    wReserved;
    DWORD   dwTime;
    HANDLE  hTask;
    DWORD   dwRet;
    WORD    wType;
    WORD    wFmt;
    HCONV   hConv;
    HSZ     hsz1;
    HSZ     hsz2;
    HDDEDATA hData;
    DWORD   dwData1;
    DWORD   dwData2;
} MONCBSTRUCT;
```

All monitor structures include a size member and a time member. The size member, cb, specifies the size of the structure. The time member, dwTime, specifies the time the DDE event occurred in milliseconds since the user booted the system. The MONCBSTRUCT contains the transaction type wType, the clipboard format wFmt, the conversation handle hConv, string handles hsz1 and hsz2, and data, hData, dwData1, and dwData2 for a transaction. The return value from the DdeCallBack() function for the specified transaction is in the dwRet member. A handle to the application instance of the application that received the transaction is in the hTask member.

A monitor application can pass any of the members to DDEML functions to get additional information. For example, to get additional information about a conversation, a monitor application can call the **DdeQueryConvInfo()** function with the hConv member of MONCBSTRUCT. String handles can be converted to strings by using the **DdeQueryString()** function. Data is a little more tricky to display in a debug application because the size and format can be almost anything. You cannot expect a monitor application to render every clipboard format. Anyway, just knowing that an application receives data is enough for debugging purposes. Displaying the data may take too much time and provide little additional information.

The MONCONVSTRUCT has the following typedef:

```
typedef struct {
    WORD    cb;
    BOOL    fConnect;
    DWORD   dwTime;
```

```
    HANDLE  hTask;
    HSZ     hszSvc;
    HSZ     hszTopic;
    HCONV   hConvClient;
    HCONV   hConvServer;
} MONCONVSTRUCT;
```

The fConnect member indicates whether a conversation is currently established. The hTask member specifies the partner in the conversation. The hszSvc and hszTopic members are the service and topic names of a conversation. By using the **DdeQueryString()** function, a monitor application can get the string values for the service and topic names. The hConvClient and hConvServer members are handles to the client and server conversations.

The MONERRSTRUCT provides information on DDEML-related errors. The wLastError member specifies the last error. The application instance that the last error occurred in is specified in the hTask member of MONERRSTRUCT. The following is the typedef of MONERRSTRUCT:

```
typedef struct {
    WORD    cb;
    WORD    wLastError;
    DWORD   dwTime;
    HANDLE  hTask;
} MONERRSTRUCT;
```

The typedef of MONHSZSTRUCT is

```
typedef struct {
    WORD    cb;
    BOOL    fsAction;
    DWORD   dwTime;
    HSZ     hsz;
    HANDLE  hTask;
    WORD    wReserved;
    char    str[1];
} MONHSZSTRUCT;
```

The hsz member is a handle to the string to which the str member points. The hTask member identifies the application instance that is performing an action on the string. The fsAction member defines the action. The fsAction can have one of the following values:

```
    #define MH_CREATE         1

    #define MH_KEEP           2
```

CHAPTER
4

```
#define MH_DELETE        3

#define MH_CLEANUP       4
```

If fsAction is MH_CREATE, the application calls **DdeCreateStringHandle()**.
MH_KEEP corresponds to the **DdeKeepStringHandle()**, and MH_DELETE corresponds to **DdeFreeStringHandle()**. If fsAction is MH_CLEANUP, the application
calls **DdeUninitialize()**. Any string handles an application creates and does
not explicitly free are deleted when the application calls **DdeUninitialize()**.

The MONLINKSTRUCT provides information on the status of an advise loop.
Monitor applications receive this structure when DDE applications start and
stop advise loops. The following is the MONLINKSTRUCT structure:

```
typedef struct {
    WORD    cb;
    DWORD   dwTime;
    HANDLE  hTask;
    BOOL    fEstablished;
    BOOL    fNoData;
    HSZ     hszSvc;
    HSZ     hszTopic;
    HSZ     hszItem;
    WORD    wFmt;
    BOOL    fServer;
    HCONV   hConvServer;
    HCONV   hConvClient;
} MONLINKSTRUCT;
```

The fEstablished member indicates whether an advise loop is established.
The fNoData member specifies whether the advise loop is a warm link or a hot
link. The hszSvc, hszTopic, and hszItem members are the service, topic, and
item names for the advise loop. The wFmt member is the clipboard format. The
hConvServer and hConvClient members are the conversation handles for
the server and client applications. When the fServer is TRUE, it indicates that
the link notification came from the server. The hTask member specifies the
application instance that is the partner in the advise loop.

The last monitor structure contains information about messages. A monitor
application receives the MONMSGSTRUCT when it specifies MF_POSTMSG or
MF_SENDMSGS in the **DdeInitialize()** function. The hwndTo member shown in
the following structure is the handle to the window that receives the DDE
message. The hTask member specifies the application instance that sent or

posted the message. The wMsg, wParam, and lParam members specify the parameters in the **SendMessage()** or **PostMessage()** function. A complete list of WM_DDE_ messages is in Chapter 1.

```
typedef struct {
    WORD    cb;
    HWND    hwndTo;
    DWORD   dwTime;
    HANDLE  hTask;
    WORD    wMsg;
    WORD    wParam;
    DWORD   lParam;
} MONMSGSTRUCT;
```

DDEMON—Example Monitor Application

The example application for this chapter is a DDEML monitor application, DDEMON.EXE. It uses an edit control in the client area to display messages. You can save the contents of the edit control to a file or print the contents of the edit control. You can also display monitor information in DBWIN or on a debug terminal.

Three dialog boxes specify monitoring options. The Monitor dialog box has options that correspond to the MF_ flags. This does not change the **DdeInitialize()** function. Each MF_ flag has a check box. If you check the check box, the option is selected; otherwise, it is not selected. When the DdeCallBack() function receives XTYP_MONITOR transactions, it checks an array of options set by the Monitor dialog box.

The Message Filters dialog box maintains an array of indicators related to WM_DDE_ messages. If you select the Posted Messages or Sent Messages option in the Monitor dialog box, DDEMON provides information about messages. You can filter the types of messages DDEMON reports by selecting only the messages you want information about in the Message Filters dialog box. The Callback Filters dialog box is similar to the Message Filters dialog box, except that it filters XTYP_ transactions rather than messages. Figure 4.1 shows the DDEMON application.

Figure 4.1.
The DDEMON
application.

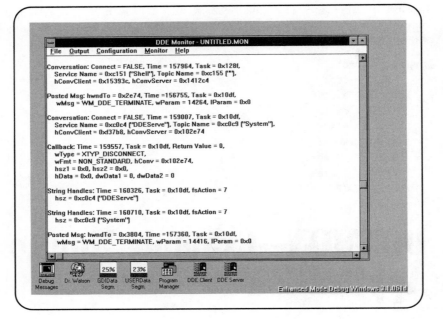

Listing 4.1. The ddemon.h header file.

```
#define NOCOMM              /* comm.drv functions not used */
#define DDEMLDB             /* Access DDEML monitor code */
#include <windows.h>
#include <ddeml.h>          /* Needed for ddeml code */
#include "resource.h"
#include "dialogs.h"

#ifndef MAIN
#define EXTERN extern
#else
#define EXTERN
#endif

/* Global Defines */
#define SZCLASSNAME 40
#define SZWINDOWTITLE 40
#define ID(x) GetWindowWord(x, GWW_ID)
#define MAXFILENAME 256
```

```
/* Global Variables */
EXTERN DWORD idInst;                        /* DDEML instance ident. */
EXTERN HINSTANCE hInst;                     /* Application instance  */
EXTERN HWND hwnd;                           /* Handle to main window */
EXTERN HWND hEditWnd;                       /* Handle to Edit control */
EXTERN HWND hAbortDlgWnd;                   /* Handle to abort dlg */

EXTERN BOOL bScreenChecked;                 /* Switch for screen output */
EXTERN BOOL bDebugChecked;                  /* Switch for debug terminal */
EXTERN BOOL bChanges;                       /* Switch for file change */
EXTERN BOOL bAbort;                         /* Switch to abort print */

EXTERN char szFileName[MAXFILENAME];  /* Current file name */
EXTERN char szFileTitle[MAXFILENAME]; /* Current file title */
EXTERN char szWindowTitle[SZWINDOWTITLE]; /* Window title */
EXTERN char szBaseWindowTitle[40];          /* Base window title */
EXTERN HCURSOR hHourGlass;            /* Handle to hourglass cursor */

EXTERN BOOL CallBackFilters[15];        /* Call back filter options */
EXTERN BOOL MessageFilters[9];          /* Message filter options */
EXTERN BOOL Monitor[7];                 /* Monitor options */

/* Global Functions */
int PASCAL WinMain(HINSTANCE, HINSTANCE, LPSTR, int);
BOOL InitApplication(HINSTANCE);
BOOL InitInstance(HINSTANCE, int);
BOOL PASCAL CreateDlgBox(HWND hWnd, LPCSTR lpTemplateName,
                         FARPROC lpDlgProc);
BOOL PASCAL NewFile(HWND);
BOOL PASCAL CommonOpenFile(HWND);
BOOL PASCAL CommonSaveFile(HWND);
BOOL PASCAL CommonSaveAs(HWND);
BOOL PASCAL QuerySaveFile(HWND);
BOOL PASCAL CommonPrint(HWND);
VOID PASCAL CommonPrintSetup(HWND);
LRESULT CALLBACK AbortDlgProc(HWND, WORD, WPARAM, LPARAM);
LRESULT CALLBACK AbortProc(HDC, int);
LRESULT CALLBACK MainWndProc(HWND, WORD, WPARAM, LPARAM);
LRESULT CALLBACK AboutDlgProc(HWND, WORD, WPARAM, LPARAM);
LRESULT CALLBACK MonitorDlgProc(HWND, WORD, WPARAM, LPARAM);
LRESULT CALLBACK CBFiltersDlgProc(HWND, WORD, WPARAM, LPARAM);
```

continues

Listing 4.1. continued

```
LRESULT CALLBACK MsgFiltersDlgProc(HWND, WORD, WPARAM, LPARAM);
HDDEDATA EXPENTRY DdeCallBack(WORD, WORD, HCONV, HSZ,
                             HSZ, HDDEDATA, DWORD, DWORD);
LRESULT CALLBACK MarkDlgProc(HWND, WORD, WPARAM, LPARAM);
```

Listing 4.2. The dialogs.h header file.

```
#define IDD_ABOUTBOX            100
#define IDD_MONITORBOX          200
#define IDD_CALLBACKS           201
#define IDD_CONVERSATIONS       202
#define IDD_ERRORS              203
#define IDD_LINKS               204
#define IDD_STRINGS             205
#define IDD_SENTMSGS            206
#define IDD_POSTEDMSG           207
#define IDD_ACK                 301
#define IDD_ADVISE              302
#define IDD_DATA                303
#define IDD_EXECUTE             304
#define IDD_INITIATE            305
#define IDD_POKE                306
#define IDD_REQUEST             307
#define IDD_TERMINATE           308
#define IDD_UNADVISE            309
#define IDD_MSGFILTERSBOX       300
#define IDD_CALLBACKBOX         400
#define IDD_XADVDATA            401
#define IDD_XADVREQ             402
#define IDD_XADVSTART           403
#define IDD_XADVSTOP            404
#define IDD_XCONNECT            405
#define IDD_XCONNECT_CONFIRM    406
#define IDD_XDISCONNECT         407
#define IDD_XERROR              408
#define IDD_XEXECUTE            409
#define IDD_XPOKE               410
#define IDD_XREGISTER           411
#define IDD_XREQUEST            412
```

```
#define IDD_XUNREGISTER          413
#define IDD_XWILDCONNECT         414
#define IDD_XXACT_COMPLETE       415
#define IDD_ABORTBOX             500
#define IDD_FILENAME             501
#define IDD_MARKBOX              600
#define IDD_MARK                 601
```

Listing 4.3. The resource.h header file.

```
#define IDM_DDEMONITORMENU       10
#define IDS_CLASSNAME            1
#define IDS_WINDOWTITLE          2

#define IDM_NEW                  100
#define IDM_OPEN                 101
#define IDM_SAVE                 102
#define IDM_SAVEAS               103
#define IDM_PRINT                104
#define IDM_PRINTSETUP           105
#define IDM_EXIT                 106

#define IDM_SCREEN               200
#define IDM_DEBUG                201
#define IDM_MARK                 202
#define IDM_CLEARSCREEN          203

#define IDM_MONITOR              300
#define IDM_MSGFILTERS           301
#define IDM_CALLBACKS            302

#define IDM_START                400

#define IDM_END                  500

#define IDM_ABOUT                600

#define IDC_EDIT                 700
```

Listing 4.4. The ddemon.c source file.

```c
#include "ddemon.h"

/* Variables global only to this module */
HMENU hMenu;
FARPROC lpDdeProc;

/* Function Prototypes for function only called from this module */
BOOL PASCAL InitializeDDEML(HWND);
BOOL PASCAL CleanUpDDEML(HWND);
VOID PASCAL SetInitialState(VOID);

/**********************************************************************/
/* Function: MainWndProc                                            */
/* Purpose: Processes messages for main window.                     */
/* Returns: Varies                                                  */
/**********************************************************************/
LRESULT CALLBACK MainWndProc(HWND hwnd, WORD message,
                             WPARAM wParam, LPARAM lParam)

    {
    switch(message)
        {
        case WM_CREATE:
            hMenu = GetMenu(hwnd);
            bScreenChecked = TRUE;
            EnableMenuItem(hMenu, IDM_END, MF_DISABLED | MF_GRAYED);
            CheckMenuItem(hMenu,IDM_SCREEN, MF_CHECKED);

            SetInitialState();

            bChanges = FALSE;

            return FALSE;

        case WM_COMMAND:
            switch((int)wParam)
                {
                case IDM_NEW:
                    if(!NewFile(hwnd))
                        return FALSE;
                    break;
```

```
case IDM_OPEN:
    if(!CommonOpenFile(hwnd))
        return FALSE;
    break;

case IDM_SAVE:
    if(CommonSaveFile(hwnd))
        break;

case IDM_SAVEAS:
    if(!CommonSaveAs(hwnd))
        return FALSE;
    break;

case IDM_PRINT:
    if(!CommonPrint(hwnd))
        return FALSE;
    break;

case IDM_PRINTSETUP:
    CommonPrintSetup(hwnd);
    break;

case IDM_EXIT:
    DestroyWindow(hEditWnd);
    PostQuitMessage(0);
    break;

case IDM_SCREEN:
    if(bScreenChecked)
        {
        bScreenChecked = FALSE;
        CheckMenuItem(hMenu,IDM_SCREEN,MF_UNCHECKED);
        }
    else
        {
        bScreenChecked = TRUE;
        CheckMenuItem(hMenu,IDM_SCREEN, MF_CHECKED);
        }
    break;

case IDM_DEBUG:
```

continues

Listing 4.4. continued

```
                            if(bDebugChecked)
                                {
                                bDebugChecked = FALSE;
                                CheckMenuItem(hMenu,IDM_DEBUG,MF_UNCHECKED);
                                }
                            else
                                {
                                bDebugChecked = TRUE;
                                CheckMenuItem(hMenu,IDM_DEBUG, MF_CHECKED);
                                }
                            break;

                    case IDM_MARK:
                        CreateDlgBox(hwnd,
                                    (LPCSTR)MAKEINTRESOURCE(IDD_MARKBOX),
                                    (FARPROC)MarkDlgProc);
                        break;

                    case IDM_CLEARSCREEN:
                        SendMessage(hEditWnd,EM_SETSEL,0,MAKELONG(0,-1));
                        SendMessage(hEditWnd,EM_REPLACESEL,0,(LONG)(LPSTR)"");
                        break;

                    case IDM_MONITOR:
                        CreateDlgBox(hwnd,
                                    (LPCSTR)MAKEINTRESOURCE(IDD_MONITORBOX),
                                    (FARPROC)MonitorDlgProc);
                        break;

                    case IDM_MSGFILTERS:
                        CreateDlgBox(hwnd,
                                    (LPCSTR)MAKEINTRESOURCE(IDD_MSGFILTERSBOX),
                                    (FARPROC)MsgFiltersDlgProc);
                        break;

                    case IDM_CALLBACKS:
                        CreateDlgBox(hwnd,
                                    (LPCSTR)MAKEINTRESOURCE(IDD_CALLBACKBOX),
                                    (FARPROC)CBFiltersDlgProc);
                        break;
```

```
case IDM_START:
    if(!InitializeDDEML(hwnd))
        MessageBox(hwnd, "DDEML Initialization Failed",
                    "Monitor",MB_OK);
    else
        {
        CheckMenuItem(hMenu, IDM_START,
                    MF_CHECKED);
        EnableMenuItem(hMenu, IDM_START,
                    MF_GRAYED);
        EnableMenuItem(hMenu, IDM_END,
                    MF_ENABLED);
        }
    return FALSE;
    break;

case IDM_END:
    if(CleanUpDDEML(hwnd))
        {
        CheckMenuItem(hMenu, IDM_START,
                    MF_UNCHECKED);
        EnableMenuItem(hMenu, IDM_END,
                    MF_GRAYED);
        EnableMenuItem(hMenu, IDM_START,
                    MF_ENABLED);
        }
    return FALSE;
    break;

case IDM_ABOUT:
    CreateDlgBox(hwnd,
            (LPCSTR)MAKEINTRESOURCE(IDD_ABOUTBOX),
            (FARPROC)AboutDlgProc);
    break;

case IDC_EDIT:
    if (HIWORD (lParam) == EN_ERRSPACE)
        MessageBox (GetFocus (), "Out of memory.",
                    "DDE Monitor Application",
                    MB_ICONHAND | MB_OK);
    break;
}
```

continues

Listing 4.4. continued

```
                break;

        case WM_SETFOCUS:
            SetFocus(hEditWnd);
            break;

        case WM_SIZE:
            MoveWindow(hEditWnd, 0, 0,
                        LOWORD(lParam), HIWORD(lParam), TRUE);
            break;

        case WM_CLOSE:
            DestroyWindow(hwnd);
            break;

        case WM_DESTROY:
            PostQuitMessage(0);
            break;

        default:
            return DefWindowProc(hwnd, message, wParam, lParam);
        }
    return FALSE;
    }


/**********************************************************************/
/* Function: InitializeDDEML                                        */
/* Purpose: This function initializes the DDEML and makes           */
/*          an instances DdeCallBack function.                      */
/**********************************************************************/
BOOL PASCAL InitializeDDEML(HWND hWnd)
    {
    lpDdeProc = MakeProcInstance((FARPROC)DdeCallBack, hInst);
    idInst = 0L;
    if(DMLERR_NO_ERROR == DdeInitialize((LPDWORD) &idInst,
                                    (PFNCALLBACK) lpDdeProc,
                                    APPCLASS_MONITOR |
                                    MF_CALLBACKS   |
                                    MF_CONV        |
                                    MF_ERRORS      |
```

```
                                        MF_HSZ_INFO        ¦
                                        MF_LINKS           ¦
                                        MF_POSTMSGS        ¦
                                        MF_SENDMSGS,
                                        0L))
        return TRUE;
    else
        return FALSE;
    }

/*********************************************************************/
/* Function: CleanUpDDEML                                         */
/* Purpose: This function uninitializes the DDEML for this app    */
/*          and frees the procedure instance for the DdeCallBack  */
/*          function.                                             */
/*********************************************************************/
BOOL PASCAL CleanUpDDEML(HWND hWnd)
    {
    DdeUninitialize(idInst);
    FreeProcInstance(lpDdeProc);
    return TRUE;
    }


/*********************************************************************/
/* Function: SetInitialState                                      */
/* Purpose: This sets the option arrays to an initial value of    */
/*          TRUE. This could be a place to retrieve the option    */
/*          values from an .ini file in the future.               */
/*********************************************************************/
VOID PASCAL SetInitialState()
    {
    int i;
    for(i = 0; i <= 6; i++)
        Monitor[i] = TRUE;

    for(i = 0; i <= 8 ; i++)
        MessageFilters[i] = TRUE;

    for(i = 0; i <= 14; i++)
        CallBackFilters[i] = TRUE;
    }
```

Listing 4.5. The dde.c source file.

```c
#include "ddemon.h"
#include <dde.h>                /* Needed for DDE messages */
#include <stdio.h>

#define SEND TRUE
#define POST FALSE
#define NEWLINE FALSE
#define DOUBLESPACE TRUE
char achBuf[80];

BOOL PASCAL MonitorCallBacks(LPVOID);
VOID PASCAL MonitorConversations(LPVOID);
VOID PASCAL MonitorErrors(LPVOID);
VOID PASCAL MonitorHszInfo(LPVOID);
VOID PASCAL MonitorLinks(LPVOID);
BOOL PASCAL MonitorMessages(LPVOID, BOOL);
VOID PASCAL GetClipBoardFormat(WORD);
VOID PASCAL GetStringHandleString(HSZ);
VOID PASCAL DisplayOutput(BOOL);
/**********************************************************************/
/* Function: DdeCallBack                                            */
/* Purpose: This is a DDE callback to monitor DDE applications.     */
/* Parameters:                                                      */
/*             WORD wType      - XTYP_MONITOR                        */
/*             WORD wFmt       - not used                           */
/*             HCONV hConv     - not used                           */
/*             HSZ hsz1        - not used                           */
/*             HSZ hsz2        - not used                           */
/*             HDDEDATA hData  - handle of a global memory object    */
/*             DWORD dwData1   - not used                           */
/*             DWORD dwData2   - DDE event                          */
/* Returns: Results vary depending on transaction type.            */
/**********************************************************************/
HDDEDATA EXPENTRY DdeCallBack(WORD wType, WORD wFmt, HCONV hConv,
                             HSZ hsz1, HSZ hsz2, HDDEDATA hData,
                             DWORD dwData1,DWORD dwData2)

    {
    LPVOID lpData;
    DWORD cb;
```

```
switch(wType)
    {
    case XTYP_MONITOR:
        if(lpData = DdeAccessData(hData, &cb))
            {
            switch(dwData2)
                {
                case MF_CALLBACKS:
                    if(Monitor[0])
                        MonitorCallBacks(lpData);
                    break;
                case MF_CONV:
                    if(Monitor[1])
                        MonitorConversations(lpData);
                    break;
                case MF_ERRORS:
                    if(Monitor[2])
                        MonitorErrors(lpData);
                    break;
                case MF_LINKS:
                    if(Monitor[3])
                        MonitorLinks(lpData);
                    break;
                case MF_HSZ_INFO:
                    if(Monitor[4])
                        MonitorHszInfo(lpData);
                    break;
                case MF_SENDMSGS:
                    if(Monitor[5])
                        MonitorMessages(lpData, SEND);
                    break;
                case MF_POSTMSGS:
                    if(Monitor[6])
                        MonitorMessages(lpData, POST);
                    break;
                }
            DdeUnaccessData(hData);
            }
        break;
    }
return ((HDDEDATA) 0);
}
```

continues

195

Listing 4.5. continued

```
/************************************************************************/
/* Function: MonitorCallBacks                                          */
/* Purpose: If callback transactions are being monitored, the          */
/*          DdeCallBack function sends the callback data here           */
/*          to be formatted and written.                               */
/************************************************************************/
BOOL PASCAL MonitorCallBacks(LPVOID lpData)
    {
    MONCBSTRUCT FAR * lpCB;
    char achTBuf[80];

    lpCB = lpData;

    switch(lpCB->wType)
        {
        case XTYP_ADVDATA:
            if(!CallBackFilters[0])
                return FALSE;
            lstrcpy(achTBuf, "XTYP_ADVDATA,");
            break;
        case XTYP_ADVREQ:
            if(!CallBackFilters[1])
                return FALSE;
            lstrcpy(achTBuf, "XTYP_ADVREQ,");
            break;
        case XTYP_ADVSTART:
            if(!CallBackFilters[2])
                return FALSE;
            lstrcpy(achTBuf, "XTYP_ADVSTART,");
            break;
        case XTYP_ADVSTOP:
            if(!CallBackFilters[3])
                return FALSE;
            lstrcpy(achTBuf, "XTYP_ADVSTOP,");
            break;
        case XTYP_CONNECT:
            if(!CallBackFilters[4])
                return FALSE;
```

```
            lstrcpy(achTBuf, "XTYP_CONNECT,");
            break;
        case XTYP_CONNECT_CONFIRM:
            if(!CallBackFilters[5])
                return FALSE;
            lstrcpy(achTBuf, "XTYP_CONNECT_CONFIRM,");
            break;
        case XTYP_DISCONNECT:
            if(!CallBackFilters[6])
                return FALSE;
            lstrcpy(achTBuf, "XTYP_DISCONNECT,");
            break;
        case XTYP_ERROR:
            if(!CallBackFilters[7])
                return FALSE;
            lstrcpy(achTBuf, "XTYP_ERROR,");
            break;
        case XTYP_EXECUTE:
            if(!CallBackFilters[8])
                return FALSE;
            lstrcpy(achTBuf, "XTYP_EXECUTE,");
            break;
        case XTYP_POKE:
            if(!CallBackFilters[9])
                return FALSE;
            lstrcpy(achTBuf, "XTYP_POKE,");
            break;
        case XTYP_REGISTER:
            if(!CallBackFilters[10])
                return FALSE;
            lstrcpy(achTBuf, "XTYP_REGISTER,");
            break;
        case XTYP_REQUEST:
            if(!CallBackFilters[11])
                return FALSE;
            lstrcpy(achTBuf, "XTYP_REQUEST,");
            break;
        case XTYP_UNREGISTER:
            if(!CallBackFilters[12])
                return FALSE;
            lstrcpy(achTBuf, "XTYP_UNREGISTER,");
            break;
```

continues

197

Listing 4.5. continued

```
            case XTYP_WILDCONNECT:
                if(!CallBackFilters[13])
                    return FALSE;
                lstrcpy(achTBuf, "XTYP_WILDCONNECT,");
                break;
            case XTYP_XACT_COMPLETE:
                if(!CallBackFilters[14])
                    return FALSE;
                lstrcpy(achTBuf, "XTYP_XACT_COMPLETE,");
                break;
            default:
                sprintf(achTBuf,"0x%x,",lpCB->wType);
                break;
            }
        sprintf(achBuf,
            "Callback: Time = %.0f, Task = 0x%x,
                Return Value = %.0f,\r\n",
            (double)lpCB->dwTime, (WORD)lpCB->hTask,
            (double)lpCB->dwRet);

    DisplayOutput(NEWLINE);

    sprintf(achBuf,"    wType = %s\r\n", achTBuf);

    DisplayOutput(NEWLINE);

    lstrcpy(achBuf,"    wFmt = ");

    GetClipBoardFormat(lpCB->wFmt);
    sprintf(achTBuf,", hConv = 0x%lx,\r\n",
            (DWORD)lpCB->hConv);
    lstrcat(achBuf,achTBuf);
    DisplayOutput(NEWLINE);

    if(!lpCB->hsz1 && !lpCB->hsz2)
        {
        sprintf(achBuf,"    hsz1 = 0x%lx, hsz2 = 0x%lx,\r\n",
                (DWORD)lpCB->hsz1, (DWORD)lpCB->hsz2);
        DisplayOutput(NEWLINE);
        }
```

```
    else
        {
        sprintf(achBuf,"     hsz1 = 0x%lx (\"", (DWORD)lpCB->hsz1);
        GetStringHandleString(lpCB->hsz1);
        lstrcat(achBuf,"\"),\r\n");
        DisplayOutput(NEWLINE);

        sprintf(achBuf,"     hsz2 = 0x%lx (\"", (DWORD)lpCB->hsz2);
        GetStringHandleString(lpCB->hsz2);
        lstrcat(achBuf,"\"),\r\n");
        DisplayOutput(NEWLINE);
        }

    sprintf(achBuf,
        "     hData = 0x%lx, dwData1 = %.0f, dwData2 = %.0f\r\n",
        (DWORD)lpCB->hData, (double)lpCB->dwData1,
        (double)lpCB->dwData2);

    DisplayOutput(DOUBLESPACE);
    return TRUE;
    }

/**********************************************************************/
/* Function: MonitorConversations                                   */
/* Purpose: If conversations are being monitored, the              */
/*          DdeCallBack function sends the conversation data here   */
/*          to be formatted and written.                            */
/**********************************************************************/
VOID PASCAL MonitorConversations(LPVOID lpData)
    {
    MONCONVSTRUCT FAR * lpCONV;
    char achTBuf[80];

    lpCONV = lpData;

    lstrcpy(achBuf,"Conversation: Connect = ");

    if(lpCONV->fConnect)
        lstrcat(achBuf,"TRUE, Time = ");
    else
        lstrcat(achBuf,"FALSE, Time = ");
```

continues

199

Listing 4.5. continued

```
        sprintf(achTBuf,"%.0f, Task = 0x%x,\r\n",
                (double)lpCONV->dwTime, (WORD)lpCONV->hTask);
        lstrcat(achBuf,achTBuf);

        DisplayOutput(NEWLINE);

        sprintf(achBuf,"    Service Name = 0x%lx (\"",
            (DWORD)lpCONV->hszSvc);

        GetStringHandleString(lpCONV->hszSvc);

        sprintf(achTBuf,"\"), Topic Name = 0x%lx (\"",
            (DWORD)lpCONV->hszTopic);
        lstrcat(achBuf,achTBuf);

        GetStringHandleString(lpCONV->hszTopic);

        lstrcat(achBuf,"\"),\r\n");

        DisplayOutput(NEWLINE);

        sprintf(achBuf,"    hConvClient = 0x%lx, hConvServer = 0x%lx\r\n",
                (DWORD)lpCONV->hConvClient,
                (DWORD)lpCONV->hConvServer);

        DisplayOutput(DOUBLESPACE);

    }

/**********************************************************************/
/* Function: MonitorErrors                                          */
/* Purpose: If DDEML errors are being monitored, the               */
/*          DdeCallBack function sends the error data here          */
/*          to be formatted and written.                           */
/**********************************************************************/
VOID PASCAL MonitorErrors(LPVOID lpData)
    {
    MONERRSTRUCT FAR * lpERR;
    char achTBuf[80];
```

```
lpERR = lpData;

switch((WORD)lpERR->wLastError)
    {
    case DMLERR_ADVACKTIMEOUT:
        lstrcpy(achBuf,"Error: DMLERR_ADVACKTIMEOUT");
        break;
    case DMLERR_BUSY:
        lstrcpy(achBuf,"Error: DMLERR_BUSY");
        break;
    case DMLERR_DATAACKTIMEOUT:
        lstrcpy(achBuf,"Error: DMLERR_DATAACKTIMEOUT");
        break;
    case DMLERR_DLL_NOT_INITIALIZED:
        lstrcpy(achBuf,"Error: DMLERR_DLL_NOT_INITIALIZED");
        break;
    case DMLERR_DLL_USAGE:
        lstrcpy(achBuf,"Error: DMLERR_DLL_USAGE");
        break;
    case DMLERR_EXECACKTIMEOUT:
        lstrcpy(achBuf,"Error: DMLERR_EXECACKTIMEOUT");
        break;
    case DMLERR_INVALIDPARAMETER:
        lstrcpy(achBuf,"Error: DMLERR_INVALIDPARAMETER");
        break;
    case DMLERR_LOW_MEMORY:
        lstrcpy(achBuf,"Error: DMLERR_LOW_MEMORY");
        break;
    case DMLERR_MEMORY_ERROR:
        lstrcpy(achBuf,"Error: DMLERR_MEMORY_ERROR");
        break;
    case DMLERR_NOTPROCESSED:
        lstrcpy(achBuf,"Error: DMLERR_NOTPROCESSED");
        break;
    case DMLERR_NO_CONV_ESTABLISHED:
      lstrcpy(achBuf,"Error: DMLERR_NO_CONV_ESTABLISHED");
        break;
    case DMLERR_POKEACKTIMEOUT:
        lstrcpy(achBuf,"Error: DMLERR_POKEACKTIMEOUT");
        break;
    case DMLERR_POSTMSG_FAILED:
        lstrcpy(achBuf,"Error: DMLERR_POSTMSG_FAILED");
```

continues

Listing 4.5. continued

```
            break;
        case DMLERR_REENTRANCY:
            lstrcpy(achBuf,"Error: DMLERR_REENTRANCY");
            break;
        case DMLERR_SERVER_DIED:
            lstrcpy(achBuf,"Error: DMLERR_SERVER_DIED");
            break;
        case DMLERR_SYS_ERROR:
            lstrcpy(achBuf,"Error: DMLERR_SYS_ERROR");
            break;
        case DMLERR_UNADVACKTIMEOUT:
            lstrcpy(achBuf,"Error: DMLERR_UNADVACKTIMEOUT");
            break;
        case DMLERR_UNFOUND_QUEUE_ID:
            lstrcpy(achBuf,"Error: DMLERR_UNFOUND_QUEUE_ID");
            break;
        default:
             lstrcpy(achBuf,"Error: UNKNOWN");
            break;
        }
    sprintf(achTBuf,", Time = %.0f, Task = 0x%x\r\n",
            (double)lpERR->dwTime, (WORD)lpERR->hTask);
    lstrcat(achBuf,achTBuf);

    DisplayOutput(DOUBLESPACE);
    }

/***********************************************************************/
/* Function: MonitorHszInfo                                          */
/* Purpose: If string information is being monitored, the            */
/*          DdeCallBack function sends the string here                */
/*          to be formatted and written.                              */
/***********************************************************************/
VOID PASCAL MonitorHszInfo(LPVOID lpData)
    {
    MONHSZSTRUCT FAR * lpHSZ;
    char achTBuf[80];

    lpHSZ = lpData;
```

```
        sprintf(achBuf,
            "String Handles: Time = %.0f, Task = 0x%x, fsAction = ",
            (double)lpHSZ->dwTime, (WORD)lpHSZ->hTask);

        switch(lpHSZ->fsAction)
            {
            case MH_CLEANUP:
                lstrcat(achBuf,"MH_CLEANUP, ");
                break;
            case MH_CREATE:
                lstrcat(achBuf,"MH_CREATE, ");
                break;
            case MH_DELETE:
                lstrcat(achBuf,"MH_DELETE, ");
                break;
            case MH_KEEP:
                lstrcat(achBuf,"MH_KEEP, ");
                break;
            default:
                sprintf(achTBuf,"%d ",(WORD)lpHSZ->fsAction);
                lstrcat(achBuf,achTBuf);
                break;
            }
        lstrcat(achBuf,"\r\n");
        DisplayOutput(NEWLINE);

        sprintf(achBuf,"    hsz = 0x%lx (\"",
                (DWORD)lpHSZ->hsz);

        GetStringHandleString(lpHSZ->hsz);

        lstrcat(achBuf,"\")\r\n");

        DisplayOutput(DOUBLESPACE);
        }

/*********************************************************************/
/* Function: MonitorLinks                                          */
/* Purpose: If links are being monitored, the                     */
/*          DdeCallBack function sends the link data here          */
/*          to be formatted and written.                          */
/*********************************************************************/
```

continues

Listing 4.5. continued

```
VOID PASCAL MonitorLinks(LPVOID lpData)
    {
    MONLINKSTRUCT FAR * lpLINK;

    char achTBuf[80];

    lpLINK = lpData;
    lstrcpy(achBuf,"Link: Established = ");
    if(lpLINK->fEstablished)
        lstrcat(achBuf,"TRUE, Time = ");
    else
        lstrcat(achBuf,"FALSE, Time = ");

    sprintf(achTBuf,"%.0f, Task = 0x%x, fNoData = ",
            (double)lpLINK->dwTime, (WORD)lpLINK->hTask);
    lstrcat(achBuf,achTBuf);

    if(lpLINK->fNoData)
        lstrcat(achBuf,"TRUE,\r\n");
    else
        lstrcat(achBuf,"FALSE,\r\n");

    DisplayOutput(NEWLINE);

    sprintf(achBuf,"    Service Name = 0x%lx (\"",
            (DWORD)lpLINK->hszSvc);

    GetStringHandleString(lpLINK->hszSvc);

    sprintf(achTBuf,"\"), Topic Name = 0x%lx (\"",
        (DWORD)lpLINK->hszTopic);
    lstrcat(achBuf,achTBuf);

    GetStringHandleString(lpLINK->hszTopic);

    lstrcat(achBuf,"\"),\r\n");

    DisplayOutput(NEWLINE);

    sprintf(achBuf,"    Item Name = 0x%lx (\"",
```

```
                    (DWORD)lpLINK->hszItem);

        GetStringHandleString(lpLINK->hszItem);

        lstrcat(achBuf,"\")\r\n");

        DisplayOutput(NEWLINE);

        lstrcpy(achBuf,"    wFmt = ");

        GetClipBoardFormat(lpLINK->wFmt);

        if(lpLINK->fServer)
            lstrcat(achBuf,", fServer = TRUE,\r\n");
        else
            lstrcat(achBuf,", fServer = FALSE,\r\n");

        DisplayOutput(NEWLINE);

        sprintf(achBuf,"    hConvClient = 0x%lx, hConvServer = 0x%lx\r\n",
                (DWORD)lpLINK->hConvClient,
                (DWORD)lpLINK->hConvServer);

        DisplayOutput(DOUBLESPACE);
        }

/************************************************************************/
/* Function: MonitorMessages                                           */
/* Purpose: If messages are being monitored, the                      */
/*          DdeCallBack function sends the message data here           */
/*          to be formatted and written.                               */
/*          If bType is SEND, then it is SendMessage data;             */
/*          otherwise it is PostMessage data.                          */
/************************************************************************/
BOOL PASCAL MonitorMessages(LPVOID lpData, BOOL bType)
    {
    MONMSGSTRUCT FAR * lpMSG;
    char achTBuf[80];

    lpMSG = lpData;

    switch(lpMSG->wMsg)
```

continues

Listing 4.5. continued

```
    {
case WM_DDE_ACK:
    if(!MessageFilters[0])
        return FALSE;
    lstrcpy(achTBuf,"WM_DDE_ACK");
    break;
case WM_DDE_ADVISE:
    if(!MessageFilters[1])
        return FALSE;
    lstrcpy(achTBuf,"WM_DDE_ADVISE");
    break;
case WM_DDE_DATA:
    if(!MessageFilters[2])
        return FALSE;
    lstrcpy(achTBuf,"WM_DDE_DATA");
    break;
case WM_DDE_EXECUTE:
    if(!MessageFilters[3])
        return FALSE;
    lstrcpy(achTBuf,"WM_DDE_EXECUTE");
    break;
case WM_DDE_INITIATE:
    if(!MessageFilters[4])
        return FALSE;
    lstrcpy(achTBuf,"WM_DDE_INITIATE");
    break;
case WM_DDE_POKE:
    if(!MessageFilters[5])
        return FALSE;
    lstrcpy(achTBuf,"WM_DDE_POKE");
    break;
case WM_DDE_REQUEST:
    if(!MessageFilters[6])
        return FALSE;
    lstrcpy(achTBuf,"WM_DDE_REQUEST");
    break;
case WM_DDE_TERMINATE:
    if(!MessageFilters[7])
        return FALSE;
    lstrcpy(achTBuf,"WM_DDE_TERMINATE");
```

```
                    break;
            case WM_DDE_UNADVISE:
                if(!MessageFilters[8])
                    return FALSE;
                lstrcpy(achTBuf,"WM_DDE_UNADVISE");
                break;
            }

        if(bType == SEND)
            sprintf(achBuf,
                "Sent Msg: hwndTo = 0x%x, Time =%.0lf, Task = 0x%x,\r\n ",
                (WORD)lpMSG->hwndTo,  (double)lpMSG->dwTime,
                (WORD)lpMSG->hTask);
        else
            sprintf(achBuf,
                "Posted Msg: hwndTo = 0x%x, Time =%.0lf,
                    Task = 0x%x,\r\n ",
                (WORD)lpMSG->hwndTo,  (double)lpMSG->dwTime,
                (WORD)lpMSG->hTask);

        DisplayOutput(NEWLINE);

        sprintf(achBuf,"    wMsg = %s, wParam = %d, lParam = 0x%lx\r\n",
                achTBuf,(WORD)lpMSG->wParam,(DWORD)lpMSG->lParam);

        DisplayOutput(DOUBLESPACE);

        return TRUE;
        }

/*********************************************************************/
/* Function: GetClipBoardFormat                                      */
/* Purpose: This function concatenates the clipboard format          */
/*          to achBuf.                                               */
/*********************************************************************/
VOID PASCAL GetClipBoardFormat(WORD wFmt)
    {
    switch(wFmt)
        {
        case CF_TEXT:
            lstrcat(achBuf,"CF_TEXT");
            break;
```

continues

Listing 4.5. continued

```c
case CF_BITMAP:
    lstrcat(achBuf,"CF_BITMAP");
    break;
case CF_METAFILEPICT:
    lstrcat(achBuf,"CF_METAFILEPICT");
    break;
case CF_SYLK:
    lstrcat(achBuf,"CF_SYLK");
    break;
case CF_DIF:
    lstrcat(achBuf,"CF_DIF");
    break;
case CF_TIFF:
    lstrcat(achBuf,"CF_TIFF");
    break;
case CF_OEMTEXT:
    lstrcat(achBuf,"CF_OEMTEXT");
    break;
case CF_DIB:
    lstrcat(achBuf,"CF_DIB");
    break;
case CF_PALETTE:
    lstrcat(achBuf,"CF_PALETTE");
    break;
case CF_PENDATA:
    lstrcat(achBuf,"CF_PENDATA");
    break;
case CF_OWNERDISPLAY:
    lstrcat(achBuf,"CF_OWNERDISPLAY");
    break;
case CF_DSPTEXT:
    lstrcat(achBuf,"CF_DSPTEXT");
    break;
case CF_DSPBITMAP:
    lstrcat(achBuf,"CF_DSPBITMAP");
    break;
case CF_DSPMETAFILEPICT:
    lstrcat(achBuf,"CF_DSPMETAFILEPICT");
    break;
case CF_PRIVATEFIRST:
    lstrcat(achBuf,"CF_PRIVATEFIRST");
```

```
                        break;
                case CF_PRIVATELAST:
                    lstrcat(achBuf,"CF_PRIVATELAST");
                    break;
                case CF_GDIOBJFIRST:
                    lstrcat(achBuf,"CF_GDIOBJFIRST");
                    break;
                case CF_GDIOBJLAST:
                    lstrcat(achBuf,"CF_GDIOBJLAST");
                    break;
                default:
                    lstrcat(achBuf,"NON_STANDARD");
                }
        }

/**********************************************************************/
/* Function: GetStringHandleString                                    */
/* Purpose: This function gets a string handle's string value         */
/*          and concatenates the string value to achBuf.              */
/**********************************************************************/
VOID PASCAL GetStringHandleString(HSZ hsz)
    {
    LOCALHANDLE hMem;
    PSTR psz;
    WORD cb;

    cb = (WORD)DdeQueryString(idInst, hsz, NULL, 0, 0) + 2;
    if(hMem = LocalAlloc(LPTR,cb))
        {
        psz = LocalLock(hMem);
        DdeQueryString(idInst, hsz, psz, cb, CP_WINANSI);
        lstrcat(achBuf,psz);
        LocalUnlock(hMem);
        }
    LocalFree(hMem);
    }

/**********************************************************************/
/* Function: DisplayOutput                                            */
/* Purpose: This function writes to the edit window and/or the        */
/*          debug terminal based on the user's preferences.           */
/**********************************************************************/
```

continues

Listing 4.5. continued

```
VOID PASCAL DisplayOutput(BOOL bSkip)
    {
    if(bScreenChecked)
        {
        bChanges = TRUE;
        SendMessage(hEditWnd, EM_REPLACESEL,0,(LONG)(LPSTR)achBuf);
        if(bSkip)
            SendMessage(hEditWnd, EM_REPLACESEL,0,(LONG)(LPSTR)"\r\n");
        }
    if(bDebugChecked)
        {
        OutputDebugString(achBuf);
        if(bSkip)
            SendMessage(hEditWnd, EM_REPLACESEL,0,(LONG)(LPSTR)"\r\n");
        }
    }
```

Listing 4.6. The dialogs.c source file.

```
#include "ddemon.h"

/***********************************************************************/
/* Function: CreateDlgBox                                              */
/* Purpose: Generic function to create dialog boxes.                   */
/* Returns: TRUE/FALSE                                                 */
/***********************************************************************/
BOOL PASCAL CreateDlgBox(HWND hWnd, LPCSTR lpTemplateName,
                         FARPROC lpDlgProc)
    {
    BOOL    bResult;

    lpDlgProc = MakeProcInstance(lpDlgProc, hInst);
    if(lpDlgProc)
        {
        DialogBox(hInst, lpTemplateName, hWnd, (DLGPROC)lpDlgProc);
        FreeProcInstance(lpDlgProc);
        bResult = TRUE;
        }
```

```
    else
        bResult = FALSE;

    return bResult;
    }

/*************************************************************************/
/* Function: MonitorDlgProc                                          */
/* Purpose: Dialog box procedure for monitor configuration.          */
/* Returns: TRUE/FALSE                                               */
/*************************************************************************/
LRESULT CALLBACK MonitorDlgProc(HWND hDlg, WORD message,
                                WPARAM wParam, LPARAM lParam)
    {
    int i;
    switch(message)
        {
        case WM_INITDIALOG:
            for(i = IDD_CALLBACKS; i <= IDD_POSTEDMSG; i++)
                if(Monitor[i-IDD_CALLBACKS] == TRUE)
                    SendDlgItemMessage(hDlg, i,
                                       BM_SETCHECK,TRUE,0L);
            return (LRESULT)TRUE;

        case WM_COMMAND:
            switch((WORD)wParam)
                {
                case IDOK:
                    for(i = IDD_CALLBACKS; i <= IDD_POSTEDMSG; i++)
                        {
                        if(IsDlgButtonChecked(hDlg,i))
                            Monitor[i-IDD_CALLBACKS] = TRUE;
                        else
                            Monitor[i-IDD_CALLBACKS] = FALSE;
                        }
                    EndDialog(hDlg,IDOK);
                    return (LRESULT)FALSE;
                    break;
                case IDCANCEL:
                    EndDialog(hDlg,IDCANCEL);
                    return (LRESULT)FALSE;
                    break;
```

continues

Listing 4.6. continued

```
                }
            break;
        }
    return FALSE;
    }


/***************************************************************************/
/* Function: MsgFiltersDlgProc                                           */
/* Purpose: Dialog box procedure for message filters.                    */
/* Returns: TRUE/FALSE                                                   */
/***************************************************************************/
LRESULT CALLBACK MsgFiltersDlgProc(HWND hDlg, WORD message,
                                   WPARAM wParam, LPARAM lParam)

    {
    int i;

    switch(message)
        {
        case WM_INITDIALOG:
            for(i = IDD_ACK; i <= IDD_UNADVISE; i++)
                if(MessageFilters[i-IDD_ACK] == TRUE)
                    SendDlgItemMessage(hDlg, i,
                                       BM_SETCHECK,TRUE,0L);
            return (LRESULT)TRUE;

        case WM_COMMAND:
            switch((WORD)wParam)
                {
                case IDOK:
                    for(i = IDD_ACK; i <= IDD_UNADVISE; i++)
                        {
                        if(IsDlgButtonChecked(hDlg,i))
                            MessageFilters[i-IDD_ACK] = TRUE;
                        else
                            MessageFilters[i-IDD_ACK] = FALSE;
                        }
                    EndDialog(hDlg,IDOK);
                    return (LRESULT)FALSE;
                    break;
                case IDCANCEL:
```

```
                            EndDialog(hDlg,IDCANCEL);
                            return (LRESULT)FALSE;
                            break;
                        }
                    break;
                }
        return FALSE;
        }


/**********************************************************************/
/* Function: CBFiltersDlgProc                                         */
/* Purpose: Dialog box procedure for callback filters.                */
/* Returns: TRUE/FALSE                                                */
/**********************************************************************/
LRESULT CALLBACK CBFiltersDlgProc(HWND hDlg, WORD message,
                                  WPARAM wParam, LPARAM lParam)
    {
    int i;
    switch(message)
        {
        case WM_INITDIALOG:
                for(i = IDD_XADVDATA; i <= IDD_XXACT_COMPLETE; i++)
                    if(CallBackFilters[i-IDD_XADVDATA] == TRUE)
                        SendDlgItemMessage(hDlg, i,
                                        BM_SETCHECK,TRUE,0L);
                return (LRESULT)TRUE;

        case WM_COMMAND:
            switch((WORD)wParam)
                {
                case IDOK:
                    for(i = IDD_XADVDATA;
                                i <= IDD_XXACT_COMPLETE; i++)
                        {
                        if(IsDlgButtonChecked(hDlg,i))
                            CallBackFilters[i-IDD_XADVDATA] = TRUE;
                        else
                            CallBackFilters[i-IDD_XADVDATA] = FALSE;
                        }
                    EndDialog(hDlg,IDOK);
                    return (LRESULT)FALSE;
                    break;
```

continues

Listing 4.6. continued

```
                     case IDCANCEL:
                          EndDialog(hDlg,IDCANCEL);
                          return (LRESULT)FALSE;
                          break;

                  }
             break;
        }
    return FALSE;
    }


/***********************************************************************/
/* Function: AboutDlgProc                                              */
/* Purpose: Handles messages for the About dialog box.                 */
/* Returns: TRUE/FALSE                                                 */
/***********************************************************************/
LRESULT CALLBACK AboutDlgProc(HWND hDlg, WORD message,
                              WPARAM wParam, LPARAM lParam)

    {
    switch(message)
        {
        case WM_INITDIALOG:
             return (LRESULT)TRUE;
        case WM_COMMAND:
             switch((WORD)wParam)
                 {
                 case IDOK:
                 case IDCANCEL:
                      EndDialog(hDlg, TRUE);
                      return (LRESULT)TRUE;
                 }
             break;
        }
    return (LRESULT)FALSE;
    }


/***********************************************************************/
/* Function: AbortProc                                                 */
/* Purpose: Dispatches messages to the Abort dialog box.               */
/* Returns: TRUE/FALSE                                                 */
/***********************************************************************/
```

```
LRESULT CALLBACK AbortProc(HDC hPr, int Code)
    {
    MSG msg;

    if (!hAbortDlgWnd)
        return (LRESULT)TRUE;

    /* Process messages intended for the abort dialog box */

    while (!bAbort && PeekMessage(&msg, NULL, NULL, NULL, TRUE))
        if (!IsDialogMessage(hAbortDlgWnd, &msg)) {
            TranslateMessage(&msg);
            DispatchMessage(&msg);
        }

    /* bAbort is TRUE (return is FALSE) if the user has aborted */

    return (LRESULT)(!bAbort);
    }

/**********************************************************************/
/* Function: AbortDlgProc                                           */
/* Purpose: Used to abort prints.                                   */
/* Returns: TRUE/FALSE                                              */
/**********************************************************************/
LRESULT CALLBACK AbortDlgProc(HWND hDlg, WORD msg,
                              WPARAM wParam, LPARAM lParam)
    {
    switch(msg)
        {
        case WM_INITDIALOG:
            SetFocus(GetDlgItem(hDlg, IDCANCEL));
            SetDlgItemText(hDlg, IDD_FILENAME, szFileName);
            return (LRESULT)TRUE;

        case WM_COMMAND:
            return (LRESULT)(bAbort = TRUE);
        }
    return (LRESULT)FALSE;
    }
```

continues

Listing 4.6. continued

```c
/******************************************************************/
/* Function: MarkDlgProc                                         */
/* Purpose: Handles messages for the Mark dialog box.            */
/* Returns: TRUE/FALSE                                           */
/******************************************************************/
LRESULT CALLBACK MarkDlgProc(HWND hDlg, WORD message,
                            WPARAM wParam, LPARAM lParam)

    {
    char achText[80];
    switch(message)
        {
        case WM_INITDIALOG:
            SendDlgItemMessage(hDlg, IDD_MARK,
                            WM_SETTEXT,0,(LONG)(LPSTR)"------");
            return (LRESULT)TRUE;
        case WM_COMMAND:
            switch((WORD)wParam)
                {
                case IDOK:
                    SendDlgItemMessage(hDlg, IDD_MARK,
                            WM_GETTEXT,80,(LONG)(LPSTR)achText);
                    if(bScreenChecked)
                        {
                        bChanges = TRUE;
                        SendMessage(hEditWnd, EM_REPLACESEL,0,
                                    (LONG)(LPSTR)achText);
                        }
                    if(bDebugChecked)
                        OutputDebugString(achText);
                    EndDialog(hDlg, TRUE);
                    return (LRESULT)TRUE;
                case IDCANCEL:
                    EndDialog(hDlg, FALSE);
                    return (LRESULT)TRUE;
                }
            break;
        }
    return (LRESULT)FALSE;
    }
```

Listing 4.7. The file.c source file.

```c
#include "ddemon.h"
#include <commdlg.h>        /* Needed for common dialogs */
#include <io.h>
#include <stdio.h>
#include <sys\types.h>
#include <sys\stat.h>

/* Variables global only to this module */
HFILE hFile;
HCURSOR hSaveCursor;
OPENFILENAME ofn;
OFSTRUCT OfStruct;
struct stat FileStatus;
HANDLE hEditBuffer;
PSTR pEditBuffer;
char szFilterSpec [128] =    /* file types */
    "Monitor Files (*.MON)\0*.MON\0All Files (*.*)\0*.*\0";

/* Function prototypes for function access by only this module */
VOID PASCAL SetEditBuffer(HWND, HANDLE);
VOID PASCAL SaveFile(HWND);
VOID SetFileName(VOID);
/**********************************************************************/
/* Function: NewFile                                                  */
/* Purpose: Queries to see if the file needs to be saved and          */
/*          then empties the edit control.                            */
/**********************************************************************/
BOOL PASCAL NewFile(HWND hwnd)
    {
    char achTemp[128];
    /* See if user wants to save current file */
    if(!QuerySaveFile(hwnd))
        return FALSE;

    bChanges = FALSE;
    szFileName[0] = 0;

    /* Set the window caption */
    sprintf(achTemp, "%s - %s", szBaseWindowTitle, "UNTITLED.MON");
    SetWindowText(hwnd, achTemp);
```

continues

```
                                                          }
```

Listing 4.7. continued

```
    /* Clear the edit control */
    SetEditBuffer(hwnd, NULL);
    return TRUE;
    }


/***********************************************************************/
/* Function: CommonOpenFile                                          */
/* Purpose: Queries to see if the file needs to be saved and         */
/*          then opens and loads a file.                             */
/***********************************************************************/
BOOL PASCAL CommonOpenFile(HWND hwnd)
    {
    char achTemp[128];

    /* Find out if the file needs to be saved. If so, save it */
    if(!QuerySaveFile(hwnd))
        return FALSE;

    /* Get the file name from the common open file dlg */
    SetFileName();
    if (!GetOpenFileName ((LPOPENFILENAME)&ofn))
        return FALSE;

    /* Open the file */
    hFile = OpenFile ((LPSTR)szFileName,
                      (LPOFSTRUCT)&OfStruct, OF_READ);
    if (!hFile)
       return FALSE;

    /* Get the file status */
    _fstat(hFile, &FileStatus);

    /* If the file is too big, don't load it */
    if (FileStatus.st_size > 65534)
        {
        MessageBox(hwnd, "Can't load files larger than 64K long",
                   NULL, MB_OK | MB_ICONEXCLAMATION);
        _lclose(hFile);
        return FALSE;
        }
```

```
        /* Allocate a buffer for the file */
        hEditBuffer = LocalAlloc(LMEM_MOVEABLE | LMEM_ZEROINIT,
                                 (WORD)FileStatus.st_size+1);

        /* This will take a moment or two */
        hSaveCursor = SetCursor(hHourGlass);

        /* Read the file into buffer */
        pEditBuffer = LocalLock(hEditBuffer);
        _lread(hFile, pEditBuffer, (WORD)FileStatus.st_size);

        /* Close the file */
        _lclose(hFile);

        LocalUnlock(hEditBuffer);

        /* Set the window caption */
        sprintf(achTemp, "%s - %s", szBaseWindowTitle, szFileTitle);
        SetWindowText(hwnd, achTemp);

        /* Set the edit buffer to the edit control */
        SetEditBuffer(hwnd, hEditBuffer);

        SetCursor(hSaveCursor);
        return TRUE;
        }

/********************************************************************/
/* Function: CommonSaveFile                                         */
/* Purpose: Uses a common dialog to save a file.                    */
/********************************************************************/
BOOL PASCAL CommonSaveFile(HWND hwnd)
    {
    if(szFileName[0])
        {
        if(bChanges)
            {
            SaveFile(hwnd);
            return TRUE;
            }
        }
    return FALSE;
    }
```

Listing 4.7. continued

```c
/***********************************************************************/
/* Function: CommonSaveAs                                              */
/* Purpose: Uses the common SaveAs dialog to save a file.              */
/***********************************************************************/
BOOL PASCAL CommonSaveAs(HWND hwnd)
    {
    char achTemp[128];

    SetFileName();
    /*  Use the common saveas dlg to get file name */
    if(!GetSaveFileName ((LPOPENFILENAME)&ofn))
        return FALSE;

    /* Set the window caption */
    sprintf(achTemp, "%s - %s", szBaseWindowTitle, szFileTitle);
    SetWindowText(hwnd, achTemp);

    /* Save the file */
    SaveFile(hwnd);
    return TRUE;
    }

/***********************************************************************/
/* Function: SetEditBuffer                                             */
/* Purpose: This function allocates a buffer for a file to be          */
/*          loaded into an edit control.                               */
/***********************************************************************/
VOID PASCAL SetEditBuffer(HWND hwnd, HANDLE hNewBuffer)
    {
    HANDLE hOldBuffer;

    /* Get and free the old edit control buffer */
    hOldBuffer = (HANDLE)SendMessage(hEditWnd, EM_GETHANDLE, 0, 0L);
    LocalFree(hOldBuffer);

    /* If we don't have a new buffer, allocate it. */
    if(!hNewBuffer)
        hNewBuffer = LocalAlloc(LMEM_MOVEABLE | LMEM_ZEROINIT, 1);
```

```
        /* Set the new buffer to the edit control */
        SendMessage(hEditWnd, EM_SETHANDLE, hNewBuffer, 0L);

        /* Set focus to edit control */
        SetFocus(hEditWnd);
        /* New file loaded--hasn't been changed yet */
        bChanges = FALSE;
        }

/**********************************************************************/
/* Function: QuerySaveFile                                            */
/* Purpose: Queries to see if the file needs to be saved and          */
/*          uses a common dialog to save the file.                    */
/**********************************************************************/
BOOL PASCAL QuerySaveFile(HWND hwnd)
    {
    int rc;
    char achTemp[128];

    /* If file has changed, see if user wants to save it */
    if (bChanges)
        {
        sprintf(achTemp, "Save changes to: %s", szFileName);
        rc = MessageBox(hwnd, achTemp,
                        "DDE Monitor",
                        MB_YESNOCANCEL |
                        MB_ICONEXCLAMATION);
        /* If yes, save it */
        if (rc == IDYES)
            {
            while(!szFileName[0])
                {
                SetFileName();
                if (!GetSaveFileName ((LPOPENFILENAME)&ofn))
                    return FALSE;
                }
            SaveFile(hwnd);
            }
        else
            /* No save, get out of here */
            if (rc == IDCANCEL)
                return FALSE;
```

continues

Listing 4.7. continued

```
        }
    else
        return TRUE;
    }

/**********************************************************************/
/* Function: SaveFile                                               */
/* Purpose: Writes a file from the edit control.                    */
/**********************************************************************/
VOID PASCAL SaveFile(HWND hwnd)
    {
    /* This could take a moment */
    hSaveCursor = SetCursor(hHourGlass);

    /* Open file to save it */
    hFile = OpenFile(szFileName, &OfStruct, OF_CANCEL | OF_CREATE);

    /* Get the edit buffer, lock it down */
    hEditBuffer = (HANDLE)SendMessage(hEditWnd, EM_GETHANDLE, 0, 0L);
    pEditBuffer = LocalLock(hEditBuffer);

    /* Write to the file and close it */
    _lwrite(hFile, pEditBuffer, lstrlen(pEditBuffer));
    _lclose(hFile);

    bChanges = FALSE;   /* File was just saved, no changes to it yet */
    LocalUnlock(hEditBuffer);

    SetCursor(hSaveCursor);
    }

/**********************************************************************/
/* Function: SetFileName                                            */
/* Purpose: Set the values in the ofn struct.                       */
/**********************************************************************/
VOID SetFileName(VOID)
    {
    ofn.lStructSize      = sizeof(OPENFILENAME);
    ofn.hwndOwner        = hwnd;
    ofn.lpstrFilter      = szFilterSpec;
    ofn.lpstrCustomFilter = NULL;
```

```
    ofn.nMaxCustFilter    = 0;
    ofn.nFilterIndex      = 1;
    ofn.lpstrFile         = szFileName;
    ofn.nMaxFile          = MAXFILENAME;
    ofn.lpstrInitialDir   = NULL;
    ofn.lpstrFileTitle    = szFileTitle;
    ofn.nMaxFileTitle     = MAXFILENAME;
    ofn.lpstrTitle        = NULL;
    ofn.lpstrDefExt       = "MON";
    ofn.Flags             = 0;
    }
```

Listing 4.8. The print.c source file.

```
#include "ddemon.h"
#include <drivinit.h>
#include <commdlg.h>      /* Needed for common dialogs */

/* Global Variables only to this module */
FARPROC lpAbortProc, lpAbortDlg;
PRINTDLG pd;

/* Function prototypes for functions only accessed from this module */
HDC GetPrinterDC(HWND);
VOID SetPrinter(HWND);
/******************************************************************/
/* Function: CommonPrint                                          */
/* Purpose: Invokes the common print dialog and prints the        */
/*          edit control buffer.                                  */
/******************************************************************/
BOOL PASCAL CommonPrint(HWND hwnd)
    {
    WORD wStatus, wPageSize, wLineSpace, wLinesPerPage;
    WORD wCurrLine, wLineLen, wLines, wIndex;
    char achLine[128];
    HDC hdcPrinter;
    HCURSOR hSaveCursor;
    TEXTMETRIC tm;

    /* This could take a while */
    hSaveCursor = SetCursor(hHourGlass);
```

continues

Listing 4.8. continued

```c
/* Display the common print dlg and get handle to
   device context for the printer */
hdcPrinter = GetPrinterDC(hwnd);
if(!hdcPrinter)
    return FALSE;

/* Allow the user to abort print */
lpAbortDlg =  MakeProcInstance((FARPROC)AbortDlgProc, hInst);
lpAbortProc = MakeProcInstance((FARPROC)AbortProc, hInst);

Escape(hdcPrinter, SETABORTPROC, NULL,
       (LPSTR)(LONG)lpAbortProc,
       (LPSTR)NULL);

if(Escape(hdcPrinter, STARTDOC, 14, "DDE Monitor Log",
   (LPSTR) NULL) < 0)
    {
    MessageBox(hwnd, "Unable to Print",
               "DDE Monitor",
               MB_OK | MB_ICONHAND);
    FreeProcInstance(lpAbortDlg);
    FreeProcInstance(lpAbortProc);
    DeleteDC(hdcPrinter);
    }
bAbort = FALSE;

/* Create and show modeless Abort dialog */
hAbortDlgWnd = CreateDialog(hInst,
                           (LPCSTR)MAKEINTRESOURCE(IDD_ABORTBOX),
                           hwnd, lpAbortDlg);
ShowWindow (hAbortDlgWnd, SW_NORMAL);

/* Disable the main window */
EnableWindow(hwnd, FALSE);
  /* Remove the hourglass */

/* Get info for TextOut and paging */
GetTextMetrics(hdcPrinter, &tm);
wLineSpace = tm.tmHeight + tm.tmExternalLeading;
wPageSize = GetDeviceCaps (hdcPrinter, VERTRES);
```

```
wLinesPerPage = wPageSize / wLineSpace - 1;
wLines = (WORD)SendMessage(hEditWnd, EM_GETLINECOUNT, 0, 0L);

/* OK, print the bad boy */
wCurrLine = 1;
wStatus = 0;
for(wIndex = 0; wIndex < wLines; wIndex++)
    {
    achLine[0] = 128;
    achLine[1] = 0;
    wLineLen = (int)SendMessage(hEditWnd, EM_GETLINE,
                                wIndex, (DWORD)(LPSTR)achLine);
    TextOut(hdcPrinter, 0, wCurrLine*wLineSpace,
            (LPSTR)achLine, wLineLen);
    if(++wCurrLine > wLinesPerPage )
        {
        wCurrLine = 1;
        wStatus = Escape(hdcPrinter, NEWFRAME, 0, 0L, 0L);
        if(wStatus < 0 ¦¦ bAbort)
            break;
        }
    }

if(wStatus >= 0 && !bAbort)
    {
    Escape(hdcPrinter, NEWFRAME, 0, 0L, 0L);
    Escape(hdcPrinter, ENDDOC, 0, 0L, 0L);
    }

/* Enable the main window */
EnableWindow(hwnd, TRUE);

/* Free Abort dialog resources */
DestroyWindow(hAbortDlgWnd);
FreeProcInstance(lpAbortDlg);
FreeProcInstance(lpAbortProc);
DeleteDC(hdcPrinter);

SetCursor(hSaveCursor);
return TRUE;
}
```

continues

Listing 4.8. continued

```
/***********************************************************************/
/* Function: CommonPrintSetup                                          */
/* Purpose: Use the common print dlg for print setup.                  */
/***********************************************************************/
VOID PASCAL CommonPrintSetup(HWND hwnd)
    {
    DWORD FlagSwitch;

    SetPrinter(hwnd);

    FlagSwitch = pd.Flags;
    pd.Flags |= PD_PRINTSETUP;
    PrintDlg((LPPRINTDLG)&pd);
    pd.Flags = FlagSwitch;
    }


/***********************************************************************/
/* Function: GetPrinterDC                                              */
/* Purpose: Get Device Context for printer and set up PRINTDLG         */
/*          struct.                                                    */
/***********************************************************************/
HDC GetPrinterDC(HWND hwnd)
    {
    LPSTR lpszDriverName, lpszDeviceName, lpszPortName;
    LPDEVMODE lpDevMode = NULL;
    LPDEVNAMES lpDevNames;
    HDC hDC;

    SetPrinter(hwnd);

    if (!PrintDlg((LPPRINTDLG)&pd))
        return FALSE;

    if(pd.hDC)
        {
        hDC = pd.hDC;
        }
    else
        {
```

```
            if (!pd.hDevNames)
                return FALSE;

            lpDevNames = (LPDEVNAMES)GlobalLock(pd.hDevNames);
            lpszDriverName = (LPSTR)lpDevNames +
                lpDevNames->wDriverOffset;
            lpszDeviceName = (LPSTR)lpDevNames +
                lpDevNames->wDeviceOffset;
            lpszPortName   = (LPSTR)lpDevNames +
                lpDevNames->wOutputOffset;
            GlobalUnlock(pd.hDevNames);

            if (pd.hDevMode)
                lpDevMode = (LPDEVMODE)GlobalLock(pd.hDevMode);

            hDC = CreateDC(lpszDriverName, lpszDeviceName,
                           lpszPortName, (LPSTR)lpDevMode);

            if (pd.hDevMode && lpDevMode)
                GlobalUnlock(pd.hDevMode);
            }

        if (pd.hDevNames)
            GlobalFree(pd.hDevNames);
        if (pd.hDevMode)
            GlobalFree(pd.hDevMode);
        return hDC;
        }

VOID SetPrinter(HWND hwnd)
        {
        pd.lStructSize      = sizeof(PRINTDLG);
        pd.hwndOwner        = hwnd;
        pd.hDevMode         = NULL;
        pd.hDevNames        = NULL;
        pd.Flags            = PD_RETURNDC | PD_NOSELECTION |
                              PD_NOPAGENUMS;
        pd.nCopies          = 1;
        }
```

Listing 4.9. The winmain.c source file.

```c
#define MAIN
#include "ddemon.h"

/***********************************************************************/
/* Function: WinMain                                                 */
/* Purpose: Main function for windows app. Initializes all instances*/
/*          of app, translates and dispatches messages.             */
/* Returns: Value of PostQuitMessage.                               */
/***********************************************************************/
int PASCAL WinMain(HINSTANCE hInstance, HINSTANCE hPrevInstance,
                   LPSTR lpszCmdLine, int nCmdShow)

    {
    MSG msg;

    /* If there isn't a previous instance of app, then initialize  */
    /* the first instance of app.                                  */
    if(!hPrevInstance)
        if(!InitApplication(hInstance))
            return FALSE;

    /* Perform initialization for all instances of application     */
    if(!InitInstance(hInstance, nCmdShow))
        return FALSE;

    /* Get messages for this application until WM_QUIT is received */
    while(GetMessage(&msg, 0, 0, 0))
        {
        TranslateMessage(&msg);
        DispatchMessage(&msg);
        }
    return (int)msg.wParam;
    }
```

Listing 4.10. The init.c source file.

```c
#include "ddemon.h"
#include <stdio.h>
```

```
/**********************************************************************/
/* Function: InitApplication                                         */
/* Purpose: Performs all initialization for first instance of app.   */
/* Returns: TRUE if successful, FALSE if failure                     */
/**********************************************************************/
BOOL InitApplication(HINSTANCE hInstance)
    {
    BOOL bResult;
    char szClassName[SZCLASSNAME];
    WNDCLASS wc;

    /* Load the window class name from resource string table */

    if(!LoadString(hInstance, IDS_CLASSNAME,
        szClassName, sizeof szClassName))
        return FALSE;

    /* Class styles */
    wc.style          = NULL;
    /* Name of message loop function for windows of this class */
    wc.lpfnWndProc    = MainWndProc;
    /* Not using Class Extra data */
    wc.cbClsExtra     = 0;
    /* Not using Window Extra data */
    wc.cbWndExtra     = 0;
    /* Instance that owns this class */
    wc.hInstance      = hInstance;
    /* Use default application icon */
    wc.hIcon          = LoadIcon(NULL, IDI_APPLICATION);
    /* Use arrow cursor */
    wc.hCursor        = LoadCursor(NULL, IDC_ARROW);
    /* Use system background color */
    wc.hbrBackground = GetStockObject(WHITE_BRUSH);
    /* Resource name for menu */
    wc.lpszMenuName   = MAKEINTRESOURCE(IDM_DDEMONITORMENU);
    /* Name given to this class */
    wc.lpszClassName = szClassName;

    /* Register the window class */
    bResult = RegisterClass(&wc);
```

continues

Listing 4.10. continued

```c
    /* Return result based on registration */
    return bResult;
    }


/**********************************************************************/
/* Function: InitInstance                                           */
/* Purpose: Performs all initialization for all instances of app.   */
/* Returns: TRUE if successful, FALSE if failure                    */
/**********************************************************************/
BOOL InitInstance (HINSTANCE hInstance, int nCmdShow)
    {
    char szClassName[SZCLASSNAME];
    char szTemp[128];
    RECT Rect;

    hInst = hInstance;

    /* Load the window class name from resource string table */
    if(!LoadString(hInst, IDS_CLASSNAME,
        szClassName, sizeof szClassName))
        return FALSE;

    /* Load the window title from resource string table */
    if(!LoadString(hInst, IDS_WINDOWTITLE,
                   szBaseWindowTitle, sizeof szBaseWindowTitle))
        return FALSE;
    sprintf(szTemp, "%s - %s", szBaseWindowTitle, "UNTITLED.MON");

    hwnd = CreateWindow(&szClassName[0],     /* Window class to create */
                        &szTemp[0],          /* Text for title bar     */
                        WS_OVERLAPPEDWINDOW, /* Window styles          */
                        CW_USEDEFAULT,       /* Default x  position    */
                        CW_USEDEFAULT,       /* Default y  position    */
                        CW_USEDEFAULT,       /* Default cx position    */
                        CW_USEDEFAULT,       /* Default cy position    */
                        0,                   /* Parent window          */
                        0,                   /* Menu                   */
                        hInstance,           /* Owning instance        */
                        NULL);               /* User-defined params    */
```

```
        /* If CreateWindow wasn't successful, return FALSE */
        if(!hwnd)
            return FALSE;

        GetClientRect(hwnd, (LPRECT) &Rect);
        hEditWnd = CreateWindow("Edit",
            NULL,
            WS_CHILD | WS_VISIBLE |
            ES_MULTILINE | ES_READONLY |
            WS_VSCROLL | WS_HSCROLL |
            ES_AUTOHSCROLL | ES_AUTOVSCROLL,
            0,
            0,
            (Rect.right-Rect.left),
            (Rect.bottom-Rect.top),
            hwnd,
            IDC_EDIT,                          /* Child control ID */
            hInstance,
            NULL);

        if (!hEditWnd) {
            DestroyWindow(hwnd);
            return (NULL);
        }

        /* Get an hourglass cursor to use during file transfers */

        hHourGlass = LoadCursor(NULL, IDC_WAIT);

        /* Show and paint window */
        ShowWindow(hwnd, nCmdShow);
        UpdateWindow(hwnd);

        return TRUE;
        }
```

Listing 4.11. The ddemon.rc resource file.

```
#include <windows.h>
#include "resource.h"
```

continues

Listing 4.11. continued

```
#include "dialogs.h"

IDM_DDEMONITORMENU MENU
    BEGIN
        POPUP         "&File"
        BEGIN
            MENUITEM   "&New",                      IDM_NEW
            MENUITEM   "&Open...",                   IDM_OPEN
            MENUITEM   "&Save",                      IDM_SAVE
            MENUITEM   "Save &As...",                IDM_SAVEAS
            MENUITEM   "&Print...",                  IDM_PRINT
            MENUITEM   "P&rint Setup...",            IDM_PRINTSETUP
            MENUITEM   SEPARATOR
            MENUITEM   "E&xit",                      IDM_EXIT
        END

        POPUP         "&Output"
        BEGIN
            MENUITEM    "&Screen",                   IDM_SCREEN
            MENUITEM    "&Debug Terminal",           IDM_DEBUG
            MENUITEM    SEPARATOR
            MENUITEM    "&Mark",                      IDM_MARK
            MENUITEM    "&Clear Screen",             IDM_CLEARSCREEN
        END

        POPUP          "&Configuration"
        BEGIN
            MENUITEM    "&Monitor ...",              IDM_MONITOR
            MENUITEM    "&Message Filters ...",      IDM_MSGFILTERS
            MENUITEM    "&Callbacks Filters ...",    IDM_CALLBACKS
        END

        POPUP          "&Monitor"
        BEGIN
            MENUITEM   "&On",                        IDM_START
            MENUITEM   "O&ff",                       IDM_END
        END

        POPUP          "&Help"
        BEGIN
```

```
                MENUITEM "&About Monitor ...",                IDM_ABOUT
            END
        END

STRINGTABLE
    BEGIN
        IDS_CLASSNAME       "DDEMonitorClass"
        IDS_WINDOWTITLE     "DDE Monitor"
    END

#include "ddemon.dlg"
```

Listing 4.12. The ddemon.dlg dialog file.

```
DLGINCLUDE RCDATA DISCARDABLE
BEGIN
    "DIALOGS.H\0"
END

IDD_ABOUTBOX DIALOG 136, 37, 152, 94
STYLE DS_MODALFRAME | WS_POPUP | WS_VISIBLE | WS_CAPTION | WS_SYSMENU
CAPTION "About DDE Monitor"
FONT 8, "Helv"
BEGIN
    CTEXT           "Microsoft Windows", -1, 42, 14, 67, 8
    CTEXT           "DDE Monitor Application", -1, 28, 33, 94, 8
    CTEXT           "Copyright \251 Jeffrey Clark, 1991",
                    -1, 21, 53, 110, 8
    PUSHBUTTON      "OK", IDOK, 55, 73, 40, 14
END

IDD_MONITORBOX DIALOG 118, 34, 160, 92
STYLE DS_MODALFRAME | WS_POPUP | WS_VISIBLE | WS_CAPTION | WS_SYSMENU
CAPTION "Monitor Configuration"
FONT 8, "Helv"
BEGIN
    CONTROL         "DDE &Callbacks", IDD_CALLBACKS, "Button",
                    BS_AUTOCHECKBOX | WS_TABSTOP, 6, 6, 65, 10
    CONTROL         "Con&versations", IDD_CONVERSATIONS, "Button",
                    BS_AUTOCHECKBOX | WS_TABSTOP, 6, 18, 60, 10
```

continues

Listing 4.12. continued

```
    CONTROL          "&Errors", IDD_ERRORS, "Button", BS_AUTOCHECKBOX ¦
                     WS_TABSTOP, 6, 30, 40, 10
    CONTROL          "&Links", IDD_LINKS, "Button", BS_AUTOCHECKBOX ¦
                     WS_TABSTOP, 6, 42, 40, 10
    CONTROL          "&String Handle Data", IDD_STRINGS, "Button",
                     BS_AUTOCHECKBOX ¦ WS_TABSTOP, 6, 54, 76, 10
    CONTROL          "Sent &Messages", IDD_SENTMSGS, "Button",
                     BS_AUTOCHECKBOX ¦ WS_TABSTOP, 6, 66, 65, 10
    CONTROL          "&Posted Messages", IDD_POSTEDMSG, "Button",
                     BS_AUTOCHECKBOX ¦ WS_TABSTOP, 6, 78, 71, 10
    PUSHBUTTON       "OK", IDOK, 116, 6, 40, 14
    PUSHBUTTON       "Cancel", IDCANCEL, 116, 25, 40, 14
END

IDD_MSGFILTERSBOX DIALOG 122, 28, 160, 116
STYLE DS_MODALFRAME ¦ WS_POPUP ¦ WS_VISIBLE ¦ WS_CAPTION ¦ WS_SYSMENU
CAPTION "Message Filters"
FONT 8, "Helv"
BEGIN
    CONTROL          "WM-DDE-A&CK", IDD_ACK, "Button", BS_AUTOCHECKBOX ¦
                     WS_TABSTOP, 6, 6, 62, 10
    CONTROL          "WM-DDE-&ADVISE", IDD_ADVISE, "Button",
                     BS_AUTOCHECKBOX ¦
                     WS_TABSTOP, 6, 18, 74, 10
    CONTROL          "WM-DDE-&DATA", IDD_DATA, "Button", BS_AUTOCHECKBOX ¦
                     WS_TABSTOP, 6, 30, 66, 10
    CONTROL          "WM-DDE-E&XECUTE", IDD_EXECUTE, "Button",
                     BS_AUTOCHECKBOX ¦ WS_TABSTOP, 6, 42, 78, 10
    CONTROL          "WM-DDE-&INITIATE", IDD_INITIATE, "Button",
                     BS_AUTOCHECKBOX ¦ WS_TABSTOP, 6, 54, 75, 10
    CONTROL          "WM-DDE-&POKE", IDD_POKE, "Button", BS_AUTOCHECKBOX ¦
                     WS_TABSTOP, 6, 66, 65, 10
    CONTROL          "WM-DDE-&REQUEST", IDD_REQUEST, "Button",
                     BS_AUTOCHECKBOX ¦ WS_TABSTOP, 6, 78, 78, 10
    CONTROL          "WM-DDE-&TERMINATE", IDD_TERMINATE, "Button",
                     BS_AUTOCHECKBOX ¦ WS_TABSTOP, 6, 90, 87, 10
    CONTROL          "WM-DDE-&UNADVISE", IDD_UNADVISE, "Button",
                     BS_AUTOCHECKBOX ¦ WS_TABSTOP, 6, 102, 82, 10
    PUSHBUTTON       "OK", IDOK, 112, 6, 40, 14
    PUSHBUTTON       "Cancel", IDCANCEL, 112, 26, 40, 14
```

```
    END

    IDD_CALLBACKBOX DIALOG 101, 24, 247, 101
    STYLE DS_MODALFRAME | WS_POPUP | WS_VISIBLE | WS_CAPTION | WS_SYSMENU
    CAPTION "Callback Filters"
    FONT 8, "Helv"
    BEGIN
        CONTROL         "XTYP-&ADVDATA", IDD_XADVDATA, "Button",
                        BS_AUTOCHECKBOX |
                        WS_TABSTOP, 4, 6, 68, 10
        CONTROL         "XTYP-ADV&REQ", IDD_XADVREQ, "Button",
                        BS_AUTOCHECKBOX |
                        WS_TABSTOP, 4, 18, 65, 10
        CONTROL         "XTYP-ADV&START", IDD_XADVSTART, "Button",
                        BS_AUTOCHECKBOX | WS_TABSTOP, 4, 30, 71, 10
        CONTROL         "XTYP-ADVS&TOP", IDD_XADVSTOP, "Button",
                        BS_AUTOCHECKBOX |
                        WS_TABSTOP, 4, 42, 67, 10
        CONTROL         "XTYP-&CONNECT", IDD_XCONNECT, "Button",
                        BS_AUTOCHECKBOX |
                        WS_TABSTOP, 4, 54, 70, 10
        CONTROL         "XTYP-C&ONNECT-CONFIRM", IDD_XCONNECT_CONFIRM,
                        "Button",
                        BS_AUTOCHECKBOX | WS_TABSTOP, 4, 66, 101, 10
        CONTROL         "XTYP-&DISCONNECT", IDD_XDISCONNECT, "Button",
                        BS_AUTOCHECKBOX | WS_TABSTOP, 4, 78, 80, 10
        CONTROL         "XTYP-&ERROR", IDD_XERROR, "Button",
                        BS_AUTOCHECKBOX |
                        WS_TABSTOP, 4, 90, 61, 10
        CONTROL         "XTYP-E&XECUTE", IDD_XEXECUTE, "Button",
                        BS_AUTOCHECKBOX |
                        WS_TABSTOP, 114, 6, 67, 10
        CONTROL         "XTYP-&POKE", IDD_XPOKE, "Button",
                        BS_AUTOCHECKBOX |
                        WS_TABSTOP, 114, 18, 52, 10
        CONTROL         "XTYP-RE&GISTER", IDD_XREGISTER, "Button",
                        BS_AUTOCHECKBOX | WS_TABSTOP, 114, 30, 71, 10
        CONTROL         "XTYP-RE&QUEST", IDD_XREQUEST, "Button",
                        BS_AUTOCHECKBOX |
                        WS_TABSTOP, 114, 42, 69, 10
```

continues

235

Listing 4.12. continued

```
    CONTROL         "XTYP-&UNREGISTER", IDD_XUNREGISTER, "Button",
                    BS_AUTOCHECKBOX ¦ WS_TABSTOP, 114, 54, 82, 10
    CONTROL         "XTYP-&WILDCONNECT", IDD_XWILDCONNECT, "Button",
                    BS_AUTOCHECKBOX ¦ WS_TABSTOP, 114, 66, 87, 10
    CONTROL         "XTYP-XACT-CO&MPLETE", IDD_XXACT_COMPLETE, "Button",
                    BS_AUTOCHECKBOX ¦ WS_TABSTOP, 114, 78, 94, 10
    PUSHBUTTON      "OK", IDOK, 201, 6, 40, 14
    PUSHBUTTON      "Cancel", IDCANCEL, 201, 24, 40, 14
END

IDD_ABORTBOX DIALOG 106, 30, 160, 84
STYLE DS_MODALFRAME ¦ WS_POPUP ¦ WS_VISIBLE ¦ WS_CAPTION ¦ WS_SYSMENU
CAPTION "DDE Monitor"
FONT 8, "Helv"
BEGIN
    PUSHBUTTON      "Cancel", IDCANCEL, 60, 66, 40, 14
    CTEXT           "Sending", -1, 35, 12, 90, 8
    CTEXT           "", IDD_FILENAME, 4, 30, 154, 8
    CTEXT           "to print spooler.", -1, 26, 48, 107, 8
END

IDD_MARKBOX DIALOG 83, 36, 152, 60
STYLE DS_MODALFRAME ¦ WS_POPUP ¦ WS_VISIBLE ¦ WS_CAPTION ¦ WS_SYSMENU
CAPTION "Add Mark to Output"
FONT 8, "Helv"
BEGIN
    LTEXT           "Mark:", -1, 8, 17, 20, 8
    EDITTEXT        IDD_MARK, 30, 15, 113, 12, ES_AUTOHSCROLL
    DEFPUSHBUTTON   "OK", IDOK, 31, 36, 40, 14
    PUSHBUTTON      "Cancel", IDCANCEL, 83, 36, 40, 14
END
```

Listing 4.13. The ddemon.def module definition file.

```
NAME DDEMON
DESCRIPTION 'DDE Monitor, Copyright Jeffrey Clark, 1991'
EXETYPE WINDOWS
STUB 'WINSTUB.EXE'
CODE PRELOAD MOVEABLE DISCARDABLE
```

```
DATA PRELOAD MOVEABLE MULTIPLE

HEAPSIZE  0x0FFF
STACKSIZE 8192

SEGMENTS
    WINMAIN_TEXT    MOVEABLE              PRELOAD
    DDEMON_TEXT     MOVEABLE              PRELOAD
    INIT_TEXT       MOVEABLE DISCARDABLE PRELOAD
    DIALOGS_TEXT    MOVEABLE DISCARDABLE LOADONCALL
    DDE_TEXT        MOVEABLE DISCARDABLE LOADONCALL
    FILE_TEXT       MOVEABLE DISCARDABLE LOADONCALL
    PRINT_TEXT      MOVEABLE DISCARDABLE LOADONCALL

EXPORTS
    MainWndProc        @1
    AboutDlgProc       @2
    DdeCallBack        @3
    MonitorDlgProc     @4
    CBFiltersDlgProc   @5
    MsgFiltersDlgProc  @6
    AbortDlgProc       @7
    AbortProc          @8
    MarkDlgProc        @9
```

Listing 4.14. The DDEMON make file.

```
CC = cl -c -AM -Gsw -Od -W3 -Zpi -Fo$@

all: ddemon.exe

ddemon.h: dialogs.h resource.h

ddemon.res: ddemon.rc ddemon.dlg dialogs.h resource.h
  rc -r ddemon

init.obj: init.c ddemon.h
    $(CC) $*.c

file.obj: file.c ddemon.h
```

continues

Listing 4.14. continued

```
    $(CC) $*.c

print.obj: print.c ddemon.h
    $(CC) $*.c

winmain.obj: winmain.c ddemon.h
    $(CC) $*.c

ddemon.obj: ddemon.c ddemon.h
    $(CC) $*.c

dde.obj: dde.c ddemon.h
    $(CC) $*.c

dialogs.obj: dialogs.c ddemon.h
    $(CC) $*.c

ddemon.exe::  init.obj winmain.obj ddemon.obj dde.obj\
              dialogs.obj file.obj\
              print.obj  ddemon.res ddemon.def
    link /CO /MAP /NOD @<<
file+
print+
init+
winmain+
ddemon+
dde+
dialogs
$@

libw mlibcew ddeml commdlg
ddemon.def
<<
    mapsym ddemon
    rc ddemon.res
```

Summary

This chapter outlined the process of creating a DDEML monitor application. The example program is a good starting point for a useful development tool that you can use to debug DDEML applications. You can add a few enhancements and customizations to the example program to make it more useful. A few ideas for enhancements are

- [ ] Add support for files greater than 64K.
- [ ] Create an MDI application and separate transaction types into individual MDI child windows.
- [ ] Add text-editing support.

Object Linking
and Embedding

PART

II

Object Linking
and Embedding
Concepts

In the context of object linking and embedding, an *object* is anything a user can manipulate with a Windows application. The accessory applications that accompany Windows 3.1 are good examples of applications that manipulate OLE objects. For example, the Paintbrush program manipulates bitmap objects, and the Sound Recorder application manipulates sound objects. Although bitmaps and sounds are completely different types of objects, OLE applications use a similar method to handle both of them.

Linking and embedding are the two methods programmers use to access OLE objects. Objects are either linked or embedded in an OLE client application's document. An *embedded* object becomes a physical part of a client application's document. A *linked* object remains separate from a client application's document. An OLE client application can edit a linked object or an embedded object by invoking the OLE server application as an editor.

This chapter covers the following object linking and embedding (OLE) topics:

- Objects and documents
- Linking and embedding objects
- Packages
- Registration
- Clipboard
- OLE client and server applications

Objects and Documents

The major thrust of OLE is a document-centered view of computing, which is contrary to the application-centered view of computing most users have. For example, a Microsoft Excel user can create a report using a spreadsheet that contains text, charts, and calculations that are all generated in Excel. Although Excel is good for calculations, it is very poor at manipulating text.

In the document-centered world of OLE, applications should be more specialized and handle one task extremely well. For example, document-centered users might create the report in the preceding example with a desktop publishing package that specializes in layout. The package could contain other features; however, it should perform document layout best. When document-centered users create text for the report, they use a word-processing application. When they create charts, they use a charting application. You get the idea. Users create each object for the final output in a specialized application.

With OLE, users do not need to leave the desktop publishing package to incorporate an object in a document. To insert objects, users can use a menu item that invokes a dialog box from which they can select the type of object they need. Selecting the object from the dialog box invokes the application that creates the object. Users do not need to know what application generates the object; they just need to know what object they require.

Launching applications from inside other applications to create an object has a slight benefit: It saves time from switching away from the current application and then finding and starting another application to create the object. The downside of a document-centered approach to computing is that users need to know how to use multiple applications. Although the Windows GUI enables users to learn new applications quickly, it may not always be cost-effective for users to learn specialized applications for tasks they perform infrequently.

Linking and Embedding

When users create a chart in one application and then copy and paste the chart to another application, the chart loses some flexibility. If the chart needs to be revised, users have to find the application that created the chart, find the file for the chart, and then edit the chart. When the revisions are complete, users must return to the document, delete the old version of the chart, and copy and paste the new version of the chart. Although this is the way Windows works without OLE, it is surely better than importing and exporting files in text-based DOS applications.

OLE does not require the manual steps used in the preceding example. When users create an OLE object, they can link or embed the object in a compound document. Linking and embedding provide a method to edit and update an object quickly. The difference between linking and embedding lies in the storage of an object. An embedded object becomes part of the compound document. The compound document for a linked object does not contain the linked object. The application that creates the linked object stores the linked object in its own file. A compound document always contains a reference to the application that creates a linked object or an embedded object.

Despite the difference in storage methods for linked objects and embedded objects, the presentation of the data is the same. The choice between linked objects and embedded objects depends on the use and life of the object. An embedded object is a copy of an object at a particular moment in time. The original object can change without affecting the embedded object. A linked object, on the other hand, can change independently of the compound document. When a linked object changes independently of the compound document, users have the choice of updating the link or using the last representation of the object.

Packages

A *package* is an object or a collection of objects in a graphical wrapper. The graphical wrapper is an icon. The package is an embedded object in a client document. The package can contain either a linked object or an embedded object. Packages provide a concise method of representing large amounts of information.

You can create a package using one of three methods. The first method is to drop a file into a client document from the File Manager. The second method is to copy a file from the File Manager to the clipboard, and then **P**aste or Paste **L**ink the file into a client document. The third method is to invoke the Object Packager applet. The user can start the Object Packager applet from within the client application with the **I**nsert Object menu item, or directly from Program Manager.

The Registration Database

The *registration database* is the mechanism that OLE programs use to get information about other OLE programs. Specifically, OLE server applications have entries in the registration database that specify the executable filenames and paths, object classes, verbs, and, optionally, an object handler. (Object handlers are discussed in Chapter 8.)

The API for registration database calls is in the SHELL.DLL. Server applications use the registration API to register as an OLE server. This process is called *registration*. Entries in the registration database provide information for the OLE libraries or other applications that interact with an OLE server application.

> **Note:** *Registration* and the *registration database* are two different things. Registration is a process, whereas a registration database is a collection of information about OLE applications and file extensions for Windows applications.

A user or a program can maintain the registration database. Typically, when a new application is installed, the installation program updates the registration database for the new application. A user can also directly edit the registration database by using the REGEDIT.EXE applet. A user can append entries to the registration database by typing the entries in the REGEDIT applet, or by merging a text file into the registration database. An example text file follows:

```
REGEDIT

HKEY_CLASSES_ROOT\Polygons = Polygons
HKEY_CLASSES_ROOT\.ply = Polygons
HKEY_CLASSES_ROOT\Polygons\protocol\StdFileEditing\server =
    c:\poly\poly.exe
HKEY_CLASSES_ROOT\Polygons\protocol\StdFileEditing\verb\0 =
    &Edit
HKEY_CLASSES_ROOT\Polygons\protocol\StdFileEditing\handler =
    c:\polyhand\polyhand.dll
```

The keyword REGEDIT identifies that the file is a registration database text file to the REGEDIT applet. The HKEY_CLASSES_ROOT keyword delimits keys in the database. The first key in the preceding example is the class name key. The value to the left of the equal sign is the class name the server uses to register itself as an OLE server. The value to the right is a descriptive version of the class name that the client application can use in menus to identify an object class.

The second key identifies the file extension associated with the class name. The third through fifth keys describe the protocol of the server application. The preceding example contains only one protocol: StdFileEditing. Two other protocols exist: StdExecute and Static. StdExecute identifies applications that support the **OleExecute()** function. The StdFileEditing protocol is the protocol for embedded and linked objects. The `Static` protocol identifies non-OLE objects.

> **Note:** The registration database can store information that is traditionally contained in .INI files. The only danger in using the registration database for this purpose is that Microsoft may change the format of the database in the future.

The keyword after `StdFileEditing` identifies the server application, a *verb* supported by the server application, and, optionally, an object handler. The values for the keywords `server` and `handler` specify a path and an executable name for the server and object handler, respectively. The keyword `verb` lists the supported verbs for an object. An object can have one or more verbs. The numbering of the verbs starts with zero. The zero verb is the primary verb. All other verbs are secondary verbs. The preceding example contains one verb— a primary verb called `&Edit`. The value of the verb is the same as it would appear on a menu; thus the `Edit` verb contains an ampersand. (Client applications use the verb value for menu items.)

Clipboard

The clipboard is an integral part of linking and embedding. OLE server applications represent objects placed in the clipboard in data formats. The four data format categories are native data, OwnerLink data, ObjectLink data, and a presentation data format. The order of the formats on the clipboard determines whether an object is a linked object or an embedded object. OLE server applications also place descriptions of the data formats on the clipboard before they place the data on the clipboard. The order of the descriptions describes the fidelity of the data formats, with the best fidelity first and the worst fidelity last.

The ObjectLink and OwnerLink formats are identical; however, their contents are not necessarily identical. The format for ObjectLink and OwnerLink is a null-terminated class name string, a null-terminated document name string, and an item name string with two terminating null characters. The OwnerLink format identifies the owner of an object, and the ObjectLink format identifies the source of data for an object.

Native data is usually meaningful only to a particular server application. Native data, to a server application, defines an object in a context that the server application understands. It is not relevant that client applications understand native data. Presentation formats, on the other hand, are formats that many Windows applications understand. Examples of presentation formats are CF_BITMAP and CF_METAFILEPICT. These formats may or may not be supported by all OLE client applications. Native data can also be presentation data. For example, if an application's purpose is to manipulate bitmaps, its native data format can be CF_BITMAP. In this instance, the application's presentation format can also be CF_BITMAP.

The order of the clipboard's contents for embedded objects is native, OwnerLink, presentation, and ObjectLink. The presentation format is optional. ObjectLink format applies to servers that support links. The clipboard contents order for linked objects is OwnerLink, presentation or native, and ObjectLink. The presentation and native formats are optional.

> **Note:** A native format cannot appear on the clipboard more than once. For example, if a native format and a presentation format are the same, they cannot both be placed on the clipboard.

The behavior of an OLE client application depends on the action of the user. For instance, if a user selects the **P**aste menu item, the client application queries the clipboard for the first compatible format for the destination of the object. The first format found is always the highest fidelity the client application can use, because the server application places the formats on the clipboard in the order of their fidelity. When the client application finds a suitable clipboard format, the program decides whether to make the object an embedded object or just part of the document.

If the client application finds a suitable clipboard format prior to the native format, the format can become part of the document. This makes sense because a user may want to use the clipboard inside an application, between two instances of the same application, or between two applications that are similar in format. It would not be beneficial, for instance, if text (an object) created in the Write applet was an embedded object in Microsoft Word. Both applications are word processors, and both have the capability to edit text objects.

If a client application does not find a suitable clipboard format prior to the native format, the object becomes embedded. To test this, use the Paintbrush and Write applets. You can see the formats copied to the clipboard through the **D**isplay menu item in the Clipboard Viewer.

OLE Applications

OLE applications communicate through the use of three dynamic-link libraries: OLECLI.DLL, OLESVR.DLL, and SHELL.DLL. As mentioned before, the SHELL.DLL provides the registration API, thus enabling applications to communicate with the registration database. The SHELL.DLL also contains the drag and drop API. It is a good idea to include drag and drop functionality in any application that uses files, because many applications will be using drag and drop, and users will come to expect it. (Besides, drag and drop functionality is very easy to implement.) The OLECLI.DLL is the OLE client library. The OLESVR.DLL is the server library. OLESVR.DLL and OLECLI.DLL provide the API for linking and embedding.

The OLE server and client libraries communicate with each other through DDE messages. The typical path of communication for an OLE function includes the call of the function, DDE messages between OLE libraries, and disseminating information to the client and server applications. Client applications use callback functions and *methods* to receive information from the OLE client library. Server applications use *methods* to receive information from the OLE server library.

Methods is the term Microsoft uses for callback functions contained in OLE structures. The term *method* is taken from its use in C++. Although C++ methods and OLE methods are not exactly the same, the term does differentiate between normal callback functions and those in OLE structures.

The OLE libraries require Windows to run in protected mode. The OLE libraries will work with Windows 3.0; however, you cannot run Windows 3.0 in real mode while running an OLE application. The OLE libraries use message-based DDE to perform communications. The reason they do not use DDEML is that OLE and DDEML were developed independently. Future changes to OLE may include the use of DDEML or some other method of interprocess communications.

The three classifications of OLE applications are clients, servers, and object handlers. Servers provide objects for linking and embedding, whereas clients use objects for linking and embedding. Object handlers are dynamic-link libraries that facilitate communication between client applications and server applications.

249

Client Applications

OLE client applications use the OLE library OLECLI.DLL. There are 55 OLE functions in the OLECLI.DLL that client applications can use. It may appear to be a large task to incorporate so many new functions into an application; however, you can implement OLE functionality into an existing application without a great amount of reworking. This is especially true if the application is modular.

When you write an OLE client application, the OLE API is implemented in three major areas. The first area is in *document management*. Most of the document-managed functions are implemented under the **F**ile menu option. When a client application creates a new document or opens an existing document, the client application must register the document with the OLE client library. Any time the document changes status, the client application must inform the OLE client of the change. Actions that cause a change in status include saving the document, renaming the document, and closing the document. Thus, under the **F**ile menu, the **N**ew, **O**pen, **S**ave, Save **A**s, and **C**lose menu items have corresponding calls to the OLE client API.

The second area for OLE API implementation is *object management*. Whenever the client application embeds, links, deletes, or changes the status of an object, there are corresponding calls to the OLE API. These actions take place under the **E**dit menu and the **F**ile menu. Although document management occurs under the **F**ile menu, some actions on files involve OLE objects. When you select **O**pen from the **F**ile menu, the application reads the file. If the file contains OLE objects, the OLE client library needs to know about the objects as well as the document. The same is true with the **F**ile **C**lose menu item. When you close a file, the OLE client library does not need to track the objects in the file; thus the program should release the objects.

The third area in which the OLE API is used is in the implementation of the OLE structures and methods. There are four data structures of interest in an OLE client application: OLECLIENT, OLECLIENTVTBL, OLESTREAM, and OLESTREAMVTBL. The OLECLIENT structure contains a pointer to an OLECLIENTVTBL structure. The OLECLIENTVTBL structure contains a pointer to an OLE client notification procedure, generally named CallBack() or ClientCallBack(). The OLESTREAM structure contains a pointer to an OLESTREAMVTBL structure. The OLESTREAMVTBL structure contains two members that contain far pointers to the stream methods: Get() and Put(). The callback functions, or methods, are a critical part of an OLE application. They receive notifications and status information from the OLE libraries.

Client applications should allocate and initialize the `OLECLIENT` and `OLESTREAM` structures when the client application starts. At the same time, the client application needs to register the clipboard formats that it requires to operate. To engage in OLE, the client application will have to call `RegisterClipboardFormat()` for the native, OwnerLink, and ObjectLink formats. Additionally, the client application can register any other clipboard formats it supports.

Client User Interface

The user interface defines the methods for creating linked and embedded objects for the user. OLE applications require changes to the **E**dit menu to implement linking and embedding. The **C**opy and C**u**t menu items remain the same. The **P**aste menu item copies an object from the clipboard to a document. From the previous discussion about clipboard formats, you know that when a client application queries the clipboard formats for an object and finds a format before it encounters the native format, an embedded object is not created. The object becomes part of the document. If this previous case is not true, the object is embedded.

The **P**aste menu item should be active only when the clipboard contains an object. The C**u**t and **C**opy menu items are active only when an object is selected in the client application. In addition to the C**u**t, **C**opy, and **P**aste menu items, there are five menu items for OLE client applications that are not found in non-OLE applications—Paste **L**ink, *classname* **O**bject, Lin**k**s, **I**nsert Object, and Paste Sp**e**cial.

The Paste **L**ink menu item is active only when the clipboard contains an object that can be linked. This occurs when the first format in the clipboard is OwnerLink. The Paste **L**ink menu item inserts a link between the document and the object's file. Linked objects require that a file exists for the object. In other words, you cannot create a linked object if you do not save the object to a file from the OLE server application.

Another **P**aste menu item, Paste Special, is optional in OLE client applications. Paste Special takes an object in the clipboard and either embeds or links the object to a document. The unique part of the Paste Special command is that the data format is chosen by the user. An example of Paste Special can be found in Microsoft Word for Windows. If you create an object in Paintbrush, save it to a file, and then copy the object to the clipboard, Paste Special in Word would enable you to link or embed the object. When Paste Special is selected, a dialog box displays a list of data formats. In this case, there are three formats:

a PC Paintbrush Picture Object, a Picture, and a Bitmap. If you choose PC Paintbrush Picture Object (native data format), you can paste the object to the document, thus creating an embedded object. If either the Picture or Bitmap data format is selected, you have a choice to create a link or to paste.

The *classname* **O**bject menu item, in which *classname* refers to the type of object, executes an object's verb. An object's verb is the type of action a user performs on an object, such as *edit* or *play*. When an object has more than one verb, the client application should display the verbs as menu items subordinate to the *classname* **O**bject menu item. The *classname* **O**bject menu item should be active only when an object is selected in the client document. The client application gets the classname and verbs from the registration database.

The **Li**nks menu item maintains established object links. This includes updating linked objects, removing links, and repairing broken links. The **Li**nks menu item should be active only when the user selects a linked object in the client document.

The **I**nsert Object menu item causes an OLE server application to create an embedded object. This menu item invokes a dialog box that has a list box that contains object names. The box does not list application names. The object names are associated with applications through the registration database.

Document Management

Document management for client applications occurs in response to user interaction with the **F**ile menu options. Because the **F**ile menu options often involve more than one file operation, it is easiest to explain document management in terms of basic functionality. For instance, when the user selects the **N**ew menu option from the **F**ile menu, the user can save and then close the existing document. Then the client application creates a new document. Thus, document management is best explained in terms of opening, closing, and saving documents.

Opening Documents

When a client application opens a document, it must register the document with the client library, OLECLI. The **OleRegisterClientDoc()** function does this registration. The client application obtains a handle to the document from the **OleRegisterClientDoc()** function it will have to use with OLE functions.

After the client application registers the document, it can read the document. When the client application encounters an OLE object, the application should call **OleLoadFromStream()** if the client is to display the object on the screen. When the client application calls **OleLoadFromStream()**, the client library uses the OLECLIENT and OLESTREAM structures—which point to OLECLIENTVTBL and OLESTREAMVTBL structures—to call the client's callback function and the Get() method.

Closing Documents

When a client application closes a document, each object in the document must be released from the server. The client application calls the **OleRelease()** function to do this. After the client application releases the objects, it must inform the client library of the document's current status. If the client application closes the document without saving—in effect reverting to the original document—the client application should call **OleRevertClientDoc()**. If the client application saves the document before closing, the application should call **OleSavedClientDoc()**. When the client application receives notification that all the objects have been released, the client application should call **OleRevokeClientDoc()**.

The **OleRelease()** function returns OLE_OK if the client library immediately releases an object. If **OleRelease()** returns OLE_WAIT_FOR_RELEASE, the client application has to wait for the client library to release the object. The client application receives notification through the ClientCallBack() function. The client application should use a counter to keep track of the number of objects in a document. As the client library releases each object, the client application can decrement the counter. Thus, when the counter reaches zero, the client application can call **OleRevokeClientDoc()**.

Saving Documents

When a client application saves a document, it must save the data for the document and the data for each object in the document. The **OleSaveToStream()** function provides the means to save objects. The client application passes a pointer to the object and to the OLESTREAM structure when it calls the **OleSaveToStream()** function. The client library uses the OLESTREAM structure, which points to the OLESTREAMVTBL structure, to call the Put() method.

After the client application saves all the objects, the client application calls **OleSavedClientDoc()**. If a document is renamed during a save operation, such as with the Save **As** option from the **F**ile menu, the client application should call **OleRenameClientDoc()** before it saves the document and the

objects. If the save is not successful—as when there isn't enough disk space—the client application has to call **OleRenameClientDoc()** a second time to revert to the old document name.

Object Management

You have already encountered some object-management processes in the document management section of this chapter. The seven key areas in object management are closing, activating, drawing, creating, deleting, maintaining the clipboard, and maintaining links.

Activating Objects

Activating an object is analogous to opening an object. When users select an object by double-clicking or through the *classname* **O**bject menu item, they ask the client application to open or activate the object. The **OleActivate()** function requests the client library to start the server application of the object class and for the specified verb. If the verb is Edit, the server application will more than likely appear in a window to enable the user to update the object. The client application can specify whether the server is displayed.

The client application should ensure that it is safe to activate an object before activating it. If the object is busy due to another operation, the client application should not attempt to activate the object. Additionally, the client application should not enable the user to activate an object while the object is already activated. The **OleQueryReleaseStatus()** function indicates whether an object is busy. It returns OLE_BUSY if an object is busy, and OLE_OK if the object is not busy. The **OleQueryOpen()** function indicates whether an object is currently activated.

Closing Objects

When the client application needs to close an activated object, it can call the **OleClose()** function. The need to do this can occur when a user has left an object open but wants to terminate the application or to save a client document.

Drawing Objects

Drawing objects is not as difficult as you might think. When the client application loads an object, it should create a window for the object and call the **OleDraw()** function. The **OleDraw()** function requires a handle to a device context and a pointer to a bounding rectangle. Because **OleDraw()** uses a device context, the client application can use **OleDraw()** to print objects as well as display objects on a monitor.

The client application typically uses the object's presentation data format to display an object. If the presentation data format is a metafile, the client application must expect notification messages sent by the client library to the client application's callback function. The client library sends OLE_QUERY_PAINT messages to the client callback function while it is drawing the object. If the client callback function returns FALSE, the client library stops drawing the object. Thus, the client application should return TRUE for OLE_QUERY_PAINT notification messages unless it wants to terminate the drawing of an object.

The OLE client library must be aware of changes to an object's environment. For instance, if the user changes the target device for an object, the client application should call **OleSetTargetDevice()**. Changing the target device can also change the size of the bounding rectangle for an object. The client application can retrieve the bounding rectangle for a target device by calling **OleQueryBounds()**. If the size of the bounding rectangle changes for an object, the client application should call **OleSetBounds()**. This does not apply to linked objects, because the size of linked objects is determined by the server document. If the client application calls **OleSetBounds()**, it should then call **OleUpdate()** followed by **OleDraw()**. The **OleUpdate()** function updates the presentation of an object.

Creating Objects

Table 5.1 shows the object-creation functions a client application can use.

Table 5.1. Object-creation functions.

Function	Purpose
OleClone()	Creates an exact copy of an object; however, the object is not connected to the server.
OleCopyFromLink()	Creates an embedded object from a copy of a linked object.
OleCreate()	Creates an embedded object by opening the server to perform the initial editing of the object.
OleCreateFromClip()	Creates an object from the clipboard.

continues

255

Table 5.1. continued

Function	Purpose
OleCreateFromFile()	Creates an object from a file.
OleCreateFromTemplate()	Creates an object using another object as a template.
OleCreateLinkFromClip()	Creates an object from the clipboard.
OleCreateLinkFromFile()	Creates an object from a file.

The **OleCreate()** function creates an embedded object. The client application calls **OleCreate()** when users select the Insert Object menu item. Selecting this item invokes the Insert Object dialog box (see Figure 5.1). The Insert Object dialog box contains a list box of OLE servers. The client application gets the list from the registration database. When the user selects a server and presses the OK button in the Insert Object dialog box, the client application should call **OleCreate()**.

Figure 5.1.
The Insert Object dialog box.

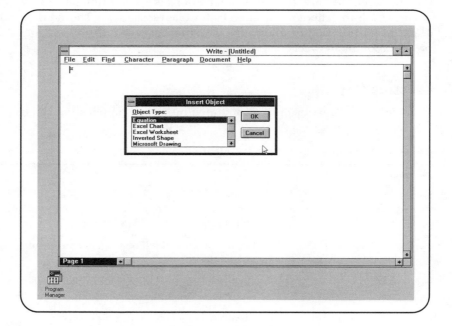

The `OleCreateLinkFromFile()` and `OleCreateFromFile()` functions are most often used when a client application supports the Create From File menu option. This enables the user to create an object from a file without showing the server application.

Deleting Objects

A client application can delete an object by calling the `OleDelete()` function. The client application does not need to close the object before deleting it because the `OleDelete()` function automatically closes the object. The `OleClone()` function is often used in conjunction with the Undo menu option. The result of `OleClone()` gives a client application a copy of an object that is not connected to the server application. Thus, if the user changes an object with a server application, a copy of the object is available to the client application if the client application calls `OleClone()` before the user activates and edits an object.

Maintaining the Clipboard

When the client application performs cut or paste clipboard functions, it should use the `OleCopyToClipboard()` function. If the client application performs a cut, it should then delete the object by calling the `OleDelete()` function.

The Paste and Paste Link menu items are one source of embedded and linked objects for client applications. The `OleQueryCreateFromClip()` and `OleQueryLinkFromClip()` functions allow a client application to enable or disable the Paste and Paste Link menu items. The `OleQueryCreateFromClip()` function determines whether the Paste menu item can be enabled, whereas the `OleQueryLinkFromClip()` determines whether the Paste Link menu item can be enabled.

If a user selects the Paste menu item, the client application should open the clipboard and call `OleCreateFromClip()`. If the user selects the Paste Link menu item, the client application should open the clipboard and call `OleCreateLinkFromClip()`.

Another menu option for client applications to have is Paste Special. The Paste Special menu item creates a dialog box that enumerates the data formats in the clipboard. The formats can be determined by calling `EnumClipBoardFormats()`. The Paste Special dialog box enables the user to select the data format of the object, thus determining whether the object is linked or embedded.

Maintaining Links

Link maintenance occurs when the user selects the Links dialog box via the Links menu item. The Links dialog box, which is shown in Figure 5.2, lists the linked objects in a document. The user can choose whether linking for an object should be automatic or manual. Additionally, the user can update a link, cancel a link, or repair a broken link.

Figure 5.2.
The Links
dialog box.

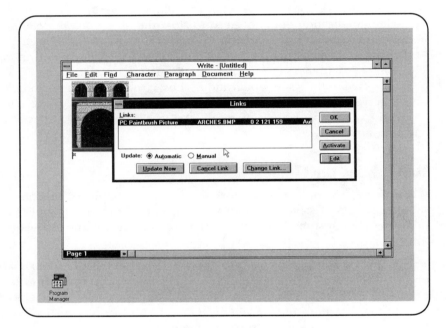

The client application can generate the list box information in one of two ways. First, the client application can store the information for each object in an array of structures. Second, the client application can call **OleGetData()** to get the object's ObjectLink data. The client application can get the descriptive name for the object through the registration database.

The type of link (either automatic or manual) is controlled by radio buttons. The client application should set these buttons by calling **OleGetLinkUpdateOptions()**. If the user changes the link update options, then the client application should update the options by calling **OleSetLinkUpdateOptions()**.

When the user pushes the **U**pdate Now button, the client application can call the **OleUpdate()** function to update the link. To cancel a link, the client application can call **OleObjectConvert()**. The Change Link... button attempts to repair broken links. The client application can retrieve link information with the **OleGetData()** function by specifying the OwnerLink format. The user can edit the link information—and the client application can store the new information into the object—by calling the **OleSetData()** function with the ObjectLink format. The client application calls **OleObjectConvert()** in response to a user pressing the Cancel Link button.

Server Applications

The structure of an OLE server application is somewhat different from an OLE client application. Applications that generate objects easily can be converted to server applications. Server applications require a few additional components that a non-OLE application does not require. The first component is in the initialization process of the server. The server must register itself with the server library: OLESRV.DLL.

Additionally, the server should register its clipboard formats. The clipboard formats should include native, OwnerLink, and ObjectLink, as well as any other supported clipboard formats. The server must also have the capability to parse the command line when the OLE server library starts the server for a particular file, as well as the capability to check an /Embedding command.

A server application must maintain its **F**ile menu according to the way the OLE server library starts the server application. This includes changing the **F**ile Save **A**s menu item to **F**ile **U**pdate. Additionally, the server application may want to change the **F**ile E**x**it menu item to E**x**it and Return to *Client application name*.

OLE server applications have six structures of interest: OLEOBJECT, OLEOBJECTVTBL, OLESERVER, OLESERVERVTBL, OLESERVERDOC, and OLESERVERDOCVTBL. The VTBL structures contain far pointers to methods. These methods handle requests from the OLESVR.DLL. The corresponding OLE structures— OLEOBJECT, OLESERVER, and OLESERVERDOC—contain pointers to the VTBL structures. The VTBL structures contain the methods listed in Table 5.2.

Table 5.2. VTBL structures and methods.

OLESERVERVTBL	OLESERVERDOCVTBL	OLEOBJECTVTBL
Create()	Close()	DoVerb()
CreateFromTemplate()	GetObject()	EnumFormats()

continues

Table 5.2. continued

OLESERVERVTBL	OLESERVERDOCVTBL	OLEOBJECTVTBL
Edit()	Execute()	GetData()
Execute()	Release()	QueryProtocol()
Exit()	Save()	Release()
Open()	SetColorScheme()	SetBounds()
Release()	SetHostNames()	SetColorScheme()
		SetData()
		SetTargetDevice()
		Show()

The three sets of structures correspond to components in an OLE server application. The OLESERVER structure contains information about the server application as a whole, whereas the OLESERVERDOC structure contains information about documents within a server application. The OLEOBJECT structure contains information about objects within documents.

Server User Interface

An OLE server requires changes to menu items under the **F**ile menu. When the server edits an embedded object, the **S**ave menu item changes to **U**pdate. Because there isn't a link with an embedded object, the changes must be reflected in the client application document. The **U**pdate menu item reflects the changes. If the server edits a linked object, the changes made within the server application automatically appear in the client document due to the link. The server application does not have an **U**pdate menu item in this case.

The E**x**it menu item can also change in an OLE server application; however, it is optional. If the server edits an embedded object, it can replace the E**x**it menu item with E**x**it and Return to *Docname*. *Docname* is the name of the client application document.

Server Management

Server applications are responsible for keeping the server library informed of their application state. When a server application starts, it should register with the server library. The **OleRegisterServer()** function informs the server library of the class name, instance, and the number of support instances of a server. The server application must perform a reverse process when terminating. The **OleRevokeServer()** function notifies the server library that the server wants to terminate any communications with client applications.

A server can block requests from the server library with the **OleBlockServer()** function. This function queues requests until the server calls the **OleUnblockServer()** function. Calling **OleBlockServer()** does not prohibit the server from processing prior requests from client applications.

Server Document Management

When a server application changes the status of a server document, it must inform the server library of the changes. These changes can occur when the server creates, saves, renames, or closes a document. The **OleRegisterServerDoc()** function registers a document with the server library. The server calls **OleRegisterServerDoc()** when a new document is created or an existing document is opened.

The **OleSavedServerDoc()** function notifies the server library that a document has been saved. If a server application renames a document, **OleRenameServerDoc()** should be called. When a server application wants to inform the server library that a document is no longer available, the server should call **OleRevokeServerDoc()**. This generally occurs when a document is closed.

Server Object Management

Server applications need to inform the server library when an object is no longer available. The **OleRevokeObject()** function informs the server library that an object is no longer available. The most common reason an object becomes unavailable is that the server application has deleted the object.

Version Control

Version control is an important topic for server applications. Server applications define the objects they produce. Over several releases of a software product, native format for an object can change to include additional features. If this occurs, you will probably want your server application to be able to handle older versions of objects. Users may want to use previous versions of objects, and perhaps even save new objects in old versions to retain compatibility with other systems in their organization.

Keep in mind that users can distribute compound documents to machines that do not contain the most recent version of software. They may have to use older versions of objects in compound documents until all people in an organization have upgraded their software. This is great for software developers. If users frequently distribute compound documents, more people in an organization will become dependent on software upgrades. The more distribution, the more upgrades!

During an upgrade period, you will want to keep users happy. The user of version control enables a new version of a server to be installed and to exist with a previous version of a server. The server program will have to update the registration database to enable two servers to exist, or one server to handle two object types.

Summary

OLE enables users to move from an application-centered view of computing to a document-centered view of computing. OLE applications can specialize in performing one task and be seamlessly integrated with other OLE applications. This enables the user to focus on the task at hand rather than the applications that complete the task. Because the OLE protocol works independently of data formats, applications can use data formats in the future that do not exist today.

Linked objects can be updated dynamically as other objects change in context to other events on the system. Documents that contain embedded objects can be printed without the embedded object's application, thus enabling easy distribution of complex documents based on a single application. The use of linked objects creates smaller files, because the linked object can be stored in its own file and shared among multiple documents.

OLE Server
Applications

This chapter provides the details of programming an OLE server application. OLE programs take a considerable amount of code; however, much of the code is homogeneous. Separating OLE code from application code is fairly easy. Given this, adding OLE to existing applications should be fairly easy. The difficult part of OLE programming is the testing and debugging phase. Because implementing OLE takes much code, it is difficult to find places to test during development. It is even more difficult to divide the example program into units for testing. Doing so would require hundreds of pages of program listings. Thus, I present the example OLE server application by modules and explain the functionality of each module. Figure 6.1 shows the example OLE server application whose code is presented in this chapter. This chapter covers the following topics:

- Polygon window processing

- Document methods and management

- Object methods and management

- Dialog box procedures

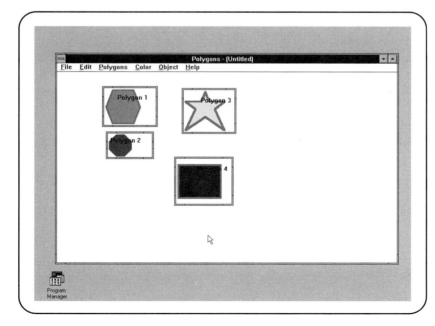

Figure 6.1.
An example
OLE server
application.

POLY.EXE: An OLE Server Application

The example OLE server application generates colored polygons; thus I call it POLY. The *Polygons* application does not do much more in terms of non-OLE functionality. The example program has the modules listed in Table 6.1.

Table 6.1. The modules of the *Polygons* program.

Module	Description
poly.h	Global header file
dialogs.h	Defines for dialog boxes
resource.h	Defines for resources
winmain.c	WinMain function
init.c	Initialization and termination code
poly.c	Main window procedure
object.c	Callback procedure for polygon windows
vtserver.c	Server methods
vtdoc.c	Document methods
docmgt.c	Document-management functions
vtobject.c	Object methods
objmgt.c	Object-management functions
file.c	File I/O and common dialogs
menu.c	Menu-control functions
misc.c	Miscellaneous functions
dialogs.c	Dialog box callbacks
poly.rc	Resource definition file
poly.def	Module definition file
poly.dlg	Dialog box definitions

Module	Description
poly.reg	Registration database merge file
POLY	Makefile

Example Program Header Files

The poly.h module contains the typical typedefs, defines, global variables, and function prototypes. The SERVER, DOC, and POLYGON structures in poly.h drive the OLE server application. There is a loose hierarchy among these structures. In general terms, they relate to server, document, and object layers in the application. One other structure, NATIVE, defines the native data for a polygon.

The SERVER structure contains an OLESERVER structure and an LHSERVER member, lhsrvr. The lhsrvr member is the handle to the server. The OLE libraries use this handle during the registration process. The OLESERVER structure contains an LPOLESERVERVTBL member that points to server methods contained in an OLESERVERVTBL structure. You can implement the OLESERVER structure and lhsrvr member as individual entities. They are in the same structure in this application because they relate to the server level of the application.

> **Note:** The OLE libraries access pointers to methods in the OLESERVERVTBL structure. You can use any structure you want to organize server information in your application; however, the OLE libraries will use an offset to use the pointers to methods. Thus, the OLESERVER structure must be the first member in your server structure.

The DOC structure has a layout similar to the SERVER structure. Its first member is oledoc, which is an OLESERVERDOC structure. The oledoc member contains a member of type LPOLESERVERDOCVTBL that points to an OLESERVERDOCVTBL structure. The OLESERVERDOCVTBL structure contains members that point to document methods. The OLE libraries require the first member to be of type OLESERVERDOC. The lhdoc member is a handle to the document. The other members—doctype, aName, hpal, and rgfObjNums—define the document.

The POLYGON structure defines the object-level data for the application. Similar to the SERVER and DOC structures, the POLYGON structure contains a structure that contains a pointer to a structure, which contains pointers to methods. This structure is OLEOBJECT. The OLEOBJECT structure contains a pointer of type LPOLEOBJECTVTBL that points to a structure of type OLEOBJECTVTBL. The hPolygon member of the POLYGON structure is a handle to a polygon object. The other members provide information about the polygon object, with the majority of information in a structure of type NATIVE.

The pointers to methods in the OLESERVERVTBL, OLESERVERDOCVTBL, and OLEOBJECTVTBL structures are pointers to callback functions that the OLE library OLESRV.DLL calls to control exchanges of OLE objects. Table 6.2 contains OLE server application methods.

Table 6.2. OLE server application methods.

Server Method	Document Method	Object Method
Create	Close	DoVerb
CreateFromTemplate	GetObject	EnumFormats
Edit	Execute	GetData
Execute	Release	QueryProtocol
Exit	Save	Release
Open	SetColorScheme	SetBounds
Release	SetHostNames	SetColorScheme
		SetData
		SetTargetDevice
		Show

Listing 6.1. The poly.h header file.

```
#define SERVERONLY
#include "windows.h"
#include "ole.h"
#include "commdlg.h"
#include "dialogs.h"
#include "resource.h"
```

```
#ifndef MAIN
#define EXTERN extern
#else
#define EXTERN
#endif


#define SZCLASSNAME       40
#define SZWINDOWTITLE     40
#define SZMESSAGE         128
#define OBJECT_WIDTH      120
#define OBJECT_HEIGHT     60
#define FILENAMEMAXLEN    256
#define VERSION           1
#define MAXCOLORS         9
#define RED               0x000000ffl
#define GREEN             0x0000ff00l
#define BLUE              0x00ff0000l
#define WHITE             0x00ffffffl
#define GRAY              0x00808080l
#define CYAN              0x00ffff00l
#define MAGENTA           0x00ff00ffl
#define YELLOW            0x0000ffffl
#define DOCNEW            0
#define DOCFROMFILE       1
#define DOCEMBEDDED       2
#define PLAY              OLEVERB_PRIMARY
#define EDIT              OLEVERB_PRIMARY+1
#define MAXOBJECTS        30
#define MAXCLIENTS        30
#define DC_SCREEN         0
#define DC_BITMAP         1
#define DC_METAFILE       2

typedef HANDLE HPOLYGON;

typedef struct
    {
    OLESERVER     olesrvr;
    LHSERVER      lhsrvr;
    } SERVER;
```

continues

Listing 6.1. continued

```
typedef struct
    {
    OLESERVERDOC oledoc;
    LHSERVERDOC  lhdoc;
    WORD         doctype;
    ATOM         aName;
    HPALETTE     hpal;
    BYTE         rgfObjNums[MAXOBJECTS+1];
    } DOC, *DOCPTR, FAR *LPDOC;

typedef struct
    {
    int  idmPoly;
    int  idmColor;
    int  nWidth;
    int  nHeight;
    int  nX;
    int  nY;
    int  nHiMetricWidth;
    int  nHiMetricHeight;
    int  version;
    char szName[32];
    } NATIVE, FAR *LPNATIVE;

typedef struct
    {
    OLEOBJECT   oleobject;
    HPOLYGON    hPolygon;
    LPOLECLIENT lpoleclient[MAXCLIENTS];
    HWND        hwnd;
    ATOM        aName;
    HPALETTE    hpal;
    NATIVE      native;
    } POLYGON, FAR *LPPOLYGON;

typedef LPVOID (CALLBACK *LPVOIDPROC)(LPOLEOBJECT, LPSTR);

/* Global variable declarations. */
EXTERN HINSTANCE        hInst;
EXTERN HWND             hWnd;
```

```
EXTERN SERVER          server;
EXTERN DOC             doc;
EXTERN HANDLE          hAccel;
EXTERN BOOL            fDocChanged;
EXTERN BOOL            fEmbedding;
EXTERN BOOL            fRevokeSrvrOnSrvrRelease;
EXTERN BOOL            fWaitingForDocRelease;
EXTERN BOOL            fWaitingForSrvrRelease;
EXTERN char            szClient[FILENAMEMAXLEN];
EXTERN HBRUSH          hbrColor[MAXCOLORS];
EXTERN int             version;
EXTERN OLECLIPFORMAT   cfObjectLink;
EXTERN OLECLIPFORMAT   cfOwnerLink;
EXTERN OLECLIPFORMAT   cfNative;
EXTERN OLESERVERDOCVTBL vtDoc;
EXTERN OLEOBJECTVTBL   vtObject;
EXTERN OLESERVERVTBL   vtServer;

/* Global Functions--Prototypes */
/* dialogs.c */
BOOL PASCAL CreateDlgBox(HWND, LPCSTR, FARPROC);
LRESULT CALLBACK AboutDlgProc(HWND, WORD, WPARAM, LPARAM);
LRESULT CALLBACK FailedUpdateDlgProc(HWND, WORD, WPARAM, LPARAM);

/* doc.c */
BOOL CreateUntitledDoc(VOID);
BOOL PASCAL CreateTitledDoc(LONG, LPSTR);
VOID DestroyDoc(VOID);
OLESTATUS RevokeDoc(VOID);

/* docmgt.c */
BOOL PASCAL AssociateClient(LPOLECLIENT, LPPOLYGON);
WORD PASCAL SaveChanges(BOOL *pfUpdateLater);
VOID PASCAL SendDocMessage(WORD);

/* file.c */
BOOL PASCAL CreateDocFromTemplate(LPSTR, LHSERVERDOC);
BOOL PASCAL CreateDocFromFile(LPSTR, LHSERVERDOC);
BOOL CommonOpenFile(VOID);
BOOL CommonSaveFile(VOID);
BOOL CommonSaveAs(VOID);
```

continues

Listing 6.1. continued

```c
/* init.c */
BOOL PASCAL InitApplication(HINSTANCE);
BOOL PASCAL InitInstance(HINSTANCE, int);
BOOL PASCAL ProcessCmdLine(LPSTR, int, HWND);
VOID CleanUp(VOID);
VOID PASCAL Terminate(BOOL);

/* menu.c */
VOID PASCAL EnableDisableMenus(WORD);
VOID PASCAL UpdateMenu(BOOL);

/* misc.c */
VOID PASCAL SetTitle(LPSTR, BOOL);
LPSTR PASCAL Abbrev(LPSTR);
OLESTATUS RevokeServer(VOID);
VOID PASCAL MsgBox(HWND, WORD, WORD);
VOID PASCAL DeviceToHiMetric(HWND, LPPOINT);
VOID PASCAL HiMetricToDevice(HWND, LPPOINT);
VOID PASCAL SetHiMetricFields(LPPOLYGON);
VOID PASCAL Wait(BOOL *);

/* object.c */
LRESULT CALLBACK ObjectWndProc(HWND, WORD, WPARAM, LPARAM);

/* objmgt.c */
LPPOLYGON CreateNewPolygon(BOOL);
VOID PASCAL DestroyPolygon(HWND);
VOID PASCAL DrawPolygon(HDC, LPPOLYGON, RECT, int);
HBITMAP PASCAL GetBitmap(LPPOLYGON);
HANDLE PASCAL GetLink(LPPOLYGON);
HANDLE PASCAL GetMetafilePict(LPPOLYGON);
HANDLE PASCAL GetNative(LPPOLYGON);
int PASCAL GetPolygonNumber(LPPOLYGON);
HANDLE PASCAL GetText(LPPOLYGON);
VOID PASCAL PaintPolygon(HWND);
VOID RevokePolygon(VOID);
VOID PASCAL SendPolygonMessage(LPPOLYGON, WORD);
VOID PASCAL SizePolygon(HWND, RECT, BOOL);
BOOL PASCAL CreatePolygonWindow(LPPOLYGON);
```

```
/* poly.c */
LRESULT CALLBACK MainWndProc(HWND, WORD, WPARAM, LPARAM);


/* vtdoc.c */
OLESTATUS CALLBACK DocClose(LPOLESERVERDOC);
OLESTATUS CALLBACK DocExecute(LPOLESERVERDOC, HANDLE);
OLESTATUS CALLBACK DocGetObject(LPOLESERVERDOC, LPSTR,
                              LPOLEOBJECT FAR *, LPOLECLIENT);
OLESTATUS CALLBACK DocRelease(LPOLESERVERDOC);
OLESTATUS CALLBACK DocSave(LPOLESERVERDOC);
OLESTATUS CALLBACK DocSetColorScheme(LPOLESERVERDOC,
                                  LPLOGPALETTE);
OLESTATUS CALLBACK DocSetDocDimensions(LPOLESERVERDOC, LPRECT);
OLESTATUS CALLBACK DocSetHostNames(LPOLESERVERDOC, LPSTR, LPSTR);


/* vtobject.c */
OLESTATUS CALLBACK ObjectDoVerb(LPOLEOBJECT, WORD, BOOL, BOOL);
OLESTATUS CALLBACK ObjectGetData(LPOLEOBJECT, OLECLIPFORMAT,
                              LPHANDLE);
LPVOID CALLBACK ObjectQueryProtocol(LPOLEOBJECT, LPSTR);
OLESTATUS CALLBACK ObjectRelease(LPOLEOBJECT);
OLESTATUS CALLBACK ObjectSetBounds(LPOLEOBJECT, LPRECT);
OLESTATUS CALLBACK ObjectSetColorScheme(LPOLEOBJECT, LPLOGPALETTE);
OLESTATUS CALLBACK ObjectSetData(LPOLEOBJECT, OLECLIPFORMAT,
                              HANDLE);
OLESTATUS CALLBACK ObjectSetTargetDevice(LPOLEOBJECT, HANDLE);
OLESTATUS CALLBACK ObjectShow(LPOLEOBJECT, BOOL);
OLECLIPFORMAT CALLBACK ObjectEnumFormats(LPOLEOBJECT,
                                      OLECLIPFORMAT);


/* vtserver.c */
OLESTATUS CALLBACK ServerCreate(LPOLESERVER, LHSERVERDOC,
    LPSTR, LPSTR, LPOLESERVERDOC FAR *);
OLESTATUS CALLBACK ServerCreateFromTemplate(LPOLESERVER,
    LHSERVERDOC, LPSTR, LPSTR, LPSTR, LPOLESERVERDOC FAR *);
OLESTATUS CALLBACK ServerEdit(LPOLESERVER, LHSERVERDOC,
    LPSTR, LPSTR, LPOLESERVERDOC FAR * );
OLESTATUS CALLBACK ServerExecute(LPOLESERVER, HANDLE);
OLESTATUS CALLBACK ServerExit(LPOLESERVER);
OLESTATUS CALLBACK ServerOpen(LPOLESERVER, LHSERVERDOC,
                            LPSTR, LPOLESERVERDOC FAR *);
OLESTATUS CALLBACK ServerRelease(LPOLESERVER);
```

continues

Listing 6.1. continued

```
/* winmain.c */
int PASCAL WinMain(HINSTANCE, HINSTANCE, LPSTR, int);
```

Listing 6.2. The resource.h header file.

```
#define IDM_MENU          1
#define IDA_ACC           1

#define IDM_NEW           100
#define IDM_OPEN          101
#define IDM_SAVE          102
#define IDM_SAVEAS        103
#define IDM_EXIT          104
#define IDM_UPDATE        105

#define IDM_CUT           200
#define IDM_COPY          201
#define IDM_DELETE        202

#define IDM_TRIANGLE      300
#define IDM_RECTANGLE     301
#define IDM_PENTAGON      302
#define IDM_HEXAGON       303
#define IDM_HEPTAGON      304
#define IDM_OCTAGON       305
#define IDM_STAR          306

#define IDM_RED           400
#define IDM_GREEN         401
#define IDM_BLUE          402
#define IDM_WHITE         403
#define IDM_GRAY          404
#define IDM_CYAN          405
#define IDM_MAGENTA       406
#define IDM_YELLOW        407

#define IDM_NEWOBJ        500
#define IDM_NEXTOBJ       501
```

```
#define IDM_ABOUT            600

#define IDS_MAINCLASSNAME      1
#define IDS_OBJCLASSNAME       2
#define IDS_WINDOWTITLE        3
#define IDS_SRVCLASSNAME       4
#define IDS_FILENOTFOUND       5
#define IDS_WRONGFORMAT        6
#define IDS_FILESAVEERROR      7
#define IDS_WAITFORREVOKE      8
#define IDS_SERIOUSERROR       9
```

Listing 6.3. The dialogs.h header file.

```
#define IDD_ABOUTBOX           100
#define IDD_FAILEDUPDATE       200
#define IDD_CONTINUEEDIT       201
#define IDD_UPDATEEXIT         202
#define IDD_TEXT               203
```

WinMain: **Application Initialization and Termination**

The `WinMain()` function is fairly standard. OLE server applications must have the ability to parse a command line because the OLE libraries start server applications with command-line options. The command-line options include a flag—-Embedding or /Embedding—and a filename. The `ProcessCmdLine()` function and the other initialization functions are in the init.c source file. Listing 6.4 is the winmain.c source file.

Listing 6.4. The winmain.c source file.

```
#define MAIN
#include "poly.h"
```

continues

Listing 6.4. continued

```
/**********************************************************************/
/* Function: WinMain                                                 */
/* Purpose: Main function for windows app. Initializes all           */
/*          instances of app, translates and dispatches messages.    */
/* Returns: Value of PostQuitMessage                                 */
/**********************************************************************/
int PASCAL WinMain(HINSTANCE hInstance, HINSTANCE hPrevInstance,
                   LPSTR lpCmdLine, int nCmdShow)
    {
    MSG msg;

    if(!hPrevInstance)
        if(!InitApplication(hInstance))
            return FALSE;

    if(!InitInstance(hInstance, nCmdShow))
        return FALSE;

    if(!ProcessCmdLine(lpCmdLine, nCmdShow, hWnd))
        {
        Terminate(FALSE);
        CleanUp();
        return FALSE;
        }

    while(GetMessage(&msg, 0, 0, 0))
        {
        if(!TranslateAccelerator(hWnd, hAccel, &msg))
            {
            TranslateMessage(&msg);
            DispatchMessage(&msg);
            }
        }

    CleanUp();

    return msg.wParam;
    }
```

The initialization process includes window class registration, method table initialization, server registration, and clipboard registration. The `InitInstance()` function performs the OLE-related initialization tasks by calling the `InitializeProcedureTables()` and `InitServer()` functions and by registering the clipboard formats.

The `InitializeProcedureTables()` function calls **`MakeProcInstance()`** for each method in the `OLESERVERVTBL`, `OLESERVERDOCVTBL`, and `OLEOBJECTVTBL` structures.

> **Note:** Additional methods are available in the `OLEOBJECTVTBL` structure that are not used in this application. Refer to the ole.h header file for a complete list of methods. The methods not used are typically used in object-handler dynamic-link libraries. The `#define SERVERONLY` statement in poly.h limits the size of the `OLEOBJECTVTBL` structure. An object handler may require additional methods, and thus the application would not define `SERVERONLY`.

The clipboard registration occurs in `InitInstance()`. OLE server applications that provide full linking and embedding must register the ObjectLink and OwnerLink clipboard formats. The Native clipboard format is a stream of bytes that the server application uses to communicate with an object handler library. (Chapter 8 develops an object handler for the polygon application.) The following is the clipboard registration code:

```
cfObjectLink = RegisterClipboardFormat("ObjectLink");
cfOwnerLink  = RegisterClipboardFormat("OwnerLink");
cfNative     = RegisterClipboardFormat("Native");
```

The `InitServer()` function registers the server with the OLE libraries. This includes a call to the **`OleRegisterServer()`** function. The **`OleRegisterServer()`** function has the following prototype:

```
OLESTATUS OleRegisterServer(LPSTR lpszClass,
    LPOLESERVER lpsrvr, LHSERVER FAR   * lplhserver,
    HANDLE hInst, OLE_SERVER_USE srvruse)
```

The `lpszClass` parameter is a pointer to the server class, which is `"Polygons"` for the example application. The `lpsrvr` parameter is a pointer to the `OLESERVER` structure. The example program uses the variable of type `SERVER`, which is called `Server`, for this parameter. The `OLESERVER` structure is in the application-defined `SERVER` structure. The third parameter is a pointer to the server handle, which is the `lhserver` member in the `SERVER` structure. The

hInst parameter is the application instance. The last parameter, srvuse, tells the OLE libraries that this is a single- or multiple-instance server. *Polygons* is a multiple-instance server; thus *Polygons* calls **OleRegisterServer()** with a value of OLE_SERVER_MULTI. Single-instance servers pass a value of OLE_SERVER_SINGLE.

Applications that support multiple classes would have to call **OleRegisterServer()** for each class. Each class would have OLESERVER structure. For instance, if the example application had two classes—for instance, polygons and lines—the application would make two calls to **OleRegisterServer()** with two different OLESERVER structures. The server structures could be named LINESERVER and POLYSERVER for clarity.

In addition to the initialization code in init.c, there is application clean-up code. Two functions provide these services: CleanUp() and Terminate(). CleanUp() simply frees the method instances and deletes the brushes used to fill the polygons. Terminate() ensures that the document is closed. When an application revokes a server, it informs the OLE libraries that it closed the registered documents. (Documents are registered in the same manner that servers are registered.) The function RevokeServer() calls **OleRevokeServer()**. **OleRevokeServer()** returns OLE_OK or OLE_WAIT_FOR_RELEASE. If **OleRevokeServer()** returns OLE_WAIT_FOR_RELEASE, the server must wait for the OLESRV library to call the ServerRelease() method. This occurs when the server and client applications are still in the process of terminating communications. At this point, the server application should enter into a message loop to process any messages in the message queue. The Wait() function provides the message loop. Listing 6.5 is the init.c source file.

Listing 6.5. The init.c source file.

```c
#include "poly.h"

BOOL PASCAL CheckEmbedding(LPSTR*);
VOID InitializeProcedureTables(VOID);
BOOL PASCAL InitServer(HWND);
/******************************************************************/
/* Function: InitApplication                                     */
/* Purpose: Performs all initialization for first instance of    */
/*          app.                                                  */
/* Returns: TRUE if successful, FALSE if failure                 */
/******************************************************************/
BOOL PASCAL InitApplication(HINSTANCE hInstance)
    {
    WNDCLASS  wc;
```

```
        char szClassName[SZCLASSNAME];

        if(!LoadString(hInstance, IDS_MAINCLASSNAME,
           szClassName, sizeof szClassName))
           return FALSE;

        wc.style          = CS_HREDRAW | CS_VREDRAW;
        wc.lpfnWndProc    = MainWndProc;
        wc.cbClsExtra     = sizeof (LPSTR);
        wc.cbWndExtra     = 0;
        wc.hInstance      = hInstance;
        wc.hIcon          = LoadIcon(hInstance, IDI_APPLICATION);
        wc.hCursor        = LoadCursor(NULL, IDC_ARROW);
        wc.hbrBackground  = GetStockObject(WHITE_BRUSH);
        wc.lpszMenuName   = MAKEINTRESOURCE(IDM_MENU);
        wc.lpszClassName  = szClassName;

        if(!RegisterClass(&wc))
            return FALSE;

        if(!LoadString(hInstance, IDS_OBJCLASSNAME,
           szClassName, sizeof szClassName))
           return FALSE;
        wc.style          = CS_HREDRAW | CS_VREDRAW | CS_DBLCLKS;
        wc.lpfnWndProc    = ObjectWndProc;
        wc.hIcon          = NULL;
        wc.cbWndExtra     = sizeof (LPSTR);
        wc.lpszMenuName   = NULL;
        wc.hCursor        = LoadCursor(NULL, IDC_CROSS);
        wc.lpszClassName  = szClassName;

        if(!RegisterClass(&wc))
            return FALSE;

    return TRUE;
    }

/**********************************************************************/
/* Function: InitInstance                                           */
/* Purpose: Performs all initialization for all instances of app.   */
/* Returns: TRUE if successful, FALSE if failure                    */
/**********************************************************************/
```

continues

Listing 6.5. continued

```
BOOL PASCAL InitInstance(HINSTANCE hInstance, int nCmdShow)
    {
    char szClassName[SZCLASSNAME];
    char szWindowTitle[SZWINDOWTITLE];
    long rglColor[MAXCOLORS] =
        {RED, GREEN, BLUE, WHITE, GRAY, CYAN, MAGENTA, YELLOW};
    int i;

    hInst = hInstance;

    fDocChanged = FALSE;
    fWaitingForDocRelease = FALSE;
    fWaitingForSrvrRelease = FALSE;
    fRevokeSrvrOnSrvrRelease = TRUE;

    InitializeProcedureTables();

    for(i = 0; i < MAXCOLORS; i++)
        hbrColor[i] = CreateSolidBrush(rglColor[i]);

    cfObjectLink = RegisterClipboardFormat("ObjectLink");
    cfOwnerLink  = RegisterClipboardFormat("OwnerLink");
    cfNative     = RegisterClipboardFormat("Native");

    hAccel = LoadAccelerators(hInst, MAKEINTRESOURCE(IDA_ACC));

    if(!LoadString(hInst, IDS_MAINCLASSNAME,
       szClassName, sizeof szClassName))
       return FALSE;

    if(!LoadString(hInst, IDS_WINDOWTITLE,
       szWindowTitle, sizeof szWindowTitle))
       return FALSE;

    hWnd = CreateWindow(szClassName,
                        szWindowTitle,
                        WS_OVERLAPPEDWINDOW,
                        CW_USEDEFAULT,
                        CW_USEDEFAULT,
                        CW_USEDEFAULT,
```

```
                        CW_USEDEFAULT,
                        NULL,
                        NULL,
                        hInstance,
                        NULL);

    if(!hWnd)
        return FALSE;

    if(!InitServer(hWnd))
        return FALSE;

    szClient[0] = NULL;
    return TRUE;
    }


/*******************************************************************/
/* Function: InitializeProcedureTables                          */
/* Purpose: To create procedure instances of methods.           */
/*******************************************************************/
VOID InitializeProcedureTables(VOID)
    {
    vtServer.Create = MakeProcInstance(ServerCreate, hInst);
    vtServer.CreateFromTemplate =
        MakeProcInstance(ServerCreateFromTemplate, hInst);
    vtServer.Edit = MakeProcInstance(ServerEdit, hInst);
    vtServer.Execute = MakeProcInstance(ServerExecute, hInst);
    vtServer.Exit = MakeProcInstance(ServerExit, hInst);
    vtServer.Open = MakeProcInstance(ServerOpen, hInst);
    vtServer.Release = MakeProcInstance(ServerRelease, hInst);

    vtDoc.Close = MakeProcInstance(DocClose, hInst);
    vtDoc.GetObject = MakeProcInstance(DocGetObject, hInst);
    vtDoc.Execute = MakeProcInstance(DocExecute, hInst);
    vtDoc.Release = MakeProcInstance(DocRelease, hInst);
    vtDoc.Save = MakeProcInstance(DocSave, hInst);
    vtDoc.SetColorScheme = MakeProcInstance(DocSetColorScheme,
                                            hInst);
    vtDoc.SetDocDimensions = MakeProcInstance(DocSetDocDimensions,
                                              hInst);
```

continues

281

Listing 6.5. continued

```
        vtDoc.SetHostNames = MakeProcInstance(DocSetHostNames, hInst);

        vtObject.DoVerb = MakeProcInstance(ObjectDoVerb, hInst);
        vtObject.EnumFormats = MakeProcInstance(ObjectEnumFormats,
                                                hInst);
        vtObject.GetData = MakeProcInstance(ObjectGetData, hInst);
        vtObject.QueryProtocol =
            (LPVOIDPROC)MakeProcInstance((FARPROC)ObjectQueryProtocol,
                                         hInst);
        vtObject.Release = MakeProcInstance(ObjectRelease, hInst);
        vtObject.SetBounds = MakeProcInstance(ObjectSetBounds, hInst);
        vtObject.SetColorScheme =
            MakeProcInstance(ObjectSetColorScheme, hInst);
        vtObject.SetData = MakeProcInstance(ObjectSetData, hInst);
        vtObject.SetTargetDevice =
            MakeProcInstance(ObjectSetTargetDevice, hInst);
        vtObject.Show = MakeProcInstance(ObjectShow, hInst);
        }

/*******************************************************************/
/* Function: InitServer                                            */
/* Purpose: To register the server.                                */
/* Returns: TRUE if successful, FALSE if failure                   */
/*******************************************************************/
BOOL PASCAL InitServer(HWND hwnd)
    {
    char szClassName[SZCLASSNAME];

    server.olesrvr.lpvtbl = &vtServer;

    if(!LoadString(hInst, IDS_SRVCLASSNAME,
        &szClassName[0], sizeof szClassName))
        return FALSE;

    if(OLE_OK != OleRegisterServer(szClassName,
                 (LPOLESERVER) &server, &server.lhsrvr, hInst,
                 OLE_SERVER_MULTI))
        return FALSE;
```

```
    else
        return TRUE;
    }


/*******************************************************************/
/* Function: ProcessCmdLine                                        */
/* Purpose: To parse the command line.                             */
/* Returns: TRUE if successful, FALSE if failure                   */
/*******************************************************************/
BOOL PASCAL ProcessCmdLine(LPSTR lpszLine, int nCmdShow, HWND hWnd)
    {
    char szBuf[FILENAMEMAXLEN];
    BOOL bEmbed = FALSE;
    OFSTRUCT of;
    int i;

    if(!*lpszLine)
        {
        if(!CreateUntitledDoc())
            return FALSE;
        CreateNewPolygon(FALSE);
        ShowWindow(hWnd, nCmdShow);
        UpdateWindow(hWnd);
        return TRUE;
        }

    while(*lpszLine && *lpszLine == ' ')
        lpszLine++;

    if(CheckEmbedding(&lpszLine))
        bEmbed = TRUE;

    while(*lpszLine && *lpszLine == ' ')
        lpszLine++;

    if(*lpszLine)
        {
        i = 0;
        while(*lpszLine && *lpszLine != ' ')
            szBuf[i++] = *lpszLine++;
        szBuf[i] = '\0';
```

continues

Listing 6.5. continued

```
        if(-1 == OpenFile(szBuf, &of, OF_READ | OF_EXIST))
            {
            if(bEmbed)
                return FALSE;
            else
                {
                MsgBox(hWnd, IDS_FILENOTFOUND , MB_OK);
                if(!CreateUntitledDoc())
                    return FALSE;
                CreateNewPolygon(FALSE);
                ShowWindow(hWnd, nCmdShow);
                UpdateWindow(hWnd);
                return TRUE;
                }
            }

        if(!CreateDocFromFile(szBuf, NULL))
            {
            if(bEmbed)
                return FALSE;
            else
                {
                MsgBox(hWnd, IDS_WRONGFORMAT , MB_OK);

                if(!CreateUntitledDoc())
                    return FALSE;
                CreateNewPolygon(FALSE);
                ShowWindow(hWnd, nCmdShow);
                UpdateWindow(hWnd);
                return TRUE;
                }
            }
        }

    if(bEmbed)
        ShowWindow(hWnd, SW_HIDE);
    else
        {
        ShowWindow(hWnd, nCmdShow);
        UpdateWindow(hWnd);
        }
```

```
    return TRUE;
    }

/*******************************************************************/
/* Function: CheckEmbedding                                        */
/* Purpose: Determines if embedding is on the Cmd line.            */
/* Returns: TRUE if successful, FALSE if failure                   */
/*******************************************************************/
BOOL PASCAL CheckEmbedding(LPSTR *lpszCmd)
    {
    BOOL rc = FALSE;
    char sz[100];
    int i = 0;

    if(**lpszCmd == '-' || **lpszCmd == '/')
        {
        (*lpszCmd)++;
        while(**lpszCmd && **lpszCmd != ' ')
            sz[i++] = *(*lpszCmd)++;
        sz[i] = '\0';
        if(!lstrcmp(sz, "Embedding"))
            rc = TRUE;
        }
    return rc;
    }

/*******************************************************************/
/* Function: CleanUp                                               */
/* Purpose: Frees method instances and objects.                   */
/* Returns: TRUE if successful, FALSE if failure                   */
/*******************************************************************/
VOID CleanUp(VOID)
    {
    int i;

    FreeProcInstance(vtServer.Create);
    FreeProcInstance(vtServer.CreateFromTemplate);
    FreeProcInstance(vtServer.Edit);
    FreeProcInstance(vtServer.Exit);
```

continues

Listing 6.5. continued

```c
    FreeProcInstance(vtServer.Open);
    FreeProcInstance(vtServer.Release);

    FreeProcInstance(vtDoc.Close);
    FreeProcInstance(vtDoc.GetObject);
    FreeProcInstance(vtDoc.Release);
    FreeProcInstance(vtDoc.Save);
    FreeProcInstance(vtDoc.SetColorScheme);
    FreeProcInstance(vtDoc.SetDocDimensions);
    FreeProcInstance(vtDoc.SetHostNames);

    FreeProcInstance(vtObject.DoVerb);
    FreeProcInstance(vtObject.EnumFormats);
    FreeProcInstance(vtObject.GetData);
    FreeProcInstance((FARPROC)vtObject.QueryProtocol);
    FreeProcInstance(vtObject.Release);
    FreeProcInstance(vtObject.SetBounds);
    FreeProcInstance(vtObject.SetColorScheme);
    FreeProcInstance(vtObject.SetData);
    FreeProcInstance(vtObject.SetTargetDevice);
    FreeProcInstance(vtObject.Show);

    for(i = 0; i < MAXCOLORS; i++)
        DeleteObject(hbrColor[i]);
    }

/********************************************************************/
/* Function: Terminate                                            */
/* Purpose: Pre-PostQuitMessage processing.                       */
/* Returns: TRUE if successful, FALSE if failure                  */
/********************************************************************/
VOID PASCAL Terminate(BOOL fUpdateLater)
    {
    if(fUpdateLater)
        SendDocMessage(OLE_CLOSED);

    if(RevokeServer() == OLE_WAIT_FOR_RELEASE)
        Wait(&fWaitingForSrvrRelease);
    if(doc.doctype != DOCEMBEDDED)
        PostQuitMessage(0);
    }
```

Main Window Processing Module

From a structural point of view, main window processing for an OLE server application is not much different than it is for a non-OLE application. The MainWndProc() callback function, with a few minor changes, could be used in a non-OLE application. The main differences are in message termination and menu item processing.

When an OLE server application terminates, it must revoke its documents. If **OleRevokeServer()** returns an OLE_WAIT_FOR_RELEASE, the server application will not want to process certain messages when it enters the Wait() function message loop. WM_COMMAND messages should not be processed, because the application is waiting to terminate, and selecting menu items has no meaning to a terminating application. Thus, the following code prevents the WM_COMMAND message from being processed when the application waits for the document to be released:

```
case WM_COMMAND:
    if(fWaitingForDocRelease)
        {
        MsgBox(hWnd, IDS_WAITFORREVOKE, MB_OK);
        return NULL;
        }
```

The other difference in MainWndProc() is when the application receives a WM_CLOSE message. When *Polygons* receives a WM_CLOSE message, it must call the Terminate() function to revoke the server.

Unlike MainWndProc(), the other local functions in poly.c closely relate to OLE. *Polygons* calls CreateNewDoc() when the user selects the **N**ew menu item from the **F**ile menu. CreateNewDoc() prompts the user to save a changed document. After the user saves the document or bypasses the save, CreateNewDoc() attempts to revoke the document by calling RevokeDoc(). RevokeDoc() calls **OleRevokeServerDoc(). OleRevokeServerDoc()** takes one parameter that is a handle to the document. The handle to the document for the example application is the lhdoc member of the DOC structure. If **OleRevokeServerDoc()** returns OLE_WAIT_FOR_RELEASE, CreateNewDoc() calls Wait() to enter a message loop until the document is released. When the document is released, CreateNewDoc() creates an untitled document and a new polygon object by calling CreateUntitledDoc() and CreateNewPolygon().

The ChangePolygon() and ChangeColor() functions are similar in that they change a polygon object's native data—the type of polygon and its color.

When the change occurs, the polygon object's window is updated. If the document type is DOCFROMFILE, the change functions call SendPolygonMessage() with a handle to the changed polygon and the OLE_CHANGED message. This enables a client application with a link to the polygon object to be updated. OLE server applications update embedded objects only when the user selects the **U**pdate menu item.

This takes you to the UpdateClient() function. When a user selects the **U**pdate menu item, the *Polygons* application calls UpdateClient(). UpdateClient() calls **OleSavedServerDoc()**. **OleSavedServerDoc()** takes one parameter: a handle to a document. This informs the OLESRV library that a document has been saved or updated. At this point, the OLE client application receives an OLE_SAVED notification in its callback function.

The remaining functions in poly.c implement the functionality for **E**dit menu items. CopyPolygon() places data on the clipboard in the correct order. The order in which data is placed on the clipboard enables the client application to determine whether the object can be linked or embedded. An object cannot be a linked object if it is not first saved to a file. The *Polygons* application uses the doctype member of the DOC structure to determine whether a document has been saved to a file. If the document type is DOCFROMFILE, the *Polygons* application should provide clipboard formats to enable the client application to create either an embedded object or a linked object.

The CutPolygon() function is similar to CopyPolygon(), except that it cannot provide clipboard formats for a client application to create a linked object. This makes sense, because when an object is cut to the clipboard, it no longer exists in a document. The following is a table of the clipboard formats placed on the clipboard by *Polygons*.

Table 6.3. Clipboard format orders.

Embedded Object	Linked Object	Rendering Function
cfNative	cfNative	GetNative()
cfOwnerLink	cfOwnerLink	GetLink()
	cfObjectLink	GetLink()
CF_METAFILEPICT	CF_METAFILEPICT	GetMetafilePict()
CF_BITMAP	CF_BITMAP	GetBitmap()

When *Polygons* calls CutPolygon() or DeletePolygon(), the polygon is removed from the document. This requires the RevokePolygon() function to be called. The RevokePolygon() function calls **OleRevokeObject()**. **OleRevokeObject()** informs the OLE libraries that the object no longer exists. Listing 6.6 is the poly.c source file.

Listing 6.6. The poly.c source file.

```
#include "poly.h"

VOID CreateNewDoc(VOID);
VOID PASCAL UpdateClient(HWND);
VOID PASCAL ChangePolygon(WPARAM);
VOID PASCAL ChangeColor(WPARAM);
BOOL ClearClipBoard(VOID);
VOID CopyPolygon(LPPOLYGON);
VOID CutPolygon(LPPOLYGON);
VOID DeletePolygon(VOID);
/******************************************************************/
/* Function: MainWndProc                                          */
/* Purpose: Main window procedure.                                */
/* Returns: Varies on message                                     */
/******************************************************************/
LRESULT CALLBACK MainWndProc(HWND hwnd, WORD message,
                             WPARAM wParam, LPARAM lParam)

    {
    LPPOLYGON       lpPolygon;

    switch(message)
        {
        case WM_COMMAND:
            if(fWaitingForDocRelease)
                {
                MsgBox(hWnd, IDS_WAITFORREVOKE, MB_OK);
                return NULL;
                }
            switch(wParam)
                {
                case IDM_NEW:
                    CreateNewDoc();
                    break;
```

continues

Listing 6.6. continued

```
case IDM_OPEN:
    CommonOpenFile();
    EnableDisableMenus(MF_ENABLED);
    break;

case IDM_SAVE:
    CommonSaveFile();
    break;

case IDM_SAVEAS:
    if(!CommonSaveAs())
        break;
    UpdateMenu(FALSE);
    break;

case IDM_UPDATE:
    UpdateClient(hwnd);
    break;

case IDM_EXIT:
    SendMessage(hwnd, WM_CLOSE, 0, 0L);
    break;

case IDM_COPY:
    CopyPolygon((LPPOLYGON)GetWindowLong(GetWindow
        (hWnd, GW_CHILD),0));
    break;

case IDM_CUT:
    CutPolygon((LPPOLYGON)GetWindowLong(GetWindow
        (hWnd, GW_CHILD),0));
    break;

case IDM_DELETE:
    DeletePolygon();
    break;
```

```
case IDM_TRIANGLE:
case IDM_RECTANGLE:
case IDM_PENTAGON:
case IDM_HEXAGON:
case IDM_HEPTAGON:
case IDM_OCTAGON:
case IDM_STAR:
    ChangePolygon(wParam);
    break;

case IDM_RED:
case IDM_GREEN:
case IDM_BLUE:
case IDM_WHITE:
case IDM_GRAY:
case IDM_CYAN:
case IDM_MAGENTA:
case IDM_YELLOW:
    ChangeColor(wParam);
    break;

case IDM_NEXTOBJ:
    lpPolygon =
        (LPPOLYGON)GetWindowLong(GetWindow(hWnd,
        GW_CHILD),0);
    SetWindowPos(lpPolygon->hwnd, 1, 0,0,0,0,
                SWP_NOMOVE | SWP_NOSIZE);
    break;

case IDM_NEWOBJ:
    CreateNewPolygon(TRUE);
    break;

case IDM_ABOUT:
    CreateDlgBox(hwnd,
            (LPCSTR)MAKEINTRESOURCE(IDD_ABOUTBOX),
            (FARPROC)AboutDlgProc);
    break;
}
break;
```

continues

291

Listing 6.6. continued

```
        case WM_QUERYENDSESSION:
            {
            BOOL fUpdateLater;

            if(SaveChanges(&fUpdateLater) == IDCANCEL)
                return FALSE;

            if(fUpdateLater)
                SendDocMessage(OLE_CLOSED);
            return TRUE;
            }

        case WM_CLOSE:
            {
            BOOL fUpdateLater;

            if(SaveChanges(&fUpdateLater) != IDCANCEL)
                Terminate(fUpdateLater);
            break;
            }

        default:
            return DefWindowProc(hwnd, message, wParam, lParam);
        }
    return NULL;
    }

/********************************************************************/
/* Function: ChangePolygon                                          */
/* Purpose: Changes native data for type of polygon.                */
/********************************************************************/
VOID PASCAL ChangePolygon(WPARAM wParam)
    {
    LPPOLYGON lpPolygon;

    lpPolygon = (LPPOLYGON)GetWindowLong(GetWindow(hWnd,
                                         GW_CHILD),0);
    lpPolygon->native.idmPoly = wParam;
```

```
        InvalidateRect(lpPolygon->hwnd, (LPRECT)NULL, TRUE);
        UpdateWindow(lpPolygon->hwnd);
        fDocChanged = TRUE;

        if(doc.doctype == DOCFROMFILE)
            SendPolygonMessage(lpPolygon, OLE_CHANGED);
        }

/*******************************************************************/
/* Function: ChangeColor                                           */
/* Purpose: Changes the native data color for a polygon.           */
/*******************************************************************/
VOID PASCAL ChangeColor(WPARAM wParam)
    {
    LPPOLYGON lpPolygon;

    lpPolygon = (LPPOLYGON)GetWindowLong(GetWindow(hWnd,
                                        GW_CHILD),0);
    lpPolygon->native.idmColor = wParam;
    InvalidateRect(lpPolygon->hwnd, (LPRECT)NULL, TRUE);
    UpdateWindow(lpPolygon->hwnd);
    fDocChanged = TRUE;

    if(doc.doctype == DOCFROMFILE)
        SendPolygonMessage(lpPolygon, OLE_CHANGED);
    }

/*******************************************************************/
/* Function: CopyPolygon                                           */
/* Purpose: Copies a polygon to the clipboard using correct        */
/*          formats.                                               */
/*******************************************************************/
VOID CopyPolygon(LPPOLYGON lpPolygon)
    {
    HANDLE      hData;

    if(ClearClipBoard())
        {
        if((hData = GetNative(lpPolygon)) != NULL)
```

continues

Listing 6.6. continued

```
                    SetClipboardData(cfNative, hData);

        if((hData = GetLink(lpPolygon)) != NULL)
            SetClipboardData(cfOwnerLink, hData);

        if(doc.doctype == DOCFROMFILE)
            {
            // Can create a link if object exists in a file.
            if((hData = GetLink(lpPolygon)) != NULL)
                SetClipboardData(cfObjectLink, hData);
            }

        if((hData = GetMetafilePict(lpPolygon)) != NULL)
            SetClipboardData(CF_METAFILEPICT, hData);

        if((hData = GetBitmap(lpPolygon)) != NULL)
            SetClipboardData(CF_BITMAP, hData);


        CloseClipboard();
        }
    }

/********************************************************************/
/* Function: CutPolygon                                           */
/* Purpose: Cuts a polygon to the clipboard using correct         */
/*          formats.                                              */
/********************************************************************/
VOID CutPolygon(LPPOLYGON lpPolygon)
    {
    HANDLE      hData;

    if(ClearClipBoard())
        {
        if((hData = GetNative(lpPolygon)) != NULL)
            SetClipboardData(cfNative, hData);

        if((hData = GetLink(lpPolygon)) != NULL)
            SetClipboardData(cfOwnerLink, hData);
```

```
        if((hData = GetMetafilePict(lpPolygon)) != NULL)
            SetClipboardData(CF_METAFILEPICT, hData);

        if((hData = GetBitmap(lpPolygon)) != NULL)
            SetClipboardData(CF_BITMAP, hData);

        CloseClipboard();

        RevokePolygon();
        DestroyWindow(GetWindow(hWnd, GW_CHILD));
        if(!GetWindow(hWnd, GW_CHILD))
            EnableDisableMenus(MF_GRAYED);
        }
    }

/*********************************************************************/
/* Function: ClearClipBoard                                        */
/* Purpose: Empties the clipboard.                                 */
/* Returns: TRUE/FALSE                                             */
/*********************************************************************/
BOOL ClearClipBoard(VOID)
    {
    if(OpenClipboard(hWnd))
        {
        EmptyClipboard();
        return TRUE;
        }
    else
        return FALSE;
    }

/*********************************************************************/
/* Function: CreateNewDoc                                          */
/* Purpose: Creates a new document--prompts to save a              */
/*          changed doc.                                           */
/*********************************************************************/
VOID CreateNewDoc(VOID)
    {
    BOOL fUpdateLater;
    OLESTATUS olestatus;
```

continues

Listing 6.6. continued

```
        if(SaveChanges(&fUpdateLater) == IDCANCEL)
            return;
        else
            if(fUpdateLater)
                SendDocMessage(OLE_CLOSED);

        fRevokeSrvrOnSrvrRelease = FALSE;

        if((olestatus = RevokeDoc()) > OLE_WAIT_FOR_RELEASE)
            {
            MsgBox(hWnd, IDS_SERIOUSERROR, MB_OK);
            return;
            }
        else
            if(olestatus == OLE_WAIT_FOR_RELEASE)
                Wait(&fWaitingForDocRelease);

        fRevokeSrvrOnSrvrRelease = TRUE;

        if(!CreateUntitledDoc())
            {
            MsgBox(hWnd, IDS_SERIOUSERROR, MB_OK);
            return;
            }

        CreateNewPolygon(FALSE);
        UpdateMenu(FALSE);
        }

/**********************************************************************/
/* Function: UpdateClient                                             */
/* Purpose: Informs client app of changes.                           */
/**********************************************************************/
VOID PASCAL UpdateClient(HWND hwnd)
    {
    switch(OleSavedServerDoc(doc.lhdoc))
        {
        case OLE_ERROR_CANT_UPDATE_CLIENT:
            if(!CreateDlgBox(hwnd,
```

```
                (LPCSTR)MAKEINTRESOURCE(IDD_FAILEDUPDATE),
                (FARPROC)FailedUpdateDlgProc))
                Terminate(TRUE);
            break;
        case OLE_OK:
            break;
        default:
            MsgBox(hWnd, IDS_SERIOUSERROR, MB_OK);
        }
    }


/********************************************************************/
/* Function: DeletePolygon                                          */
/* Purpose: Deletes a polygon and updates the menu.                 */
/********************************************************************/
VOID DeletePolygon(VOID)
    {
    RevokePolygon();
    DestroyWindow(GetWindow(hWnd, GW_CHILD));
    if(!GetWindow(hWnd, GW_CHILD))
        EnableDisableMenus(MF_GRAYED);
    }
```

Polygon Window Processing

The object.c module doesn't contain too much OLE code. However, OLE does slightly impact the code. When a document is being revoked, you do not want the user to size or move a polygon window. Thus, when the ObjectWndProc() function receives a WM_SIZE or a WM_LBUTTONDOWN message, check the fWaitingForDocRelease flag. If the flag is set, the application notifies the user to wait and returns before processing any more code.

```
if(fWaitingForDocRelease)
    {
    MsgBox(hWnd, IDS_WAITFORREVOKE, MB_OK);
    return NULL;
    }
```

Listing 6.7. The object.c source file.

```c
#include "poly.h"

/********************************************************************/
/* Function: ObjectWndProc                                         */
/* Purpose: Callback procedure for polygon windows.                */
/* Returns: Varies                                                 */
/********************************************************************/
LRESULT CALLBACK ObjectWndProc(HWND hwnd, WORD message,
                               WPARAM wParam, LPARAM lParam)

    {
    static BOOL    fCapture = FALSE;
    static struct  {RECT rect; POINT pt;} drag;
    static RECT    rectMain;

    switch(message)
        {
        case WM_CREATE:
            {
            LPPOLYGON lpPolygon;
            LPCREATESTRUCT lpcs;

            lpcs = (LPCREATESTRUCT)lParam;
            lpPolygon = (LPPOLYGON)lpcs->lpCreateParams;

            lpPolygon->hwnd = hwnd;
            SetWindowLong(hwnd, 0, (LONG)lpPolygon);
            EnableDisableMenus(MF_ENABLED);
            break;
            }
        case WM_SIZE:
            {
            RECT rect;
            if(fWaitingForDocRelease)
                {
                MsgBox(hWnd, IDS_WAITFORREVOKE, MB_OK);
                return NULL;
                }
            GetWindowRect(hwnd, (LPRECT)&rect);
            ScreenToClient(hWnd, (LPPOINT)&rect);
            ScreenToClient(hWnd, (LPPOINT)&rect.right);
```

```
        SizePolygon(hwnd, rect, TRUE);
        /* Fall through */
        }
case WM_PAINT:
    PaintPolygon(hwnd);
    break;

case WM_LBUTTONDOWN:
    if(fWaitingForDocRelease)
        {
        MsgBox(hWnd, IDS_WAITFORREVOKE, MB_OK);
        return NULL;
        }
    BringWindowToTop(hwnd);

    GetWindowRect(hwnd, (LPRECT) &drag.rect);
    ScreenToClient(hWnd, (LPPOINT)&drag.rect.left);
    ScreenToClient(hWnd, (LPPOINT)&drag.rect.right);

    drag.pt.x = LOWORD(lParam);
    drag.pt.y = HIWORD(lParam);

    ClientToScreen(hwnd, (LPPOINT)&drag.pt);
    ScreenToClient(hWnd, (LPPOINT)&drag.pt);

    GetClientRect(hWnd, (LPRECT) &rectMain);

    SetCapture(hwnd);
    fCapture = TRUE;
    break;

case WM_MOUSEMOVE:
    {
    HDC   hdc;
    POINT pt;

    if(!fCapture)
        break;

    fDocChanged = TRUE;
    pt.x = LOWORD(lParam);
```

continues

299

Listing 6.7. continued

```
                     pt.y = HIWORD(lParam);

                     ClientToScreen(hwnd, (LPPOINT)&pt);
                     ScreenToClient(hWnd, (LPPOINT)&pt);

                     if(!PtInRect(&rectMain, pt))
                         break;

                     hdc = GetDC(hWnd);

                     InvertRect(hdc, (LPRECT)&drag.rect);

                     OffsetRect(&drag.rect, pt.x - drag.pt.x,
                             pt.y - drag.pt.y);

                     drag.pt.x = pt.x;
                     drag.pt.y = pt.y;

                     InvertRect(hdc, (LPRECT)&drag.rect);
                     ReleaseDC(hWnd, hdc);
                     break;
                     }

            case WM_LBUTTONUP:
                     {
                     LPPOLYGON lpPolygon;
                     if(!fCapture)
                         return TRUE;

                     fCapture = FALSE;
                     ReleaseCapture();

                     MoveWindow(hwnd, drag.rect.left, drag.rect.top,
                             drag.rect.right - drag.rect.left,
                             drag.rect.bottom - drag.rect.top, TRUE);
                     InvalidateRect(hwnd, (LPRECT)NULL, TRUE);
                     lpPolygon = (LPPOLYGON)GetWindowLong(hwnd, 0);
                     lpPolygon->native.nX = drag.rect.left;
                     lpPolygon->native.nY = drag.rect.top;
                     break;
```

```
        }

    case WM_DESTROY:
        DestroyPolygon(hwnd);
        return DefWindowProc(hwnd, message, wParam, lParam);

    default:
        return DefWindowProc(hwnd, message, wParam, lParam);
    }
    return NULL;
}
```

Server Methods

The OLESRV library calls server methods when the OLESRV library receives notification from the OLECLI library that a client application needs an object. The *Polygons* application uses six of these methods. A seventh, ServerExecute(), is included for documentation purposes. Each server method is directly related to an activity in the client application.

OLESRV calls the ServerOpen() method when the user activates a linked object in an OLE client application. The call originates when the client application calls **OleActivate()**. When OLESRV calls ServerOpen(), the server application is responsible for opening and reading a document file, thus creating a document. ServerOpen() calls CreateDocFromFile() to create the document. After the server creates the document, it then stores a pointer to the OLESERVERDOC structure in the lplpoledoc parameter of ServerOpen(). Note that the *Polygons* application's OLESERVERDOC structure is a member in the DOC structure. If ServerOpen() is successful, it returns OLE_OK. ServerOpen() returns OLE_ERROR_OPEN if the document cannot be created. Note that the server should not be visible after ServerOpen() returns. The ObjectShow() method will display the server.

OLESRV calls the ServerCreate() method when an OLE client application calls **OleCreate()**. This occurs when the user selects the **I**nsert Object menu item in the client application. ServerCreate() creates a new document by calling CreateTitledDoc(). If CreateTitledDoc() successfully creates the document, ServerCreate() stores a pointer to the OLESERVERDOC structure (DOC structure) in the lplpoledoc parameter of ServerCreate() and returns OLE_OK. Otherwise, ServerCreate() returns OLE_ERROR_NEW.

ServerCreateFromTemplate() is called by OLESRV when a client application creates a new object by specifying a template in the **OleCreateFromTemplate()** function. This is a cross between ServerOpen() and ServerCreate() because a new document is created from an existing document. The ServerCreateFromTemplate() method calls CreateDocFromTemplate() to create the new document. Similar to the previously discussed methods, ServerCreateFromTemplate() stores a pointer to the OLESERVERDOC structure in the lplpoledoc parameter of ServerCreateFromTemplate().

OLESRV calls the ServerEdit() method when a user activates an embedded object in a client application. This is almost the same as the ServerCreate() method. The only difference is that if the call to CreateTitleDoc() fails, ServerEdit() returns OLE_ERROR_EDIT. Note that the server should not be visible after ServerOpen() returns. The ObjectShow() method will display the server.

The ServerExit() method revokes the server by calling RevokeServer(). OLESRV calls ServerExit() when a fatal error requires the server to terminate.

The last method *Polygons* uses is ServerRelease(). OLESRV calls ServerRelease when it is safe to close the server. This happens after the server application calls **OleRevokeServer()** and there are no more OLE or DDE conversations associated with the server. The server application should terminate if there isn't a handle to the server. Listing 6.8 is the vtserver.c source file.

Listing 6.8. The vtserver.c source file.

```
#include "poly.h"

/*******************************************************************/
/* Function: ServerOpen                                           */
/* Purpose: Opens an existing file.                               */
/* Returns: OLE_OK if successful, OLE_ERROR_OPEN if failed        */
/*******************************************************************/
OLESTATUS CALLBACK ServerOpen(LPOLESERVER lpolesrvr,
                              LHSERVERDOC lhdoc, LPSTR lpszDoc,
                              LPOLESERVERDOC FAR *lplpoledoc)

    {
    if(!CreateDocFromFile(lpszDoc, lhdoc))
        return OLE_ERROR_OPEN;

    *lplpoledoc = (LPOLESERVERDOC) &doc;
    return OLE_OK;
```

```
    }

/*******************************************************************/
/* Function: ServerCreate                                        */
/* Purpose: Creates a new document.                              */
/* Returns: OLE_OK if successful, OLE_ERROR_NEW if unsuccessful  */
/*******************************************************************/
OLESTATUS CALLBACK ServerCreate(LPOLESERVER lpolesrvr,
    LHSERVERDOC lhdoc, LPSTR lpszClassName,
    LPSTR lpszDoc, LPOLESERVERDOC FAR *lplpoledoc)
    {
    if(!CreateTitledDoc(lhdoc, lpszDoc))
        return OLE_ERROR_NEW;

    CreateNewPolygon(TRUE);
    *lplpoledoc = (LPOLESERVERDOC)&doc;
    UpdateMenu(TRUE);
    return OLE_OK;
    }


/*******************************************************************/
/* Function: ServerCreateFromTemplate                            */
/* Purpose: Creates a new document from an existing file.        */
/* Returns: OLE_OK if successful, OLE_ERROR_TEMPLATE if          */
/*          unsuccessful                                         */
/*******************************************************************/
OLESTATUS CALLBACK ServerCreateFromTemplate(LPOLESERVER lpolesrvr,
    LHSERVERDOC lhdoc, LPSTR lpszClassName,
    LPSTR lpszDoc, LPSTR lpszTemplate,
    LPOLESERVERDOC FAR *lplpoledoc)
    {
    if(!CreateDocFromTemplate(lpszTemplate, lhdoc))
        return OLE_ERROR_TEMPLATE;

    *lplpoledoc = (LPOLESERVERDOC)&doc;

    fDocChanged = TRUE;
    UpdateMenu(TRUE);
    return OLE_OK;
    }
```

continues

303

Listing 6.8. continued

```c
/*******************************************************************/
/* Function: ServerEdit                                           */
/* Purpose: Edits an existing document.                           */
/* Returns: OLE_OK if successful, OLE_ERROR_EDIT if unsuccessful  */
/*******************************************************************/
OLESTATUS CALLBACK ServerEdit(LPOLESERVER lpolesrvr,
    LHSERVERDOC lhdoc, LPSTR lpszClassName,
    LPSTR lpszDoc, LPOLESERVERDOC FAR *lplpoledoc)
    {
    if(!CreateTitledDoc(lhdoc, lpszDoc))
        return OLE_ERROR_EDIT;

    fDocChanged = FALSE;
    *lplpoledoc = (LPOLESERVERDOC)&doc;
    UpdateMenu(TRUE);
    return OLE_OK;
    }


/*******************************************************************/
/* Function: ServerExit                                           */
/* Purpose: Close down app.                                       */
/* Returns: OLE_OK                                                */
/*******************************************************************/
OLESTATUS CALLBACK ServerExit(LPOLESERVER lpolesrvr)
    {
    if(server.lhsrvr)
        RevokeServer();

    return OLE_OK;
    }


/*******************************************************************/
/* Function: ServerRelease                                        */
/* Purpose: Notifies app it is safe to terminate.                 */
/* Returns: OLE_OK                                                */
/*******************************************************************/
OLESTATUS CALLBACK ServerRelease(LPOLESERVER lpolesrvr)
    {
    if(server.lhsrvr)
        {
```

```
        if(fRevokeSrvrOnSrvrRelease &&
           (doc.doctype == DOCEMBEDDED ¦¦
           !IsWindowVisible(hWnd)))
            RevokeServer();
        }
    else
        {
        fWaitingForSrvrRelease = FALSE;
        PostQuitMessage(0);
        }
    return OLE_OK;
    }


/**********************************************************************/
/* Function: ServerExecute--used for DDE executes.                    */
/* Purpose: Not used in the app--here for documentation               */
/*          purposes.                                                 */
/* Returns: OLE_ERROR_COMMAND                                         */
/**********************************************************************/
OLESTATUS CALLBACK ServerExecute(LPOLESERVER lpolesrvr,
                                 HANDLE hCommands)
    {
    return OLE_ERROR_COMMAND;
    }
```

Document Methods

Document methods control file-level access to objects. There are eight document methods. *Polygons* uses seven of the methods and includes the DocExecute() method for documentation purposes. (DocExecute(), if active, would perform DDE executes.)

The DocSave() method directs the server to save a linked file. This occurs when a client application closes or saves a document that contains a linked object. The *Polygons* application calls CommonSaveFile(), which contains the common Save As dialog. If the file was successfully saved, DocSave() returns OLE_OK. Otherwise, it returns OLE_ERROR_GENERIC.

OLESRV calls the DocClose() method when a client application terminates. This always occurs before the DocRelease() method is called. The DocClose()

method is responsible for calling **OleRevokeServerDoc()**, which is in the
RevokeDoc() function.

The DocSetHostNames() method provides the server with the name of the
client application's document and object names. When OLESRV calls
DocSetHostNames(), the server title bar should change to reflect the client
document and object names. This occurs only for embedded objects.

OLESRV calls the DocSetDocDimensions() method to inform the server of the
bounds of the target device for rendering the object. This is useful only
for embedded objects because linked objects are based on files. The
DocSetDocDimensions() method receives the bounds in a pointer to a RECT
structure. The bounds are in MM_HIMETRIC units. Thus, if a server application
does not use the MM_HIMETRIC mapping mode, the server must call a conversion routine, such as HiMetricToDevice().

> **Note:** The OLE libraries expect the use of MM_HIMETRIC when dealing
> with coordinates. An application can use any mapping mode as long
> as it expresses its coordinates to the OLE libraries in terms of
> MM_HIMETRIC.

The DocGetObject() method retrieves an object when a client application
creates an object. The lpszObjectName parameter is the name of the object. If
lpszObjectName is NULL, the entire document is the object. The server application must save the lpoleclient parameter so that it can later send notification
to the client application's callback function. (An example of this would be
OLE_CHANGED when an object changes.) DocGetObject() calls AssociateClient()
to accomplish this. The server application updates the lplpoleobject parameter with the pointer to the OLEOBJECT structure, which is a member of the
POLYGON structure in the example program. If the server application cannot
find the object, DocGetObject() should return OLE_ERROR_NAME. If the server
application cannot render the object, DocGetObject() should return
OLE_ERROR_MEMORY. Otherwise, DocGetObject() returns OLE_OK.

OLESRV calls the DocRelease() method after the server calls **OleRevokeServer()**
or **OleRevokeServerDoc()**. Additionally, if there is a DDE conversation with an
object, the OLESRV will call DocRelease(). (*Polygons* does not support any DDE
conversations.) When OLESRV calls DocRelease(), the server should free all
resources associated with the specified document.

The DocSetColorScheme() method sets the palette used to render the document to the client application's preferred palette. The client palette is passed

in the lppal parameter of the DocSetColorScheme() method. The server application should delete the old palette and replace it with the preferred palette.

Listing 6.9. The vtdoc.c source file.

```
#include "poly.h"

/*******************************************************************/
/* Function: DocSave                                               */
/* Purpose: Save the Document.                                     */
/* Returns: OLE_OK                                                 */
/*******************************************************************/
OLESTATUS CALLBACK DocSave(LPOLESERVERDOC lpoledoc)
    {
    if(doc.doctype == DOCFROMFILE)
        return CommonSaveFile() ? OLE_OK : OLE_ERROR_GENERIC;
    else
        return OLE_ERROR_GENERIC;
    }


/*******************************************************************/
/* Function: DocClose                                              */
/* Purpose: Close the document--unconditionally.                   */
/* Returns: Result from RevokeDoc                                  */
/*******************************************************************/
OLESTATUS CALLBACK DocClose(LPOLESERVERDOC lpoledoc)
    {
    return RevokeDoc();
    }


/*******************************************************************/
/* Function: DocSetHostNames                                       */
/* Purpose: Receive window title from client.                      */
/* Returns: OLE_OK                                                 */
/*******************************************************************/
OLESTATUS CALLBACK DocSetHostNames(LPOLESERVERDOC lpoledoc,
    LPSTR lpszClient, LPSTR lpszDoc)
    {
    SetTitle(lpszDoc, TRUE);
    lstrcpy((LPSTR) szClient, lpszClient);
```

continues

307

Listing 6.9. continued

```c
    return OLE_OK;
    }

/**********************************************************************/
/* Function: DocSetDocDimensions                                      */
/* Purpose: Set document dimensions.                                  */
/* Returns: OLE_OK                                                    */
/**********************************************************************/
OLESTATUS CALLBACK DocSetDocDimensions(LPOLESERVERDOC lpoledoc,
                                        LPRECT lprect)

    {
    if(doc.doctype == DOCEMBEDDED)
        {
        RECT rect = *lprect;
        HiMetricToDevice(hWnd, (LPPOINT) &rect.left);
        HiMetricToDevice(hWnd, (LPPOINT) &rect.right);
        MoveWindow(GetWindow(hWnd, GW_CHILD), 0, 0,
                    rect.right - rect.left + 2 *
                    GetSystemMetrics(SM_CXFRAME),
                    rect.bottom - rect.top + 2 *
                    GetSystemMetrics(SM_CYFRAME),
            TRUE);
        }
    return OLE_OK;
    }


/**********************************************************************/
/* Function: DocGetObject                                             */
/* Purpose: Create an object.                                         */
/* Returns: OLE_OK if successful, varies if not successful            */
/**********************************************************************/
OLESTATUS CALLBACK DocGetObject(LPOLESERVERDOC lpoledoc,
    LPSTR lpszObjectName, LPOLEOBJECT FAR *lplpoleobject,
    LPOLECLIENT lpoleclient)
    {
    HWND   hwnd;
    ATOM   aName;
    LPPOLYGON lpPolygon;

    if(lpszObjectName == NULL || lpszObjectName[0] == '\0')
```

```
    {
    hwnd = GetWindow(hWnd, GW_CHILD);
    lpPolygon = hwnd ? (LPPOLYGON)GetWindowLong(hwnd, 0) :
                CreateNewPolygon(FALSE);
    *lplpoleobject = (LPOLEOBJECT) lpPolygon;
    if(!AssociateClient(lpoleclient, lpPolygon))
        return OLE_ERROR_MEMORY;
    return OLE_OK;
    }

if(!(aName = GlobalFindAtom(lpszObjectName)))
    return OLE_ERROR_NAME;


hwnd = GetWindow(hWnd, GW_CHILD);

while(hwnd)
    {
    lpPolygon = (LPPOLYGON)GetWindowLong(hwnd, 0);

    if(aName == lpPolygon->aName)
        {
        *lplpoleobject = (LPOLEOBJECT) lpPolygon;
        if(!AssociateClient(lpoleclient, lpPolygon))
            return OLE_ERROR_MEMORY;
        return OLE_OK;
        }
    hwnd = GetWindow(hwnd, GW_HWNDNEXT);
    }

if(((LPDOC)lpoledoc)->doctype == DOCEMBEDDED)
    {
    lpPolygon = CreateNewPolygon(FALSE);
    *lplpoleobject = (LPOLEOBJECT) lpPolygon;

    if(!AssociateClient(lpoleclient, lpPolygon))
        return OLE_ERROR_MEMORY;
    return OLE_OK;
    }

return OLE_ERROR_NAME;
}
```

continues

Listing 6.9. continued

```
/********************************************************************/
/* Function: DocRelease                                           */
/* Purpose: It is now OK to destroy the document.                 */
/* Returns: OLE_OK                                                */
/********************************************************************/
OLESTATUS CALLBACK DocRelease(LPOLESERVERDOC lpoledoc)
    {
    fWaitingForDocRelease = FALSE;
    DestroyDoc();
    return OLE_OK;
    }


/********************************************************************/
/* Function: DocSetColorScheme                                    */
/* Purpose: Preferred client palette.                             */
/* Returns: OLE_OK if successful, OLE_ERROR_PALETTE if not        */
/********************************************************************/
OLESTATUS CALLBACK DocSetColorScheme(LPOLESERVERDOC lpoledoc,
                                     LPLOGPALETTE lppal)

    {
    HPALETTE hpal = CreatePalette(lppal);

    if(hpal==NULL)
        return OLE_ERROR_PALETTE;

    if(doc.hpal)
        DeleteObject(doc.hpal);
    doc.hpal = hpal;
    return OLE_OK;
    }


/********************************************************************/
/* Function: DocExecute                                           */
/* Purpose: DDE execute strings--here only for documentation      */
/*          purposes.                                             */
/* Returns: OLE_ERROR_COMMAND--server does not support this.      */
/********************************************************************/
OLESTATUS CALLBACK DocExecute(LPOLESERVERDOC lpoledoc,
                              HANDLE hCommands)
```

```
{
return OLE_ERROR_COMMAND;
}
```

Document Management

The document-management functions for *Polygons* aid in the creation and destruction of documents. This is different than reading and writing from document files. (File I/O is covered in a later section in this chapter.)

The CreateTitledDoc() and CreateUntitledDoc() functions create documents with and without titles. These functions call the **OleRegisterServerDoc()** function to register the document with OLESRV. Additionally, the create functions initialize the DOC document structure. The **OleRegisterServerDoc()** function has the following prototype:

```
OLESTATUS OleRegisterServerDoc(LHSERVER lhsrvr,
    LPSTR lpszDocName, LPOLESERVERDOC lpdoc,
    LHSERVERDOC FAR * lplhdoc)
```

The lhsrvr parameter is a handle to the server. The lpszDocName parameter specifies the document name. The lpdoc parameter is a pointer to the OLESERVERDOC structure, which is the first member of the DOC structure. The lplhdoc parameter points to the handle of the document, which is the second member of the DOC structure, doc.lhdoc.

The CreateTitleDoc() and CreateUntitledDoc() functions differ in that the CreateTitleDoc() structure creates an embedded document and the CreateUntitledDoc() creates a new document that is not linked or embedded.

The DestroyDoc() function deletes all polygon windows, deletes the document name from the atom table, and deletes the palette for the document. Note that *Polygons* uses the atom table to store the document name. *Polygons* stores the atom for a document name in the DOC structure. This is an easy method to store a variable-length string in a structure without wasting memory.

The RevokeDoc() function calls **OleRevokeServerDoc()** and then DestroyDoc(). **OleRevokeServerDoc()** informs the OLE libraries that the document is no longer available to client applications. This is the opposite of calling **OleRegisterServerDoc()**. **OleRevokeServerDoc()** has the following prototype:

```
OLESTATUS OleRevokeServerDoc(LHSERVERDOC lhdoc)
```

The lhdoc parameter is the handle to the document that was registered with the **OleRegisterServerDoc()** function. **OleRevokeServerDoc()** returns OLE_OK if successful, or OLE_ERROR_HANDLE if an incorrect handle is specified in the call. It can also return OLE_WAIT_FOR_RELEASE if communications between client applications and the server have not terminated. Server applications must wait for OLESRV to call the ServerRelease() method before destroying the document. *Polygons* simply waits for OLE_OK and then destroys the document.

When OLESRV calls the DocGetObject() method, DocGetObject() calls the AssociateClient() function and stores the handle to a client application in the POLYGON structure. Because there can be many clients and many polygons, the AssociateClient() function ensures that the correct client-polygon association is formed.

The SendDocMessage() function calls SendPolygonMessage() for each polygon in a document. The SendPolygonMessage() sends a message to the associated client application callback function for a given polygon.

Listing 6.10. The docmgt.c source file.

```
#include "poly.h"

/******************************************************************/
/* Function: CreateUntitledDoc                                    */
/* Purpose: Creates an untitled document.                         */
/* Returns: TRUE/FALSE                                            */
/******************************************************************/
BOOL CreateUntitledDoc(VOID)
    {
    int i;

    if(OLE_OK != OleRegisterServerDoc(server.lhsrvr,
                            "(Untitled)",
                            (LPOLESERVERDOC) &doc,
                            (LHSERVERDOC FAR *) &doc.lhdoc))
        return FALSE;

    doc.doctype       = DOCNEW;
    doc.oledoc.lpvtbl = &vtDoc;

    for(i=1; i <= MAXOBJECTS; i++)
        doc.rgfObjNums[i] = FALSE;
```

```
    fDocChanged = FALSE;

    SetTitle("(Untitled)", FALSE);
    return TRUE;
    }

/**********************************************************************/
/* Function: CreateTitleDoc                                           */
/* Purpose: Creates a titled document.                                */
/* Returns: TRUE/FALSE                                                */
/**********************************************************************/
BOOL PASCAL CreateTitledDoc(LONG lhdoc, LPSTR lpszDoc)
    {
    int i;

    if(lhdoc == NULL)
        {
        if(OLE_OK != OleRegisterServerDoc(server.lhsrvr,
                            lpszDoc,
                            (LPOLESERVERDOC) &doc,
                            (LHSERVERDOC FAR *) &doc.lhdoc))
                return FALSE;
        }
    else
        doc.lhdoc = lhdoc;

    doc.doctype = DOCEMBEDDED;
    doc.oledoc.lpvtbl= &vtDoc;

    for(i=1; i <= MAXOBJECTS; i++)
        doc.rgfObjNums[i] = FALSE;

    fDocChanged = FALSE;

    SetTitle(lpszDoc, TRUE);
    return TRUE;
    }


/**********************************************************************/
/* Function: DestroyDoc                                               */
/* Purpose: Deletes all polygons and frees doc resources.             */
/**********************************************************************/
```

continues

313

Listing 6.10. continued

```
VOID DestroyDoc(VOID)
    {
    HWND hwnd;
    HWND hwndNext;

    hwnd = GetWindow(hWnd, GW_CHILD);
    while(hwnd)
        {
        hwndNext = GetWindow(hwnd, GW_HWNDNEXT);
        DestroyWindow(hwnd);
        hwnd = hwndNext;
        }

    if(doc.aName)
        {
        GlobalDeleteAtom(doc.aName);
        doc.aName = NULL;
        }

    if(doc.hpal)
        DeleteObject(doc.hpal);
    }

/*******************************************************************/
/* Function: RevokeDoc                                             */
/* Purpose: Attempts to revoke a server document.                  */
/* Returns: olestatus                                              */
/*******************************************************************/
OLESTATUS RevokeDoc(VOID)
    {
    OLESTATUS olestatus;

    if((olestatus = OleRevokeServerDoc(doc.lhdoc)) >
        OLE_WAIT_FOR_RELEASE)
        DestroyDoc();

    doc.lhdoc = NULL;

    return olestatus;
    }
```

```
/********************************************************************/
/* Function: AssociateClient                                        */
/* Purpose: Associates a client to an object.                       */
/* Returns: TRUE/FALSE                                              */
/********************************************************************/
BOOL PASCAL AssociateClient(LPOLECLIENT lpoleclient,
                            LPPOLYGON lpPolygon)
    {
    int i;

    for(i=0; i < MAXCLIENTS; i++)
        {
        if(lpPolygon->lpoleclient[i]==lpoleclient)
            return TRUE;

        if(lpPolygon->lpoleclient[i]==NULL)
            {
            lpPolygon->lpoleclient[i]=lpoleclient;
            return TRUE;
            }
        }
    return FALSE;
    }


/********************************************************************/
/* Function: SendDocMessage                                         */
/* Purpose: Sends a message to polygons within a document.          */
/********************************************************************/
VOID PASCAL SendDocMessage(WORD wMessage)
    {
    HWND    hwnd;

    hwnd = GetWindow(hWnd, GW_CHILD);

    while(hwnd)
        {
        SendPolygonMessage((LPPOLYGON)GetWindowLong(hwnd, 0),
                           wMessage);
        hwnd = GetWindow(hwnd, GW_HWNDNEXT);
        }
    }
```

Object Methods

Object methods deal with the object level of the application. The `ObjectQueryProtocol()` method identifies the supported protocol of the server to the `OLESRV` library. *Polygons* has only one supported protocol: `"StdFileEditing"`. `ObjectQueryProtocol()` has two parameters: `lpoleobject` and `lpszProtocol`. When `OLESRV` calls `ObjectQueryProtocol()`, it queries the server application for a supported protocol for a particular object. Because *Polygons* supports one protocol for one object type, it compares only the protocol specified in `lpszProtocol` to `"StdFileEditing"`. If `lpszProtocol` is `"StdFileEditing"`, `ObjectQueryProtocol()` returns a pointer to the `OLEOBJECT` structure that `OLESRV` passes to `ObjectQueryProtocol()`.

`OLESRV` calls `ObjectRelease()` after *Polygons* revokes the server, document, or object. `OLESRV` will also call `ObjectRelease()` if a client application removes an object by calling **`OleDelete()`**. `ObjectRelease()` removes the association between the object and client by placing a `NULL` value in the `lpoleclient` member of the `OLEOBJECT` structure.

The `ObjectShow()` method makes an object visible. `OLESRV` calls this method after it calls `ServerOpen()` or `ServerEdit()`. `ObjectShow()` has two parameters: `lpoleobject` and `fTakeFocus`. The `lpoleobject` parameter specifies the object to show. The `fTakeFocus` parameter is a flag to indicate to the server to set the focus to itself. Although this is not a problem with *Polygons,* if an object is not visible within the document, the document should scroll to display the object. If the object is a selectable area of the document, the server should select the object.

The `ObjectDoVerb()` method instructs the server to execute the specified verb. `OLESRV` calls `ObjectDoVerb()` when a client application activates an embedded object with the **`OleActivate()`** function. `ObjectDoVerb()` has four parameters: `lpoleobject`, `wVerb`, `fTakeFocus`, and `fShow`. The `fTakeFocus` and `fShow` parameters specify to the server application to set the focus to itself and show the object. The `lpoleobject` parameter is a pointer to the object for which the server application executes the verb specified in `wVerb`. `wVerb` is the value of the verb from the registration database. The primary verb is always 0. Secondary verbs are numbered 1 through *n*. *Polygons* has two verbs: `Play` and `Edit`. `Play` is the primary verb. The primary verb is typically activated in the client application by double-clicking the embedded object.

`OLESRV` calls the `ObjectGetData()` method any time the client application needs to display an object. `ObjectGetData()` has three parameters: `lpoleobject`, `cfFormat`, and `lphandle`. The `lpoleobject` specifies the object for the server to render. The `cfFormat` parameter specifies the format of the object. The `lphandle` parameter receives a handle to the rendered object. *Polygons* can render its objects for the following clipboard formats: Native data, CF_METAFILEPICT, CF_BITMAP, CF_TEXT, cfObjectLink, and cfOwnerLink. The *Object Management* section of this chapter covers the functions that render these clipboard formats.

The ObjectSetData() method provides the server with the data of an object embedded in a client document. *Polygons* accepts only native data, so other formats are ignored. OLESRV calls ObjectSetData() with three parameters: lpoleobject, cfFormat, and lphandle. The lpoleobject parameter is a pointer to an OLEOBJECT structure that identifies the object. The cfFormat parameter is the clipboard format of the data contained in the lphandle parameter.

OLESRV calls the ObjectSetBounds() method, which instructs the server to set the bounds for an object. The ObjectSetBounds() method has two parameters: lpoleobject and lprect. The lpoleobject parameter identifies the object. The lprect parameter contains the bounds for the object in MM_HIMETRIC units. If a server application does not use MM_HIMETRIC units, it should convert the bounds from MM_HIMETRIC to whatever units it does use. ObjectSetBounds() calls the conversion function HiMetricToDevice(). ObjectSetBounds() sets bounds only for embedded objects because bounds for linked objects are specified in the object's file.

OLESRV calls the ObjectEnumFormats() method to enumerate a server's clipboard formats. OLESRV will call ObjectEnumFormats() until the server application returns an appropriate format or it runs out of formats, thus returning NULL.

The ObjectSetColorScheme() method is similar to the DocSetColorScheme() method, except the palette specified is for the object rather than the document. OLESRV calls ObjectSetColorScheme() with two parameters: lpoleobject and lppal. The lpoleobject parameter specifies the object for which the palette is to be updated. The lppal parameter specifies the client application's preferred palette. Note that you should delete the old palette before you assign the new palette.

Listing 6.11. The vtobject.c source file.

```
#include "poly.h"

/******************************************************************/
/* Function: ObjectQueryProtocol                                  */
/* Purpose: Identifies supported protocol for app.                */
/* Returns: LPVOID                                                */
/******************************************************************/
```

continues

Listing 6.11. continued

```
LPVOID CALLBACK ObjectQueryProtocol(LPOLEOBJECT lpoleobject,
                                    LPSTR lpszProtocol)
   {
   return lstrcmp(lpszProtocol,"StdFileEditing") ? NULL :
       lpoleobject;
   }


/********************************************************************/
/* Function: ObjectRelease                                        */
/* Purpose:  Free objects.                                        */
/* Returns: OLE_OK                                                */
/********************************************************************/
OLESTATUS CALLBACK ObjectRelease(LPOLEOBJECT lpoleobject)
   {
   int i;

   for(i=0; i < MAXCLIENTS; i++)
       ((LPPOLYGON)lpoleobject)->lpoleclient[i] = NULL;

   return OLE_OK;
   }


/********************************************************************/
/* Function: ObjectShow                                           */
/* Purpose: To show the specified object.                         */
/* Returns: OLE_OK                                                */
/********************************************************************/
OLESTATUS CALLBACK ObjectShow(LPOLEOBJECT lpoleobject,
                              BOOL fTakeFocus)
   {
   LPPOLYGON lpPolygon;
   HWND hwndOldFocus;

   hwndOldFocus = GetFocus();
   lpPolygon = (LPPOLYGON)lpoleobject;

   ShowWindow(hWnd, SW_SHOWNORMAL);
```

```
    BringWindowToTop(lpPolygon->hwnd);
    SetFocus(fTakeFocus ? lpPolygon->hwnd : hwndOldFocus);
    return OLE_OK;
    }

/********************************************************************/
/* Function: ObjectDoVerb                                           */
/* Purpose: Take appropriate action for specified verb.             */
/* Returns: OLE_OK                                                  */
/********************************************************************/
OLESTATUS CALLBACK ObjectDoVerb(LPOLEOBJECT lpoleobject,
                                WORD wVerb, BOOL fShow,
                                BOOL fTakeFocus)

    {
    int i;
    switch(wVerb)
        {
        case PLAY:
            for(i=0; i<25; i++) MessageBeep(0);
            break;

        case EDIT:
            if(fShow)
                return vtObject.Show(lpoleobject, fTakeFocus);
            else
                break;
        default:
            return OLE_ERROR_DOVERB;
        }
    return OLE_OK;
    }

/********************************************************************/
/* Function: ObjectGetData                                          */
/* Purpose: Retrieve data for clipboard format.                     */
/* Returns: OLE_OK if successful, OLE_ERROR_FORMAT if               */
/*          unsuccessful                                            */
/********************************************************************/
OLESTATUS CALLBACK ObjectGetData(LPOLEOBJECT lpoleobject,
    WORD cfFormat, LPHANDLE lphandle)
    {
```

continues

319

Listing 6.11. continued

```
LPPOLYGON lpPolygon;

lpPolygon = (LPPOLYGON)lpoleobject;

if(cfFormat == cfNative)
    {
    if(!(*lphandle = GetNative(lpPolygon)))
        return OLE_ERROR_MEMORY;
    fDocChanged = FALSE;
    return OLE_OK;
    }

if(cfFormat == CF_METAFILEPICT)
    {
    if(!(*lphandle = GetMetafilePict(lpPolygon)))
        return OLE_ERROR_MEMORY;
    return OLE_OK;
    }

if(cfFormat == CF_BITMAP)
    {
    if(!(*lphandle = (HANDLE)GetBitmap(lpPolygon)))
        return OLE_ERROR_MEMORY;
    return OLE_OK;
    }

if(cfFormat == CF_TEXT)
    {
    if(!(*lphandle = GetText(lpPolygon)))
        return OLE_ERROR_MEMORY;
    return OLE_OK;
    }

if(cfFormat == cfObjectLink)
    {
    if(!(*lphandle = GetLink(lpPolygon)))
        return OLE_ERROR_MEMORY;
    return OLE_OK;
    }
```

```
        if(cfFormat == cfOwnerLink)
            {
            if(!(*lphandle = GetLink(lpPolygon)))
                return OLE_ERROR_MEMORY;
            return OLE_OK;
            }

        return OLE_ERROR_FORMAT;
        }

/*********************************************************************/
/* Function: ObjectSetData                                           */
/* Purpose: Stores an object in a specified format.                  */
/* Returns: OLE_OK                                                   */
/*********************************************************************/
OLESTATUS CALLBACK ObjectSetData(LPOLEOBJECT lpoleobject,
    OLECLIPFORMAT cfFormat, HANDLE hdata)
    {
    LPNATIVE  lpnative;
    LPPOLYGON lpPolygon;

    lpPolygon = (LPPOLYGON)lpoleobject;

    if(cfFormat != cfNative)
        return OLE_ERROR_FORMAT;

    lpnative = (LPNATIVE)GlobalLock(hdata);

    if(lpnative)
        {
        lpPolygon->native = *lpnative;
        if(lpPolygon->aName)
            GlobalDeleteAtom(lpPolygon->aName);
        lpPolygon->aName = GlobalAddAtom(lpnative->szName);
        doc.rgfObjNums[1] = FALSE;
        doc.rgfObjNums[GetPolygonNumber(lpPolygon)] = TRUE;

        MoveWindow(lpPolygon->hwnd, 0, 0,
                   lpPolygon->native.nWidth + 2 *
                   GetSystemMetrics(SM_CXFRAME),
                   lpPolygon->native.nHeight+ 2 *
                   GetSystemMetrics(SM_CYFRAME),
```

continues

321

Listing 6.11. continued

```
            FALSE);
        GlobalUnlock(hdata);
        }
    GlobalFree(hdata);
    return lpnative ? OLE_OK : OLE_ERROR_MEMORY;
    }


/*********************************************************************/
/* Function: ObjectSetTargetDevice                                   */
/* Purpose: Here for documentation purposes.                         */
/* Returns: OLE_OK                                                   */
/*********************************************************************/
OLESTATUS CALLBACK ObjectSetTargetDevice(LPOLEOBJECT lpoleobject,
                                         HANDLE hdata)
    {
    if(hdata != NULL)
        {
        LPSTR lpstd = (LPSTR)GlobalLock(hdata);
        GlobalUnlock(hdata);
        GlobalFree(hdata);
        }
    return OLE_OK;
    }


/*********************************************************************/
/* Function: ObjectSetBounds                                         */
/* Purpose: Set Bounds for an object.                                */
/* Returns: OLE_OK                                                   */
/*********************************************************************/
OLESTATUS CALLBACK ObjectSetBounds(LPOLEOBJECT lpoleobject,
                                   LPRECT lprect)
    {
    if(doc.doctype == DOCEMBEDDED)
        {
        RECT rect = *lprect;
        LPPOLYGON lpPolygon = (LPPOLYGON) lpoleobject;
        HiMetricToDevice(hWnd, (LPPOINT) &rect.left);
        HiMetricToDevice(hWnd, (LPPOINT) &rect.right);
        MoveWindow(lpPolygon->hwnd,
                   lpPolygon->native.nX,
```

```
                        lpPolygon->native.nY,
                        rect.right - rect.left + 2 *
                        GetSystemMetrics(SM_CXFRAME),
                        rect.bottom - rect.top + 2 *
                        GetSystemMetrics(SM_CYFRAME),
                        TRUE);
        }
    return OLE_OK;
    }


/***********************************************************************/
/* Function: ObjectEnumFormats                                         */
/* Purpose: Enumerates supported clipboard formats.                    */
/* Returns: Clipboard format                                           */
/***********************************************************************/
OLECLIPFORMAT CALLBACK ObjectEnumFormats(LPOLEOBJECT lpoleobject,
    OLECLIPFORMAT cfFormat)
    {
    if(cfFormat == 0)
        return cfNative;

    if(cfFormat == cfNative)
        return cfOwnerLink;

    if(cfFormat == cfOwnerLink)
        return CF_METAFILEPICT;

    if(cfFormat == CF_METAFILEPICT)
        return CF_BITMAP;

    if(cfFormat == CF_BITMAP)
        return cfObjectLink;

    if(cfFormat == cfObjectLink)
        return NULL;

    return NULL;
    }
```

continues

323

Listing 6.11. continued

```
/********************************************************************/
/* Function: ObjectSetColorScheme                                   */
/* Purpose: Set color palette recommended by client app.            */
/* Returns: OLE_OK if successful, OLE_ERROR_PALETTE if not          */
/********************************************************************/
OLESTATUS CALLBACK ObjectSetColorScheme(LPOLEOBJECT lpoleobject,
                                              LPLOGPALETTE lppal)

    {
    HPALETTE hpal = CreatePalette(lppal);
    LPPOLYGON lpPolygon = (LPPOLYGON)lpoleobject;

    if(hpal==NULL)
        return OLE_ERROR_PALETTE;

    if(lpPolygon->hpal)
        DeleteObject(lpPolygon->hpal);
    lpPolygon->hpal = hpal;

    return OLE_OK;
    }
```

Object Management

The objmgt.c source file contains the object-management functions for *Polygons*. These functions create, delete, size, and render polygon objects. The CreateNewPolygon() function allocates memory for a POLYGON structure, defines the default data for the structure, and then creates the polygon window. The DestroyPolygon() function deletes the polygon object name from the atom table, deletes the palette associated with the polygon object, and frees memory allocated to the POLYGON structure.

The DrawPolygon() function renders a polygon object for a given format. The GetBitmap(), GetMetafilePict(), and PaintPolygon() functions call the DrawPolygon() function. The ObjectWndProc() function calls PaintPolygon() every time it receives a WM_PAINT message. The GetBitmap() function requests DrawPolygon() to render the polygon in CF_BITMAP format. The GetMetafilePict() function requests DrawPolygon() to render the polygon in CF_METAFILEPICT format.

The GetLink(), GetNative(), and GetText() functions return ObjectLink, native, and text formats of a polygon object. The copy/cut functions and the ObjectGetData() method require these formats of the polygon.

The RevokePolygon() function calls **OleRevokeObject()**. The **OleRevokeObject()** revokes client access to the object. **OleRevokeObject()** has one parameter that points to the OLE client. After the server calls **OleRevokeObject()**, the OLE libraries know that the object is no longer available to client applications.

When an object changes status (in other words, the user changes the color or type of polygon, or saves the polygon to file), the OLE client application associated with the object needs to be notified of the change. The SendPolygonMessage() function calls the OLE client callback function with a message to inform the client of a change in status. The following is an example of the call:

```
lpPolygon->lpoleclient[i]->lpvtbl->CallBack
lpPolygon->lpoleclient[i], wMessage,(LPOLEOBJECT)lpPolygon);
```

The pointer to the client application is stored in the POLYGON structure in the lpoleclient member (the AssociateClient() function performs this assignment). The lpoleclient member points to an OLECLIENT structure. The OLECLIENT structure's first member points to the client application's CallBack method. The CallBack() function has three parameters: lpoleclient, wMessage, and lpoleobject. The lpoleclient parameter points to the client application's OLECLIENT structure. The lpoleobject parameter points to the OLEOBJECT structure. This is lpPolygon for the preceding example. The wMessage parameter contains the notification message. wMessage can have any of the values in Table 6.4.

Table 6.4. Client callback notification messages.

Notification Message	Description
OLE_CHANGED	Notifies the client that a linked object has changed.
OLE_CLOSED	The server has closed the object.
OLE_QUERY_PAINT	Informs the client that a lengthy rendering operation is occurring.
OLE_QUERY_RETRY	Notifies the client that the server is busy.
OLE_RELEASE	Informs the client that an object has been released because an asynchronous operation has finished.

continues

325

Table 6.4. continued

Notification Message	Description
OLE_RENAMED	Informs the client that a linked object has been renamed.
OLE_SAVED	The server has saved a linked object.

The SizePolygon() function handles the sizing of a polygon. The ObjectWndProc() function calls SizePolygon() when it receives a WM_SIZE message. If the polygon is a linked object in a client document, SizePolygon() calls SendPolygonMessage() with a notification message of OLE_CHANGED.

Listing 6.12. The objmgt.c source file.

```c
#include "poly.h"

/*******************************************************************/
/* Function: CreateNewPolygon                                      */
/* Purpose: Creates a new polygon.                                 */
/* Returns: Handle to the new polygon                              */
/*******************************************************************/
LPPOLYGON CreateNewPolygon(BOOL fDoc_Changed)
    {
    HPOLYGON hPolygon = NULL;
    LPPOLYGON  lpPolygon = NULL;
    int     ifObj = 0;

    if((hPolygon = LocalAlloc(LMEM_MOVEABLE | LMEM_ZEROINIT,
        sizeof(POLYGON))) == NULL)
        return NULL;

    if((lpPolygon = (LPPOLYGON) LocalLock(hPolygon)) == NULL)
        {
        LocalFree(hPolygon);
        return NULL;
        }

    for(ifObj=1; ifObj <= MAXOBJECTS; ifObj++)
        {
        if(doc.rgfObjNums[ifObj]==FALSE)
```

```
            {
            doc.rgfObjNums[ifObj]=TRUE;
            break;
            }
        }

    if(ifObj== MAXOBJECTS+1)
        {
        MessageBeep(0);
        return NULL;
        }

    wsprintf(lpPolygon->native.szName, "Polygon %d", ifObj);

    lpPolygon->aName = GlobalAddAtom(lpPolygon->native.szName);
    lpPolygon->hPolygon = hPolygon;
    lpPolygon->oleobject.lpvtbl = &vtObject;
    lpPolygon->native.idmPoly = IDM_TRIANGLE;
    lpPolygon->native.idmColor = IDM_RED;
    lpPolygon->native.version = VERSION;
    lpPolygon->native.nWidth = OBJECT_WIDTH;
    lpPolygon->native.nHeight = OBJECT_HEIGHT;
    SetHiMetricFields(lpPolygon);

    lpPolygon->native.nX = (ifObj - 1) * 20;
    lpPolygon->native.nY = (ifObj - 1) * 20;

    if(!CreatePolygonWindow(lpPolygon))
        return FALSE;

    fDocChanged = fDoc_Changed;

    return lpPolygon;
    }
/********************************************************************/
/* Function: DestroyPolygon                                         */
/* Purpose: Frees resources associated with a polygon.              */
/********************************************************************/
VOID PASCAL DestroyPolygon(HWND hwnd)
    {
```

continues

327

Listing 6.12. continued

```
        LPPOLYGON lpPolygon = (LPPOLYGON)GetWindowLong(hwnd, 0);

        if(lpPolygon->aName)
            {
            GlobalDeleteAtom(lpPolygon->aName);
            lpPolygon->aName = NULL;
            }

        if(lpPolygon->hpal)
            DeleteObject(lpPolygon->hpal);

        doc.rgfObjNums[GetPolygonNumber(lpPolygon)] = FALSE;

        LocalUnlock(lpPolygon->hPolygon);
        LocalFree(lpPolygon->hPolygon);
        }

/**********************************************************************/
/* Function: DrawPolygon                                            */
/* Purpose: Draws a polygon for a given format.                     */
/**********************************************************************/
VOID PASCAL DrawPolygon(HDC hdc, LPPOLYGON lpPolygon, RECT rc,
                        int dctype)
    {
    static  POINT tript[] =
    {-100, -100, 0, 100, 100, -100};
    static POINT rectpt[] =
    {-100, -80, -100, 80, 100, 80, 100, -80};
    static POINT pentpt[] =
    {-100, 0, -60, 100, 60, 100, 100, 0, 0, -100};
    static POINT hexpt[] =
    {-60, -100, -100, 0, -60, 100, 60, 100, 100, 0, 60, -100};
    static POINT heptpt[] =
    {-40, -100, -100, -40, -100, 40, 0, 100, 100, 40, 100, -40,
     40, -100};
    static POINT octpt[] =
    { -40, -100, -100, -40, -100, 40, -40, 100, 40, 100, 100,
     40, 100, -40, 40, -100};
    static POINT starpt[] =
```

```
{ -100, -100, -50, 10, -100, 50, -20, 50, 0, 100, 20, 50,
 100, 50, 50, 10, 100, -100, 0, -30, -100, -100};
HPEN     hpen;
HPEN     hpenOld;
HPALETTE hpalOld = NULL;

if(dctype == DC_METAFILE)
    {
    SetWindowOrg(hdc, 0, 0);
    SetWindowExt(hdc, rc.right, rc.bottom);
    }

if(lpPolygon->hpal)
    {
    hpalOld = SelectPalette(hdc, lpPolygon->hpal, TRUE);
    RealizePalette(hdc);
    }

SelectObject(hdc, hbrColor [lpPolygon->native.idmColor-
             IDM_RED]);

hpen = CreatePen(PS_SOLID, (rc.bottom-rc.top) / 10,
                 0x00808080);
hpenOld = SelectObject(hdc, hpen);

SetMapMode(hdc, MM_ISOTROPIC);
SetWindowExt(hdc, 220, -220);
SetViewportExt(hdc, rc.right, rc.bottom);
SetWindowOrg(hdc, -110, 110);
SetPolyFillMode(hdc, ALTERNATE);

switch(lpPolygon->native.idmPoly)
    {
    case IDM_TRIANGLE:
        Polygon(hdc, tript, sizeof(tript) / sizeof(POINT));
        break;

    case IDM_RECTANGLE:
        Polygon(hdc, rectpt, sizeof(rectpt) / sizeof(POINT));
        break;
```

continues

329

Listing 6.12. continued

```c
        case IDM_PENTAGON:
            Polygon(hdc, pentpt, sizeof(pentpt) / sizeof(POINT));
            break;

        case IDM_HEXAGON:
            Polygon(hdc, hexpt, sizeof(hexpt) / sizeof(POINT));
            break;

        case IDM_HEPTAGON:
            Polygon(hdc, heptpt, sizeof(heptpt) / sizeof(POINT));
            break;

        case IDM_OCTAGON:
            Polygon(hdc, octpt, sizeof(octpt) / sizeof(POINT));
            break;

        case IDM_STAR:
            Polygon(hdc, starpt, sizeof(starpt) / sizeof(POINT));
            break;
        }

    SetBkMode(hdc, TRANSPARENT);
    SetTextAlign(hdc, TA_BASELINE | TA_CENTER);
    TextOut(hdc, rc.right / 2, (rc.top+rc.bottom) / 2,
            lpPolygon->native.szName,
            lstrlen(lpPolygon->native.szName));

    SelectObject(hdc,
                (dctype == DC_METAFILE)
                    ? GetStockObject(BLACK_PEN) : hpenOld);
    if(hpalOld)
        {
        SelectPalette(hdc,
                    (dctype == DC_METAFILE)
                        ? GetStockObject(DEFAULT_PALETTE) : hpalOld,
                    TRUE);
        }

    DeleteObject(hpen);
    }
```

```
/********************************************************************/
/* Function: GetBitmap                                             */
/* Purpose: Gets the bitmap format of a polygon.                   */
/* Returns: Handle to a bitmap                                     */
/********************************************************************/
HBITMAP PASCAL GetBitmap(LPPOLYGON lpPolygon)
    {
    HDC         hdcObj;
    HDC         hdcMem;
    RECT        rc;
    HBITMAP     hbitmap;
    HBITMAP     hbitmapOld;

    hdcObj = GetDC(lpPolygon->hwnd);
    hdcMem = CreateCompatibleDC(hdcObj);
    GetClientRect(lpPolygon->hwnd, (LPRECT)&rc);
    hbitmap = CreateCompatibleBitmap
      (hdcObj, rc.right - rc.left, rc.bottom - rc.top);
    hbitmapOld = SelectObject(hdcMem, hbitmap);

    DrawPolygon(hdcMem, lpPolygon, rc, DC_BITMAP);

    hbitmap = SelectObject(hdcMem, hbitmapOld);
    DeleteDC(hdcMem);
    ReleaseDC(lpPolygon->hwnd, hdcObj);
    return hbitmap;
    }

/********************************************************************/
/* Function: GetLink                                               */
/* Purpose: Generates owner/object link strings for a polygon.     */
/* Returns: Handle to owner/object link format                     */
/********************************************************************/
HANDLE PASCAL GetLink(LPPOLYGON lpPolygon)
    {
    char    sz[FILENAMEMAXLEN];
    LPSTR   lpszLink = NULL;
    HANDLE  hLink = NULL;
    int     cchLen;
    int     i;
```

continues

Listing 6.12. continued

```c
    LoadString(hInst, IDS_SRVCLASSNAME, sz, sizeof sz);

    cchLen = lstrlen(sz) + 1;

    cchLen += GlobalGetAtomName
                (doc.aName, (LPSTR)sz + cchLen,
                 FILENAMEMAXLEN - cchLen) + 1;

    lstrcpy(sz + cchLen, lpPolygon->native.szName);
    cchLen += lstrlen(lpPolygon->native.szName) + 1;

    sz[cchLen++] = 0;

    hLink = GlobalAlloc(GMEM_DDESHARE ¦ GMEM_ZEROINIT, cchLen);
    if(hLink == NULL)
      return NULL;
    if((lpszLink = GlobalLock(hLink)) == NULL)
        {
        GlobalFree(hLink);
        return NULL;
        }

    for(i=0; i < cchLen; i++)
        lpszLink[i] = sz[i];

    GlobalUnlock(hLink);

    return hLink;
    }

/*****************************************************************/
/* Function: GetMetafilePict                                     */
/* Purpose: Generates a metafilepict format of a polygon.        */
/* Returns: A handle to a metafile                               */
/*****************************************************************/
HANDLE PASCAL GetMetafilePict(LPPOLYGON lpPolygon)
    {
    LPMETAFILEPICT  lppict = NULL;
    HANDLE          hpict = NULL;
    HANDLE          hMF = NULL;
```

```
    RECT            rc;
    HDC             hdc;

    hdc = CreateMetaFile(NULL);

    GetClientRect(lpPolygon->hwnd, (LPRECT)&rc);

    DrawPolygon(hdc, lpPolygon, rc, DC_METAFILE);

    if((hMF = CloseMetaFile(hdc)) == NULL)
      return NULL;

    if(!(hpict = GlobalAlloc(GMEM_DDESHARE,
        sizeof (METAFILEPICT))))
        {
        DeleteMetaFile(hMF);
        return NULL;
        }

    if((lppict = (LPMETAFILEPICT)GlobalLock(hpict)) == NULL)
        {
        DeleteMetaFile(hMF);
        GlobalFree(hpict);
        return NULL;
        }

    DeviceToHiMetric(hWnd, (LPPOINT) &rc.left);
    DeviceToHiMetric(hWnd, (LPPOINT) &rc.right);

    lppict->mm   =  MM_ANISOTROPIC;
    lppict->hMF  =  hMF;
    lppict->xExt =  rc.right - rc.left;
    lppict->yExt =  rc.top - rc.bottom;
    GlobalUnlock(hpict);
    return hpict;
    }

/******************************************************************/
/* Function: GetNative                                          */
/* Purpose: Gets the native format of a polygon.               */
/* Returns: A handle to native format                          */
/******************************************************************/
```

continues

333

Listing 6.12. continued

```
HANDLE PASCAL GetNative(LPPOLYGON lpPolygon)
    {
    LPNATIVE lpnative = NULL;
    HANDLE   hNative  = NULL;

    hNative = GlobalAlloc(GMEM_DDESHARE | GMEM_ZEROINIT,
                          sizeof(NATIVE));
    if(hNative == NULL)
        return NULL;
    if((lpnative = (LPNATIVE) GlobalLock(hNative)) == NULL)
        {
        GlobalFree(hNative);
        return NULL;
        }

    *lpnative = lpPolygon->native;

    GlobalUnlock(hNative);
    return hNative;
    }

/********************************************************************/
/* Function: GetPolygonNumber                                       */
/* Purpose: Gets the number of a polygon.                           */
/* Returns: The polygon number                                      */
/********************************************************************/
int PASCAL GetPolygonNumber(LPPOLYGON lpPolygon)
    {
    LPSTR lpsz;
    int n = 0;

    lpsz = lpPolygon->native.szName + 7;
    while(*lpsz && *lpsz>='0' && *lpsz<='9')
        n = 10*n + *lpsz++ - '0';
    return n;
    }
```

```
/*******************************************************************/
/* Function: GetText                                           */
/* Purpose: Gets the text format of a polygon--its name.       */
/* Returns: A handle to the text format                        */
/*******************************************************************/
HANDLE PASCAL GetText(LPPOLYGON lpPolygon)
    {
    HANDLE hText    = NULL;
    LPSTR  lpszText = NULL;

    if(!(hText = GlobalAlloc(GMEM_DDESHARE,
        sizeof(lpPolygon->native.szName))))
        return NULL;

    if(!(lpszText = GlobalLock(hText)))
        return NULL;

    lstrcpy(lpszText, lpPolygon->native.szName);

    GlobalUnlock(hText);

    return hText;
    }


/*******************************************************************/
/* Function: PaintPolygon                                      */
/* Purpose: Paint routine for Polygons.                        */
/*******************************************************************/
VOID PASCAL PaintPolygon(HWND hwnd)
    {
    LPPOLYGON       lpPolygon;
    RECT        rc;
    HDC         hdc;
    PAINTSTRUCT paintstruct;

    BeginPaint(hwnd, &paintstruct);
    hdc = GetDC(hwnd);

    lpPolygon = (LPPOLYGON)GetWindowLong(hwnd, 0);
    GetClientRect(hwnd, (LPRECT) &rc);
```

continues

Listing 6.12. continued

```
    DrawPolygon(hdc, lpPolygon, rc, DC_SCREEN);

    ReleaseDC(hwnd, hdc);
    EndPaint(hwnd, &paintstruct);
    }

/********************************************************************/
/* Function: RevokePolygon                                          */
/* Purpose: Revokes a polygon.                                      */
/********************************************************************/
VOID RevokePolygon(VOID)
    {
    LPPOLYGON lpPolygon;
    int i;

    lpPolygon = (LPPOLYGON)GetWindowLong(GetWindow(hWnd,
                                    GW_CHILD),0);

    for(i=0; i< MAXCLIENTS; i++)
        {
        if(lpPolygon->lpoleclient[i])
            OleRevokeObject(lpPolygon->lpoleclient[i]);
        else
            break;
        }
    }

/********************************************************************/
/* Function: SendPolygonMessage                                     */
/* Purpose: Sends a message to the client callback function.    */
/********************************************************************/
VOID PASCAL SendPolygonMessage(LPPOLYGON lpPolygon, WORD wMessage)
    {
    int i;

    for(i=0; i < MAXCLIENTS; i++)
        {
        if(lpPolygon->lpoleclient[i])
            {
            lpPolygon->lpoleclient[i]->lpvtbl->CallBack
```

```
                    (lpPolygon->lpoleclient[i], wMessage,
                    (LPOLEOBJECT)lpPolygon);
                    }
            else
                break;
            }
        }

/*********************************************************************/
/* Function: SizePolygon                                             */
/* Purpose: Handles sizing of a polygon window.                      */
/*********************************************************************/
VOID PASCAL SizePolygon(HWND hwnd, RECT rect, BOOL fMove)
    {
    LPPOLYGON lpPolygon;

    lpPolygon = (LPPOLYGON)GetWindowLong(hwnd, 0);
    if(fMove)
        {
        lpPolygon->native.nX = rect.left;
        lpPolygon->native.nY = rect.top;
        }
    lpPolygon->native.nWidth  = rect.right  - rect.left;
    lpPolygon->native.nHeight = rect.bottom - rect.top ;
    SetHiMetricFields(lpPolygon);
    InvalidateRect(hwnd, (LPRECT)NULL, TRUE);
    fDocChanged = TRUE;
    if(doc.doctype == DOCFROMFILE)
        SendPolygonMessage(lpPolygon, OLE_CHANGED);
    }


/*********************************************************************/
/* Function: CreatePolygonWindow                                     */
/* Purpose: Creates the window for a polygon.                        */
/* Returns: TRUE/FALSE                                               */
/*********************************************************************/
BOOL PASCAL CreatePolygonWindow(LPPOLYGON lpPolygon)
    {
    char szClassName[SZCLASSNAME];
```

continues

```
if(!LoadString(hInst, IDS_OBJCLASSNAME,
                szClassName, sizeof szClassName))
                return FALSE;

if(!CreateWindow(szClassName,
                NULL,
                WS_BORDER ¦ WS_THICKFRAME ¦ WS_CHILD ¦
                WS_CLIPSIBLINGS ¦ WS_VISIBLE,
                lpPolygon->native.nX,
                lpPolygon->native.nY,
                lpPolygon->native.nWidth,
                lpPolygon->native.nHeight,
                hWnd,
                NULL,
                hInst,
                (LPSTR)lpPolygon))
    return FALSE;
else
    return TRUE;
}
```

File Input and Output

The file.c module contains the major file input and output routines. The CreateDocFromTemplate() and CreateDocFromFile() functions are called from server methods. The CommonOpenFile(), CommonSaveFile(), and CommonSaveAs() functions are called from the MainWndProc() callback function.

The polygon file format contains a header and is followed by native data. The HEADER structure identifies a file type and file version. It has the following typedef:

```
typedef struct
    {
    char szFileSignature[FILESIGMAXLEN];
    int  version;
    char rgfObjNums[MAXOBJECTS+1];
    } HEADER;
```

When the server reads the file, it starts by reading the file for the size of the HEADER structure. The server then compares the szFileSignature member to a string with the value "Polygons" to determine whether the file is the correct type. The version member of the HEADER structure identifies the version of the file. Because *Polygons* is a new application, it has a version of "1". The version member enables an application to support prior versions of the file format. An old version of the file format could contain different native data and would require a different I/O routine. The rgfObjNums member identifies the number of the polygon objects.

After the server reads the HEADER and has determined that the file is in a correct format, it reads native data until the end of the file is reached. The native data is stored in the file from the NATIVE structure. Thus, reading the file for the size of the NATIVE structure loads one polygon object.

When the server opens a file, the server registers the document with the OLESRV library with the **OleRegisterServerDoc()** function. When the server saves a file under a different name—CommonSaveAs()—the OLESRV library needs to be informed of the new name. The **OleRenameServerDoc()** function provides this information. The **OleRenameServerDoc()** function has the following prototype:

```
OLESTATUS OleRenameServerDoc(LHSERVERDOC lhDoc,
                             LPSTR lpszDocName)
```

The lhDoc parameter is a handle to the document. This the second member of the DOC structure. The lpszDocName parameter points to the new filename. Listing 6.13 is the file.c source file.

Listing 6.13. The file.c source file.

```
#include "poly.h"

#define FILESIGMAXLEN 9

char szFileSignature[FILESIGMAXLEN] =  "Polygons";
char szDefExt[4] = "PLY";
char szFilterSpec[128] =
    "Polygon Files (*.PLY)\0*.PLY\0All Files (*.*)\0*.*\0";
OPENFILENAME ofn;
```

continues

Listing 6.13. continued

```
typedef struct
    {
    char szFileSignature[FILESIGMAXLEN];
    int  version;
    char rgfObjNums[MAXOBJECTS+1];
    } HEADER;

VOID SetFileName(VOID);
BOOL SaveFile(VOID);
LPPOLYGON PASCAL ReadPolygons(HFILE);
BOOL PASCAL CloseFileOnError(HFILE);
BOOL PASCAL FileSaveError(HFILE);
/********************************************************************/
/* Function: CreateDocFromTemplate                                  */
/* Purpose: Creates a document from a template.                     */
/* Returns: TRUE or FALSE                                           */
/********************************************************************/
BOOL PASCAL CreateDocFromTemplate(LPSTR lpszDoc, LHSERVERDOC lhdoc)
    {
    HEADER  header;
    HFILE   hFile;
    int     i;

    if((hFile = _lopen(lpszDoc, OF_READ)) == -1)
        return FALSE;

    if(_lread(hFile, (LPSTR)&header, sizeof(HEADER)) <
        sizeof(HEADER))
        CloseFileOnError(hFile);

    if(lstrcmp(header.szFileSignature, szFileSignature) ||
        (header.version != VERSION))
        CloseFileOnError(hFile);

    if(lhdoc == NULL)
        {
        if(OLE_OK != OleRegisterServerDoc(server.lhsrvr,
                            lpszDoc,
                            (LPOLESERVERDOC) &doc,
                            (LHSERVERDOC FAR *) &doc.lhdoc))
        CloseFileOnError(hFile);
```

```
        }
    else
        doc.lhdoc = lhdoc;

    doc.doctype     = DOCEMBEDDED;
    doc.oledoc.lpvtbl= &vtDoc;

    fDocChanged = FALSE;

    SetTitle(lpszDoc, TRUE);

    for(i=1; i <= MAXOBJECTS; i++)
        doc.rgfObjNums[i] = header.rgfObjNums[i];

    for(i=0; ReadPolygons(hFile); i++);

    _lclose(hFile);

    fDocChanged = FALSE;
    return TRUE;
    }

/*********************************************************************/
/* Function: CreateDocFromFile                                       */
/* Purpose: Creates a document from a file.                          */
/* Returns: TRUE or FALSE                                            */
/*********************************************************************/
BOOL PASCAL CreateDocFromFile(LPSTR lpszDoc, LHSERVERDOC lhdoc)
    {
    HEADER  header;
    HFILE   hFile;
    int     i;

    if((hFile =_lopen(lpszDoc, OF_READ)) == -1)
        return FALSE;

    if(_lread(hFile, (LPSTR)&header, sizeof(HEADER)) <
       sizeof(HEADER))
       CloseFileOnError(hFile);
```

continues

Listing 6.13. continued

```
    if(lstrcmp(header.szFileSignature, szFileSignature) ||
        (header.version != VERSION))
        CloseFileOnError(hFile);

    if(lhdoc == NULL)
        {
        if(OLE_OK != OleRegisterServerDoc(server.lhsrvr,
                            lpszDoc,
                            (LPOLESERVERDOC) &doc,
                            (LHSERVERDOC FAR *) &doc.lhdoc))
        CloseFileOnError(hFile);
        }
    else
        doc.lhdoc = lhdoc;

    doc.doctype     = DOCFROMFILE;
    doc.oledoc.lpvtbl= &vtDoc;

    fDocChanged = FALSE;

    SetTitle(lpszDoc, TRUE);

    for(i=1; i <= MAXOBJECTS; i++)
        doc.rgfObjNums[i] = header.rgfObjNums[i];

    for(i=0; ReadPolygons(hFile); i++);

    _lclose(hFile);

    fDocChanged = FALSE;
    return TRUE;
    }

/*******************************************************************/
/* Function: CloseFileOnError                                      */
/* Purpose: Closes a file & returns FALSE to be returned by        */
/*          calling function.                                      */
/* Returns: Always FALSE                                           */
/*******************************************************************/
BOOL PASCAL CloseFileOnError(HFILE hFile)
    {
```

```
    _lclose(hFile);
    return FALSE;
    }

/******************************************************************/
/* Function: CommonOpenFile                                       */
/* Purpose: Uses common dialog to open a document.                */
/* Returns: TRUE or FALSE                                         */
/******************************************************************/
BOOL CommonOpenFile(VOID)
    {
    char        szDoc[FILENAMEMAXLEN];
    BOOL        fUpdateLater;
    OLESTATUS   olestatus;

    if(SaveChanges(&fUpdateLater) == IDCANCEL)
        return FALSE;

    SetFileName();
    ofn.Flags |= OFN_FILEMUSTEXIST;

    wsprintf(szDoc, "*.%s", (LPSTR) szDefExt);

    ofn.lpstrFile = szDoc;

    if(!GetOpenFileName(&ofn))
        return FALSE;

    if(fUpdateLater)
        SendDocMessage(OLE_CLOSED);

    fRevokeSrvrOnSrvrRelease = FALSE;

    if((olestatus = RevokeDoc()) > OLE_WAIT_FOR_RELEASE)
        return FALSE;
    else
        if(olestatus == OLE_WAIT_FOR_RELEASE)
            Wait(&fWaitingForDocRelease);

    fRevokeSrvrOnSrvrRelease = TRUE;
    UpdateMenu(FALSE);
```

continues

Listing 6.13. continued

```c
    if(!CreateDocFromFile(szDoc, NULL))
        {
        MsgBox(hWnd, IDS_WRONGFORMAT, MB_OK | MB_ICONEXCLAMATION);
        CreateUntitledDoc();
        CreateNewPolygon(FALSE);
        return FALSE;
        }
    fDocChanged = FALSE;
    return TRUE;
    }


/*********************************************************************/
/* Function: ReadPolygons                                          */
/* Purpose: Reads the native data for a polygon from a document.   */
/* Returns: Handle to a polygon if successful, FALSE if             */
/*          unsuccessful                                           */
/*********************************************************************/
LPPOLYGON PASCAL ReadPolygons(HFILE hFile)
    {
    HPOLYGON  hPolygon = NULL;
    LPPOLYGON lpPolygon = NULL;

    hPolygon = LocalAlloc(LMEM_MOVEABLE | LMEM_ZEROINIT,
                        sizeof(POLYGON));

    if(hPolygon == NULL)
        return NULL;

    lpPolygon = (LPPOLYGON)LocalLock(hPolygon);

    if(lpPolygon == NULL)
        {
        LocalFree(hPolygon);
        return NULL;
        }

    if(_lread(hFile, (LPSTR)&lpPolygon->native,
        sizeof(NATIVE)) < sizeof(NATIVE))
        {
```

```
           LocalUnlock(hPolygon);
           LocalFree(hPolygon);
           return NULL;
           }

      lpPolygon->hPolygon = hPolygon;
      lpPolygon->oleobject.lpvtbl = &vtObject;
      lpPolygon->aName = GlobalAddAtom(lpPolygon->native.szName);

      if(!CreatePolygonWindow(lpPolygon))
          {
          LocalUnlock(hPolygon);
          LocalFree(hPolygon);
          return NULL;
          }
      return lpPolygon;
      }

/********************************************************************/
/* Function: CommonSaveFile                                         */
/* Purpose: If a doc is new, invoke the Common Dialog for SaveAs.   */
/*          Otherwise, just save the doc to a file.                 */
/* Returns: TRUE or FALSE                                           */
/********************************************************************/
BOOL CommonSaveFile(VOID)
    {
    if(doc.doctype == DOCNEW)
        return CommonSaveAs();
    else
        return SaveFile();
    }

/********************************************************************/
/* Function: CommonSaveAs                                           */
/* Purpose: Invokes the common Save As dialog and saves a file.     */
/* Returns: TRUE or FALSE                                           */
/********************************************************************/
BOOL CommonSaveAs(VOID)
    {
    char szDoc[FILENAMEMAXLEN];
    char szDocOld[FILENAMEMAXLEN];
    BOOL fUpdateLater = FALSE;
```

continues

345

CHAPTER 6

Listing 6.13. continued

```c
    if(doc.doctype == DOCEMBEDDED)
        if(SaveChanges(&fUpdateLater) == IDCANCEL)
            return FALSE;

    SetFileName();

    ofn.Flags |= OFN_PATHMUSTEXIST;
    wsprintf(szDoc, "*.%s", (LPSTR)szDefExt);
    ofn.lpstrFile = szDoc;

    if(GetSaveFileName(&ofn))
        {
        if(fUpdateLater)
            SendDocMessage(OLE_CLOSED);

        SetTitle(szDoc, FALSE);
        OleRenameServerDoc(doc.lhdoc, szDoc);

        if(SaveFile())
            return TRUE;
        else
            {
            SetTitle(szDocOld, FALSE);
            OleRenameServerDoc(doc.lhdoc, szDocOld);
            return FALSE;
            }
        }
    else
        return FALSE;
    }

/*********************************************************************/
/* Function: SaveFile                                              */
/* Purpose: Saves the current document into a file.                */
/* Returns: TRUE or FALSE                                          */
/*********************************************************************/
BOOL SaveFile(VOID)
    {
    HWND     hwnd;
    HFILE    hFile;
```

346

```
LPPOLYGON lpPolygon;
char      szDoc[FILENAMEMAXLEN];
HEADER    header;
int       i;

hwnd = GetWindow(hWnd, GW_CHILD);

if(!hwnd)
    return FileSaveError(NULL);

GlobalGetAtomName(doc.aName, szDoc, FILENAMEMAXLEN);
if((hFile =_lcreat(szDoc, 0)) == -1)
    return FileSaveError(NULL);

lstrcpy(header.szFileSignature, szFileSignature);
header.version = VERSION;
for(i=1; i <= MAXOBJECTS; i++)
    header.rgfObjNums[i] = doc.rgfObjNums[i];

if(_lwrite(hFile, (LPSTR)&header, sizeof(HEADER)) <
   sizeof(HEADER))
   return FileSaveError(hFile);

while(hwnd)
    {
    lpPolygon = (LPPOLYGON)GetWindowLong(hwnd, 0);
    if(_lwrite(hFile, (LPSTR)&lpPolygon->native,
       sizeof(NATIVE))
     < sizeof(NATIVE))
        return FileSaveError(hFile);

    hwnd = GetWindow(hwnd, GW_HWNDNEXT);
    }
_lclose(hFile);

doc.doctype = DOCFROMFILE;
fDocChanged = FALSE;

OleSavedServerDoc(doc.lhdoc);

return TRUE;
}
```

continues

347

Listing 6.13. continued

```
/*******************************************************************/
/* Function: FileSaveError                                       */
/* Purpose: Closes file and posts an error message box for save   */
/*          error.                                               */
/* Returns: Always FALSE                                         */
/*******************************************************************/
BOOL PASCAL FileSaveError(HFILE hFile)
    {
    if(hFile)
        _lclose(hFile);

    MsgBox(hWnd, IDS_FILESAVEERROR, MB_OK | MB_ICONEXCLAMATION);
    return FALSE;
    }


/*******************************************************************/
/* Function: SaveChanges                                         */
/* Purpose: Prompts user to save changes.                        */
/* Returns: User's choice: yes, no, or cancel                    */
/*******************************************************************/
WORD PASCAL SaveChanges(BOOL *pfUpdateLater)
    {
    int  rc;
    char szBuf[FILENAMEMAXLEN];

    *pfUpdateLater = FALSE;

    if(fDocChanged)
        {
        char szTmp[FILENAMEMAXLEN];

        if(doc.aName)
            GlobalGetAtomName(doc.aName, szTmp, FILENAMEMAXLEN);
        else
            szTmp[0] = NULL;

        if(doc.doctype == DOCEMBEDDED)
            wsprintf(szBuf, "Update %s before closing?",
                    Abbrev(szTmp));
        else
            lstrcpy(szBuf, (LPSTR) "Save changes?");
```

```
            rc = MessageBox(hWnd, szBuf, "Polygons",
                        MB_ICONEXCLAMATION ¦ MB_YESNOCANCEL);

        switch(rc)
            {
            case IDYES:
                if(doc.doctype != DOCEMBEDDED)
                    CommonSaveFile();
                else
                    switch(OleSavedServerDoc(doc.lhdoc))
                        {
                        case OLE_ERROR_CANT_UPDATE_CLIENT:
                            *pfUpdateLater = TRUE;
                            break;
                        case OLE_OK:
                            break;
                        default:
                            MsgBox(hWnd, IDS_SERIOUSERROR, MB_OK);
                        }
                return IDYES;
            case IDNO:
                return IDNO;
            case IDCANCEL:
                return IDCANCEL;
            }
        }
    return TRUE;
    }

/********************************************************************/
/* Function: SetFileName                                          */
/* Purpose: Sets the default values for the ofn struct.          */
/********************************************************************/
VOID SetFileName()
    {
    static char szFileTitle[13];

    ofn.lStructSize       = sizeof(OPENFILENAME);
    ofn.hwndOwner         = hWnd;
    ofn.lpstrFilter       = szFilterSpec;
    ofn.lpstrCustomFilter = NULL;
    ofn.nMaxCustFilter    = 0L;
```

continues

Listing 6.13. continued

```
ofn.nFilterIndex      = 1L;
ofn.lpstrFile         = NULL;
ofn.nMaxFile          = FILENAMEMAXLEN;
ofn.lpstrInitialDir   = NULL;
ofn.lpstrFileTitle    = szFileTitle;
ofn.hInstance         = hInst;
ofn.lCustData         = NULL;
ofn.lpfnHook          = NULL;
ofn.lpTemplateName    = NULL;
ofn.lpstrTitle        = NULL;
ofn.lpstrDefExt       = szDefExt;
ofn.Flags             = 0;
ofn.nFileOffset       = 0;
ofn.nFileExtension    = 0;
}
```

Menu and Miscellaneous Processing

Two menu functions, EnableDisableMenus() and UpdateMenu(), relate to OLE. EnableDisableMenus() controls the *Polygons* menu based on the state of the document and objects. If a document contains no objects, EnableDisableMenus() is called to gray the **File S**ave, **File S**ave **A**s, **Edit C**opy, **Edit C**ut, **Edit D**elete, and **O**bject **N**ext Object menu items. When the server creates a new document, a default polygon object is also created. At this point, EnableDisableMenus() is called to enable the menu items.

The server calls the UpdateMenu() function when it has been activated for an embedded object. The UpdateMenu() function then displays the **File U**pdate menu item in place of the **File S**ave menu item. Additionally, it grays the **O**bject menu option and the **Edit C**ut and **Edit D**elete menu items. The **Edit C**ut and **Edit D**elete menu items are grayed because the object is embedded in a client document and it should not be deleted by the server.

Two other functions are of interest in the misc.c module: RevokeServer() and Wait(). RevokeServer() sets the server handle to NULL, hides the server, and returns the return value from **OleRevokeServer()**. **OleRevokeServer()** has one parameter, which is a handle to the server. Because the RevokeServer()

function set the server handle to NULL, a temporary variable is set with the value of the server handle for the call to **OleRevokeServer()**.

The server calls the Wait() function when **OleRevokeServer()** returns OLE_WAIT_FOR_RELEASE. The OLE_WAIT_FOR_RELEASE flag indicates that the server and client applications are still in the process of terminating communications. The Wait() function allows messages to be processed until the OLESRV library calls the ServerRelease() method. Listings 6.14 and 6.15 are the menu.c and misc.c source files.

Listing 6.14. The menu.c source file.

```c
#include "poly.h"

/********************************************************************/
/* Function: EnableDisableMenus                                     */
/* Purpose: Controls menu items.                                    */
/********************************************************************/
VOID PASCAL EnableDisableMenus(WORD wEnable)
    {
    HMENU       hMenu;

    hMenu = GetMenu(hWnd);
    EnableMenuItem(hMenu, 3, MF_BYPOSITION | wEnable);
    EnableMenuItem(hMenu, 2, MF_BYPOSITION | wEnable);

    hMenu = GetSubMenu(GetMenu(hWnd), 0);
    EnableMenuItem(hMenu, IDM_SAVE,   MF_BYCOMMAND | wEnable);
    EnableMenuItem(hMenu, IDM_SAVEAS, MF_BYCOMMAND | wEnable);

    hMenu = GetSubMenu(GetMenu(hWnd), 1);
    EnableMenuItem(hMenu, IDM_CUT,    MF_BYCOMMAND | wEnable);
    EnableMenuItem(hMenu, IDM_COPY,   MF_BYCOMMAND | wEnable);
    EnableMenuItem(hMenu, IDM_DELETE, MF_BYCOMMAND | wEnable);

    hMenu = GetSubMenu(GetMenu(hWnd), 4);
    EnableMenuItem(hMenu, IDM_NEXTOBJ, MF_BYCOMMAND | wEnable);

    DrawMenuBar(hWnd);
    }
```

continues

Listing 6.14. continued

```c
/********************************************************************/
/* Function: UpdateMenu                                           */
/* Purpose:  Updates menu items.                                  */
/********************************************************************/
VOID PASCAL UpdateMenu(BOOL bEmbed)
    {
    HMENU hMenu = GetMenu(hWnd);

    if(bEmbed)
        {
        ModifyMenu(hMenu, IDM_SAVE, MF_BYCOMMAND | MF_STRING,
                   IDM_UPDATE, "&Update");
        EnableMenuItem(hMenu, 4, MF_BYPOSITION | MF_GRAYED);
        EnableMenuItem(hMenu, IDM_CUT,    MF_BYCOMMAND |
                       MF_GRAYED);
        EnableMenuItem(hMenu, IDM_DELETE,  MF_BYCOMMAND |
                       MF_GRAYED);
        }
    else
        {
        ModifyMenu(hMenu, IDM_UPDATE, MF_BYCOMMAND | MF_STRING,
                   IDM_SAVE, "&Save");
        EnableMenuItem(hMenu, 4, MF_BYPOSITION | MF_ENABLED);
        }
    DrawMenuBar(hWnd);
    }
```

Listing 6.15. The misc.c source file.

```c
#include "poly.h"

/********************************************************************/
/* Function: SetTitle                                             */
/* Purpose: Sets the Main window caption.                         */
/********************************************************************/
VOID PASCAL SetTitle(LPSTR lpszDoc, BOOL fEmbedded)
    {
    char szBuf[FILENAMEMAXLEN];
```

```
        if(lpszDoc && lpszDoc[0])
            {
            if(doc.aName)
                GlobalDeleteAtom(doc.aName);
            doc.aName = GlobalAddAtom(lpszDoc);
            }

        if(fEmbedded)
            {
            if(lpszDoc && lpszDoc[0])
                {
                wsprintf(szBuf, "Polygons - Polygon in %s",
                        Abbrev(lpszDoc));
                }
            else
                {
                char szDoc [FILENAMEMAXLEN];

                GlobalGetAtomName(doc.aName, szDoc, FILENAMEMAXLEN);
                wsprintf(szBuf, "Polygons - Polygon in %s",
                        Abbrev(szDoc));
                }
            SetWindowText(hWnd, (LPSTR)szBuf);
            }
        else
            if(lpszDoc && lpszDoc[0])
                {
                wsprintf(szBuf, "Polygons - %s", Abbrev(lpszDoc));
                SetWindowText(hWnd, szBuf);
                }
        }

/*******************************************************************/
/* Function: Abbrev                                               */
/* Purpose: Truncates path from filename.                         */
/* Returns: New filename                                          */
/*******************************************************************/
LPSTR PASCAL Abbrev(LPSTR lpsz)
    {
    LPSTR lpszTemp;

    lpszTemp = lpsz + lstrlen(lpsz) - 1;
```

continues

Listing 6.15. continued

```
    while(lpszTemp > lpsz && lpszTemp[-1] != '\\')
        lpszTemp--;
    return lpszTemp;
    }


/**********************************************************************/
/* Function: RevokeServer                                           */
/* Purpose: Hide Window and call OleRevokeServer.                   */
/* Returns: OLESTATUS                                               */
/**********************************************************************/
OLESTATUS RevokeServer(VOID)
    {
    LHSERVER lhserver;

    ShowWindow(hWnd, SW_HIDE);
    lhserver = server.lhsrvr;
    server.lhsrvr = NULL;
    return (OleRevokeServer(lhserver));
    }


/**********************************************************************/
/* Function: MsgBox                                                 */
/* Purpose: Creates a message box.                                  */
/**********************************************************************/
VOID PASCAL MsgBox(HWND hwnd, WORD wMsg, WORD wType)
    {
    char szWindowTitle[SZWINDOWTITLE];
    char szMessage[SZMESSAGE];

    LoadString(hInst, IDS_WINDOWTITLE,
               szWindowTitle, sizeof szWindowTitle);
    LoadString(hInst, wMsg,
               szMessage, sizeof szMessage);
    MessageBox(hwnd, szMessage, szWindowTitle, wType);
    }


/**********************************************************************/
/* Function: DeviceToHiMetric                                       */
/* Purpose: Converts device units to MM_HIMETRIC.                   */
/**********************************************************************/
```

```
VOID PASCAL DeviceToHiMetric(HWND hwnd, LPPOINT lppt)
    {
    HDC   hdc;
    int   nMapMode;

    hdc = GetDC(hwnd);
    nMapMode = SetMapMode (hdc, MM_HIMETRIC);
    DPtoLP(hdc, lppt, 1);
    SetMapMode(hdc, nMapMode);
    ReleaseDC(hwnd, hdc);
    }

/*********************************************************************/
/* Function: HiMetricToDevice                                        */
/* Purpose: Converts MM_HIMETRIC to device units.                    */
/*********************************************************************/
VOID PASCAL HiMetricToDevice(HWND hwnd, LPPOINT lppt)
    {
    HDC   hdc;
    int   nMapMode;

    hdc = GetDC(hwnd);
    nMapMode = SetMapMode(hdc, MM_HIMETRIC);
    LPtoDP(hdc, lppt, 1);
    SetMapMode(hdc, nMapMode);
    ReleaseDC(hwnd, hdc);
    }

/*********************************************************************/
/* Function: SetHiMetricFields                                       */
/* Purpose: Converts native data to MM_HIMETRIC.                     */
/*********************************************************************/
VOID PASCAL SetHiMetricFields(LPPOLYGON lpPolygon)
    {
    POINT pt;

    pt.x = lpPolygon->native.nWidth;
    pt.y = lpPolygon->native.nHeight;
    DeviceToHiMetric(hWnd, &pt);
    lpPolygon->native.nHiMetricWidth  = pt.x;
```

continues

Listing 6.15. continued

```
    lpPolygon->native.nHiMetricHeight = - pt.y;
    }


/******************************************************************/
/* Function: Wait                                              */
/* Purpose: MessageLoop.                                       */
/******************************************************************/
VOID PASCAL Wait(BOOL *pf)
    {
    MSG msg;
    BOOL fMoreMsgs = FALSE;

    *pf = TRUE;
    while(*pf==TRUE)
        OleUnblockServer(server, 1hsrvr, &f More Msgs);
        {
        if(!fMoreMsgs)
            {
            if(GetMessage(&msg, NULL, NULL, NULL))
                {
                TranslateMessage (&msg);
                DispatchMessage (&msg);
                }
            }
        }
    }
```

Dialog Box Procedures

The two dialog boxes for the *Polygons* application are the About dialog box and the Failed Update dialog box. The UpdateClient() function activates the Failed Update dialog box when **OleSavedServerDoc()** returns OLE_ERROR_CANT_UPDATE_CLIENT. The Failed Update dialog box enables the user to continue editing the document or to update and exit. Listing 6.16 is the dialogs.c source file.

Listing 6.16. The dialogs.c source file.

```c
#include "poly.h"

/********************************************************************/
/* Function: CreateDlgBox                                          */
/* Purpose: Generic function to create dialog boxes.               */
/* Returns: TRUE/FALSE                                             */
/********************************************************************/
BOOL PASCAL CreateDlgBox(HWND hwnd, LPCSTR lpTemplateName,
                         FARPROC lpDlgProc)
    {
    BOOL    bResult = TRUE;

    lpDlgProc = MakeProcInstance(lpDlgProc, hInst);
    if(lpDlgProc)
        {
        if(!DialogBox(hInst, lpTemplateName, hwnd,
                      (DLGPROC)lpDlgProc))
            bResult = FALSE;
        FreeProcInstance(lpDlgProc);
        }
    else
        bResult = FALSE;

    return bResult;
    }


/********************************************************************/
/* Function: AboutDlgProc                                          */
/* Purpose: Handles messages for the About dialog box.            */
/* Returns: TRUE/FALSE                                             */
/********************************************************************/
LRESULT CALLBACK AboutDlgProc(HWND hDlg, WORD message,
                              WPARAM wParam, LPARAM lParam)
    {
    switch(message)
        {
        case WM_INITDIALOG:
            return (LRESULT)TRUE;
        case WM_COMMAND:
```

continues

Listing 6.16. continued

```
            switch((WORD)wParam)
                {
                case IDOK:
                case IDCANCEL:
                    EndDialog(hDlg, TRUE);
                    return (LRESULT)TRUE;
                }
            break;
        }
    return (LRESULT)FALSE;
    }

/*******************************************************************/
/* Function: FailedUpdateDlgProc                                   */
/* Purpose: Handles messages for the Failed Update dialog box.     */
/* Returns: TRUE/FALSE                                             */
/*******************************************************************/
LRESULT CALLBACK FailedUpdateDlgProc(HWND hDlg, WORD message,
                                    WPARAM wParam, LPARAM lParam)

    {
    switch(message)
        {
        case WM_INITDIALOG:
            {
            char szMsg[200];

            szMsg[0] = NULL;

            wsprintf(szMsg,
                "This %s document can only be updated when
                 you exit %s.",
                (LPSTR) szClient,
                "Polygons");

            SetDlgItemText(hDlg, IDD_TEXT, szMsg);
            return TRUE;
            }

        case WM_COMMAND:
            switch(wParam)
```

358

```
            {
            case IDCANCEL:
            case IDD_CONTINUEEDIT:
                EndDialog(hDlg, TRUE);
                break;

            case IDD_UPDATEEXIT:
                EndDialog(hDlg, FALSE);
                break;
            }
        break;

    default:
        break;
    }
    return FALSE;
}
```

Supporting Modules

The poly.reg file is the only new file type for OLE applications. It is a registration database merge file. You will have to merge this file into the registration database so that the client application can access the *Polygons* application. The Regedit applet that comes with Windows 3.1 enables you to merge files into the registration database.

An alternative method for updating the registration database is through the use of an install program. An install program can use the registration API to insert records into the database.

Listing 6.17. The poly.reg registration file.

```
REGEDIT

HKEY_CLASSES_ROOT\.ply = Polygons
HKEY_CLASSES_ROOT\Polygons = Polygons
HKEY_CLASSES_ROOT\Polygons\protocol\StdFileEditing\server =
    c:\poly\poly.exe
HKEY_CLASSES_ROOT\Polygons\protocol\StdFileEditing\verb\0 = &Play
HKEY_CLASSES_ROOT\Polygons\protocol\StdFileEditing\verb\1 = &Edit
```

Listing 6.18. The poly.rc resource definition file.

```
#include "windows.h"
#include "resource.h"
#include "dialogs.h"

IDM_MENU MENU
BEGIN
    POPUP "&File"
    BEGIN
        MENUITEM "&New",              IDM_NEW
        MENUITEM "&Open...",          IDM_OPEN
        MENUITEM "&Save",             IDM_SAVE
        MENUITEM "Save &As...",       IDM_SAVEAS
        MENUITEM SEPARATOR
        MENUITEM "E&xit",             IDM_EXIT
    END

    POPUP "&Edit"
    BEGIN
        MENUITEM "Cu&t\tShift+Del", IDM_CUT
        MENUITEM "&Copy\tCtrl+Ins", IDM_COPY
        MENUITEM "&Delete\tDel",    IDM_DELETE
    END

    POPUP        "&Polygons"
    BEGIN
        MENUITEM    "&Triangle",              IDM_TRIANGLE
        MENUITEM    "&Rectangle",             IDM_RECTANGLE
        MENUITEM    "&Pentagon",              IDM_PENTAGON
        MENUITEM    "He&xagon",               IDM_HEXAGON
        MENUITEM    "&Heptagon",              IDM_HEPTAGON
        MENUITEM    "&Octagon",               IDM_OCTAGON
        MENUITEM    "&Star",                  IDM_STAR
    END

    POPUP "&Color"
    BEGIN
        MENUITEM "&Red",              IDM_RED
        MENUITEM "&Green",            IDM_GREEN
        MENUITEM "&Blue",             IDM_BLUE
```

```
            MENUITEM "&White",          IDM_WHITE
            MENUITEM "Gr&ay",           IDM_GRAY
            MENUITEM "&Cyan",           IDM_CYAN
            MENUITEM "&Magenta",        IDM_MAGENTA
            MENUITEM "&Yellow",         IDM_YELLOW
        END

        POPUP "&Object"
        BEGIN
            MENUITEM "&New",            IDM_NEWOBJ
            MENUITEM "Ne&xt",           IDM_NEXTOBJ
        END

        POPUP "&Help"
        BEGIN
            MENUITEM "A&bout...",       IDM_ABOUT
        END
    END
END

IDA_ACC ACCELERATORS
BEGIN
    VK_DELETE, IDM_CUT,    VIRTKEY, SHIFT
    VK_INSERT, IDM_COPY,   VIRTKEY, CONTROL
    VK_DELETE, IDM_DELETE, VIRTKEY
END

STRINGTABLE
    BEGIN
        IDS_MAINCLASSNAME   "MainClass"
        IDS_OBJCLASSNAME    "ObjClass"
        IDS_WINDOWTITLE     "Polygons"
        IDS_SRVCLASSNAME    "Polygons"
        IDS_FILENOTFOUND    "File Not Found"
        IDS_WRONGFORMAT     "Incorrect File Format"
        IDS_FILESAVEERROR   "Cannot Save File"
        IDS_WAITFORREVOKE   "Wait for document to be revoked"
        IDS_SERIOUSERROR    "Serious Error"
    END

#include "poly.dlg"
```

Listing 6.19. The poly.def module definition file.

```
NAME           Polygons

DESCRIPTION    'An OLE Server Application'

EXETYPE        WINDOWS

STUB           'WINSTUB.EXE'

CODE           PRELOAD MOVEABLE DISCARDABLE
DATA           PRELOAD MOVEABLE MULTIPLE DISCARDABLE

HEAPSIZE       1000
STACKSIZE      16000

SEGMENTS
    DIALOGS_TEXT    MOVEABLE DISCARDABLE LOADONCALL
    DOC_TEXT        MOVEABLE DISCARDABLE LOADONCALL
    DOCMGT_TEXT     MOVEABLE DISCARDABLE LOADONCALL
    FILE_TEXT       MOVEABLE DISCARDABLE LOADONCALL
    INIT_TEXT       MOVEABLE DISCARDABLE PRELOAD
    MENU_TEXT       MOVEABLE DISCARDABLE LOADONCALL
    MISC_TEXT       MOVEABLE DISCARDABLE LOADONCALL
    OBJECT_TEXT     MOVEABLE DISCARDABLE LOADONCALL
    OBJMGT_TEXT     MOVEABLE DISCARDABLE LOADONCALL
    POLY_TEXT       MOVEABLE             PRELOAD
    VTDOC_TEXT      MOVEABLE DISCARDABLE LOADONCALL
    VTOBJECT_TEXT   MOVEABLE DISCARDABLE LOADONCALL
    VTSERVER_TEXT   MOVEABLE DISCARDABLE LOADONCALL
    WINMAIN_TEXT    MOVEABLE             PRELOAD

EXPORTS
    MainWndProc               @1
    ObjectWndProc             @2
    AboutDlgProc              @3
    FailedUpdateDlgProc       @4
    ServerCreate              @5
    ServerCreateFromTemplate  @6
    ServerEdit                @7
    ServerExecute             @8
    ServerExit                @9
```

```
    ServerOpen              @10
    ServerRelease           @11
    DocClose                @12
    DocExecute              @13
    DocGetObject            @14
    DocRelease              @15
    DocSave                 @16
    DocSetColorScheme       @17
    DocSetDocDimensions     @18
    DocSetHostNames         @19
    ObjectDoVerb            @20
    ObjectEnumFormats       @21
    ObjectGetData           @22
    ObjectQueryProtocol     @23
    ObjectRelease           @24
    ObjectSetBounds         @25
    ObjectSetColorScheme    @26
    ObjectSetData           @27
    ObjectSetTargetDevice   @28
    ObjectShow              @29
```

Listing 6.20. The poly.dlg dialog definition file.

```
DLGINCLUDE RCDATA DISCARDABLE
BEGIN
    "DIALOGS.H\0"
END


IDD_ABOUTBOX DIALOG 101, 49, 160, 81
STYLE DS_MODALFRAME ¦ WS_POPUP ¦ WS_VISIBLE ¦ WS_CAPTION ¦
    WS_SYSMENU
CAPTION "About Polygons"
FONT 8, "MS Sans Serif"
BEGIN
    PUSHBUTTON      "OK", IDOK, 58, 62, 40, 14
    LTEXT           "Polygons", -1, 64, 10, 31, 8
    LTEXT           "An OLE Server Application", -1, 37, 25, 92, 8
    LTEXT           "Copyright _ 1992, Jeffrey Clark",
                    -1, 30, 42, 106, 8
END
```

continues

Listing 6.20. continued

```
IDD_FAILEDUPDATE DIALOG 9, 26, 251, 55
STYLE DS_MODALFRAME ¦ WS_POPUP ¦ WS_VISIBLE ¦ WS_CAPTION ¦
    WS_SYSMENU
CAPTION "Object Update"
FONT 8, "MS Sans Serif"
BEGIN
    DEFPUSHBUTTON    "&Continue Editing", IDD_CONTINUEEDIT,
                     77, 36, 68, 14,
                     WS_GROUP
    PUSHBUTTON       "Update && E&xit", IDD_UPDATEEXIT, 6, 36, 55, 14
    LTEXT            "", IDD_TEXT, 9, 9, 233, 20
END
```

Listing 6.21. The POLY make file.

```
CC = cl -c -AM -Gsw -Od -W3 -Zpi -Fo$@

all: poly.exe

poly.h: dialogs.h resource.h

poly.res: poly.rc poly.dlg dialogs.h resource.h
  rc -r poly

dialogs.obj: dialogs.c poly.h
  $(CC) $*.c

docmgt.obj: docmgt.c poly.h
  $(CC) $*.c

file.obj: file.c poly.h
 $(CC) $*.c

init.obj: init.c poly.h
  $(CC) $*.c

menu.obj: menu.c poly.h
  $(CC) $*.c
```

```
misc.obj: misc.c poly.h
 $(CC) $*.c

object.obj: object.c poly.h
  $(CC) $*.c

objmgt.obj: objmgt.c poly.h
  $(CC) $*.c

poly.obj: poly.c poly.h
  $(CC) $*.c

vtdoc.obj: vtdoc.c poly.h
 $(CC) $*.c

vtobject.obj: vtobject.c poly.h
 $(CC) $*.c

vtserver.obj: vtserver.c poly.h
 $(CC) $*.c

winmain.obj: winmain.c poly.h
  $(CC) $*.c

poly.exe:: dialogs.obj docmgt.obj file.obj init.obj\
           menu.obj misc.obj object.obj objmgt.obj poly.obj\
           vtdoc.obj vtobject.obj vtserver.obj winmain.obj\
           poly.res poly.def
    link /CO /MAP /NOD @<<
dialogs+
docmgt+
file+
init+
menu+
misc+
object+
objmgt+
poly+
vtdoc+
vtobject+
vtserver+
```

continues

Listing 6.21. continued

```
winmain
$@

libw mlibcew olesvr commdlg
poly.def
<<
    mapsym poly
    rc poly.res
```

Summary

This chapter describes the details of developing an OLE server application. Developing OLE applications is difficult because there are few stopping points to test and debug applications during development. There are, however, some ways to ease OLE application development. The first approach is to create modular programs. Even if you cannot test the OLE code, you can compile and link it, thus removing syntactical errors from the program. The second approach is to build OLE functionality into methods gradually. For the most part, the methods in the *Polygons* application are rather generic. You can use generic methods to start development and expand their functionality to meet the needs of your applications.

Another method to ease OLE application development is to program a non-OLE application first, but remembering how OLE code fits into the application. This will enable you to test and debug the core functionality of the application, thus isolating bugs related only to the non-OLE application code. When you are finished testing the base application, you can then add OLE code.

OLE Client
Applications

This chapter explores OLE client applications. I take an approach similar to the approach I took in Chapter 6, because the example program is large. The discussion of OLE client applications starts with the structures for the example program, OLECLNT.EXE. After I discuss the structures, I discuss the individual code modules. I have attempted to organize the code modules by functional area. For the most part, I was able to do so. Some modules, however, call functions in a completely different functional area. In such cases, I describe what the code does rather than how the code works. Figure 7.1 shows an example OLE client application.

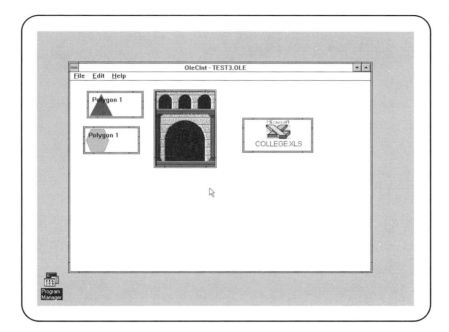

Figure 7.1.
An example OLE client application.

OLECLNT.EXE: An OLE Client Application

The example program, OLECLNT.EXE, unfortunately doesn't have a unique name; however, it does describe what the program does. The program is a

basic OLE client application that serves no real purpose. If you have glanced ahead, you have found pages and pages of code. All of this code represents a basic implementation of OLE. For the most part, you can probably use the code presented in this chapter to form the basis of other OLE applications. The program consists of the modules in Table 7.1.

Table 7.1. OLECLNT program modules.

Module	Description
oleclnt.h	Global header file
dialogs.h	Defines for dialog boxes
resource.h	Defines for resources
clipbord.c	Handles clipboard processing
dialogs.c	Dialog box callbacks
docmgt.c	Document management
dragdrop.c	Drag and drop processing
file.c	File I/O and common dialogs
init.c	Initialization code
links.c	Linking code
mem.c	Memory-management functions
misc.c	Miscellaneous functions
object.c	Object window callback
objmgt.c	Object-management functions
oleclnt.c	Main window callback
register.c	Registration database functions
vtclient.c	Client callback
vtstream.c	Stream methods
winmain.c	WinMain function
oleclnt.rc	Resource definition file
oleclnt.def	Module definition file
oleclnt.dlg	Dialog box definitions
OLECLNT	Make file

Example Program Header Files

The major items of concern in the header files are the following structures: OBJWIN, OBJECT, DOC, STREAM, and FILEOBJECT. The OBJWIN and OBJECT structures contain OLECLIENTVTBL structures as their first members. Thus, these structures can be passed to OLE functions in place of the OLECLIENT structure. The OBJWIN structure contains additional information for object window management. The OBJECT structure contains information for embedded and linked objects that are contained in the object window.

The DOC structure contains also an OLECLIENTVTBL structure for its first member. The OLECLNT application uses this structure for document-management functions. The last three members of the DOC structure are scratch memory areas. The OLECLNT application allocates memory for these members when OLECLNT starts.

The STREAM structure is an adaptation of the OLESTREAM structure. Because the STREAM structure contains an OLESTREAMVTBL for its first member, it can be used for any OLE function call that requires an OLESTREAM structure. The only other member of STREAM is a file handle. The file handle is associated to the current document. The DOC structure contains a member of type STREAM, which OLECLNT uses to call OLE functions that require OLESTREAM structures for parameters. This logically groups the OLESTREAM structure with the DOC structure, because stream processing and document processing are closely related. Nothing prohibits you from implementing these structures independently.

The FILEOBJECT structure contains members that relate to objects saved in a document. There is one FILEOBJECT for each object in a document. Each FILEOBJECT contains the base information for an object. This includes the window rectangle coordinates, the name, a window ID, and the size of the object. Listings 7.1, 7.2, and 7.3 show the oleclnt.h, dialogs.h, and resource.h header files.

Listing 7.1. The oleclnt.h header file.

```
#include <windows.h>
#include <ole.h>
#include <shellapi.h>
#include <commdlg.h>
#include "resource.h"
#include "dialogs.h"
```

continues

Listing 7.1. continued

```
#ifndef MAIN
#define EXTERN extern
#else
#define EXTERN
#endif

/* defines */
#define SZCLASSNAME         40
#define SZWINDOWTITLE       40
#define SZMESSAGE           128
#define FILENAMEMAXLEN      256
#define LINK                TRUE
#define NOLINK              FALSE
#define NOTIFY_SIZED        1
#define NOTIFY_CHANGED      2
#define NOTIFY_ACTIVATED    3
#define PM_MSGS             WM_USER+99
#define PM_GETRECT          PM_MSGS
#define PM_GETOBJECT        PM_MSGS+1
#define PM_NOTIFYOBJECT     PM_MSGS+2
#define PM_EXECUTE          PM_MSGS+3

#define CBSCRATCH           1024
#define CSCRATCH            3

#define OLEUPDATE_UNAVAILABLE   -2
#define OLEUPDATE_STATIC        -1
#define ENUMLINK_SELECTED       0
#define ENUMLINK_UNSELECTED     1
#define ENUMLINK_ALL            2

/* structures */
typedef struct
    {
    RECT        rc;
    WORD        wID;
    char        szName[40];
    DWORD       cbObject;
    } FILEOBJECT, FAR *LPFILEOBJECT;
```

```
typedef struct
    {
    LPOLESTREAMVTBL     pvt;
    HANDLE              hFile;
    } STREAM, FAR *LPSTREAM;

typedef struct _DOC
    {
    LPOLECLIENTVTBL     pvt;
    LHCLIENTDOC         lh;
    ATOM                aCaption;
    ATOM                aFile;
    LPSTREAM            pStream;
    HWND                hWnd;
    WORD                cObjects;
    struct _OBJECT FAR *pObjFirst;
    struct _OBJECT FAR *pObjLast;
    HWND                hList;
    HWND                cxList;
    WORD                cLinks;
    WORD                cWait;
    HANDLE              hData;
    LPSTR               pszData1;
    LPSTR               pszData2;
    LPSTR               pszData3;
    } DOC, FAR *LPDOC;

typedef struct _OBJECT
    {
    LPOLECLIENTVTBL     pvt;
    LPOLEOBJECT         pObj;
    BOOL                fRelease;
    BOOL                fOpen;
    struct _OBJECT FAR *pPrev;
    struct _OBJECT FAR *pNext;
    LPDOC               pDoc;
    ATOM                aName;
    ATOM                aClass;
    ATOM                aLink;
    ATOM                aSel;
```

continues

373

Listing 7.1. continued

```
    DWORD              dwType;
    OLEOPT_UPDATE      dwLink;
    BOOL               fNoMatch;
    LPOLEOBJECT        pObjUndo;
    BOOL               fUndoOpen;
    BOOL               fLinkChange;
    HANDLE             hData;
    } OBJECT, FAR *LPOBJECT;

typedef struct
    {
    LPOBJECT           pObj;
    BOOL               fOpen;
    BOOL               fUserResize;
    RECT               rc;
    POINT              ptDrag;
    BOOL               fDrag;
    } OBJWIN, *POBJWIN, FAR *LPOBJWIN;

/* typedefs */
typedef int (CALLBACK *LPCLIENTCALLBACK)(LPOLECLIENT,
    OLE_NOTIFICATION, LPOLEOBJECT);
typedef DWORD (CALLBACK *LPSTREAMMETHOD)(LPOLESTREAM, LPSTR,
                                         DWORD);
typedef BOOL (CALLBACK *LPFNLINKENUM)(HWND, WORD, LPOBJECT, DWORD);
typedef BOOL FAR *LPBOOL;

/* global variables */
EXTERN HWND          hWnd;
EXTERN HANDLE        hInst;
EXTERN LPSTR         pszCmdLine;
EXTERN HANDLE        hMemStrings;
EXTERN HANDLE        hAccel;
EXTERN BOOL          fDocChanged;
EXTERN BOOL          fOpenFile;
EXTERN char          szFile[FILENAMEMAXLEN];
EXTERN HWND          hWndLastActive;
EXTERN OLECLIPFORMAT cfObjectLink;
```

```
EXTERN OLECLIPFORMAT cfOwnerLink;
EXTERN OLECLIPFORMAT cfNative;
EXTERN LPDOC        pDoc;
EXTERN OLESTATUS     olestatus;

/* function prototypes */
/* clipbord.c */
BOOL CutObject(VOID);
BOOL PASCAL CopyObject(VOID);
BOOL PASCAL PasteObject(BOOL);

/* dialogs.c */
BOOL PASCAL CreateDlgBox(HWND, LPCSTR, FARPROC);
LRESULT CALLBACK AboutDlgProc(HWND, WORD, WPARAM, LPARAM);
BOOL PASCAL CreateInsertDlgBox(VOID);
LRESULT CALLBACK InsertObjectDlgProc(HWND, WORD, WPARAM, LPARAM);
LRESULT CALLBACK LinksDlgProc(HWND, WORD, WPARAM, LPARAM);
VOID PASCAL EnableLinkButtons(HWND, HWND);

/* docmgt.c */
BOOL RevokeDoc(VOID);
VOID FreeDoc(VOID);
BOOL SetDocName(VOID);
BOOL PASCAL ProcessMessages(LPMSG);

/* dragdrop.c */
BOOL PASCAL GetDroppedFiles(HANDLE);

/* file.c */
BOOL OpenPassedFile(VOID);
BOOL SaveChanges(VOID);
BOOL CreateNewDoc(VOID);
BOOL CommonOpenFile(VOID);
BOOL PASCAL CommonSaveFile(BOOL);
BOOL CommonSaveAs(VOID);
BOOL PASCAL ChangeLink(HWND);

/* init.c */
BOOL PASCAL InitApplication(HINSTANCE);
BOOL PASCAL InitInstance(HINSTANCE, int);
BOOL PASCAL InitClient(LPSTR);
```

continues

Listing 7.1. continued

```
VOID PASCAL ProcessCmdLine(LPSTR);
BOOL PASCAL Terminate(VOID);

/* links.c */
BOOL PASCAL QueryLinks(VOID);
BOOL PASCAL EnumLinks(HWND, LPFNLINKENUM, WORD, DWORD);
BOOL PASCAL LinksInit(LPOBJECT);
BOOL PASCAL ChangeLinkOptions(HWND, WORD, LPOBJECT, DWORD);
BOOL PASCAL UpdateLinks(HWND, WORD, LPOBJECT, DWORD);
BOOL PASCAL CancelLinks(HWND, WORD, LPOBJECT, DWORD);
BOOL PASCAL ChangeLinks(HWND, WORD, LPOBJECT, DWORD);
BOOL PASCAL FindLinks(HWND, WORD, LPOBJECT, DWORD);
BOOL PASCAL UndoLinks(HWND, WORD, LPOBJECT, DWORD);
BOOL PASCAL CleanupClones(HWND, WORD, LPOBJECT, DWORD);
BOOL PASCAL AutoUpdateLinks(LPDOC, LPOBJECT);

/* misc.c */
LPSTR PASCAL Abbrev(LPSTR);
VOID PASCAL MsgBox(HWND hwnd, WORD wMsg, WORD wType);
OLESTATUS PASCAL ErrHandler(OLESTATUS, LPDOC, LPOBJECT, BOOL);
LPSTR PASCAL GetFileFromPath(LPSTR);
LPSTR PASCAL GetExtFromFile(LPSTR);
VOID  PASCAL ConvertRectMappings(LPRECT, WORD, WORD);
BOOL PASCAL Wait(BOOL, LPOBJECT);

/* mem.c */
LPOLECLIENTVTBL AllocClientVtbl(VOID);
LPSTREAM AllocStream(VOID);
BOOL FreeClientVtbl(VOID);
BOOL FreeStream(VOID);

/* menu.c */
VOID PASCAL InitMenuPopup(WPARAM, LPARAM);

/* object.c */
LRESULT CALLBACK ObjectWndProc(HWND, WORD, WPARAM, LPARAM);

/* oleclnt.c */
LRESULT CALLBACK MainWndProc(HWND, WORD, WPARAM, LPARAM);
```

```
/* objmgt.c */
LPOBJECT PASCAL AllocObject(VOID);
LPOBJECT PASCAL InitializeObject(LPOBJECT, LPDOC);
LPOBJECT PASCAL FreeObject(LPDOC, LPOBJECT);
VOID PASCAL ClearObject(LPARAM);
VOID ClearAllObjects(VOID);
BOOL PASCAL CloseObjects(LPOBJECT);
BOOL PASCAL UpdateObjects(LPOBJECT);
BOOL PASCAL DeleteObjects(LPOBJECT);
VOID PASCAL SetFileObject(LPFILEOBJECT);
HWND PASCAL CreateObjectWindow(LPFILEOBJECT, BOOL, LPOBJECT);
LPRECT PASCAL GetObjectWindowRect(HWND, LPRECT, HWND);
BOOL PASCAL PaintObject(HDC, LPRECT, LPOBJECT);
BOOL PASCAL SetObjectRect(LPDOC, LPOBJECT, LPRECT, WORD);
BOOL PASCAL GetObjectRect(LPOBJECT, LPRECT, WORD);
BOOL PASCAL GetObjectData(LPOBJECT, WORD, LPSTR);
BOOL PASCAL SetObjectData(LPOBJECT, WORD, LPSTR);

/* register.c */
WORD PASCAL LoadClassList(HWND);
WORD PASCAL GetClassFromDesc(LPSTR, LPSTR, WORD);
WORD PASCAL GetDescFromClass(LPSTR, LPSTR, WORD);
WORD PASCAL GetClassFromExt(LPSTR, LPSTR, WORD);
WORD PASCAL BuildVerbList(LPSTR, LPSTR, WORD);

/* vtclient.c */
int CALLBACK ClientCallback(LPOBJECT, OLE_NOTIFICATION,
                            LPOLEOBJECT);

/* vtstream.c */
DWORD CALLBACK StreamGet(LPSTREAM, LPBYTE, DWORD);
DWORD CALLBACK StreamPut(LPSTREAM, LPBYTE, DWORD);

/* winmain.c */
int PASCAL WinMain(HINSTANCE, HINSTANCE, LPSTR, int);
```

Listing 7.2. The dialogs.h header file.

```
#define IDD_ABOUTBOX            100

#define IDD_INSERTOBJECTBOX     200
#define IDD_OBJECTLIST          201

#define IDD_LINKSBOX            300
#define IDD_LINKLIST            301
#define IDD_AUTOMATIC           302
#define IDD_MANUAL              303
#define IDD_UPDATENOW           304
#define IDD_CANCELLINK          305
#define IDD_CHANGELINK          306
```

Listing 7.3. The resource.h header file.

```
#define IDS_MAINCLASSNAME       1
#define IDS_OBJCLASSNAME        2
#define IDS_WINDOWTITLE         3
#define IDS_QUERYSAVEFILE       4
#define IDS_QUERYLINKS          5
#define IDS_UPDATINGLINKS       6
#define IDS_BADFILELINK         7
#define IDS_BUSY                8
#define IDS_CANNOTINSERT        9
#define IDS_CHANGELINK1         10
#define IDS_CHANGELINK2         11

#define IDM_MENU                1
#define IDA_ACC                 1

#define IDM_NEW                 100
#define IDM_OPEN                101
#define IDM_SAVE                102
#define IDM_SAVEAS              103
#define IDM_EXIT                104

#define IDM_CUT                 200
#define IDM_COPY                201
#define IDM_PASTE               202
```

```
#define IDM_PASTELINK      203
#define IDM_LINKS          204
#define IDM_INSERTOBJECT   205
#define IDM_CLEAR          207
#define IDM_CLEARALL       208
#define IDM_FIRSTVERB      250
#define IDM_LASTVERB       299

#define IDM_ABOUT          300
```

WinMain: **Application Initialization and Termination**

The application initialization code for OLECLNT is rather generic. WinMain() calls InitApplication() and InitInstance() to perform the usual application initialization. The InitInstance() function, however, performs some critical OLE application initialization. In particular, InitInstance() calls InitClient() and registers the clipboard formats for the application.

The InitClient() function allocates the DOC and STREAM structures. Because OLECLNT uses the DOC structure as the OLECLIENT structure, OLECLNT calls **MakeProcInstance()** for the ClientCallback() function. The same is true for the pointer to StreamGet() and StreamPut() methods contained in the OLESTREAMVTBL member of the STREAM structure. Additional memory is allocated for the last three members of the DOC structure: pszData1, pszData2, and pszData3. OLECLNT uses these scratch areas throughout its processing. Allocating memory once here and freeing it when the application terminates reduces the amount of memory management throughout the program.

If a command-line parameter is passed to OLECLNT, the ProcessCmdLine() function will open the passed file. If the file is a valid OLECLNT file, the document is registered with the OLE client library through the **OleRegisterClientDoc()** function. Otherwise, an "Untitled" document is registered with OLECLI.

The init.c source file contains also termination code in the Terminate() function. This function queries the user to save the current document if the document has changed, and it also calls the RevokeDoc() function. The

RevokeDoc() function calls **OleRevokeClientDoc()** after it revokes each of the objects contained in the document. Listings 7.4 and 7.5 show the winmain.c and init.c source modules.

Listing 7.4. The winmain.c source module.

```
#define MAIN
#include "oleclnt.h"

/*********************************************************************/
/* Function: WinMain                                                 */
/* Purpose: Main function for windows app. Initializes all           */
/*          instances of app, translates and dispatches messages. */
/* Returns: Value of PostQuitMessage                                 */
/*********************************************************************/
int PASCAL WinMain(HINSTANCE hInstance, HINSTANCE hPrevInstance,
                   LPSTR lpCmdLine, int nCmdShow)
    {
    MSG msg;

    if(!hPrevInstance)
        if(!InitApplication(hInstance))
            return FALSE;

    if(!InitInstance(hInstance, nCmdShow))
        return FALSE;

    ProcessCmdLine(lpCmdLine);

    while(GetMessage(&msg, 0, 0, 0))
        {
        if(!TranslateAccelerator(hWnd, hAccel, &msg))
            {
            TranslateMessage(&msg);
            DispatchMessage(&msg);
            }
        }

    FreeDoc();

    return msg.wParam;
    }
```

Listing 7.5. The init.c source module.

```c
#include "oleclnt.h"

/*********************************************************************/
/* Function: InitApplication                                        */
/* Purpose: Performs all initialization for first instance of app.*/
/* Returns: TRUE if successful, FALSE if failure                    */
/*********************************************************************/
BOOL PASCAL InitApplication(HINSTANCE hInstance)
    {
    WNDCLASS  wc;
    char szClassName[SZCLASSNAME];

    if(!LoadString(hInstance, IDS_MAINCLASSNAME,
        szClassName, sizeof szClassName))
        return FALSE;

    wc.style         = CS_HREDRAW | CS_VREDRAW;
    wc.lpfnWndProc   = MainWndProc;
    wc.cbClsExtra    = 0;
    wc.cbWndExtra    = 0;
    wc.hInstance     = hInstance;
    wc.hIcon         = LoadIcon(hInstance, IDI_APPLICATION);
    wc.hCursor       = LoadCursor(NULL, IDC_ARROW);
    wc.hbrBackground = GetStockObject(WHITE_BRUSH);
    wc.lpszMenuName  = MAKEINTRESOURCE(IDM_MENU);
    wc.lpszClassName = szClassName;

    if(!RegisterClass(&wc))
        return FALSE;

    if(!LoadString(hInstance, IDS_OBJCLASSNAME,
        szClassName, sizeof szClassName))
        return FALSE;

    wc.style         = CS_HREDRAW | CS_VREDRAW | CS_DBLCLKS;
    wc.lpfnWndProc   = ObjectWndProc;
    wc.hIcon         = NULL;
    wc.cbWndExtra    = sizeof (LPSTR);
```

continues

Listing 7.5. continued

```
    wc.lpszMenuName  = NULL;
    wc.hCursor       = LoadCursor(NULL, IDC_CROSS);
    wc.lpszClassName = szClassName;

    if(!RegisterClass(&wc))
        return FALSE;

    return TRUE;
    }


/***********************************************************************/
/* Function: InitInstance                                            */
/* Purpose: Performs all initialization for all instances of app. */
/* Returns: TRUE if successful, FALSE if failure                     */
/***********************************************************************/
BOOL PASCAL InitInstance(HINSTANCE hInstance, int nCmdShow)
    {
    char szClassName[SZCLASSNAME];
    char szWindowTitle[SZWINDOWTITLE];

    hInst = hInstance;

    cfObjectLink = RegisterClipboardFormat("ObjectLink");
    cfOwnerLink  = RegisterClipboardFormat("OwnerLink");
    cfNative     = RegisterClipboardFormat("Native");

    hAccel = LoadAccelerators(hInst, MAKEINTRESOURCE(IDA_ACC));

    if(!LoadString(hInst, IDS_MAINCLASSNAME,
        szClassName, sizeof szClassName))
        return FALSE;

    if(!LoadString(hInst, IDS_WINDOWTITLE,
        szWindowTitle, sizeof szWindowTitle))
        return FALSE;

    if(!InitClient(szWindowTitle))
        return FALSE;
```

```
        hWnd = CreateWindow(szClassName,
                            szWindowTitle,
                            WS_OVERLAPPEDWINDOW,
                            CW_USEDEFAULT,
                            CW_USEDEFAULT,
                            CW_USEDEFAULT,
                            CW_USEDEFAULT,
                            NULL,
                            NULL,
                            hInstance,
                            NULL);

    if(!hWnd)
        return FALSE;

    pDoc->hWnd = hWnd;
    ShowWindow(hWnd, nCmdShow);
    UpdateWindow(hWnd);
    fDocChanged = FALSE;
    return TRUE;
    }

/*****************************************************************/
/* Function: InitClient                                        */
/* Purpose: Initializes client document.                       */
/* Returns: Pointer to document                                */
/*****************************************************************/
BOOL PASCAL InitClient(LPSTR pszCaption)
    {
    HANDLE hMem;

    if(NULL == hInst || NULL == pszCaption)
        return FALSE;

    hMem = LocalAlloc(LPTR, sizeof(DOC));

    if(!hMem)
        return FALSE;

    pDoc=(LPDOC)(PSTR)hMem;
```

continues

Listing 7.5. continued

```
    pDoc->aCaption = AddAtom(pszCaption);
    pDoc->pvt = AllocClientVtbl();
    pDoc->pStream = AllocStream();

    pDoc->hData = GlobalAlloc(GHND, CSCRATCH*CBSCRATCH);

    if(!pDoc->hData)
        return FALSE;

    pDoc->pszData1 = GlobalLock(pDoc->hData);
    pDoc->pszData2 = pDoc->pszData1+CBSCRATCH;
    pDoc->pszData3 = pDoc->pszData2+CBSCRATCH;

    return TRUE;
    }


/********************************************************************/
/* Function: ProcessCmdLine                                         */
/* Purpose: Parse command line.                                     */
/* Returns: TRUE if successful, FALSE if failure                    */
/********************************************************************/
VOID PASCAL ProcessCmdLine(LPSTR lpszLine)
    {
    int i;

    while(*lpszLine && *lpszLine == ' ')
        lpszLine++;

    if(*lpszLine)
        {
        i = 0;
        while(*lpszLine && *lpszLine != ' ')
            szFile[i++] = *lpszLine++;
        szFile[i] = '\0';
        }
     OpenPassedFile();
    }
```

```
/*********************************************************************/
/* Function: Terminate                                               */
/* Purpose: Pre-PostQuitMessage processing.                          */
/* Returns: TRUE if successful, FALSE if failure                     */
/*********************************************************************/
BOOL PASCAL Terminate(VOID)
    {
    if(fDocChanged)
        if(!SaveChanges())
            return FALSE;

    RevokeDoc();
    return TRUE;
    }
```

Main Window Processing Module

The `MainWndProc()` function is the callback function for OLECLNT's main window. This function does not contain any OLE functions; however, it calls functions that handle document and object management. The `MainWndProc()` calls document-management functions when it receives `WM_CREATE`, `WM_CLOSE`, `WM_DESTROY`, and `WM_COMMAND` messages for the **F**ile menu items.

When `MainWndProc()` receives a `WM_CREATE` message, it calls `CreateNewDoc()` if `fOpenFile` is FALSE. `fOpenFile` is a global variable, and it will be set to TRUE if a file is passed on the command line. `MainWndProc()` also calls the **DragAcceptFiles()** function when it receives a `WM_CREATE` message. The **DragAcceptFiles()** function registers the window to accept dropped files. The **DragAcceptFiles()** function has the following prototype:

```
VOID DragAcceptFiles(HWND hwnd, BOOL fAccept);
```

The `hwnd` parameter is the handle to the window to accept dropped files. The `fAccept` parameter indicates whether dropped files should be accepted. If `fAccept` is TRUE, the window specified in the `hwnd` parameter will receive `WM_DROPFILES` messages when a user drops a file on the window. If `fAccept` is FALSE, Windows will filter `WM_DROPFILES` messages for the given window.

Windows sends the `WM_COMMAND` message to `MainWndProc()` when the user selects a menu item. The menu items fall into two categories: those associated

with the **F**ile menu, and those associated with the **E**dit menu. The functions
associated with the **F**ile menu items are OLE document-related functions.
The functions associated with the **E**dit menu items are OLE object-related
functions. Listing 7.6 is the oleclnt.c source module.

Listing 7.6. The oleclnt.c source module.

```
#include "oleclnt.h"

/********************************************************************/
/* Function: MainWndProc                                          */
/* Purpose: Main window procedure.                                */
/* Returns: Varies on message                                     */
/********************************************************************/
LRESULT CALLBACK MainWndProc(HWND hwnd, WORD Message,
                             WPARAM wParam, LPARAM lParam)
    {
    switch(Message)
        {
        case WM_CREATE:
            hWndLastActive = NULL;
            fDocChanged = FALSE;
            DragAcceptFiles(hwnd, TRUE);
            if(!fOpenFile)
                {
                if(!CreateNewDoc())
                    PostMessage(hwnd, WM_CLOSE, 0, 0L);
                }
            break;

        case WM_INITMENUPOPUP:
            InitMenuPopup(wParam, lParam);
            break;

        case WM_CLOSE:
            if(!Terminate())
                break;
            DestroyWindow(hwnd);
            break;
```

```
case WM_DESTROY:
    DragAcceptFiles(hwnd, FALSE);
    PostQuitMessage(0);
    break;

case WM_MOVE:
case WM_SIZE:
    fDocChanged = TRUE;
    break;

case WM_KEYDOWN:
    if(VK_RETURN==wParam)
        SendMessage(hWndLastActive, PM_EXECUTE, 0, 0L);
    break;

case WM_DROPFILES:
    GetDroppedFiles((HANDLE)wParam);
    break;

case WM_COMMAND:
    if(wParam >= IDM_FIRSTVERB && wParam <= IDM_LASTVERB)
        {
        SendMessage(hWndLastActive, PM_EXECUTE,
                    wParam-IDM_FIRSTVERB, 0L);
        break;
        }

    if(wParam >=1000 && NOTIFY_ACTIVATED == HIWORD(lParam))
        {
        if(NULL!=hWndLastActive)
            SendMessage(hWndLastActive, WM_NCACTIVATE,
                        FALSE, 0L);

        hWndLastActive=(HWND)LOWORD(lParam);
        }

    if(wParam >=1000 && (NOTIFY_ACTIVATED != HIWORD(lParam)))
        fDocChanged = TRUE;

    switch(wParam)
        {
```

continues

387

Listing 7.6. continued

```c
case IDM_NEW:
    CreateNewDoc();
    break;

case IDM_OPEN:
    CommonOpenFile();
    break;

case IDM_SAVE:
    CommonSaveFile(FALSE);
    break;

case IDM_SAVEAS:
    CommonSaveAs();
    break;

case IDM_EXIT:
    PostMessage(hwnd, WM_CLOSE, 0, 0L);
    break;

case IDM_CUT:
    CutObject();
    break;

case IDM_COPY:
    CopyObject();
    break;

case IDM_PASTE:
    PasteObject(NOLINK);
    break;

case IDM_PASTELINK:
    PasteObject(LINK);
    break;

case IDM_LINKS:
    if(CreateDlgBox(hwnd,
            (LPCSTR)MAKEINTRESOURCE(IDD_LINKSBOX),
```

```
                          (FARPROC)LinksDlgProc))
                    fDocChanged = TRUE;
                break;

            case IDM_INSERTOBJECT:
                CreateInsertDlgBox();
                break;

            case IDM_CLEAR:
                ClearObject(lParam);
                break;

            case IDM_CLEARALL:
                ClearAllObjects();
                break;

            case IDM_ABOUT:
                CreateDlgBox(hwnd,
                        (LPCSTR)MAKEINTRESOURCE(IDD_ABOUTBOX),
                        (FARPROC)AboutDlgProc);
                break;
        }
    default:
        return (DefWindowProc(hwnd, Message, wParam, lParam));
    }
    return 0L;
}
```

Drag and Drop

Drag and drop functionality is very easy to implement. As described in the previous section, the main window callback function receives WM_DROPFILES messages when a user drops a file on the main window. The wParam for the WM_DROPFILES message contains a handle to the dropped file or files. The MainWndProc() function calls GetDroppedFiles() when it receives a WM_DROPFILES message. GetDroppedFiles() creates OLE packages for the dropped file.

The GetDroppedFiles() function calls **DragQueryFile()** to determine the number of files dropped on the main window. This first call to **DragQueryFile()** has a −1 for the second parameter. This instructs the **DragQueryFile()**

389

function to return the number of files dropped. The following lines show the function prototype for **DragQueryFile()**:

```
WORD DragQueryFile(HANDLE hDrop, WORD iFile,
                   LPSTR lpszFile, WORD cb);
```

The first parameter, hDrop, is a handle that identifies an internal structure that contains the file names of the dropped files. The second parameter, iFile, is an index to the files. The first file is zero. If iFile has the value of −1, **DragQueryFile()** returns the number of files dropped. The third parameter, lpszFile, points to a null-terminated string that contains the name of the file when **DragQueryFile()** returns. The last parameter, cb, specifies the size of lpszFile. The lpszFile and cb parameters can be set to NULL and zero respectively to determine the required size of lpszFile when **DragQueryFile()** is called with a valid iFile parameter.

When GetDroppedFiles() knows the number of dropped files, it loops for the number of files and calls DragQueryFile() to retrieve the file names. Then GetDroppedFiles() allocates an OBJECT structure by calling AllocObject(). After the OBJECT structure is allocated for the file, GetDroppedFiles() calls **OleCreateFromFile()** to create a package. **OleCreateFromFile()** has the following prototype:

```
OLESTATUS OleCreateFromFile(LPSTR lpszProtocol,
     LPOLECLIENT lpClient, LPSTR lpszClass, LPSTR lpszFile,
     LHCLIENTDOC lhClientDoc, LPSTR lpszObjname,
     LPOLEOBJECT FAR *lplpObject, OLEOPT_REDNER renderopt,
     OLECLIPFORMAT cfFormat);
```

The lpszProtocol parameter contains a pointer to a protocol name. In this instance, the protocol name is "StdFileEditing". The lpClient parameter points to the client structure. The pObj variable points to an OBJECT structure, and the first member of the OBJECT structure is an OLECLIENT structure. By passing pObj to **OleCreateFromFile()**, the OLECLI library is informed of the ClientCallback() function. The third parameter, lpszClass, is the class name of the object. Because you are creating packages, the class name is "Package".

The lpszClass parameter could be NULL in other situations. In such a case, the client library would use the file extension of the fourth parameter, lpszFile, to determine the class name from the registration database. The lpszFile parameter specifies the file to create the object. The fifth parameter, lhClientDoc, is a handle to the client document that is gotten by a call to **OleRegisterClientDoc()**. The lpszObjname parameter is the name of the object. The name must be unique. The SetFileObject() function creates a unique name for an object, as well as other default information.

The `lplpObject` parameter points to a variable where `OLECLI` will store a pointer to the new object. The `renderopt` parameter determines how the object will be rendered. The simplest rendering method is `olerender_draw`. When a client application specifies `olerender_draw`, it needs only to call **OleDraw()** to render an object. There are two other render options: `olerender_none` and `olerender_format`. When a client application specifies `olerender_none`, the client library does not render the object. Instead of calling **OleDraw()**, the client application should call **OleGetData()** for ObjectLink, OwnerLink, and Native data formats.

The `olerender_format` option enables the client application to compute the data instead of drawing it. Additionally, a client application can use the `olerender_format` option to change an implementation of a data format or to use a nonstandard data format.

The last parameter in **OleCreateFromFile()** supports the `olerender_format` option. The `cfFormat` specifies the format of the data retrieved by the subsequent call to **OleGetData()**. If the clipboard format is `CF_DIB`, `CF_BITMAP`, or `CF_METAFILEPICT`, OLECLI can manage the drawing of the object. The client library does not support any other formats.

After `GetDroppedFiles()` calls **OleCreateFromFile()**, it checks the return value with the `ErrHandler()` function. If the call is successful, `GetDroppedFiles()` calls `CreateObjectWindow()`. The `CreateObjectWindow()` function simply creates the window for the object. After `GetDropFiles()` repeats this process for every file dropped, it then calls **DragFinish()**.

The `GetDroppedFiles()` calls the **DragFinish()** function with the handle to the dropped files, `hDrop`. **DragFinish()** uses the handle to delete the global block of memory allocated by Windows to transfer the file name to the client application. Listing 7.7 is the dragdrop.c source module.

Listing 7.7. The dragdrop.c source module.

```
#include "oleclnt.h"

/******************************************************************/
/* Function: GetDroppedFiles                                      */
/* Purpose: Creates packages from dropped files.                  */
/* Returns: TRUE/FALSE                                            */
/******************************************************************/
BOOL PASCAL GetDroppedFiles(HANDLE hDrop)
    {
```

continues

Listing 7.7. continued

```
LPOBJECT pObj;
FILEOBJECT fo;
HWND hWndT;
char szPath[FILENAMEMAXLEN];
WORD cFiles;
WORD i;
BOOL rc = TRUE;

cFiles = DragQueryFile(hDrop, (WORD)-1, szPath, FILENAMEMAXLEN);

for(i = 0; i< cFiles; i++)
    {
    DragQueryFile(hDrop, i, szPath, FILENAMEMAXLEN);

    SetFileObject(&fo);
    pObj = AllocObject();
    if(!pObj)
        {
        FreeObject(pDoc, pObj);
        rc = FALSE;
        continue;
        }

    olestatus = OleCreateFromFile("StdFileEditing",
                        (LPOLECLIENT)pObj, "Package",
                        szPath, pDoc->lh, fo.szName,
                        &pObj->pObj, olerender_draw, 0);

    if(OLE_OK != ErrHandler(olestatus, pDoc, pObj, TRUE))
        {
        FreeObject(pDoc, pObj);
        rc = FALSE;
        continue;
        }

    hWndT = CreateObjectWindow(&fo, TRUE, pObj);
```

```
        if(NULL == hWndT)
            rc = FALSE;
    }

    DragFinish(hDrop);
    return rc;
    }
```

Object Window Processing

The ObjectWndProc() callback function handles the object window messages. When an object window is created, the ObjectWndProc() receives a WM_NCCREATE message followed by a WM_CREATE message. When it receives the WM_NCCREATE message, ObjectWndProc() allocates an OBJWIN structure and then sets the extra windows memory with **SetWindowWord()**.

On subsequent calls to ObjectWndProc(), you access the OBJWIN structure at the beginning of the function by calling **GetWindowWord()**. Thus, when ObjectWndProc() receives the WM_CREATE message, it can initialize pObjwin, which points to the OBJWIN structure.

ObjectWndProc() handles several private messages. Table 7.2 lists these private messages.

Table 7.2. Private messages for ObjectWndProc()**.**

Message	Description
PM_GETRECT	Request to get rectangle coordinates for the object window.
PM_GETOBJECT	Request for an object structure.
PM_NOTIFYOBJECT	Notifies an object that it has been saved, changed, or renamed.
PM_EXECUTE	Request to activate the object.

The PM_GETRECT and PM_GETOBJECT messages are obvious; however, PM_NOTIFYOBJECT and PM_EXECUTE are a little more complex. When ObjectWndProc() receives a PM_NOTIFYOBJECT, one of the object-management

functions has made a change to the object by saving the object, renaming it, or physically changing the object's appearance. If the object was renamed, wParam contains OLE_RENAMED, and ObjectWndProc() calls InitializeObject(). The InitializeObject() function changes the object name in the OBJWIN structure. If the object was saved or changed, wParam contains either OLE_SAVED or OLE_CHANGED. In this situation, ObjectWndProc() adjusts the object window and then sends a message to notify the main window of the change.

The ObjectWndProc() receives a PM_EXECUTE message when the user has selected a verb for an object from the **E**dit menu or has double-clicked an object. When ObjectWndProc() receives the PM_EXECUTE message, it checks to see whether the object is busy by calling OleQueryReleaseStatus(). If the object is not busy, ObjectWndProc() calls **OleActivate()**.

The **OleQueryReleaseStatus()** function has one parameter, a pointer to an OLEOBJECT structure. If the object is busy, **OleQueryReleaseStatus()** returns OLE_BUSY. The **OleActivate()** function has the following prototype:

```
OLESTATUS OleActivate(LPOLEOBJECT lpObject, WORD iVerb,
    BOOL fShow, BOOL fTakeFocus, HWND hwnd, LPRECT lpBounds);
```

The first parameter, lpObject, is a pointer to the object to activate. The second parameter is the verb. The fShow parameter specifies to the server application whether to show the window. The fTakeFocus parameter specifies whether the server application receives the focus. The hwnd parameter specifies the window for the document that contains the object. The last parameter, lpBounds, is the bounding rectangle of the object window. Listing 7.8 is the object.c source module.

Listing 7.8. The object.c source module.

```c
#include "oleclnt.h"

/*********************************************************************/
/* Function: ObjectWndProc                                          */
/* Purpose: Callback function to handle object window messages.     */
/* Returns: Varies                                                  */
/*********************************************************************/
LRESULT CALLBACK ObjectWndProc(HWND hwnd, WORD message,
                               WPARAM wParam, LPARAM lParam)

   {
   LPCREATESTRUCT  pCreate;
   POBJWIN pObjwin;
   HANDLE hMem;
   HWND hWndParent;
```

```
HDC hDC;
PAINTSTRUCT ps;
RECT rc;
WORD cx, cy;

hWndParent = GetParent(hwnd);
pObjwin = (POBJWIN)GetWindowWord(hwnd, 0);

switch(message)
    {
    case WM_NCCREATE:
        hMem = LocalAlloc(LPTR, sizeof(OBJWIN));

        if(NULL == hMem)
            return FALSE;

        SetWindowWord(hwnd, 0, (HANDLE)hMem);
        return (DefWindowProc(hwnd, message, wParam, lParam));

    case WM_CREATE:
        pCreate = (LPCREATESTRUCT)lParam;
        pObjwin->pObj = (LPOBJECT)pCreate->lpCreateParams;

        if(!InitializeObject(pObjwin->pObj,
                             pObjwin->pObj->pDoc))
            {
            pObjwin->pObj = NULL;
            return -1L;
            }
        pObjwin->pObj->hData = hwnd;
        pObjwin->fDrag = FALSE;
        return TRUE;

    case PM_GETRECT:
        if(!lParam)
            break;
        GetObjectWindowRect(hwnd, (LPRECT)lParam, hWndParent);
        return TRUE;
        break;

    case PM_GETOBJECT:
        return (DWORD)pObjwin->pObj;
```

continues

Listing 7.8. continued

```
            case PM_NOTIFYOBJECT:
                if(wParam == OLE_RENAMED)
                    {
                    InitializeObject(pObjwin->pObj,
                                    pObjwin->pObj->pDoc);
                    break;
                    }

                if(wParam == OLE_SAVED || wParam == OLE_CHANGED)
                    {
                    if(GetObjectRect(pObjwin->pObj, &rc, MM_TEXT))
                        {
                        if(!pObjwin->fUserResize)
                            {
                            AdjustWindowRect(&rc,
                                    WS_BORDER | WS_THICKFRAME,
                                    FALSE);

                            SetWindowPos(hwnd, NULL, 0, 0,
                                    rc.right-rc.left,
                                    rc.bottom-rc.top,
                                    SWP_NOMOVE | SWP_NOZORDER);
                            }
                        wParam = GetWindowWord(hwnd, GWW_ID);
                        lParam = MAKELONG(hwnd, NOTIFY_CHANGED);
                        SendMessage(hWndParent, WM_COMMAND,
                                    wParam, lParam);
                        }
                    }
                InvalidateRect(hwnd, NULL, TRUE);
                UpdateWindow(hwnd);
                break;

            case PM_EXECUTE:
                GetClientRect(hwnd, &rc);

                olestatus = OleQueryReleaseStatus(pObjwin->pObj->pObj);
                olestatus = ErrHandler(olestatus, pObjwin->pObj->pDoc,
                                    pObjwin->pObj, TRUE);

                if(OLE_OK != olestatus)
                    break;
```

```
        olestatus = OleActivate(pObjwin->pObj->pObj, wParam,
                                TRUE, TRUE, hWndParent, &rc);

    if(OLE_OK == ErrHandler(olestatus, pObjwin->pObj->pDoc,
                            pObjwin->pObj, TRUE))
        {
        pObjwin->pObj->fOpen = TRUE;
        InvalidateRect(hwnd, NULL, TRUE);
        UpdateWindow(hwnd);
        }
    break;

case WM_NCDESTROY:
    if(NULL !=  pObjwin->pObj);
        FreeObject(pObjwin->pObj->pDoc, pObjwin->pObj);

    if(NULL != pObjwin)
        LocalFree((HANDLE)pObjwin);
    break;

case WM_NCACTIVATE:
    if(1 == wParam)
        {
        wParam = GetWindowWord(hwnd, GWW_ID);
        lParam = MAKELONG(hwnd, NOTIFY_ACTIVATED);
        SendMessage(hWndParent, WM_COMMAND, wParam, lParam);
        }

    return (DefWindowProc(hwnd, message, wParam, lParam));

case WM_SIZE:
    fDocChanged = TRUE;
    if(pObjwin->fUserResize)
        {
        GetWindowRect(hwnd, &rc);

        cx = GetSystemMetrics(SM_CXFRAME);
        cy = GetSystemMetrics(SM_CYFRAME);
        InflateRect(&rc, -cx, -cy);

        SetObjectRect(pObjwin->pObj->pDoc,
                    pObjwin->pObj, &rc, MM_TEXT);
```

continues

Listing 7.8. continued

```
                    pObjwin->fUserResize = FALSE;

                    wParam = GetWindowWord(hwnd, GWW_ID);
                    lParam = MAKELONG(hwnd, NOTIFY_SIZED);
                    SendMessage(hWndParent, WM_COMMAND,
                                wParam, lParam);
                }
            break;

        case WM_PAINT:
            hDC = BeginPaint(hwnd, &ps);
            GetClientRect(hwnd, &rc);
            PaintObject(hDC, &rc, pObjwin->pObj);
            EndPaint(hwnd, &ps);
            break;

        case WM_NCLBUTTONDBLCLK:
            SendMessage(hwnd, PM_EXECUTE, 0, 0L);
            return (DefWindowProc(hwnd, message, wParam, lParam));

        case WM_NCHITTEST:
            lParam = DefWindowProc(hwnd, message, wParam, lParam);
            if((LONG)HTCLIENT == lParam)
                lParam = (LONG)HTCAPTION;
            return lParam;

        case WM_NCLBUTTONDOWN:
            fDocChanged = TRUE;
            BringWindowToTop(hwnd);
            SendMessage(hwnd, WM_NCACTIVATE, 1, 0L);
            return (DefWindowProc(hwnd, message, wParam, lParam));

        case WM_SYSCOMMAND:
            if(SC_SIZE == (wParam & 0xfff0))
                pObjwin->fUserResize = TRUE;
            return (DefWindowProc(hwnd, message, wParam, lParam));

        default:
            return (DefWindowProc(hwnd, message, wParam, lParam));
```

```
    }
  return FALSE;
  }
```

Client Callback and Stream Methods

The OLECLI library uses the client callback function to notify the client application of the status of objects. The client callback function receives a pointer to an OLEOBJECT structure, a notification code, and a pointer to the OLEOBJECT structure that contains information on the object that caused the notification.

The notification codes are summarized in Table 7.3.

Table 7.3. OLE notification codes.

Notification Code	Description
OLE_CHANGED	The server application changed the object.
OLE_CLOSED	The server application closed an embedded object it was editing.
OLE_QUERY_PAINT	A lengthy drawing operation is taking place on an object.
OLE_QUERY_RETRY	An OLE function called by the client application returned OLE_BUSY.
OLE_RELEASE	An object that was previously busy in an asynchronous event is free for other processing.
OLE_RENAMED	The server application has renamed a linked object.
OLE_SAVED	The server application has saved a linked object or updated an embedded object.

When the ClientCallback() function receives an OLE_CLOSED, OLE_SAVED, OLE_CHANGED, or OLE_RENAMED notification, the ClientCallback() function posts a message to the object window using the PM_NOTIFYOBJECT message. If the notification is OLE_CLOSED, the ClientCallback() function takes back the focus before posting the message.

The OLE_RELEASE notification enables the client application to set a flag that the object has been busy and decrement the wait counter. The OLE_QUERY_PAINT message must return TRUE, or else the client library stops drawing the object. Listing 7.9 is the vtclient.c source module.

Listing 7.9. The vtclient.c source module.

```
#include "oleclnt.h"

/********************************************************************/
/* Function: ClientCallback                                        */
/* Purpose: Notification callback procedure.                       */
/* Returns: TRUE/FALSE                                             */
/********************************************************************/
int CALLBACK ClientCallback(LPOBJECT pObj, OLE_NOTIFICATION wCode,
                        LPOLEOBJECT pOLEObj)

    {
    switch(wCode)
        {
        case OLE_CLOSED:
            SetFocus(hWnd);
            pObj->fOpen = FALSE;
            PostMessage((HWND)pObj->hData, PM_NOTIFYOBJECT,
                        wCode, (LONG)pObj);
            break;

        case OLE_SAVED:
        case OLE_CHANGED:
        case OLE_RENAMED:
            PostMessage((HWND)pObj->hData, PM_NOTIFYOBJECT,
                        wCode, (LONG)pObj);
            break;

        case OLE_RELEASE:
            pObj->fRelease = TRUE;
            pObj->pDoc->cWait--;
            break;

        case OLE_QUERY_RETRY:
            break;
```

```
        case OLE_QUERY_PAINT:
            return TRUE;

        default:
            break;
        }
    return FALSE;
    }
```

Listing 7.10, the vtstream.c source module, contains the stream methods. These methods are called by the client library when the client application needs to read and write an object. The StreamGet() method reads an object, and the StreamPut() method writes an object. The implementation in this example program calls the **_hread()** and **_hwrite()** functions.

> **Note:** The **_hread()** and **_hwrite()** functions can read and write objects that are greater than 64K. Because objects can be anything, a good client application should take into account that it may need to read and write objects that are greater than 64K. The **_hread()** and **_hwrite()** functions are new to Windows 3.1. These functions do not work with Windows 3.0. Thus, if you want your applications to run under both Windows 3.0 and 3.1, you have to write an implementation of a huge read and write.

Listing 7.10. The vtstream.c source module.

```
#include "oleclnt.h"

/********************************************************************/
/* Function: StreamGet                                            */
/* Purpose: Get method.                                           */
/* Returns: Number of bytes read                                  */
/********************************************************************/
DWORD CALLBACK StreamGet(LPSTREAM pStream, LPBYTE pb, DWORD cb)
    {
    DWORD dw;
```

continues

Listing 7.10. continued

```
    if(NULL == pStream->hFile)
        return 0L;

    dw = _hread(pStream->hFile, (LPVOID)pb, cb);

    return dw;
    }


/********************************************************************/
/* Function: StreamPut                                           */
/* Purpose: Put method.                                          */
/* Returns: Number of bytes written                             */
/********************************************************************/
DWORD CALLBACK StreamPut(LPSTREAM pStream, LPBYTE pb, DWORD cb)
    {
    DWORD dw;

    if(NULL == pStream->hFile)
        return 0L;

    dw = _hwrite(pStream->hFile, (LPVOID)pb, cb);

    return dw;
    }
```

Document Management

The document-management functions in docmgt.c control some of the interaction with the client library that is required for an OLE document. There are essentially two sides to document management: registering the document and revoking the document. When a client application opens a document, it calls **OleRegisterClientDoc()** to register the document with the client library. The **OleRegisterClientDoc()** function has the following prototype:

```
OLESTATUS OleRegisterClientDoc(LPSTR lpszClass, LPSTR lpszDoc,
    LONG reserved, LHCLIENTDOC FAR *lplhDoc);
```

The first parameter, lpszClass, is a pointer to a string that contains the class name. The example program uses its name, "Oleclnt". The lpszDoc parameter is a pointer to a string that contains the document name. The reserved parameter is not used; however, it must be zero. The last parameter receives a handle to the client document when **OleRegisterClientDoc()** returns. The OLECLNT application calls **OleRegisterClientDoc()** in CreateNewDoc() and CommonOpenFile() functions.

When a client application renames a document, it should call **OleRenameClientDoc()**. This function has the following prototype:

```
OLESTATUS OleRenameClientDoc(LHCLIENTDOC lhClientDoc,
                   LPSTR lpszNewDocname);
```

The first parameter in **OleRenameClientDoc()** is the handle to the client document that was gotten from a previous call to **OleRegisterClientDoc()**. The second parameter is a pointer to a string that contains the new document name. OLECLNT calls **OleRenameClientDoc()** in the CommonOpenFile() function.

Although I am discussing document-management functions, I have to spend some time on a couple of object-related functions because they are used in conjunction with document operations. When the client application saves a document, it has to save the information for the objects in the document. The **OleSaveToStream()** function provides the method to save the objects. The **OleSaveToStream()** function has the following prototype:

```
OLESTATUS OleSaveToStream(LPOLEOBJECT lpObject,
                   LPOLESTREAM lpStream);
```

The lpObject parameter is a pointer to the object to save. The lpStream is a pointer to the OLESTREAM structure. When OLECLNT calls **OleSaveToStream()**, the client library uses the pointer to the STREAM structure that points to the OLESTREAMVTBL structure to get the put method, StreamPut().

The opposite of **OleSaveToStream()** is **OleLoadFromStream()**. The function prototype for **OleLoadFromStream()** is

```
OLESTATUS OleLoadFromStream(LPOLESTREAM lpStream,
     LPSTR lpszProtocol, LPOLECLIENT lpClient,
     LHCLIENTDOC lhClientDoc, LPSTR lpszObjname,
     LPOLEOBJECT FAR *lplpObject);
```

The lpStream parameter is a pointer to an OLESTREAM structure. The second parameter, lpszProtocol, is a pointer to a string that defines the protocol name. This can be "StdFileEditing" or "Static". The lpClient parameter points to an OLECLIENT structure. The lhClientDoc parameter is a handle to the client document. The fifth parameter, lpszObjname, contains a pointer to a string for the object name. The lplpObject parameter is a pointer to a pointer to an object. The client library stores a pointer to the loaded object in the lplpObject parameter.

After a client application saves a document, it should inform the client library that the document has been saved with the **OleSavedClientDoc()** function. **OleSaveClientDoc()** takes a parameter, a handle to the client document gotten from the **OleRegisterClientDoc()** call. **OleSavedClientDoc()** is called in the CommonSaveFile() function.

The **OleRevertClientDoc()** function informs the client library that a document has been reverted to a previously saved state. The **OleRevertClientDoc()** has one parameter, which is a handle to the client document. The SaveChanges() function calls **OleRevertClientDoc()** when it queries a user to save a file on termination of the application and the user chooses not to save the file.

When a client application needs to close a document, it will have to close the individual objects in the document and then revoke the document. The RevokeDoc() function performs these services. RevokeDoc() calls **OleRevokeClientDoc()**. **OleRevokeClientDoc()** has one parameter, which is a handle to the client document. Listings 7.11, 7.12, and 7.13 are the docmgt.c, mem.c, and file.c source modules.

Listing 7.11. The docmgt.c source module.

```
#include "oleclnt.h"

/*******************************************************************/
/* Function: RevokeDoc                                           */
/* Purpose: Closes all objects and revokes client doc.           */
/* Returns: TRUE/FALSE                                           */
/*******************************************************************/
BOOL RevokeDoc(VOID)
    {
    LPOBJECT pObj;

    pDoc->cWait = 0;
    pObj = pDoc->pObjFirst;
```

```
    while(NULL != pObj)
        {
        if(!CloseObjects(pObj))
            break;

        pObj = pObj->pNext;
        }

    Wait(TRUE, NULL);

    SendMessage(hWnd, WM_COMMAND, IDM_CLEARALL, 0L);

    olestatus = OleRevokeClientDoc(pDoc->lh);

    fOpenFile = FALSE;
    fDocChanged = FALSE;
    return (OLE_OK == olestatus);
    }

/*******************************************************************/
/* Function: FreeDoc                                               */
/* Purpose: Frees the DOCUMENT structure and vtbls.                */
/*******************************************************************/
VOID FreeDoc(VOID)
    {
    if(NULL != pDoc->hData)
        GlobalFree(pDoc->hData);

    if(pDoc->aCaption)
        DeleteAtom(pDoc->aCaption);

    FreeStream();
    FreeClientVtbl();

    LocalFree((HANDLE)(DWORD)pDoc);
    }

/*******************************************************************/
/* Function: SetDocName                                            */
/* Purpose: Sets a new document for the DOCUMENT structure.        */
/* Returns: TRUE                                                   */
/*******************************************************************/
```

continues

Listing 7.11. continued

```
BOOL SetDocName(VOID)
    {
    if(pDoc->aFile)
        DeleteAtom(pDoc->aFile);

    pDoc->aFile=AddAtom(szFile);
    return TRUE;
    }


/******************************************************************/
/* Function: ProcessMessages                                      */
/* Purpose: Message loop.                                         */
/* Returns: TRUE                                                  */
/******************************************************************/
BOOL PASCAL ProcessMessages(LPMSG pMsg)
    {
    if(!TranslateAccelerator(hWnd, hAccel, pMsg))
        {
        TranslateMessage(pMsg);
        DispatchMessage(pMsg);
        }
    return TRUE;
    }
```

Listing 7.12. The mem.c source module.

```
#include "oleclnt.h"

LPOLESTREAMVTBL AllocStreamVtbl(VOID);
BOOL PASCAL FreeStreamVtbl(VOID);
/******************************************************************/
/* Function: AllocClientVtbl                                      */
/* Purpose: Allocates structure and makes instance of             */
/*          ClientCallback.                                       */
/* Returns: Pointer to OLECLIENTVTBL structure                    */
/******************************************************************/
LPOLECLIENTVTBL AllocClientVtbl(VOID)
    {
    LPOLECLIENTVTBL        pvt;
    HANDLE                 hMem;
```

```
    hMem = LocalAlloc(LPTR, sizeof(OLECLIENTVTBL));

    if(!hMem)
        return NULL;

    pvt = (LPOLECLIENTVTBL)(PSTR)hMem;

    pvt->CallBack = (LPCLIENTCALLBACK)
        MakeProcInstance((FARPROC)ClientCallback, hInst);

    return pvt;
    }

/******************************************************************/
/* Function: AllocStream                                        */
/* Purpose: Allocates STREAM structure.                         */
/* Returns: Pointer to STREAM structure                         */
/******************************************************************/
LPSTREAM AllocStream(VOID)
    {
    HANDLE          hMem;
    LPSTREAM        pStream;

    hMem = LocalAlloc(LPTR, sizeof(STREAM));

    if(!hMem)
        return NULL;

    pStream = (LPSTREAM)(PSTR)hMem;

    pStream->pvt = AllocStreamVtbl();
    return pStream;
    }

/******************************************************************/
/* Function: AllocStreamVtbl                                    */
/* Purpose: Allocates structure, makes instances for           */
/*          StreamGet/Put.                                      */
/* Returns: Pointer to OLESTREAMVTBL structure                  */
/******************************************************************/
```

continues

407

Listing 7.12. continued

```
LPOLESTREAMVTBL AllocStreamVtbl(VOID)
    {
    LPOLESTREAMVTBL pvt;
    HANDLE hMem;

    hMem = LocalAlloc(LPTR, sizeof(OLESTREAMVTBL));

    if(!hMem)
        return NULL;

    pvt = (LPOLESTREAMVTBL)(PSTR)hMem;

    pvt->Get = (LPSTREAMMETHOD)
            MakeProcInstance((FARPROC)StreamGet, hInst);
    pvt->Put = (LPSTREAMMETHOD)
            MakeProcInstance((FARPROC)StreamPut, hInst);

    return pvt;
    }

/*********************************************************************/
/* Function: FreeClientVtbl                                         */
/* Purpose: Frees structure and CallBack proc.                      */
/* Returns: TRUE/FALSE                                              */
/*********************************************************************/
BOOL FreeClientVtbl(VOID)
    {
    if(!pDoc->pvt)
        return FALSE;

    if(pDoc->pvt->CallBack)
        FreeProcInstance((FARPROC)pDoc->pvt->CallBack);

    if(!LocalFree((HANDLE)(DWORD)pDoc->pvt))
        return FALSE;

    return TRUE;
    }
```

```
/********************************************************************/
/* Function: FreeStream                                           */
/* Purpose: Frees structure.                                      */
/* Returns: TRUE/FALSE                                            */
/********************************************************************/
BOOL FreeStream(VOID)
    {
    if(!pDoc->pStream)
        return FALSE;

    if(!FreeStreamVtbl())
        return FALSE;

    if(!LocalFree((HANDLE)(DWORD)pDoc->pStream))
        return FALSE;

    return TRUE;
    }

/********************************************************************/
/* Function: FreeStreamVtbl                                       */
/* Purpose: Frees structure and Proc instances for StreamGet/Put. */
/* Returns: TRUE/FALSE                                            */
/********************************************************************/
BOOL PASCAL FreeStreamVtbl(VOID)
    {
    if(!pDoc->pStream->pvt)
        return FALSE;

    if(pDoc->pStream->pvt->Get)
        FreeProcInstance((FARPROC)pDoc->pStream->pvt->Get);

    if(pDoc->pStream->pvt->Put)
        FreeProcInstance((FARPROC)pDoc->pStream->pvt->Put);

    if(!LocalFree((HANDLE)(DWORD)pDoc->pStream->pvt))
        return FALSE;

    return TRUE;
    }
```

Listing 7.13. The file.c source module.

```c
#include "oleclnt.h"

#define FILESIGMAXLEN 8

char szFileSignature[FILESIGMAXLEN] =  "OleClnt";
char szDefExt[4] = "OLE";
char szFilterSpec[128] =
    "OleClnt Files (*.OLE)\0*.OLE\0All Files (*.*)\0*.*\0";
OPENFILENAME ofn;

typedef struct
    {
    char szFileSignature[FILESIGMAXLEN];
    int         version;
    DWORD       dwState;
    DWORD       cObjects;
    } HEADER, FAR *LPHEADER;

VOID SetTitle(VOID);
VOID SetFileName(VOID);
BOOL PASCAL ReadFile(LPHEADER);
BOOL PASCAL WriteFile(LPHEADER);
BOOL PASCAL WriteObject(LPOBJECT, DWORD);
/*******************************************************************/
/* Function: OpenPassedFile                                       */
/* Purpose: Opens a file passed on the command line.             */
/* Returns: TRUE/FALSE                                            */
/*******************************************************************/
BOOL OpenPassedFile (VOID)
    {
    HEADER hdr;
    BOOL rc;

    SetTitle ();
    olestatus = OleRegisterClientDoc("OleClnt", szFile,
                                     OL, &pDoc->lh);
```

```
        if (OLE_OK != olestatus)
            return FALSE;

    if(ReadFile (&hdr))
        {
        fOpenfile = TRUE;
        QueryLinks ();
        rc = TRUE;
        }
    else
        {
        lstrcpy(szFile, "Untitled)");
        SetTitle();

        olestatus - OleRenameClientDoc (pDoc->lh, szfile);

        rc - (OLE_OK == olestatus);
         }
    Set Doc Name ();
    fDocChanged  = FALSE;
    return rc;
    }
/********************************************************************/
/* Function: CreateNewDoc                                         */
/* Purpose: Registers a new document.                             */
/* Returns: TRUE/FALSE                                            */
/********************************************************************/
BOOL CreateNewDoc(VOID)
    {
    if(fDocChanged)
        if(!SaveChanges())
            return FALSE;

    RevokeDoc();

    lstrcpy(szFile, "(Untitled)");
    SetTitle();

    olestatus = OleRegisterClientDoc("OleClnt", szFile,
                                 0L, &pDoc->lh);
```

continues

411

Listing 7.13. continued

```
    if(OLE_OK != olestatus)
        return FALSE;

    SetDocName();
    fDocChanged = FALSE;
    return TRUE;
    }

/*******************************************************************/
/* Function: CommonOpenFile                                        */
/* Purpose: Uses common dlgs File Open to open a doc and read it.  */
/* Returns: TRUE/FALSE                                             */
/*******************************************************************/
BOOL CommonOpenFile(VOID)
    {
    char szDoc[40];
    HEADER hdr;
    BOOL rc = TRUE;

    if(fDocChanged)
        if(!SaveChanges())
            return FALSE;

    SetFileName();
    ofn.Flags |= OFN_FILEMUSTEXIST;

    wsprintf(szDoc, "*.%s", (LPSTR) szDefExt);

    ofn.lpstrFile = szDoc;

    if(!GetOpenFileName(&ofn))
        return FALSE;
    lstrcpy(szFile, ofn.lpstrFile);

    RevokeDoc();

    SetTitle();
```

```
    olestatus = OleRegisterClientDoc("OleClnt", szFile,
                                    0L, &pDoc->lh);

if(OLE_OK != olestatus)
    return FALSE;

if(ReadFile(&hdr))
    {
    fOpenFile = TRUE;
    QueryLinks();
    rc = TRUE;
    }
else
    {
    lstrcpy(szFile, "(Untitled)");
    SetTitle();

    olestatus = OleRenameClientDoc(pDoc->lh, szFile);

    rc = (OLE_OK == olestatus);
    }

SetDocName();
fDocChanged = FALSE;
return rc;
}

/*****************************************************************/
/* Function: CommonSaveFile                                      */
/* Purpose: Saves a file and/or invokes common dlg SaveAs.       */
/* Returns: TRUE/FALSE                                           */
/*****************************************************************/
BOOL PASCAL CommonSaveFile(BOOL fSaveAs)
    {
    HEADER hdr;

    if(!fOpenFile && !fSaveAs)
        return CommonSaveAs();
```

continues

Listing 7.13. continued

```
    hdr.version = 1;
    hdr.cObjects = pDoc->cObjects;
    if(!WriteFile(&hdr))
        return FALSE;

    if(fSaveAs)
        {
        olestatus = OleRenameClientDoc(pDoc->lh, szFile);
        SetDocName();
        }
    else
        olestatus = OleSavedClientDoc(pDoc->lh);

    fDocChanged = FALSE;
    fOpenFile = TRUE;
    return TRUE;
    }

/******************************************************************/
/* Function: CommonSaveAs                                         */
/* Purpose: Invokes common dlg SaveAs to save a file.            */
/* Returns: TRUE/FALSE                                            */
/******************************************************************/
BOOL CommonSaveAs(VOID)
    {
    SetFileName();

    ofn.Flags |= OFN_PATHMUSTEXIST;
    wsprintf(szFile, "*.%s", (LPSTR)szDefExt);
    ofn.lpstrFile = szFile;

    if(GetSaveFileName(&ofn))
        {
        if(fOpenFile = CommonSaveFile(TRUE))
            SetTitle();
        }
    return fOpenFile;
    }
```

```
/*******************************************************************/
/* Function: ChangeLink                                          */
/* Purpose: Invokes File Open common dlg to change link.         */
/* Returns: TRUE/FALSE                                           */
/*******************************************************************/
BOOL PASCAL ChangeLink(HWND hList)
    {
    LPSTR pszLinkFile;
    LPSTR pszFile;
    LPSTR pszExt;
    LPSTR psz;
    HINSTANCE hInst;
    HWND hWndParent;
    BOOL rc;
    ATOM aFileOld;
    ATOM aFileNew;
    WORD cch;
    WORD wTemp;
    char szFile[FILENAMEMAXLEN];
    char szFilter[80];
    WORD cch1;
    WORD cch2;
    char sz1[64];
    char sz2[64];

    hWndParent = GetParent(hList);
    hInst = GetWindowWord(hWndParent, GWW_HINSTANCE);

    EnumLinks(hList, FindLinks,
            ENUMLINK_SELECTED, MAKELONG(1,1));

    pszFile = pDoc->pszData1 + lstrlen(pDoc->pszData1) + 1;
    lstrcpy(szFile, pszFile);
    aFileOld = AddAtom(pszFile);
    DeleteAtom(aFileOld);

    pszExt = GetExtFromFile(pszFile);

    GetClassFromExt(pszExt, pDoc->pszData2, FILENAMEMAXLEN);
    GetDescFromClass(pDoc->pszData2, pDoc->pszData1,
                    FILENAMEMAXLEN);
```

continues

415

Listing 7.13. continued

```
wsprintf(pDoc->pszData2, " (%s)", pszExt);
lstrcat(pDoc->pszData1, pDoc->pszData2);

if('.' == *pszExt)
    pszExt++;

SetFileName();
ofn.Flags |= OFN_FILEMUSTEXIST;
ofn.lpstrTitle = "Change Link";
ofn.lpstrDefExt = pszExt;

lstrcpy(szFilter, pDoc->pszData1);
cch1=1+lstrlen(szFilter);

cch2 = wsprintf(pszFile, "*.%s", pszExt);
lstrcpy(szFilter+cch1, pszFile);

*(szFilter+cch1+cch2+1)=0;
ofn.lpstrFilter = szFilter;

rc = GetOpenFileName(&ofn);
if(!rc)
    return FALSE;

aFileNew = AddAtom(szFile);
EnumLinks(hList, ChangeLinks,
        ENUMLINK_SELECTED, MAKELONG(aFileNew, 0));

EnumLinks(hList, UpdateLinks, ENUMLINK_SELECTED,
        MAKELONG(0, IDIGNORE));

rc = EnumLinks(hList, FindLinks,
            ENUMLINK_UNSELECTED, MAKELONG(aFileOld, 0));

if(rc)
    {
    DeleteAtom(aFileNew);
    return TRUE;
    }
```

416

```
       psz = pDoc->pszData2;
       pszLinkFile = GetFileFromPath(szFile);

       GetAtomName(pDoc->aFile, pDoc->pszData3, FILENAMEMAXLEN);
       pszFile = GetFileFromPath(pDoc->pszData3);

       LoadString(hInst, IDS_CHANGELINK1,
                   sz1, sizeof sz1);
       LoadString(hInst, IDS_CHANGELINK2,
                   sz2, sizeof sz2);

       cch = wsprintf(psz, sz1, pszLinkFile, pszFile);
       wsprintf(psz+cch, sz2, pszLinkFile);

       wTemp = MessageBox(hWndParent, psz, "Change Link",
                           MB_YESNO | MB_ICONEXCLAMATION);

       if(IDYES == wTemp)
           {
           EnumLinks(hList, ChangeLinks,
                       ENUMLINK_UNSELECTED,
                       MAKELONG(aFileNew, aFileOld));

           aFileOld = aFileNew;

           EnumLinks(hList, UpdateLinks, ENUMLINK_UNSELECTED,
                       MAKELONG(aFileOld, IDIGNORE));
           }

       DeleteAtom(aFileNew);
       return TRUE;
       }

/*******************************************************************/
/* Function: ReadFile                                             */
/* Purpose: Reads a document.                                     */
/* Returns: TRUE/FALSE                                            */
/*******************************************************************/
```

continues

Listing 7.13. continued

```
BOOL PASCAL ReadFile(LPHEADER lphdr)
    {
    HFILE hFile;
    OFSTRUCT of;
    WORD cbW;
    DWORD cObjects;
    FILEOBJECT fo;
    LPOBJECT pObj;
    HWND hwndChild;

    hFile = OpenFile(szFile, &of, OF_READ);

    if(-1 == hFile)
        return FALSE;

    cbW = _lread(hFile, (LPVOID)lphdr, sizeof(HEADER));

    if(sizeof(HEADER) != cbW)
        {
        _lclose(hFile);
        return FALSE;
        }

    pDoc->pStream->hFile = hFile;
    pDoc->cLinks = 0;
    cObjects = lphdr->cObjects;

    while(cObjects)
        {
        cObjects--;
        cbW = _lread(hFile, (LPSTR)&fo, sizeof(FILEOBJECT));
        if(cbW != sizeof(FILEOBJECT))
            break;

        pObj = AllocObject();

        if(!pObj)
            {
```

```
                FreeObject(pDoc, pObj);
                break;
                }

        olestatus = OleLoadFromStream((LPOLESTREAM)pDoc->pStream,
                                "StdFileEditing",
                                (LPOLECLIENT)pObj,
                                pDoc->lh,
                                fo.szName,
                                &pObj->pObj);

        if(OLE_OK != ErrHandler(olestatus, pDoc, pObj, TRUE))
            {
            FreeObject(pDoc, pObj);
            break;
            }

        hwndChild = CreateObjectWindow(&fo, TRUE, pObj);

        if(NULL == hwndChild)
            break;

        if(OT_LINK == pObj->dwType)
            {
            if(!AutoUpdateLinks(pDoc, pObj))
                pDoc->cLinks++;
            }
        }

_lclose(hFile);

hwndChild = GetWindow(hWnd, GW_CHILD);

if(!hwndChild)
    {
    BringWindowToTop(hwndChild);
    SendMessage(hwndChild, WM_NCACTIVATE, TRUE, 0L);
    }
```

continues

Listing 7.13. continued

```
    return TRUE;
    }

/********************************************************************/
/* Function: WriteFile                                          */
/* Purpose: Writes a document.                                  */
/* Returns: TRUE/FALSE                                          */
/********************************************************************/
BOOL PASCAL WriteFile(LPHEADER lphdr)
    {
    HFILE hFile;
    OFSTRUCT of;
    DWORD cb;
    LPOBJECT pObj;

    hFile = OpenFile(szFile, &of, OF_CREATE ¦ OF_WRITE);

    if(-1 == hFile)
        return FALSE;

    cb = _lwrite(hFile, (LPSTR)lphdr, sizeof(HEADER));

    if((DWORD)sizeof(HEADER) != cb)
        {
        _lclose(hFile);
        return FALSE;
        }
    pDoc->pStream->hFile = hFile;
    pObj = pDoc->pObjFirst;

    while(NULL != pObj)
        {
        if(!WriteObject(pObj, 0L))
            break;

        pObj = pObj->pNext;
        }

    _lclose(hFile);
    return (NULL == pObj);
    }
```

```
/********************************************************************/
/* Function: WriteObject                                            */
/* Purpose: Writes an object to the document.                       */
/* Returns: TRUE/FALSE                                              */
/********************************************************************/
BOOL PASCAL WriteObject(LPOBJECT pObj, DWORD dw)
    {
    FILEOBJECT fo;
    HWND hwndObject;
    WORD cb;

    hwndObject = (HWND)pObj->hData;

    SendMessage(hwndObject, PM_GETRECT, 0, (LONG)(LPSTR)&fo.rc);
    GetWindowText(hwndObject, fo.szName, 40);
    fo.wID = GetWindowWord(hwndObject, GWW_ID);

    olestatus = OleQuerySize(pObj->pObj, &fo.cbObject);

    if(OLE_OK != olestatus)
        return FALSE;

    cb = _lwrite(pDoc->pStream->hFile,
                (LPSTR)&fo, sizeof(FILEOBJECT));

    if(cb != sizeof(FILEOBJECT))
        return FALSE;

    olestatus = OleSaveToStream(pObj->pObj,
                                (LPOLESTREAM)pDoc->pStream);

    return (OLE_OK == olestatus);
    }


/********************************************************************/
/* Function: SetTitle                                               */
/* Purpose: Sets window caption.                                    */
/********************************************************************/
VOID SetTitle(VOID)
    {
    char szTitle[FILENAMEMAXLEN];
```

continues

Listing 7.13. continued

```c
    wsprintf(szTitle, "%s - %s", (LPSTR)"OleClnt", Abbrev(szFile));
    SetWindowText(hWnd, szTitle);
    return;
    }


/******************************************************************/
/* Function: SaveChanges                                        */
/* Purpose: Asks user to save a changed document.               */
/* Returns: TRUE/FALSE                                          */
/******************************************************************/
BOOL SaveChanges(VOID)
    {
    DWORD dwrc;
    char szWindowTitle[SZWINDOWTITLE];
    char szMessage[SZMESSAGE];

    LoadString(hInst, IDS_WINDOWTITLE,
               szWindowTitle, sizeof szWindowTitle);
    LoadString(hInst, IDS_QUERYSAVEFILE,
               szMessage, sizeof szMessage);

    dwrc = (DWORD)MessageBox(hWnd,
                             szMessage,
                             szWindowTitle,
                             MB_YESNOCANCEL);

    switch(LOWORD(dwrc))
        {
        case IDYES:
            return CommonSaveFile(FALSE);
            break;

        case IDNO:
            olestatus = OleRevertClientDoc(pDoc->lh);
            return (OLE_OK == olestatus);
            break;

        case IDCANCEL:
            return FALSE;
            break;
```

```
            }
        }

/*******************************************************************/
/* Function: SetFileName                                           */
/* Purpose: Sets the default values for the ofn struct.            */
/*******************************************************************/
VOID SetFileName(VOID)
    {
    static char szFileTitle[13];

    ofn.lStructSize        = sizeof(OPENFILENAME);
    ofn.hwndOwner          = hWnd;
    ofn.lpstrFilter        = szFilterSpec;
    ofn.lpstrCustomFilter  = NULL;
    ofn.nMaxCustFilter     = 0L;
    ofn.nFilterIndex       = 1L;
    ofn.lpstrFile          = NULL;
    ofn.nMaxFile           = FILENAMEMAXLEN;
    ofn.lpstrInitialDir    = NULL;
    ofn.lpstrFileTitle     = szFileTitle;
    ofn.hInstance          = hInst;
    ofn.lCustData          = NULL;
    ofn.lpfnHook           = NULL;
    ofn.lpTemplateName     = NULL;
    ofn.lpstrTitle         = NULL;
    ofn.lpstrDefExt        = szDefExt;
    ofn.Flags              = 0;
    ofn.nFileOffset        = 0;
    ofn.nFileExtension     = 0;
    }
```

Object Management

The objmgt.c source module contains a dozen different OLE function calls.
Table 7.4 lists the OLE functions within the program functions. Some OLE
functions are called in multiple functions, so to avoid redundancy, I list the
OLE functions only once.

Table 7.4. OLE object-management functions.

OLE Function Name	Program Function Name
OleQueryName()	InitializeObject()
OleQueryType()	InitializeObject()
OleSetHostNames()	InitializeObject()
OleGetLinkUpdateOptions()	InitializeObject()
OleDelete()	DeleteObjectWIndow()
OleRelease()	CloseObjects()
OleUpdate()	UpdateObjects()
OleDraw()	PaintObjects()
OleSetBounds()	SetObjectRect()
OleQueryBounds()	GetObjectRect()
OleGetData()	GetObjectData()
OleSetData()	SetObjectData()

The **OleQueryName()** function gets the name of an object. It has the following prototype:

```
OLESTATUS OleQueryName(LPOLEOBJECT  lpObject,
                    LPSTR lpszObject, WORD FAR *lpwBuffSize);
```

The first parameter points to the OLEOBJECT structure. The second parameter, lpszObject, is a buffer to receive the object name. The third parameter points to a variable that specifies the size of the second parameter. The InitializeObject() uses the OleQueryName() function to store the name of the object for application use.

The **OleQueryType()** function identifies the type of an object. It takes two parameters. The first parameter points to the OLEOBJECT structure, whereas the second points to a LONG variable that receives OT_EMBEDDED, OT_LINK, or OT_STATIC.

Client applications must call **OleSetHostNames()** before calling **OleActivate()**. The **OleSetHostNames()** function provides the client library with the client application's name so that the server application can set the window title bars. It is necessary to call **OleSetHostNames()** only once before all **OleActivate()**

function calls, and each time the client's name for the object changes. **OleSetHostNames()** has the following prototype:

```
OLESTATUS OleSetHostNames(LPOLEOBJECT lpObject,
                    LPSTR lpszClient, LPSTR lpszClientObj);
```

The first parameter points to the OLEOBJECT structure. The lpszClient parameter is the name of the client application. The lpszClientObj parameter is the name that the client application uses for the object.

The **OleGetLinkUpdateOptions()** function facilitates the use of the Links dialog box. **OleGetLinkUpdateOptions()** has two parameters, the first being a pointer to the OLEOBJECT structure. The second parameter receives the link-update option. The link-update option can be oleupdate_always, oleupdate_onsave, or oleupdate_oncall. The oleupdate_always link-update option corresponds with the *Automatic* radio button in the Links dialog box. This means that the link should be updated whenever possible. The oleupdate_oncall option corresponds with the *Manual* radio button. The oleupdate_onsave option means that the link should be updated when the source document of the object is saved.

The **OleDelete()** function deletes the object identified by the only parameter, a pointer to an OLEOBJECT structure. If the object is currently open, **OleDelete()** closes the object and then deletes the object. The function should be called any time an object window is destroyed, because the **OleDelete()** function frees memory associated with the object and informs the client library that the object has been permanently removed.

A related function to **OleDelete()** is **OleRelease()**. **OleRelease()** releases an object from memory and closes it if it is open. **OleRelease()** does not indicate that the object has been permanently removed.

The **OleUpdate()** function updates the object specified by the pointer to the OLEOBJECT structure. The client application calls **OleDraw()** when it needs to repaint an object. The **OleDraw()** function has the following prototype:

```
OLESTATUS OleDraw(LPOLEOBJECT lpObject, HDC hdc,
    LPRECT lprcBounds, LPRECT lprcWBounds, HDC hdcFormat);
```

The first parameter is a pointer to the OLEOBJECT structure. The second parameter is a handle to the device context for drawing the object. The lprcBounds parameter specifies the bounding rectangle for the client library to draw the object. The lprcWBounds parameter is used for a bounding rectangle for a metafile device context. The last parameter, hdcFormat, contains a device context for formatting the object.

OleSetBounds() and **OleQueryBounds()** are opposite functions. They both point to an OLEOBJECT structure in the first parameter, and the second

parameter is a pointer to a RECT structure. The bounds of an object are defined by the bounding rectangle. **OleSetBounds()** can set the bounds for an embedded object. It cannot, however, set the bounds for a linked object because linked objects are defined by the source document. The coordinates for the bounds are always given in MM_HIMETRIC units.

Another set of opposite functions is **OleSetData()** and **OleGetData()**. Client applications use these functions to get and set an object's data. These functions have three parameters: a pointer to an OLEOBJECT, an OLECLIPBOARDFORMAT, and a handle to the data. Listing 7.14 is the objmgt.c source module.

Listing 7.14. The objmgt.c source module.

```
#include "oleclnt.h"

WORD PASCAL GetNextWindowID(BOOL);
LPRECT PASCAL GetNextObjectWindowRect(LPRECT, BOOL);
VOID PASCAL DeleteObjectWindow(HWND, HWND);
/*******************************************************************/
/* Function: AllocObject                                           */
/* Purpose:  Allocates an OBJECT structure.                        */
/* Returns: Pointer to OBJECT structure                            */
/*******************************************************************/
LPOBJECT PASCAL AllocObject(VOID)
    {
    HANDLE          hMem;
    LPOBJECT        pObj;

    if(NULL == pDoc)
        return NULL;

    hMem = LocalAlloc(LPTR, sizeof(OBJECT));

    if(NULL == hMem)
        return FALSE;

    pObj = (LPOBJECT)(PSTR)hMem;

    pObj->pvt = pDoc->pvt;

    if(NULL == pDoc->pObjFirst)
        pDoc->pObjFirst=pObj;
```

426

```
        pObj->pPrev = pDoc->pObjLast;

        if(NULL!=pObj->pPrev)
            {
            pObj->pNext = pObj->pPrev->pNext;
            pObj->pPrev->pNext = pObj;
            }
        else
            pObj->pNext = NULL;

        if(NULL != pObj->pNext)
            pObj->pNext->pPrev = pObj;

        pDoc->pObjLast = pObj;

        pObj->pDoc = pDoc;

        pDoc->cObjects++;
        return pObj;
        }

/*********************************************************************/
/* Function: InitializeObject                                        */
/* Purpose: Initializes an OBJECT structure.                         */
/* Returns: Pointer to OBJECT structure                              */
/*********************************************************************/
LPOBJECT PASCAL InitializeObject(LPOBJECT pObj, LPDOC pDoc)
    {
    WORD wTemp;
    LPSTR pszT;

    if(NULL == pObj || NULL == pDoc)
        return NULL;

    wTemp = CBSCRATCH;
    olestatus = OleQueryName(pObj->pObj, pDoc->pszData1, &wTemp);

    if(OLE_OK != olestatus)
        return NULL;

    if(pObj->aName)
        DeleteAtom(pObj->aName);
```

continues

427

Listing 7.14. continued

```
pObj->aName = AddAtom(pDoc->pszData1);

olestatus = OleQueryType(pObj->pObj, &pObj->dwType);

if(OLE_OK != olestatus)
    return NULL;

if(OT_EMBEDDED == pObj->dwType)
    {
    GetAtomName(pDoc->aCaption, pDoc->pszData2, CBSCRATCH);
    olestatus = OleSetHostNames(pObj->pObj, pDoc->pszData2,
                                pDoc->pszData1);

    if(OLE_OK != ErrHandler(olestatus, pDoc, pObj, TRUE))
        return NULL;
    }

if(OT_LINK==pObj->dwType)
    {
    olestatus = OleGetLinkUpdateOptions(pObj->pObj,
                                        &pObj->dwLink);

    if(OLE_OK != olestatus)
        return NULL;

    if(!GetObjectData(pObj, cfObjectLink, pDoc->pszData1))
        return NULL;

    pszT=pDoc->pszData1;

    if(pObj->aClass)
        DeleteAtom(pObj->aClass);

    pObj->aClass=AddAtom(pszT);

    pszT += lstrlen(pszT) + 1;

    if(pObj->aLink)
        DeleteAtom(pObj->aLink);

    pObj->aLink = AddAtom(pszT);
```

```
        pszT += lstrlen(pszT) + 1;

        if(pObj->aSel)
            DeleteAtom(pObj->aSel);

        pObj->aSel = AddAtom(pszT);
        }

    return pObj;
    }

/*******************************************************************/
/* Function: FreeObject                                            */
/* Purpose: Frees OBJECT structure.                                */
/* Returns: NULL if successful                                     */
/*******************************************************************/
LPOBJECT PASCAL FreeObject(LPDOC pDoc, LPOBJECT pObj)
    {
    LPOBJECT pPrev;
    LPOBJECT pNext;

    if(!pObj)
        return NULL;

    if(!LocalHandle((HANDLE)(DWORD)pObj))
        return NULL;

    pPrev = pObj->pPrev;
    pNext = pObj->pNext;

    if(pObj->aSel)
        DeleteAtom(pObj->aSel);

    if(pObj->aLink)
        DeleteAtom(pObj->aLink);

    if(pObj->aClass)
        DeleteAtom(pObj->aClass);

    if(pObj->aName)
        DeleteAtom(pObj->aLink);
```

continues

429

Listing 7.14. continued

```
    if(pObj->pObjUndo)
        {
        olestatus = OleDelete(pObj->pObjUndo);

        pObj->pObj = pObj->pObjUndo;
        ErrHandler(olestatus, pDoc, pObj, TRUE);
        }

    if(LocalFree((HANDLE)(DWORD)pObj))
        return pObj;

    if(pDoc->pObjFirst == pObj)
        pDoc->pObjFirst = pNext;

    if(pDoc->pObjLast == pObj)
        pDoc->pObjLast = pPrev;

    if(pPrev)
        pPrev->pNext = pNext;

    if(pNext)
        pNext->pPrev = pPrev;

    pDoc->cObjects--;
    return NULL;
    }

/******************************************************************/
/* Function: ClearObject                                          */
/* Purpose: Clears one object window.                             */
/******************************************************************/
VOID PASCAL ClearObject(LPARAM lParam)
    {
    if(0 == LOWORD(lParam))
        DeleteObjectWindow(hWndLastActive, hWnd);
    else
        DeleteObjectWindow((HWND)LOWORD(lParam), hWnd);
    fDocChanged = TRUE;
    }
```

```
/******************************************************************/
/* Function: ClearAllObjects                                      */
/* Purpose: Clears all object windows.                            */
/******************************************************************/
VOID ClearAllObjects(VOID)
    {
    LPOBJECT pObj;

    pDoc->cWait = 0;

    pObj = pDoc->pObjFirst;

    while(NULL != pObj)
        {
        if(!DeleteObjects(pObj))
            break;
        pObj = pObj->pNext;
        }
    Wait(TRUE, NULL);
    hWndLastActive = NULL;
    fDocChanged = TRUE;
    }


/******************************************************************/
/* Function: CloseObjects                                         */
/* Purpose: Releases an object.                                   */
/* Returns: TRUE                                                  */
/******************************************************************/
BOOL PASCAL CloseObjects(LPOBJECT pObj)
    {
    olestatus = OleRelease(pObj->pObj);
    ErrHandler(olestatus, pDoc, pObj, FALSE);
    return TRUE;
    }


/******************************************************************/
/* Function: UpdateObjects                                        */
/* Purpose: Updates an object.                                    */
/* Returns: TRUE                                                  */
/******************************************************************/
BOOL PASCAL UpdateObjects(LPOBJECT pObj)
```

continues

431

Listing 7.14. continued

```
    {
    pDoc->cWait = 0;

    if(OT_LINK == pObj->dwType)
        {
        olestatus = OleUpdate(pObj->pObj);
        if(OLE_OK != ErrHandler(olestatus, pDoc, pObj, TRUE))
            {
            pObj->dwLink = OLEUPDATE_UNAVAILABLE;
            pDoc->cLinks++;
            }
        }
    return TRUE;
    }

/**********************************************************************/
/* Function: DeleteObjects                                          */
/* Purpose: Deletes an object.                                      */
/* Returns: TRUE                                                    */
/**********************************************************************/
BOOL PASCAL DeleteObjects(LPOBJECT pObj)
    {
    HWND hwnd;

    hwnd = (HWND)pObj->hData;

    olestatus = OleDelete(pObj->pObj);

    if(OLE_ERROR_OBJECT != olestatus)
        ErrHandler(olestatus, pDoc, pObj, FALSE);

    DestroyWindow(hwnd);
    return TRUE;
    }

/**********************************************************************/
/* Function: SetFileObject                                          */
/* Purpose: Sets defaults in FILEOBJECT structure.                 */
/**********************************************************************/
VOID PASCAL SetFileObject(LPFILEOBJECT pFO)
    {
    char szClassName[SZCLASSNAME];
```

```
    pFO->wID = GetNextWindowID(FALSE);
    GetNextObjectWindowRect(&pFO->rc, FALSE);

    LoadString(hInst, IDS_OBJCLASSNAME,
                szClassName, sizeof szClassName);

    wsprintf(pFO->szName, "%s[%d]", szClassName, pFO->wID);
    return;
    }

/*******************************************************************/
/* Function: CreateObjectWindow                                    */
/* Purpose: Creates a window for an object.                        */
/* Returns: Handle to the window                                   */
/*******************************************************************/
HWND PASCAL CreateObjectWindow(LPFILEOBJECT pFO, BOOL fShow,
                                LPOBJECT pObj)
    {
    char szClassName[SZCLASSNAME];
    FILEOBJECT  fo;
    HWND hwndChild=NULL;
    HANDLE hInst;
    DWORD dwStyle;

    if(NULL == hWnd ¦¦ NULL == pObj)
        return NULL;

    if(NULL == pFO)
        {
        pFO = &fo;
        SetFileObject(pFO);
        }

    hInst = GetWindowWord(hWnd, GWW_HINSTANCE);

    dwStyle = WS_BORDER ¦ WS_CHILD ¦
            WS_CLIPSIBLINGS ¦ WS_THICKFRAME;
    dwStyle ¦= (fShow) ? WS_VISIBLE : 0L;

    LoadString(hInst, IDS_OBJCLASSNAME,
                szClassName, sizeof szClassName);
```

continues

Listing 7.14. continued

```c
            hwndChild = CreateWindow(szClassName,
                            pFO->szName,
                            dwStyle,
                            pFO->rc.left,
                            pFO->rc.top,
                            pFO->rc.right-pFO->rc.left,
                            pFO->rc.bottom-pFO->rc.top,
                            hWnd,
                            pFO->wID,
                            hInst,
                            (LPVOID)pObj);

    if(NULL != hwndChild && fShow)
        {
        BringWindowToTop(hwndChild);
        SendMessage(hwndChild, WM_NCACTIVATE, TRUE, 0L);
        fDocChanged = TRUE;
        }

    if(NULL == hwndChild)
        {
        olestatus = OleDelete(pObj->pObj);
        ErrHandler(olestatus, pObj->pDoc, pObj, TRUE);
        FreeObject(pObj->pDoc, pObj);
        }

    return hwndChild;
    }

/*********************************************************************/
/* Function: GetObjectWindowRect                                     */
/* Purpose: Gets rect coordinates for an object window.              */
/* Returns: Rectangle structure                                      */
/*********************************************************************/
LPRECT PASCAL GetObjectWindowRect(HWND hWnd, LPRECT pRect,
                            HWND hWndParent)

    {
    POINT       pt;
```

```
    if((LPRECT)NULL==pRect)
        return pRect;

    GetWindowRect(hWnd, pRect);

    pt.x=pRect->left;
    pt.y=pRect->top;
    ScreenToClient(hWndParent, &pt);
    pRect->left=pt.x;
    pRect->top=pt.y;

    pt.x=pRect->right;
    pt.y=pRect->bottom;
    ScreenToClient(hWndParent, &pt);
    pRect->right=pt.x;
    pRect->bottom=pt.y;

    return pRect;
    }

/********************************************************************/
/* Function: GetNextWindowID                                      */
/* Purpose: Maintains windows IDs with a static counter.          */
/* Returns: Next window ID                                        */
/********************************************************************/
WORD PASCAL GetNextWindowID(BOOL fReset)
    {
    static WORD wID = 999;

    if(fReset)
        {
        wID=1000;
        return wID;
        }

    return ++wID;
    }
```

continues

Listing 7.14. continued

```
/*******************************************************************/
/* Function: GetNextObjectWindowRect                             */
/* Purpose: Creates a default RECT struct for a new object window.*/
/* Returns: Object window rectangle                              */
/*******************************************************************/
LPRECT PASCAL GetNextObjectWindowRect(LPRECT pRect, BOOL fReset)
    {
    static WORD x = 0, y = 0;
    static WORD cx = 100, cy = 100;

    if(fReset)
        {
        x=0;
        y=0;
        cx=150;
        cy=150;

        if((LPRECT)NULL == pRect)
            SetRect(pRect, x, y, x+cx, x+cy);

        return pRect;
        }

    if((LPRECT)NULL == pRect)
        return (LPRECT)NULL;

    SetRect(pRect, x, y, x+cx, y+cy);

    x+=10;

    if(x > 200)
        x=0;

    y+=10;

    if(y > 150)
        y=0;

    cx=150;
    cy=150;
```

```
    return pRect;
    }

/********************************************************************/
/* Function: DeleteObjectWindow                                     */
/* Purpose: Deletes an object window.                               */
/********************************************************************/
VOID PASCAL DeleteObjectWindow(HWND hwnd, HWND hWndParent)
    {
    HWND hWndNext;
    HWND hWndPrev;
    HWND hWndT;
    LPOBJECT pObj;

    hWndNext = GetWindow(hwnd, GW_HWNDNEXT);
    hWndPrev = GetWindow(hwnd, GW_HWNDPREV);
    hWndT = hWndNext;

    if(!hWndT)
        hWndT = hWndPrev;

    if(!hWndT)
        hWndT = GetWindow(hWndParent, GW_CHILD);

    pObj = (LPOBJECT)SendMessage(hwnd, PM_GETOBJECT, 0, 0L);

    olestatus = OleDelete(pObj->pObj);
    olestatus = ErrHandler(olestatus, pDoc, pObj, TRUE);

    if(hWndT == hwnd)
        hWndT = NULL;

    DestroyWindow(hwnd);

    if(hWndT)
        {
        BringWindowToTop(hWndT);
        SendMessage(hWndT, WM_NCACTIVATE, TRUE, 0L);
        }
    else
        hWndLastActive=NULL;
```

continues

437

Listing 7.14. continued

```
    return;
    }

/********************************************************************/
/* Function: PaintObject                                          */
/* Purpose: Draws an object window.                               */
/* Returns: TRUE/FALSE                                            */
/********************************************************************/
BOOL PASCAL PaintObject(HDC hDC, LPRECT pRect, LPOBJECT pObj)
    {
    olestatus = OleDraw(pObj->pObj, hDC, pRect, NULL, NULL);
    olestatus = ErrHandler(olestatus, pObj->pDoc, pObj, TRUE);

    if(OLE_OK != olestatus)
        return FALSE;

    return TRUE;
    }

/********************************************************************/
/* Function: SetObjectRect                                        */
/* Purpose: Sets object window rectangle for a given mapping mode.*/
/* Returns: TRUE/FALSE                                            */
/********************************************************************/
BOOL PASCAL SetObjectRect(LPDOC pDoc, LPOBJECT pObj,
                          LPRECT pRect, WORD mm)
    {
    if(NULL == pObj || NULL == pRect)
        return FALSE;

    ConvertRectMappings(pRect, mm, MM_HIMETRIC);

    olestatus = OleSetBounds(pObj->pObj, pRect);
    if(OLE_OK != ErrHandler(olestatus, pDoc, pObj, TRUE))
        return FALSE;

    olestatus = OleUpdate(pObj->pObj);
    if(OLE_OK != ErrHandler(olestatus, pDoc, pObj, TRUE))
        return FALSE;
```

```
    return TRUE;
    }

/*******************************************************************/
/* Function: GetObjectRect                                         */
/* Purpose: Gets object window rectangle for the given mapping     */
/*          mode.                                                  */
/* Returns: TRUE/FALSE                                             */
/*******************************************************************/
BOOL PASCAL GetObjectRect(LPOBJECT pObj, LPRECT pRect, WORD mm)
    {
    RECT Rect;

    if(NULL==pObj ¦¦ NULL==pRect)
        return FALSE;

    olestatus=OleQueryBounds(pObj->pObj, &Rect);
    if(OLE_OK!=olestatus)
        return FALSE;

    ConvertRectMappings(&Rect, MM_HIMETRIC, mm);
    CopyRect(pRect, &Rect);
    return TRUE;
    }

/*******************************************************************/
/* Function: GetObjectData                                         */
/* Purpose: Gets an object's data.                                 */
/* Returns: TRUE/FALSE                                             */
/*******************************************************************/
BOOL PASCAL GetObjectData(LPOBJECT pObj, WORD cf, LPSTR psz)
    {
    HANDLE hLink;
    LPSTR pszLink;
    WORD cch;

    if(NULL == pObj ¦¦ NULL == psz)
        return FALSE;

    olestatus = OleGetData(pObj->pObj, cf, &hLink);
    if(OLE_OK!=olestatus && OLE_WARN_DELETE_DATA!=olestatus)
        return FALSE;
```

continues

Listing 7.14. continued

```c
    pszLink = GlobalLock(hLink);

    if(pszLink)
        {
        lstrcpy(psz, pszLink);
        cch = lstrlen(pszLink)+1;
        lstrcpy(psz+cch, pszLink+cch);
        cch += lstrlen(pszLink+cch)+1;
        lstrcpy(psz+cch, pszLink+cch);
        cch += lstrlen(pszLink+cch)+1;
        *(psz+cch) = 0;
        }

    GlobalUnlock(hLink);

    if(OLE_WARN_DELETE_DATA == olestatus)
        GlobalFree(hLink);

    if(NULL == pszLink)
        return FALSE;

    return TRUE;
    }


/*********************************************************************/
/* Function: SetObjectData                                          */
/* Purpose: Sets an object's data for a given clipboard format.     */
/* Returns: TRUE/FALSE                                              */
/*********************************************************************/
BOOL PASCAL SetObjectData(LPOBJECT pObj, WORD cf, LPSTR pszDoc)
    {
    HANDLE hMem;
    LPSTR pszT;

    if(NULL == pObj || NULL == pszDoc)
        return FALSE;

    hMem = GlobalAlloc(GHND | GMEM_DDESHARE, 1024);
```

```
if(!hMem)
    return FALSE;

pszT = GlobalLock(hMem);

pszT += GetAtomName(pObj->aClass, pszT, 256) + 1;

if(pObj->aLink)
    DeleteAtom(pObj->aLink);

pObj->aLink = AddAtom(pszDoc);
lstrcpy(pszT, pszDoc);
pszT += lstrlen(pszT)+1;

pszT += GetAtomName(pObj->aSel, pszT, 512) +1;

*(pszT) = 0;

GlobalUnlock(hMem);

olestatus = OleSetData(pObj->pObj, cf, hMem);
if(OLE_OK!=ErrHandler(olestatus, pDoc, pObj, TRUE))
    return FALSE;

return TRUE;
}
```

Dialogs and Object Insertion

There are three dialog boxes in the example client application: an About box, a Links box, and an Insert Object box. This list, of course, does not include the common dialogs for file I/O. For my discussion of this part of the application, I focus on the Insert Object dialog box. Many other functions are associated with the Links dialog box, so that will be a topic unto itself.

The Insert Object dialog box contains a list box that has all the object servers from the registration database. When the InsertObjectDlgProc() function receives the WM_INITDIALOG message, it calls the LoadClassList() function in the register.c source file. If the user selects an object, the dialog box returns to CreateInsertDlgProc(), and **OleCreate()** is called. **OleCreate()** creates an

embedded object for the class of object selected from the list box. **OleCreate()** has the following prototype:

```
OLESTATUS OleCreate(LPSTR lpszProtocol, LPOLECLIENT lpClient,
     LPSTR lpszClass, LHCLIENTDOC lhClientDoc,
     LPSTR lpszObjname, LPOLEOBJECT FAR *lplpObject,
     OLEOPT_RENDER renderopt, OLECLIPFORMAT cfFormat);
```

The first parameter, lpszProtocol, can have a value of "StdFileEditing" or "Static". The second parameter points to an OLECLIENT structure. The lhClientDoc parameter is a handle to the client document. The lpszObjname is the client application's name of the object. The lplpObject is a pointer to a pointer to an OLEOBJECT structure. This parameter receives the new object. The renderopt parameter can be olerender_none, olerender_draw, or olerender_format. The last parameter is the clipboard format specified for subsequent calls to OleGetData() when a renderopt of olerender_format is specified.

If **OleCreate()** returns with a valid status, OLECLNT creates an object window. Otherwise, a message box is posted to inform the user that the object cannot be created. Listing 7.15 is the dialogs.c source module.

Listing 7.15. The dialogs.c source module.

```
#include "oleclnt.h"

/********************************************************************/
/* Function: CreateDlgBox                                           */
/* Purpose: Generic function to create dialog boxes.                */
/* Returns: TRUE/FALSE                                              */
/********************************************************************/
BOOL PASCAL CreateDlgBox(HWND hwnd, LPCSTR lpTemplateName,
                         FARPROC lpDlgProc)

    {
    BOOL bResult = TRUE;

    lpDlgProc = MakeProcInstance(lpDlgProc, hInst);
    if(lpDlgProc)
        {
        if(!DialogBox(hInst, lpTemplateName, hwnd,
                    (DLGPROC)lpDlgProc))
            bResult = FALSE;
        FreeProcInstance(lpDlgProc);
        }
```

```
    else
        bResult = FALSE;

    return bResult;
    }

/********************************************************************/
/* Function: AboutDlgProc                                        */
/* Purpose: Handles messages for the About dialog box.           */
/* Returns: TRUE/FALSE                                           */
/********************************************************************/
LRESULT CALLBACK AboutDlgProc(HWND hDlg, WORD message,
                             WPARAM wParam, LPARAM lParam)
    {
    switch(message)
        {
        case WM_INITDIALOG:
            return (LRESULT)TRUE;
        case WM_COMMAND:
            switch((WORD)wParam)
                {
                case IDOK:
                case IDCANCEL:
                    EndDialog(hDlg, TRUE);
                    return (LRESULT)TRUE;
                }
            break;
        }
    return (LRESULT)FALSE;
    }

/********************************************************************/
/* Function: CreateInsertDlgBox                                  */
/* Purpose: Creates Insert dialog and object if selected.        */
/* Returns: TRUE/FALSE                                           */
/********************************************************************/
BOOL PASCAL CreateInsertDlgBox(VOID)
    {
    LPOBJECT  pObj;
    FILEOBJECT  fo;
    HWND hWndT;
```

continues

Listing 7.15. continued

```
if (NULL == pDOC || NULL == hInst)
    return FALSE;
SetFileObject(&fo);
CreateDlgBox(hWnd,(LPCSTR)MAKEINTRESOURCE(IDD_INSERTOBJECTBOX),
             (FARPROC)InsertObjectDlgProc);
pObj = AllocObject();

if(!pObj)
    {
    FreeObject(pDoc, pObj);
    return NULL;
    }

olestatus = OleCreate("StdFileEditing", (LPOLECLIENT)pObj,
                      pDoc->pszData1,
                      pDoc->lh, fo.szName,
                      &pObj->pObj, olerender_draw, 0);

if(OLE_OK != ErrHandler(olestatus, pDoc, pObj, TRUE))
    {
    MsgBox(hWnd, IDS_CANNOTINSERT,  MB_OK |
MB_ICONEXCLAMATION);

    FreeObject(pDoc, pObj);
    return NULL;
    }
else
    pObj->fOpen = TRUE;

if(NULL == pObj)
    return FALSE;

hWndT = CreateObjectWindow(&fo, TRUE, pObj);

if(NULL == hWndT)
    return FALSE;

return TRUE;
    }
```

```
/****************************************************************/
/* Function: InsertObjectDlgProc                                */
/* Purpose: Handles messages for the About dialog box.          */
/* Returns: TRUE/FALSE                                          */
/****************************************************************/
LRESULT CALLBACK InsertObjectDlgProc(HWND hDlg, WORD message,
                                     WPARAM wParam, LPARAM lParam)
    {
    WORD wListIndex;
    HWND hList;
    char szTemp[256];

    switch(message)
        {
        case WM_INITDIALOG:
            hList = GetDlgItem(hDlg, IDD_OBJECTLIST);
            LoadClassList(hList);
            return TRUE;

        case WM_COMMAND:
            switch(wParam)
                {
                case IDCANCEL:
                    EndDialog(hDlg, FALSE);
                    break;

                case IDD_OBJECTLIST:
                    if(LBN_DBLCLK != HIWORD(lParam))
                        break;

                case IDOK:
                    hList = GetDlgItem(hDlg, IDD_OBJECTLIST);
                    wListIndex = (WORD)SendMessage(hList,
                            LB_GETCURSEL, 0, 0L);

                    SendMessage(hList, LB_GETTEXT,
                            wListIndex,
                            (LONG)(LPSTR)szTemp);
                    GetClassFromDesc(szTemp,
                            pDoc->pszData1, 256);
                    EndDialog(hDlg, TRUE);
                    break;
```

continues

Listing 7.15. continued

```
            }
        break;
        }
    return FALSE;
    }

/**********************************************************************/
/* Function: LinksDlgProc                                           */
/* Purpose: Dlg box to handle link options.                         */
/* Returns: TRUE/FALSE                                              */
/**********************************************************************/
LRESULT CALLBACK LinksDlgProc(HWND hDlg, WORD message,
                              WPARAM wParam, LPARAM lParam)

    {
    LPOBJECT pObj;
    BOOL fLinks;
    HWND hList;
    WORD cxTabs[3];
    RECT rc;
    WORD cx;
    DWORD dwBase;
    OLEOPT_UPDATE dwUpdate;


    hList = GetDlgItem(hDlg, IDD_LINKLIST);


    switch(message)
        {
        case WM_INITDIALOG:
            pDoc->hList = hList;
            GetClientRect(hList, &rc);
            pDoc->cxList = ((rc.right-rc.left) >> 2)-8;
            dwBase = GetDialogBaseUnits();
            cx = ((rc.right-rc.left) * 4)/LOWORD(dwBase);
            cxTabs[0]=cx >> 2;
            cxTabs[1]=cx >> 1;
            cxTabs[2]=(cx * 3) >> 2;

            SendMessage(hList, LB_SETTABSTOPS, 3,
                    (LONG)(LPSTR)&cxTabs);
```

```
        pObj = pDoc->pObjFirst;
        fLinks = TRUE;
        while(NULL != pObj)
            {
            if(!LinksInit(pObj))
                {
                fLinks = FALSE;
                break;
                }
            pObj = pObj->pNext;
            }

        if(!fLinks)
            EndDialog(hDlg, -1);

        SendMessage(hList, LB_SETSEL, 1, 0L);

        EnableLinkButtons(hDlg, hList);
        return TRUE;

case WM_COMMAND:
    switch(wParam)
        {
        case IDD_UPDATENOW:
            EnumLinks(hList, UpdateLinks,
                        ENUMLINK_SELECTED, MAKELONG(0, IDOK));
            EnumLinks(hList, UpdateLinks, ENUMLINK_ALL,
                        MAKELONG(0, IDCANCEL));

            EnableLinkButtons(hDlg, hList);
            break;

        case IDD_CANCELLINK:
            EnumLinks(hList, CancelLinks,
                        ENUMLINK_SELECTED, 0L);
            EnableLinkButtons(hDlg, hList);
            break;

        case IDD_CHANGELINK:
            ChangeLink(hList);
            EnableLinkButtons(hDlg, hList);
            break;
```

continues

Listing 7.15. continued

```
                case IDD_AUTOMATIC:
                case IDD_MANUAL:
                    dwUpdate= (IDD_AUTOMATIC == wParam) ?
                            oleupdate_always : oleupdate_oncall;

                    if(0L != SendMessage(LOWORD(lParam),
                                    BM_GETCHECK, 0, 0L))
                        {
                        EnumLinks(hList, ChangeLinkOptions,
                                ENUMLINK_SELECTED, dwUpdate);
                        EnableLinkButtons(hDlg, hList);
                        }
                    break;

                case IDD_LINKLIST:
                    if(HIWORD(lParam) == LBN_SELCHANGE)
                        EnableLinkButtons(hDlg, hList);
                    break;

                case IDCANCEL:
                    EnumLinks(hList, UndoLinks,
                            ENUMLINK_ALL, 0L);
                    EndDialog(hDlg, FALSE);
                    break;

                case IDOK:
                    EnumLinks(hList, CleanupClones,
                            ENUMLINK_ALL, 0L);

                    EndDialog(hDlg, TRUE);
                    break;
                }
            break;
        }
    return FALSE;
    }
```

```
/*******************************************************************/
/* Function: EnableLinkButtons                                     */
/* Purpose: Enables buttons in Links dialog.                       */
/*******************************************************************/
VOID PASCAL EnableLinkButtons(HWND hDlg, HWND hList)
    {
    LPOBJECT pObj;
    WORD i;
    ATOM aCurLink = 0;
    WORD cAuto = 0;
    WORD cManual = 0;
    WORD cStatic = 0;
    WORD cUnavailable = 0;
    WORD cLinks;
    BOOL fAuto;
    BOOL fManual;
    BOOL fUnavailable;
    BOOL fNone;
    BOOL fAutoOnly;
    BOOL fManualOnly;
    BOOL fUnavailableOnly;
    BOOL fUpdate;
    BOOL fChangeLink=TRUE;

    cLinks = (WORD)SendMessage(hList, LB_GETCOUNT, 0, 0L);

    for(i = 0; i < cLinks; i++)
        {
        if(SendMessage(hList, LB_GETSEL, i, 0L))
            {
            pObj = (LPOBJECT)SendMessage(hList,
                                LB_GETITEMDATA, i, 0L);

            if(OT_STATIC == pObj->dwType)
                cStatic++;
            else
                {
                switch(pObj->dwLink)
                    {
                    case oleupdate_always:
                        cAuto++;
                        break;
```

continues

449

Listing 7.15. continued

```
                case oleupdate_oncall:
                    cManual++;
                    break;

                case OLEUPDATE_UNAVAILABLE:
                    cUnavailable++;
                    break;
                }

            if(0 == aCurLink)
                aCurLink = pObj->aLink;
            else
                {
                if(aCurLink != pObj->aLink)
                    fChangeLink = FALSE;
                }
            }
        }
    }

fAuto = (0 != cAuto);
fManual = (0 != cManual);
fUnavailable = (0 != cUnavailable);
fNone = (0==cLinks ¦¦ !(fAuto ¦¦ fManual ¦¦ fUnavailable));
fAutoOnly = (fAuto && !fManual);
fManualOnly = (fManual && !fAuto);
fUnavailableOnly = ((0!=cUnavailable) && !fAuto && !fManual);
fChangeLink = (fChangeLink ¦¦ fUnavailableOnly) && !fNone;
fUpdate=(fAuto ¦¦ fManual) && !fUnavailable;
EnableWindow(GetDlgItem(hDlg, IDD_UPDATENOW),
            !fNone && fUpdate);
EnableWindow(GetDlgItem(hDlg, IDD_CANCELLINK),
            !fNone && (fAuto ¦¦ fManual));
EnableWindow(GetDlgItem(hDlg, IDD_CHANGELINK), fChangeLink);
CheckDlgButton(hDlg, IDD_AUTOMATIC,    !fNone && fAutoOnly);
CheckDlgButton(hDlg, IDD_MANUAL, !fNone && fManualOnly);
EnableWindow(GetDlgItem(hDlg, IDD_AUTOMATIC),   !fNone);
EnableWindow(GetDlgItem(hDlg, IDD_MANUAL), !fNone);
}
```

Clipboard Processing

Clipboard processing is very easy for client applications. The client application has to respond to user requests to Cut, Copy, Paste, and Paste Link. When the user selects the Cut menu option, the MainWndProc() calls CutObject(). CutObject() first calls CopyObject() and then deletes the object by sending a message with IDM_CLEAR as wParam. When MainWndProc() receives this message, it calls ClearObject(). ClearObject() calls DeleteObjectWindow(), which calls **OleDelete()**.

The CopyObject() function is called for both the Cut and the Copy menu options. CopyObject() calls **OleCopyToClipboard()**. **OleCopyToClipboard()** has one parameter, a pointer to an OLEOBJECT structure. When called, the client library copies to the clipboard the object specified by the OLEOBJECT structure.

The Paste and Paste Link menu options are handled by one function: PasteObject(). The PasteObject() function handles three types of objects: linked, embedded, and static. Static objects can be considered non-OLE objects. The PasteObject() function calls **OleCreateLinkFromClip()** to create a linked object. **OleCreateLinkFromClip()** has the following prototype:

```
OLESTATUS OleCreateLinkFromClip(LPSTR lpszProtocol,
    LPOLECLIENT lpClient, LHCLIENTDOC lhClientDoc,
    LPSTR lpszObjname, LPOLEOBJECT FAR *lplpObject,
    OLEOPT_RENDER renderopt, OLECLIPFORMAT cfFormat);
```

If the object is an embedded object or a static object, PasteObject() calls **OleCreateFromClip()**. **OleCreateFromClip()** has the following prototype:

```
OLESTATUS OleCreateFromClip(LPSTR lpszProtocol,
    LPOLECLIENT lpClient, LHCLIENTDOC lhClientDoc,
    LPSTR lpszObjname, LPOLEOBJECT FAR *lplpObject,
    OLEOPT_RENDER renderopt, OLECLIPFORMAT cfFormat);
```

If the object in the clipboard is an embedded object, the lpszProtocol parameter contains a pointer to the string "StdFileEditing". If the object in the clipboard is static, the lpszProtocol is "Static". Listing 7.16 is the clipbord.c source module.

Listing 7.16. The clipbord.c source module.

```
#include "oleclnt.h"

/********************************************************************/
/* Function: CutObject                                           */
/* Purpose:  Copies an object to the clipboard and then deletes  */
/*           it.                                                  */
/* Returns: TRUE/FALSE                                           */
/********************************************************************/
BOOL CutObject(VOID)
    {
    if(!CopyObject())
        return FALSE;
    SendMessage(hWnd, WM_COMMAND, IDM_CLEAR, 0L);
    return TRUE;
    }


/********************************************************************/
/* Function: CopyObject                                          */
/* Purpose: Copies an object to the clipboard.                   */
/* Returns: TRUE/FALSE                                           */
/********************************************************************/
BOOL PASCAL CopyObject(VOID)
    {
    LPOBJECT pObj;
    BOOL rc = FALSE;

    if(!OpenClipboard(hWnd))
        return FALSE;

    pObj = (LPOBJECT)SendMessage(hWndLastActive,
                               PM_GETOBJECT, 0, 0L);
    if(OLE_OK == OleCopyToClipboard(pObj->pObj))
        rc = TRUE;

    CloseClipboard();
    return rc;
    }
```

```
/**********************************************************************/
/* Function: PasteObject                                              */
/* Purpose: Handles Paste, Paste Link, and static paste (non-OLE).*/
/* Returns: TRUE/FALSE                                                */
/**********************************************************************/
BOOL PASCAL PasteObject(BOOL fLink)
    {
    HWND hwndChild;
    FILEOBJECT fo;
    LPOBJECT pObj;

    if(!OpenClipboard(hWnd))
        return FALSE;

    SetFileObject(&fo);
    pObj = AllocObject();

    if(!pObj)
        {
        FreeObject(pDoc, pObj);
        CloseClipboard();
        return FALSE;
        }

    if(fLink)
        {
        olestatus = OleCreateLinkFromClip("StdFileEditing",
                                          (LPOLECLIENT)pObj,
                                          pDoc->lh,
                                          fo.szName,
                                          &pObj->pObj,
                                          olerender_draw, 0);

        olestatus = ErrHandler(olestatus, pDoc, pObj, TRUE);

        if(OLE_OK!=olestatus)
            fLink = FALSE;
        }

    if(!fLink)
        {
```

continues

453

Listing 7.16. continued

```
            olestatus = OleCreateFromClip("StdFileEditing",
                                          (LPOLECLIENT)pObj,
                                          pDoc->lh,
                                          fo.szName,
                                          &pObj->pObj,
                                          olerender_draw, 0);

        olestatus = ErrHandler(olestatus, pDoc, pObj, TRUE);

        if(OLE_OK != olestatus)
            {
            olestatus = OleCreateFromClip("Static",
                                          (LPOLECLIENT)pObj,
                                          pDoc->lh,
                                          fo.szName,
                                          &pObj->pObj,
                                          olerender_draw, 0);

            olestatus = ErrHandler(olestatus, pDoc, pObj, TRUE);
            }
        }

    CloseClipboard();

    if(OLE_OK != olestatus)
        {
        FreeObject(pDoc, pObj);
        return FALSE;
        }

    hwndChild = CreateObjectWindow(&fo, TRUE, pObj);

    if(hwndChild == NULL)
        return FALSE;

    SendMessage(hwndChild, PM_NOTIFYOBJECT, OLE_CHANGED,
                (LONG)pObj);
    return TRUE;
    }
```

Link Management

The links.c source file contains functions relating to linked objects. The functions in this module call OLE functions I have not yet covered, which are shown in Table 7.5.

Table 7.5. OLE functions and application functions for linking.

OLE Functions	Application Functions
OleClone()	LinksInit()
OleQueryOpen()	LinksInit()
OleSetLinkUpdateOptions()	ChangeLinkOptions()
OleObjectConvert()	CancelLinks()
OleRename()	UndoLinks()
OleReconnect()	UndoLinks()

Most of the functions in this module are called by EnumLinks(). EnumLinks() simply loops for all objects in a document and calls an enumeration function such as LinksInit() or UndoLinks(). The main source for EnumLinks() calls is from the Links dialog box. The enumeration functions are quite easy to understand, given the coverage of new OLE functions.

The **OleClone()** function makes a copy of an object, but the object is not connected to a server. **OleClone()** has the following prototype:

```
OLESTATUS OleClone(LPOLEOBJECT lpObject, LPOLECLIENT lpClient,
                   LHCLIENTDOC lhClientDoc, LPSTR lpszObjname,
                   LPOLEOBJECT FAR *lplpObject);
```

The first parameter is the source object to clone. The second parameter is a pointer to an OLECLIENT structure for the new object. The lhClientDoc parameter is a handle to the client document. The lpszObjname parameter is the name of the object. The last parameter is a pointer to a pointer to the new OLEOBJECT structure.

When a client application calls **OleQueryOpen()**, it checks to see whether the specified object has been activated by a call to **OleActivate()**.

The **OleSetLinkUpdateOptions()** function sets the link-update option for a given object. This function is used with the Link dialog box when the *Automatic*

and *Manual* radio buttons change. **OleSetLinkUpdateOptions()** has two parameters. The first is a pointer to the OLEOBJECT structure. The second is the link-update option. The link-update option can have a value of oleupdate_always, oleupdate_onsave, or oleupdate_oncall.

The CancelLinks() enumeration function calls the **OleObjectConvert()** function. **OleObjectConvert()** creates a new static object from a linked object or an embedded object. CancelLinks() calls **OleObjectConvert()** to create the new object and deletes the old linked object. The net effect of this is the removal of a link. **OleObjectConvert()** has the following prototype:

```
OLESTATUS OleObjectConvert(LPOLEOBJECT lpObject,
     LPSTR lpszProtocol, LPOLECLIENT lpClient,
     LHCLIENTDOC lhClientDoc, LPSTR lpszObjname,
     LPOLEOBJECT FAR *lplpObject);
```

The **OleRename()** function changes the name of an object. The first parameter of this function is a pointer to the OLEOBJECT structure. The second parameter is the new name. The name must be unique. The last new OLE function in this module is **OleReconnect()**. The **OleReconnect()** function reestablishes an open link to an object. **OleReconnect()** takes one parameter: a pointer to an OLEOBJECT structure. Listing 7.17 is the links.c source module.

Listing 7.17. The links.c source module.

```
#include "oleclnt.h"

WORD PASCAL CreateLinkString(LPOBJECT);
VOID PASCAL ChangeLinkString(HWND, WORD, LPSTR);
/*******************************************************************/
/* Function: QueryLinks                                          */
/* Purpose: Queries user to update links.                        */
/* Returns: TRUE/FALSE                                           */
/*******************************************************************/
BOOL PASCAL QueryLinks(VOID)
    {
    char szMessage[SZMESSAGE];
    char szCaption[SZWINDOWTITLE];
    WORD wYesNo;
    LPOBJECT pObj;

    if(0 == pDoc->cLinks)
        return TRUE;
```

```
LoadString(hInst, IDS_QUERYLINKS,
           szMessage, sizeof szMessage);

LoadString(hInst, IDS_UPDATINGLINKS,
           szCaption, sizeof szCaption);

wYesNo = MessageBox(hWnd, szMessage, szCaption,
                    MB_YESNO | MB_ICONEXCLAMATION);

if(IDYES != wYesNo)
    return FALSE;


pDoc->cLinks=0;

pObj = pDoc->pObjFirst;

while(NULL != pObj)
    {
    if(!UpdateObjects(pObj))
        break;

    pObj = pObj->pNext;
    }
Wait(TRUE, NULL);

if(!pDoc->cLinks)
    return TRUE;

LoadString(hInst, IDS_BADFILELINK,
           szMessage, sizeof szMessage);

LoadString(hInst, IDS_WINDOWTITLE,
           szCaption, sizeof szCaption);

wYesNo = MessageBox(hWnd, szMessage, szCaption,
                    MB_YESNO | MB_ICONEXCLAMATION);

if(wYesNo == IDNO)
    return FALSE;

return CreateDlgBox(hWnd,
```

continues

Listing 7.17. continued

```
                    (LPCSTR)MAKEINTRESOURCE(IDD_LINKSBOX),
                    (FARPROC)LinksDlgProc);
    }

/**********************************************************************/
/* Function: EnumLinks                                              */
/* Purpose: General driver that calls an enumeration function.      */
/* Returns: TRUE/FALSE                                              */
/**********************************************************************/
BOOL PASCAL EnumLinks(HWND hList, LPFNLINKENUM pfn,
                    WORD wSelection, DWORD dwData)

    {
    WORD cLinks;
    LPOBJECT pObj;
    WORD i;
    BOOL fSel;
    BOOL fRet = TRUE;

    cLinks = (WORD)SendMessage(hList, LB_GETCOUNT, 0, 0L);

    for(i = 0; i < cLinks; i++)
        {
        fSel = (BOOL)SendMessage(hList, LB_GETSEL, i, 0L);
        pObj = (LPOBJECT)SendMessage(hList,
                                    LB_GETITEMDATA, i, 0L);

        if(ENUMLINK_ALL != wSelection &&
          OT_STATIC == pObj->dwType)
            continue;

        if((fSel && ENUMLINK_SELECTED == wSelection) ||
            (!fSel && ENUMLINK_UNSELECTED == wSelection) ||
            (ENUMLINK_ALL == wSelection))
            {
            if(!(*pfn)(hList, i, pObj, dwData))
                {
                fRet = FALSE;
                break;
                }
            }
        }
```

```
    return fRet;
    }

/*******************************************************************/
/* Function: LinksInit                                          */
/* Purpose: Adds links to list box.                             */
/* Returns: TRUE/FALSE                                          */
/*******************************************************************/
BOOL PASCAL LinksInit(LPOBJECT pObj)
    {
    static WORD iClone=0;
    WORD i;
    char szClone[40];

    if(OT_LINK == pObj->dwType)
        {
        CreateLinkString(pObj);

        i = (WORD)SendMessage(pDoc->hList,
                            LB_ADDSTRING, 0,
                            (LONG)pDoc->pszData1);
        SendMessage(pDoc->hList,
                    LB_SETITEMDATA,
                    i, (LONG)(LPSTR)pObj);

        wsprintf(szClone, "Clone #%d", iClone);

        olestatus = OleClone(pObj->pObj,
                            (LPOLECLIENT)pObj,
                            pDoc->lh, szClone,
                            &pObj->pObjUndo);

        pDoc->cWait = 0;
        ErrHandler(olestatus, pDoc, pObj, FALSE);
        Wait(TRUE, NULL);

        olestatus = OleQueryOpen(pObj->pObj);
        pObj->fUndoOpen = (OLE_OK == olestatus);

        pObj->fLinkChange=FALSE;
        }
```

continues

459

Listing 7.17. continued

```
    iClone++;
    return TRUE;
    }

/**********************************************************************/
/* Function: ChangeLinkOptions                                      */
/* Purpose: Updates link options.                                   */
/* Returns: TRUE/FALSE                                              */
/**********************************************************************/
BOOL PASCAL ChangeLinkOptions(HWND hList, WORD i, LPOBJECT pObj,
                              DWORD dw)

    {
    if((OLEOPT_UPDATE)dw == pObj->dwLink)
        return TRUE;

    pObj->dwLink = (OLEOPT_UPDATE)dw;
    olestatus = OleSetLinkUpdateOptions(pObj->pObj,
                                        (OLEOPT_UPDATE)dw);

    if(OLE_OK == ErrHandler(olestatus, pDoc, pObj, TRUE))
        {
        CreateLinkString(pObj);
        ChangeLinkString(hList, i, pDoc->pszData1);
        pObj->fLinkChange=TRUE;
        }

    return TRUE;
    }

/**********************************************************************/
/* Function: UpdateLinks                                            */
/* Purpose: Enumeration function to update links.                   */
/* Returns: TRUE/FALSE                                              */
/**********************************************************************/
BOOL PASCAL UpdateLinks(HWND hList, WORD i, LPOBJECT pObj, DWORD dw)
    {
    LPSTR psz;
    LPSTR pszLinkFile;
    LPSTR pszFile;
    BOOL  fRet;
    WORD  wTemp;
```

```
        DWORD dwT;
        WORD  cch;
        HWND  hWndParent;

        switch(HIWORD(dw))
            {
            case IDIGNORE:
                if(0 != LOWORD(dw))
                    {
                    if(LOWORD(dw)!=pObj->aLink)
                        return TRUE;
                    }
                break;

            case IDRETRY:
                if(LOWORD(dw) == pObj->aLink)
                    pObj->fNoMatch=TRUE;

                return TRUE;

            case IDCANCEL:
                pObj->fNoMatch = FALSE;
                return TRUE;
            }

        olestatus = OleUpdate(pObj->pObj);
        olestatus = ErrHandler(olestatus, pDoc, pObj, TRUE);

        pObj->fLinkChange = TRUE;

        dwT = pObj->dwLink;

        if(OLE_OK != olestatus)
            pObj->dwLink = OLEUPDATE_UNAVAILABLE;
        else
            {
            if(OLEUPDATE_UNAVAILABLE == pObj->dwLink)
                pObj->dwLink = oleupdate_always;
            }

        if((DWORD)pObj->dwLink != dwT)
```

continues

461

Listing 7.17. continued

```
        {
        CreateLinkString(pObj);
        ChangeLinkString(hList, i, pDoc->pszData1);
        }

    if(IDIGNORE == HIWORD(dw))
        return TRUE;

    if(pObj->fNoMatch)
        return TRUE;

    fRet = EnumLinks(hList, FindLinks,
                    ENUMLINK_UNSELECTED,
                    MAKELONG(pObj->aLink, 0));

    if(fRet)
        return TRUE;

    GetAtomName(pObj->aLink, pDoc->pszData1, CBSCRATCH);
    pszLinkFile = GetFileFromPath(pDoc->pszData1);
    cch = lstrlen(pDoc->pszData1)+1;

    GetAtomName(pDoc->aFile, pDoc->pszData1+cch, CBSCRATCH-cch);
    pszFile = GetFileFromPath(pDoc->pszData1+cch);

    psz = pDoc->pszData2;

    cch = wsprintf(psz,
        "The selected links to %s have been\nupdated. %s contains ",
        pszLinkFile, pszFile);
    wsprintf(psz+cch,
        "additional links\nto %s.\n\nUpdate addtional links?",
        pszLinkFile);

    hWndParent = GetParent(hList);
    wTemp = MessageBox(hWndParent, psz, "Updating Links",
                    MB_YESNO | MB_ICONEXCLAMATION);

    EnumLinks(hList, UpdateLinks, ENUMLINK_SELECTED,
            MAKELONG(pObj->aLink, IDRETRY));
```

462

```
        if(IDYES == wTemp)
            {
            EnumLinks(hList, UpdateLinks, ENUMLINK_UNSELECTED,
                    MAKELONG(pObj->aLink, IDIGNORE));
            }
        return TRUE;
        }


/******************************************************************/
/* Function: CancelLinks                                          */
/* Purpose: Enumeration function to cancel links.                 */
/* Returns: TRUE/FALSE                                            */
/******************************************************************/
BOOL PASCAL CancelLinks(HWND hList, WORD i, LPOBJECT pObj, DWORD dw)
    {
    LPOLEOBJECT        pOLEObj;

    GetAtomName(pObj->aName, pDoc->pszData1, 80);
    olestatus = OleObjectConvert(pObj->pObj, "Static",
                                 (LPOLECLIENT)pObj,
                                 pDoc->lh, pDoc->pszData1,
                                 &pOLEObj);

    if(OLE_OK != olestatus)
        return TRUE;

    olestatus = OleDelete(pObj->pObj);

    if(OLE_OK == ErrHandler(olestatus, pDoc, pObj, TRUE))
        {
        pObj->pObj = pOLEObj;
        pObj->dwLink = -1;
        pObj->dwType = OT_STATIC;

        CreateLinkString(pObj);
        ChangeLinkString(hList, i, pDoc->pszData1);
        pObj->fLinkChange = TRUE;
        }

    return TRUE;
    }
```

continues

Listing 7.17. continued

```
/*********************************************************************/
/* Function: ChangeLinks                                           */
/* Purpose: Enumeration function to change links.                  */
/* Returns: TRUE/FALSE                                             */
/*********************************************************************/
BOOL PASCAL ChangeLinks(HWND hList, WORD i, LPOBJECT pObj, DWORD dw)
    {
    if(0 != HIWORD(dw))
        {
        if((ATOM)HIWORD(dw) != pObj->aLink)
            return TRUE;
        }

    GetAtomName(LOWORD(dw), pDoc->pszData1, FILENAMEMAXLEN);

    if(SetObjectData(pObj, cfObjectLink, pDoc->pszData1))
        {
        if(OLEUPDATE_UNAVAILABLE == pObj->dwLink)
            pObj->dwLink = oleupdate_always;

        CreateLinkString(pObj);
        ChangeLinkString(hList, i, pDoc->pszData1);
        pObj->fLinkChange = TRUE;
        }

    return TRUE;
    }


/*********************************************************************/
/* Function: FindLinks                                             */
/* Purpose: Enumeration function to find links.                    */
/* Returns: TRUE/FALSE                                             */
/*********************************************************************/
BOOL PASCAL FindLinks(HWND hList, WORD i, LPOBJECT pObj, DWORD dw)
    {
    if(0 == HIWORD(dw))
        if((ATOM)LOWORD(dw) != pObj->aLink)
            return TRUE;
    GetObjectData(pObj, cfObjectLink, pDoc->pszData1);
    return FALSE;
    }
```

```
/******************************************************************/
/* Function: UndoLinks                                          */
/* Purpose: Enumeration function to undo links.                 */
/* Returns: TRUE/FALSE                                          */
/******************************************************************/
BOOL PASCAL UndoLinks(HWND hList, WORD i, LPOBJECT pObj, DWORD dw)
    {
    char szObject[128];

    if(!pObj->fLinkChange)
        {
        olestatus = OleDelete(pObj->pObjUndo);
        ErrHandler(olestatus, pDoc, pObj, TRUE);
        return TRUE;
        }

    GetAtomName(pObj->aName, szObject, 128);

    olestatus = OleDelete(pObj->pObj);
    olestatus = ErrHandler(olestatus, pDoc, pObj, TRUE);

    if(OLE_OK != olestatus)
        return TRUE;

    pObj->pObj = pObj->pObjUndo;
    pObj->pObjUndo = NULL;

    OleRename(pObj->pObj, szObject);

    InitializeObject(pObj, pDoc);

    if(pObj->fUndoOpen)
        {
        olestatus = OleReconnect(pObj->pObj);
        ErrHandler(olestatus, pDoc, pObj, TRUE);
        }

    (*pObj->pvt->CallBack)((LPOLECLIENT)pObj,
                           OLE_CHANGED, pObj->pObj);

    return TRUE;
    }
```

continues

465

Listing 7.17. continued

```c
/*********************************************************************/
/* Function: CleanupClones                                          */
/* Purpose: Enumeration function to delete cloned objects.          */
/* Returns: TRUE                                                    */
/*********************************************************************/
BOOL PASCAL CleanupClones(HWND hList, WORD i, LPOBJECT pObj, DWORD dw)
    {
    olestatus = OleDelete(pObj->pObjUndo);
    olestatus = ErrHandler(olestatus, pDoc, pObj, TRUE);
    return TRUE;
    }


/*********************************************************************/
/* Function: AutoUpdateLinks                                        */
/* Purpose: Updates links.                                          */
/* Returns: TRUE/FALSE                                              */
/*********************************************************************/
BOOL PASCAL AutoUpdateLinks(LPDOC pDoc, LPOBJECT pObj)
    {
    if(NULL == pObj)
        return FALSE;

    if(oleupdate_always != pObj->dwLink)
        return FALSE;

    olestatus = OleQueryOpen(pObj->pObj);

    if(OLE_OK != olestatus)
        return FALSE;

    olestatus = OleUpdate(pObj->pObj);

    return (OLE_OK == ErrHandler(olestatus, pDoc, pObj, TRUE));
    }


/*********************************************************************/
/* Function: CreateLinkString                                       */
/* Purpose: Creates the list box selection string for a link.       */
/* Returns: Length of string                                        */
/*********************************************************************/
WORD PASCAL CreateLinkString(LPOBJECT pObj)
```

```
{
HDC hDC;
WORD cch;
LPSTR pszFile;
char szTemp[FILENAMEMAXLEN];

GetAtomName(pObj->aClass, szTemp, FILENAMEMAXLEN);
cch = GetDescFromClass(szTemp, pDoc->pszData1,
                       FILENAMEMAXLEN);

if(0 == cch)
    return 0;

hDC = GetDC(pDoc->hList);
lstrcat(pDoc->pszData1, "\t");
GetAtomName(pObj->aLink, szTemp, FILENAMEMAXLEN);
pszFile = GetFileFromPath(szTemp);
lstrcat(pDoc->pszData1, pszFile);
lstrcat(pDoc->pszData1, "\t");
GetAtomName(pObj->aSel, szTemp, FILENAMEMAXLEN);
lstrcat(pDoc->pszData1, szTemp);
lstrcat(pDoc->pszData1, "\t");

switch(pObj->dwLink)
    {
    case oleupdate_always:
        lstrcat(pDoc->pszData1,"Automatic");
        break;

    case oleupdate_oncall:
        lstrcat(pDoc->pszData1,"Manual");
        break;

    case OLEUPDATE_STATIC:
        lstrcat(pDoc->pszData1,"Static");
        break;

    case OLEUPDATE_UNAVAILABLE:
        lstrcat(pDoc->pszData1,"Unavailable");
        break;
    }
```

continues

467

Listing 7.17. continued

```
    ReleaseDC(pDoc->hList, hDC);
    return lstrlen(pDoc->pszData1);
    }


/********************************************************************/
/* Function: ChangeLinkString                                       */
/* Purpose: Changes a link's string in list box.                   */
/********************************************************************/
VOID PASCAL ChangeLinkString(HWND hList, WORD i, LPSTR psz)
    {
    DWORD dw;
    DWORD dwSel;

    dw = SendMessage(hList, LB_GETITEMDATA,  i, 0L);
    dwSel = SendMessage(hList, LB_GETSEL, i, 0L);

    SendMessage(hList, LB_DELETESTRING, i, 0L);
    SendMessage(hList, LB_INSERTSTRING, i, (LONG)psz);
    SendMessage(hList, LB_SETITEMDATA,  i, dw);

    if(0L != dwSel)
        SendMessage(hList, LB_SETSEL, TRUE, MAKELONG(i, 0));

    return;
    }
```

Registration Database Access

The registration database is a primary source of information for the Insert Object and Links dialog boxes. The following source module, register.c, contains functions to access class names and class descriptions. The LoadClassList() function creates the list box in the Insert Object dialog box. The GetClassFromDesc() gets a class name from the registration database for a given description. The GetClassFromExt() gets a class name from the registration database for a file extension. The GetDescFromClass() gets a class description for the registration database for a given class name. The last function in this module, BuildVerbList(), generates a list of verbs for an object class. This list is used in the **O**bject *classname* menu option.

All these functions call registration database functions. There are four registration database functions of interest for this source module: **RegOpenKey()**, **RegCloseKey()**, **RegQueryValue()**, and **RegEnumKey()**. The **RegOpenKey()** function opens a key in the registration database. For our purposes, the first parameter for **RegOpenKey()** is HKEY_CLASSES_ROOT. You can specify a second parameter, such as a classname, to open a subkey. The last parameter of **RegOpenKey()** points to the handle of the key that is open.

The **RegQueryValue()** function retrieves a text associated with a key. **RegQueryValue()** has the following prototype:

```
LONG RegQueryValue(HKEY hkey, LPSTR lpszSubKey, LPSTR lpszValue,
                   LONG FAR *lpcb);
```

The hkey parameter is the handle of the key to query. The lpszSubKey is the subkey for the query. If the subkey is NULL and the query is successful for hkey, the lpszSubKey will contain the value of the hkey key. The lpszValue is a buffer that contains the result of the query when the function returns. The last parameter specifies the length of the third parameter.

The **RegEnumKey()** function copies the names of subkeys into a buffer. This function has four parameters. The first parameter is the key for which subkey information is gotten. The second parameter is an index to the subkey. The number of the index starts at zero. The last two parameters are the receiving string buffer and the length of the buffer. The RegEnumKey() function must be called for an open key.

> **Note:** The HKEY_CLASSES_ROOT key is always open and available.

The **RegCloseKey()** function simply closes a key. By closing all keys in the registration database, the database is updated; however, you are not updating the registration database in the example program in Listing 7.18.

Listing 7.18. The register.c source module.

```
#include "oleclnt.h"

#define MAXKEYLEN 256

DWORD dw;
WORD i;
```

continues

Listing 7.18. continued

```c
WORD cStrings;
HKEY hKey;
LONG rc;
char szExec[MAXKEYLEN];
char szClass[MAXKEYLEN];
char szKey[MAXKEYLEN];
/*********************************************************************/
/* Function: LoadClassList                                          */
/* Purpose: Loads list box with object classes for registration     */
/*          db.                                                      */
/* Returns: Number of objects in list box                           */
/*********************************************************************/
WORD PASCAL LoadClassList(HWND hList)
    {
    SendMessage(hList, LB_RESETCONTENT, 0, 0L);

    rc = RegOpenKey(HKEY_CLASSES_ROOT, NULL, &hKey);

    if((LONG)ERROR_SUCCESS != rc)
        return -1;

    cStrings=0;
    rc = RegEnumKey(hKey, cStrings++, szClass, MAXKEYLEN);

    while((LONG)ERROR_SUCCESS == rc)
        {
        lstrcpy(szExec, szClass);
        lstrcat(szExec, "\\protocol\\StdFileEditing\\server");

        dw = MAXKEYLEN;
        rc = RegQueryValue(hKey, szExec, szKey, &dw);

        if((LONG)ERROR_SUCCESS == rc)
            {
            dw = MAXKEYLEN;
            rc = RegQueryValue(hKey, szClass, szKey, &dw);

            if((LONG)ERROR_SUCCESS == rc)
                SendMessage(hList, LB_ADDSTRING,
                            0, (DWORD)(LPSTR)szKey);
            }
```

```
        rc = RegEnumKey(hKey, cStrings++, szClass, MAXKEYLEN);
        }

    RegCloseKey(hKey);

    return cStrings;
    }

/*******************************************************************/
/* Function: GetClassFromDesc                                      */
/* Purpose: Gets the object class name given a description.        */
/* Returns: Count of bytes copied                                  */
/*******************************************************************/
WORD PASCAL GetClassFromDesc(LPSTR psz, LPSTR pszClass, WORD cb)
    {
    rc = RegOpenKey(HKEY_CLASSES_ROOT, NULL, &hKey);

    if((LONG)ERROR_SUCCESS != rc)
        return 0;

    i = 0;
    rc = RegEnumKey(hKey, i++, szClass, MAXKEYLEN);

    while((LONG)ERROR_SUCCESS == rc)
        {
        dw = (DWORD)cb;
        rc = RegQueryValue(hKey, szClass, pszClass, &dw);

        if((LONG)ERROR_SUCCESS == rc)
            {
            if(!lstrcmp(pszClass, psz))
                break;
            }

        rc = RegEnumKey(hKey, i++, szClass, MAXKEYLEN);
        }

    if((LONG)ERROR_SUCCESS == rc)
        lstrcpy(pszClass, szClass);
    else
        dw = 0L;
```

continues

471

Listing 7.18. continued

```
    RegCloseKey(hKey);
    return (WORD)dw;
    }


/*********************************************************************/
/* Function: GetClassFromExt                                       */
/* Purpose: Gets an object class name given a file extension.      */
/* Returns: Count of bytes copied.                                 */
/*********************************************************************/
WORD PASCAL GetClassFromExt(LPSTR pszExt, LPSTR psz, WORD cb)
    {
    rc = RegOpenKey(HKEY_CLASSES_ROOT, NULL, &hKey);

    if((LONG)ERROR_SUCCESS != rc)
        return FALSE;

    dw = (DWORD)cb;
    rc = RegQueryValue(hKey, pszExt, psz, &dw);

    RegCloseKey(hKey);

    if((LONG)ERROR_SUCCESS != rc)
        return FALSE;

    return (WORD)dw;
    }


/*********************************************************************/
/* Function: GetDescFromClass                                      */
/* Purpose: Gets an object description given a class name.         */
/* Returns: Count of bytes copied                                  */
/*********************************************************************/
WORD PASCAL GetDescFromClass(LPSTR pszClass, LPSTR psz, WORD cb)
    {
    rc = RegOpenKey(HKEY_CLASSES_ROOT, NULL, &hKey);

    if((LONG)ERROR_SUCCESS != rc)
        return FALSE;

    dw = (DWORD)cb;
    rc = RegQueryValue(hKey, pszClass, psz, &dw);
```

472

```
    RegCloseKey(hKey);

    psz += lstrlen(psz)+1;
    *psz = 0;

    if((LONG)ERROR_SUCCESS != rc)
        return FALSE;

    return (WORD)dw;
    }

/********************************************************************/
/* Function: BuildVerbList                                          */
/* Purpose: Builds a list of verbs for a given object class.        */
/* Returns: Number of verbs in list                                 */
/********************************************************************/
WORD PASCAL BuildVerbList(LPSTR pszClass, LPSTR pszVerbs, WORD cbMax)
    {
    HKEY hKeyVerb;
    char szVerbNum[10];
    HANDLE hMem=NULL;

    rc = RegOpenKey(HKEY_CLASSES_ROOT, pszClass, &hKey);

    if(rc != (LONG)ERROR_SUCCESS)
        return FALSE;

    rc = RegOpenKey(hKey, "protocol\\StdFileEditing\\verb",
                    &hKeyVerb);

    RegCloseKey(hKey);

    if(rc != (LONG)ERROR_SUCCESS)
        return FALSE;

    i = 0;
    dw = 0L;

    while(rc == (LONG)ERROR_SUCCESS && cbMax > 0)
        {
        pszVerbs += dw;
```

continues

473

Listing 7.18. continued

```
        cbMax  -= dw;
        dw = cbMax;

        wsprintf(szVerbNum, "%d", i++);
        rc = RegQueryValue(hKeyVerb, szVerbNum, pszVerbs, &dw);
        }

    *pszVerbs=0;

    RegCloseKey(hKeyVerb);

    return --i;
    }
```

Menu Processing

There are three menu-processing functions: `InitMenuPopup()`, `EnableClipboardMenu()`, and `AppendVerbToMenu()`. The `MainWndProc()` function calls `InitMenuPopup()` when it receives a `WM_INITPOPUP` message. The `InitMenuPopup()` function calls the `EnableClipboardMenu()` and `AppendVerbToMenu()` functions to alter the **E**dit menu. The program changes the **F**ile menu when there is an open file.

The `EnableClipboardMenu()` function calls two OLE functions to determine the status of the clipboard. It determines whether the clipboard contains a linked, embedded, or static object and sets a flag for each type. The **OleQueryCreateFromClip()** detects embedded objects. By specifying a protocol of `"StdFileEditing"` and olerender_draw, **OleQueryCreateFromClip()** will return `OLE_OK` if there is an embedded object on the clipboard. The same is true to check for a static object. For that case, the protocol should be `"Static"`.

The **OleQueryLinkFromClip()** can detect whether linked objects are on the clipboard. **OleQueryLinkFromClip()** should be called with `"StdFileEditing"` and olerender_draw. Based on the results of the calls to **OleQueryLinkFromClip()** and **OleQueryCreateFromClip()**, the clipboard menu items can be set.

The `AppendVerbToMenu()` function controls the **O**bject *classname* menu item for the currently selected object. `AppendVerbToMenu()` calls `BuildVerbList()` to generate a list of verbs from the registration database for a class name. When

AppendVerbToMenu() has the list, it adds the menu items to the Edit menu.
Listing 7.19 is the menu.c source module.

Listing 7.19. The menu.c source module.

```
#include "oleclnt.h"

VOID PASCAL EnableClipboardMenu(HMENU);
VOID PASCAL AppendVerbToMenu(HMENU, LPOBJECT);
/*******************************************************************/
/* Function: InitMenuPopup                                         */
/* Purpose: Handles WM_INITMENUPOPUP message.                      */
/*******************************************************************/
VOID PASCAL InitMenuPopup(WPARAM wParam, LPARAM lParam)
    {
    LPOBJECT pObj;
    WORD wTemp;

    if(0 == LOWORD(lParam))
        {
        wTemp = (fOpenFile) ? MF_ENABLED :
            (MF_DISABLED ¦ MF_GRAYED);
        EnableMenuItem((HMENU)wParam, IDM_SAVE,
                    wTemp ¦ MF_BYCOMMAND);
        }

    if(1 == LOWORD(lParam))
        {
        pObj = (LPOBJECT)SendMessage(hWndLastActive,
                                PM_GETOBJECT,
                                0, 0L);
        AppendVerbToMenu((HMENU)wParam, pObj);
        EnableClipboardMenu((HMENU)wParam);
        }
    }

/*******************************************************************/
/* Function: EnableClipboardMenu                                   */
/* Purpose: Enables/disables the clipboard menu.                   */
/*******************************************************************/
VOID PASCAL EnableClipboardMenu(HMENU hMenu)
```

continues

Listing 7.19. continued

```
{
LPOBJECT pObj;
BOOL fEmbed = FALSE;
BOOL fLink = FALSE;
BOOL fStatic = FALSE;
WORD wTemp;

if(OLE_OK == OleQueryCreateFromClip("StdFileEditing",
    olerender_draw, 0))
    fEmbed = TRUE;

if(OLE_OK == OleQueryLinkFromClip("StdFileEditing",
    olerender_draw, 0))
    fLink = TRUE;

if(OLE_OK == OleQueryCreateFromClip("Static",
    olerender_draw, 0))
    fStatic = TRUE;

wTemp = (fEmbed | fStatic) ? MF_ENABLED :
            (MF_DISABLED | MF_GRAYED);
EnableMenuItem(hMenu, IDM_PASTE, wTemp | MF_BYCOMMAND);

wTemp = (fLink) ? MF_ENABLED :
            (MF_DISABLED | MF_GRAYED);
EnableMenuItem(hMenu, IDM_PASTELINK, wTemp | MF_BYCOMMAND);

fLink = FALSE;
pObj = pDoc->pObjFirst;

while(NULL != pObj)
    {
    if(OT_LINK == pObj->dwType)
        {
        fLink = TRUE;
        break;
        }
    pObj = pObj->pNext;
    }

wTemp = (fLink) ? MF_ENABLED : (MF_DISABLED | MF_GRAYED);
```

```
    EnableMenuItem(hMenu, IDM_LINKS, wTemp ¦ MF_BYCOMMAND);

    wTemp = (NULL!=hWndLastActive) ? MF_ENABLED :
        (MF_DISABLED ¦ MF_GRAYED);
    EnableMenuItem(hMenu, IDM_COPY, wTemp ¦ MF_BYCOMMAND);
    EnableMenuItem(hMenu, IDM_CUT, wTemp ¦ MF_BYCOMMAND);
    EnableMenuItem(hMenu, IDM_CLEAR, wTemp ¦ MF_BYCOMMAND);
    EnableMenuItem(hMenu, IDM_CLEARALL, wTemp ¦ MF_BYCOMMAND);
    }

/********************************************************************/
/* Function: AppendVerbToMenu                                       */
/* Purpose: Creates menu items for an object's verbs.              */
/********************************************************************/
VOID PASCAL AppendVerbToMenu(HMENU hMenu, LPOBJECT pObj)
    {
    LPSTR pszClass;
    LPSTR pszVerbs;
    WORD cf;
    WORD cVerbs;
    HMENU hMenuT;
    WORD wMenuId = IDM_FIRSTVERB;

    if(hMenu == NULL)
        return;

    DeleteMenu(hMenu, 11, MF_BYPOSITION);

    if(pDoc ==NULL)
        return;

    if(pObj == NULL)
        {
        InsertMenu(hMenu, 11,
                   MF_DISABLED ¦ MF_GRAYED ¦
                   MF_STRING ¦ MF_BYPOSITION,
                   IDM_FIRSTVERB, "Object");

        return;
        }

    cf = (OT_LINK==pObj->dwType) ? cfObjectLink : cfOwnerLink;
```

continues

477

Listing 7.19. continued

```
if(!GetObjectData(pObj, cf, pDoc->pszData1))
    {
    InsertMenu(hMenu, 11,
               MF_DISABLED | MF_GRAYED |
               MF_STRING | MF_BYPOSITION,
               IDM_FIRSTVERB, "Object");
    return;
    }

pszClass = pDoc->pszData1;
pszVerbs = pDoc->pszData2;
cVerbs = BuildVerbList(pszClass, pszVerbs, CBSCRATCH);

if(0==cVerbs)
    {
    cVerbs=1;
    lstrcpy(pszVerbs, "Edit");
    }

lstrcpy(pDoc->pszData3, pszClass);
GetDescFromClass(pDoc->pszData3, pszClass, CBSCRATCH);

if(1 == cVerbs)
    {
    wsprintf(pDoc->pszData3, "%s %s &Object", pszVerbs,
             pszClass);
    InsertMenu(hMenu, 11, MF_STRING | MF_BYPOSITION,
               IDM_FIRSTVERB, pDoc->pszData3);
    }
else
    {
    hMenuT=CreatePopupMenu();

    wsprintf(pDoc->pszData3, "%s &Object", pszClass);
    InsertMenu(hMenu, 11,
               MF_STRING | MF_POPUP |
               MF_BYPOSITION,
               hMenuT, pDoc->pszData3);

    while(*pszVerbs)
        {
```

```
            InsertMenu(hMenuT, -1, MF_STRING ¦ MF_BYPOSITION,
                        wMenuId++,  pszVerbs);
            pszVerbs += lstrlen(pszVerbs)+1;
            }
        }
    return;
    }
```

Supporting Modules

The two most important supporting functions for the client application are the error handler—ErrHandler()—and the Wait() function. After many of the calls to OLE functions, the ErrHandler() is called. The client and server libraries communicate asynchronously, which often means that a client application has to wait for an object to be released when there is heavy traffic on a system.

When this occurs, the ErrHandler() receives an OLE_WAIT_FOR_RELEASE status. If the fWait global variable is set to TRUE, the Wait() function is called. The Wait() function processes messages until the objects are released. This enables the user to continue using the applications; however, the user cannot do anything OLE-oriented until the object or objects are released.

The ErrHandler() function covers two OLE functions not yet discussed. The **OleQueryReleaseMethod()** and **OleQueryReleaseError()** both have one parameter, which is a pointer to an OLEOBJECT structure. The **OleQueryReleaseMethod()** function determines whether a server method has completed. It returns an ID representing the name of the method for an object. Client applications should call the **OleQueryReleaseError()** function to detect whether an asynchronous operation for an object has completed successfully. If there is an error, **OleQueryReleaseError()** returns OLE_ERROR_OBJECT. Listing 7.20 is the misc.c source module. Listing 7.21 is the oleclnt.dlg dialog definition file, and Listing 7.22 is the oleclnt.rc resource definition file. The chapter concludes after Listings 7.23 and 7.24, oleclnt.def and the OLECLNT make file.

Listing 7.20. The misc.c source module.

```c
#include "oleclnt.h"

/********************************************************************/
/* Function: Abbrev                                                 */
/* Purpose: Truncates path from file name.                          */
/* Returns: New file name                                           */
/********************************************************************/
LPSTR PASCAL Abbrev(LPSTR lpsz)
    {
    LPSTR lpszTemp;

    lpszTemp = lpsz + lstrlen(lpsz) - 1;
    while(lpszTemp > lpsz && lpszTemp[-1] != '\\')
        lpszTemp--;
    return lpszTemp;
    }


/********************************************************************/
/* Function: MsgBox                                                 */
/* Purpose: Creates a message box.                                  */
/********************************************************************/
VOID PASCAL MsgBox(HWND hwnd, WORD wMsg, WORD wType)
    {
    char szWindowTitle[SZWINDOWTITLE];
    char szMessage[SZMESSAGE];

    LoadString(hInst, IDS_WINDOWTITLE,
                szWindowTitle, sizeof szWindowTitle);
    LoadString(hInst, wMsg,
                szMessage, sizeof szMessage);
    MessageBox(hwnd, szMessage, szWindowTitle, wType);
    }


/********************************************************************/
/* Function: ErrHandler                                             */
/* Purpose: An error handler.                                       */
/* Returns: OLESTATUS                                               */
/********************************************************************/
OLESTATUS PASCAL ErrHandler(OLESTATUS olestatus, LPDOC pDoc,
                            LPOBJECT pObj, BOOL fWait)
    {
    switch(olestatus)
```

```
        {
    case OLE_OK:
        break;

    case OLE_BUSY:
        MsgBox(pDoc->hWnd, IDS_BUSY, MB_OK);
        break;

    case OLE_WARN_DELETE_DATA:
        break;

    case OLE_WAIT_FOR_RELEASE:
        if(!fWait)
            {
            pDoc->cWait++;
            olestatus = OLE_OK;
            break;
            }
        else
            {
            pObj->fRelease = FALSE;
            Wait(FALSE, pObj);

            olestatus = OleQueryReleaseError(pObj->pObj);
            }
        if(OLE_OK == olestatus)
            break;

    default:
        OleQueryReleaseMethod(pObj->pObj);
        break;
    }
    return olestatus;
    }

/******************************************************************/
/* Function: GetFileFromPath                                      */
/* Purpose: Gets the file name at the end of a path.             */
/* Returns: File name                                             */
/******************************************************************/
LPSTR PASCAL GetFileFromPath(LPSTR pszPath)
```

continues

Listing 7.20. continued

```
    {
    LPSTR psz = NULL;

    if(NULL!=pszPath)
        {
        psz = pszPath + lstrlen(pszPath)-1;

        while((psz > pszPath) && (psz[-1] != '\\'))
            psz--;
        }

    return psz;
    }

/********************************************************************/
/* Function: GetExtFromFile                                         */
/* Purpose: Gets the extension of a file name.                      */
/* Returns: A file extension                                        */
/********************************************************************/
LPSTR PASCAL GetExtFromFile(LPSTR pszFile)
    {
    LPSTR psz;
    LPSTR pszT = NULL;

    if(NULL != pszFile)
        {
        pszT = pszFile + lstrlen(pszFile);
        psz  = pszT-1;

        while((psz > pszFile) && (psz[-1] != '\\') &&
            (psz[-1] != '.'))
            psz--;

        if('.' == psz[-1])
            return --psz;
        }

    return pszT;
    }
```

482

```
/**********************************************************************/
/* Function: ConvertRectMappings                                      */
/* Purpose: Converts rectangle of one logical mapping to another.     */
/**********************************************************************/
VOID PASCAL ConvertRectMappings(LPRECT pRect, WORD mmSrc, WORD mmDst)
    {
    HDC       hDC;
    POINT     rgpt[2];
    WORD      mmTemp;

    if(NULL == pRect)
        return;

    hDC = GetDC(NULL);

    rgpt[0].x = pRect->left;
    rgpt[0].y = pRect->top;
    rgpt[1].x = pRect->right;
    rgpt[1].y = pRect->bottom;

    mmTemp=SetMapMode(hDC, mmSrc);
    LPtoDP(hDC, rgpt, 2);

    SetMapMode(hDC, mmDst);
    DPtoLP(hDC, rgpt, 2);

    pRect->left = rgpt[0].x;
    pRect->top = rgpt[0].y;
    pRect->right = rgpt[1].x;
    pRect->bottom = rgpt[1].y;

    SetMapMode(hDC, mmTemp);
    ReleaseDC(NULL, hDC);
    return;
    }


/**********************************************************************/
/* Function: Wait                                                     */
/* Purpose: Processes messages until objects are released.            */
/* Returns: TRUE/FALSE                                                */
/**********************************************************************/
```

continues

Listing 7.20. continued

```
BOOL PASCAL Wait(BOOL fWaitForAll, LPOBJECT pObj)
    {
    BOOL rc = FALSE;
    MSG  msg;

    while(TRUE)
        {
        if(fWaitForAll)
            {
            if(!pDoc->cWait)
                break;
            }
        else
            {
            if(pObj->fRelease)
                break;
            }
        if(PeekMessage(&msg, NULL, NULL, NULL, PM_REMOVE))
            ProcessMessages(&msg);
        else
            {
            WaitMessage();
            rc = TRUE;
            }
        }
    return rc;
    }
```

Listing 7.21. The oleclnt.dlg dialog definition file.

```
DLGINCLUDE RCDATA DISCARDABLE
BEGIN
    "DIALOGS.H\0"
END

IDD_ABOUTBOX DIALOG 101, 49, 160, 81
STYLE DS_MODALFRAME ¦ WS_POPUP ¦ WS_VISIBLE ¦ WS_CAPTION
    ¦ WS_SYSMENU
CAPTION "About OleClnt"
FONT 8, "MS Sans Serif"
```

```
BEGIN
    PUSHBUTTON      "OK", IDOK, 58, 62, 40, 14
    LTEXT           "OleClnt", -1, 65, 10, 28, 8
    LTEXT           "An OLE Client Application", -1, 37, 25, 92, 8
    LTEXT           "Copyright © 1992, Jeffrey Clark",
                    -1, 30, 42, 106, 8
END

IDD_INSERTOBJECTBOX DIALOG 19, 30, 175, 90
STYLE DS_MODALFRAME ¦ WS_POPUP ¦ WS_VISIBLE ¦ WS_CAPTION ¦
    WS_SYSMENU
CAPTION "Insert Object"
FONT 8, "MS Sans Serif"
BEGIN
    LTEXT           "&Object Type:", -1, 4, 4, 52, 8
    LISTBOX         IDD_OBJECTLIST, 4, 14, 123, 76, LBS_SORT ¦
                    WS_VSCROLL ¦
                    WS_TABSTOP
    DEFPUSHBUTTON   "OK", IDOK, 133, 9, 36, 14
    PUSHBUTTON      "Cancel", IDCANCEL, 133, 26, 36, 14
END

IDD_LINKSBOX DIALOG 9, 24, 312, 91
STYLE DS_MODALFRAME ¦ WS_POPUP ¦ WS_VISIBLE ¦ WS_CAPTION ¦
    WS_SYSMENU
CAPTION "Links"
FONT 8, "MS Sans Serif"
BEGIN
    LTEXT           "&Links:", -1, 2, 3, 27, 8
    LISTBOX         IDD_LINKLIST, 2, 14, 265, 43, LBS_USETABSTOPS ¦
                    LBS_EXTENDEDSEL ¦ WS_VSCROLL ¦ WS_TABSTOP
    LTEXT           "Update:", -1, 3, 58, 28, 8
    CONTROL         "Au&tomatic", IDD_AUTOMATIC, "Button",
                    BS_AUTORADIOBUTTON ¦ WS_GROUP ¦ WS_TABSTOP, 39,
                    56, 46, 12
    CONTROL         "&Manual", IDD_MANUAL, "Button",
                    BS_AUTORADIOBUTTON ¦
                    WS_TABSTOP, 93, 56, 42, 12
    PUSHBUTTON      "&Update Now", IDD_UPDATENOW, 17, 71, 52,
                    14, WS_GROUP
    PUSHBUTTON      "&Cancel Link", IDD_CANCELLINK, 76, 71, 52, 14
    PUSHBUTTON      "C&hange Link...", IDD_CHANGELINK, 136,
                    70, 52, 14
```

continues

Listing 7.21. continued

```
    PUSHBUTTON      "OK", IDOK, 274, 6, 32, 14
    PUSHBUTTON      "Cancel", IDCANCEL, 274, 25, 32, 14
END
```

Listing 7.22. The oleclnt.rc resource definition file.

```
#include <windows.h>
#include "resource.h"
#include "dialogs.h"

IDM_MENU MENU MOVEABLE DISCARDABLE
BEGIN
    POPUP "&File"
    BEGIN
        MENUITEM "&New",                    IDM_NEW
        MENUITEM "&Open...",                IDM_OPEN
        MENUITEM "&Save",                   IDM_SAVE
        MENUITEM "Save &As...",             IDM_SAVEAS
        MENUITEM SEPARATOR
        MENUITEM "E&xit",                   IDM_EXIT
    END

    POPUP "&Edit"
    BEGIN
        MENUITEM "Cu&t\tShift+Del",         IDM_CUT
        MENUITEM "&Copy\tCtrl+Ins",         IDM_COPY
        MENUITEM "&Paste\tShift+Ins",       IDM_PASTE
        MENUITEM "Paste &Link",             IDM_PASTELINK
        MENUITEM SEPARATOR
        MENUITEM "Lin&ks...",               IDM_LINKS
        MENUITEM "&Insert Object...",       IDM_INSERTOBJECT
        MENUITEM SEPARATOR
        MENUITEM "Cle&ar\tDel",             IDM_CLEAR
        MENUITEM "Clear &All",              IDM_CLEARALL
        MENUITEM SEPARATOR
    END

    POPUP "&Help"
    BEGIN
```

```
            MENUITEM "&About...",              IDM_ABOUT
        END
END

STRINGTABLE
BEGIN
    IDS_MAINCLASSNAME,   "MainWndClass"
    IDS_OBJCLASSNAME,    "ObjectWndClass"
    IDS_WINDOWTITLE,     "Ole Client"
    IDS_QUERYSAVEFILE,   "This document has changed.\nSave
        Current Changes?"
    IDS_QUERYLINKS,      "The file contains links to\nother
        documents.\nUpdate links now?"
    IDS_UPDATINGLINKS,   "Updating Links"
    IDS_BADFILELINK,     "Some linked files are not
        available.\nAttempt to Update Links?"
    IDS_BUSY,            "Object is busy.\nCannot process last
        request."
    IDS_CANNOTINSERT     "Could not insert new object or
        start object server."
    IDS_CHANGELINK1      "The selected links to %s have
        been\nchanged. %s contains "
    IDS_CHANGELINK2      "additional links\nto %s.\n\nChange
        additional links?"
END


IDA_ACC ACCELERATORS
BEGIN
    VK_DELETE,     IDM_CUT, SHIFT, VIRTKEY
    VK_INSERT,     IDM_COPY, CONTROL, VIRTKEY
    VK_INSERT,     IDM_PASTE, SHIFT, VIRTKEY
    VK_DELETE,     IDM_CLEAR, VIRTKEY
END

#include "oleclnt.dlg"
```

Listing 7.23. The oleclnt.def module definition file.

```
NAME            OLECLNT

DESCRIPTION     'Example Ole Client Application'

EXETYPE         WINDOWS

STUB            'WINSTUB.EXE'

CODE            PRELOAD MOVEABLE DISCARDABLE
DATA            PRELOAD MOVEABLE MULTIPLE

HEAPSIZE        8192
STACKSIZE       4096

SEGMENTS
    CLIPBORD_TEXT   MOVEABLE DISCARDABLE LOADONCALL
    DIALOGS_TEXT    MOVEABLE DISCARDABLE LOADONCALL
    DOCMGT_TEXT     MOVEABLE DISCARDABLE LOADONCALL
    DRAGDROP_TEXT   MOVEABLE DISCARDABLE LOADONCALL
    FILE_TEXT       MOVEABLE DISCARDABLE LOADONCALL
    INIT_TEXT       MOVEABLE DISCARDABLE PRELOAD
    LINKS_TEXT      MOVEABLE DISCARDABLE LOADONCALL
    MEM_TEXT        MOVEABLE DISCARDABLE LOADONCALL
    MENU_TEXT       MOVEABLE DISCARDABLE LOADONCALL
    MISC_TEXT       MOVEABLE DISCARDABLE LOADONCALL
    OBJECT_TEXT     MOVEABLE             PRELOAD
    OLECLNT_TEXT    MOVEABLE             PRELOAD
    OBJMGT_TEXT     MOVEABLE DISCARDABLE LOADONCALL
    REGISTER_TEXT   MOVEABLE DISCARDABLE LOADONCALL
    VTCLIENT_TEXT   MOVEABLE DISCARDABLE LOADONCALL
    VTSTREAM_TEXT   MOVEABLE DISCARDABLE LOADONCALL
    WINMAIN_TEXT    MOVEABLE             PRELOAD

EXPORTS
    MainWndProc         @1
    ObjectWndProc       @2
    ClientCallback      @3
    StreamGet           @4
    StreamPut           @5
    AboutDlgProc        @6
```

```
    InsertObjectDlgProc    @7
    LinksDlgProc           @8
```

Listing 7.24. The OLECLNT make file.

```
CC = cl -c -AM -Gsw -Od -W3 -Zpi -Fo$@

all: oleclnt.exe

oleclnt.h: dialogs.h resource.h

oleclnt.res: oleclnt.rc oleclnt.dlg dialogs.h resource.h
  rc -r oleclnt

clipbord.obj: clipbord.c oleclnt.h
  $(CC) $*.c

dialogs.obj: dialogs.c oleclnt.h
  $(CC) $*.c

docmgt.obj: docmgt.c oleclnt.h
  $(CC) $*.c

dragdrop.obj: dragdrop.c oleclnt.h
  $(CC) $*.c

file.obj: file.c oleclnt.h
  $(CC) $*.c

init.obj: init.c oleclnt.h
  $(CC) $*.c

links.obj: links.c oleclnt.h
  $(CC) $*.c

mem.obj: mem.c oleclnt.h
  $(CC) $*.c

menu.obj: menu.c oleclnt.h
  $(CC) $*.c
```

continues

489

Listing 7.24. continued

```
misc.obj: misc.c oleclnt.h
  $(CC) $*.c

oleclnt.obj: oleclnt.c oleclnt.h
  $(CC) $*.c

object.obj: object.c oleclnt.h
  $(CC) $*.c

objmgt.obj: objmgt.c oleclnt.h
  $(CC) $*.c

register.obj: register.c oleclnt.h
  $(CC) $*.c

vtclient.obj: vtclient.c oleclnt.h
  $(CC) $*.c

vtstream.obj: vtstream.c oleclnt.h
  $(CC) $*.c

winmain.obj: winmain.c oleclnt.h
  $(CC) $*.c

oleclnt.exe:: clipbord.obj dialogs.obj docmgt.obj\
              dragdrop.obj file.obj init.obj links.obj\
              mem.obj menu.obj misc.obj object.obj\
              objmgt.obj oleclnt.obj register.obj\
              vtclient.obj vtstream.obj winmain.obj\
              oleclnt.res oleclnt.def
    link /CO /MAP /NOD @<<
clipbord+
dialogs+
docmgt+
dragdrop+
file+
init+
links+
mem+
menu+
misc+
```

```
object+
objmgt+
oleclnt+
register+
vtclient+
vtstream+
winmain
$@

libw shell olecli commdlg mlibcew
oleclnt.def
<<
    mapsym oleclnt
    rc oleclnt.res
```

Summary

It is easy to see that programming an OLE client application requires much code to implement just the base OLE functionality. The example program in this chapter can provide you with a starting place for your OLE client applications. The functions implemented in the example program, for the most part, are just the start of a real application. There are no application-specific functions in the sample program. By adding application-specific functions around the example program, you will begin to have an application that does something more than display objects.

Object
Handlers

Object handlers are dynamic-link libraries (DDLs) that supplement or replace OLE functionality that is normally provided by OLECLI and server applications. Object handlers act as intermediaries between the OLE libraries and OLE applications. For instance, when a client application calls an object-creation function, the call goes to OLECLI. If the class for the object has an associated object handler, OLECLI loads and calls the object handler to create the object.

This chapter covers the development of an object handler and contains a review of dynamic-link libraries. Specifically, it covers the following topics:

- Dynamic-link library concepts
- Import libraries
- polyhand.dll: an example object handler

Dynamic-Link Library Concepts

A *dynamic-link library* is a form of an executable Windows program. DLLs contain functions and resources that Windows programs can access. DLLs cannot be executed directly. Windows applications call the functions contained in DLLs. DLLs typically have the file extension .DLL, but they can also have other file extensions, such as .FON, .DRV, .EXE, and .SYS.

DLLs enable Windows applications to employ *dynamic linking*. Dynamic linking occurs when an application links with a DLL at run time. This is the opposite of *static linking*, which is when an application is linked to a library by the LINK utility. Static linking incorporates functions called by an application into the executable module of the application. This tends to be inefficient when two or more applications call the same statically linked function. When the applications run simultaneously, you have duplicate copies of the same function in memory at the same time. Windows applications can use DLLs to share functions. DLLs allow one copy of a function to be shared among many Windows applications.

Import Libraries

All Windows programs use dynamic-link libraries. When an application calls a Windows API function, DLLs are used. Windows has three primary DLLs: KERNEL.EXE, GDI.EXE, and USER.EXE. When the *Polygons* application calls the **Polygon()** function to draw an object in a window, the application accesses the GDI.EXE DLL.

Because Windows applications use DLLs for many purposes, it is logical to ask how the linker knows when a function is in a DLL and when a function is in a static-link library. The linker differentiates between functions contained in DLLs and those contained in static-link libraries by using an additional library, which is called an *import library*.

At link time, the linker searches static-link libraries for object modules to resolve external references. If an external reference is resolved by a static-link library, the linker binds the object module for the external reference from the static-link library. If the external reference is not resolved by a static-link library, it may be resolved by an import library. The key difference in the linking processes when you access an import library is that there is no object module in the import library to link. Import libraries contain import records rather than object modules.

An *import record* contains information about a function. It does not contain any code or data. The import record specifies the dynamic-link library and the name of the function in the DLL or the ordinal value of the function in the DLL. When the linker finds an import record for an external reference, it copies the information from the import record to create a dynamic link.

> **Note:** Libraries can contain both import records and object modules. It is a good practice, however, to separate import libraries and object libraries.

Another method of resolving external reference to functions in DLLs is by using the IMPORTS section of the module definition file. In a sense, each line in the IMPORTS section of the module definition file is equivalent to an import record in an import library. Functions can be referenced by name or ordinal value in the IMPORTS section. For example, the **Polygon()** function could be referenced by the two following IMPORTS sections:

```
IMPORTS
     Polygon = GDI.36
```

or

```
IMPORTS
     GDI.Polygon
```

Two utilities are useful in dealing with import libraries and DLLs. The first utility is EXEHDR.EXE. EXEHDR is the utility I used to find the ordinal value of the **Polygon()** function. EXEHDR lists the names, addresses, and ordinal values of functions in executable files. If you run EXEHDR on the GDI.EXE, you will see information pertaining to GDI functions. You can also see information on undocumented GDI functions. These functions have interesting names, such as DEATH and RESURRECTION.

The second utility of interest is IMPLIB.EXE. IMPLIB creates import libraries from the EXPORTS section of a module definition file. This is convenient to have when you create a DLL that exports functions for use in many other applications. Instead of having an IMPORTS section in the module definition file for each application, you can use the import library created by IMPLIB.

Components of Dynamic-Link Libraries

Dynamic-link libraries are slightly different from normal Windows executables. The first difference is the entry point of a DLL. The entry point for a DLL is LibEntry(). The SDK contains the source code for LibEntry() in the file LIBENTRY.ASM. Microsoft C compilers, in versions greater than 5.1, contain the start-up code for normal C programs. You can find information about the start-up code for C programs in the file STARTUP.DOC. Non-DLL Windows programs also have a different entry point. The SDK does not, however, provide the start-up code for normal Windows programs.

The main point to the discussion of start-up code is that the LIBENTRY.OBJ module must be linked to DLLs. The LibEntry() function generates the code segment INIT_TEXT, initializes the local heap if one exists, and then calls LibMain(). LibMain() is the WinMain() function of DLLs. Thus, all DLLs must have a LibMain() function. From a functional point of view, LibMain() is the start of a DLL.

```
int FAR PASCAL LibMain(HANDLE hInstance, WORD wDataSeg,
                    WORD wHeapSize, LPSTR lpszCmdLine)
```

The `LibMain()` function should perform DLL-specific initialization. This generally entails initializing global variables and saving the instance handle so that you can access resources later. Another general practice is to unlock the local heap if the `wHeapSize` parameter is greater than zero. The `LibEntry()` function leaves the local heap locked when the `wHeapSize` parameter is greater than zero. Unlocking the segment allows Windows to move the segment in memory.

After the `LibMain()` function successfully performs the initialization tasks, it should return `TRUE`. The `LibEntry()` function receives this value and returns it to Windows, thus indicating that start-up was successful.

In addition to different start-up code, DLLs require an exit routine. This is the `WEP()` function. The prototype for `WEP()` is

```
int FAR PASCAL WEP(int nParameter)
```

Windows can call the `WEP()` function for two events. When Windows terminates, it passes a value of `WEP_SYSTEM_EXIT` to `WEP()`. When the last Windows module no longer requires the services of a DLL, Windows passes a value to `WEP_FREE_DLL` to `WEP()`. At this time, the `WEP()` function performs any required clean-up activities for the DLL and returns `TRUE`.

The `WEP()` function must be included in the `EXPORTS` section of the module definition file. An ordinal value and the `RESIDENTNAME` keyword should be assigned to the `WEP()` `EXPORT` record. The ordinal value allows Windows to find the `WEP()` function quickly. The `RESIDENTNAME` keyword causes the information for `WEP()` to remain in memory.

Advantages of Dynamic-Link Libraries

Dynamic-link libraries have two major advantages over static-link libraries. The advantages become greater as the size and number of applications that access a DLL increase. The first advantage is more efficient use of memory. This is an advantage only when more than one application executes code in a DLL at the same time. This advantage could occur, for instance, when a developer has a suite of Windows applications that can be used on the same computer at the same time.

The second advantage is seen in program maintenance and updates. You can use DLLs to modularize an application. Instead of having one large executable file, an application can consist of a smaller executable file and several

DLLs. If a function in a DLL breaks, the developer can easily update the function and distribute only the DLL. This is even more advantageous when several applications use the same DLL. A bug in a function that is common to several applications would require rebuilding several applications instead of fixing it once in a DLL and distributing the DLL.

POLYHAND.DLL: Object Handler Dynamic-Link Library

Creating an object handler is a fairly straightforward process when you have an understanding of DLLs. The example program, POLYHAND.DLL, provides a generic shell for an object handler. POLYHAND.DLL is purely an example program because it really doesn't provide any tangible benefits other than serving as a shell for other object handlers.

Object Handler Registration

An OLE server application that provides an object handler must register the object handler with the system registration database. This involves inserting a record into the registration database with the keyword handler. The server application can call registration API functions to insert the record, or you can manually insert the record with the REGEDIT.EXE applet. To use REGEDIT, just merge the file in Listing 8.1 with the registration database.

Listing 8.1. The polyhand.reg registration database merge file.

```
REGEDIT

HKEY_CLASSES_ROOT\Polygons\protocol\StdFileEditing\handler =
    c:\polyhand\polyhand.dll
```

The client library, OLECLI.DLL, searches the registration database for object handlers when OLE client applications call object-creation functions. If the client library finds an object handler for an object class, it loads and calls the

object handler. The object handler can either create the object or call the client library default object-creation functions.

Object Handler Import and Export Functions

Object handlers can import functions from the client library. The client library exports the object-creation function API with alias names that use the prefix Def. Thus, for example, **OleCreate()** becomes DefCreate(). Object handlers are required to import the functions listed in Table 8.1.

Table 8.1. Required imports for object handlers.

IMPORT Function Name

DefCreate()

DefCreateFromClip()

DefCreateFromFile()

DefCreateFromTemplate()

DefCreateLinkFromClip()

DefLoadFromStream()

These functions must appear in the IMPORTS section of the module definition file. Here's a sample IMPORTS record:

```
IMPORTS
     DefCreate=olecli.DefCreate
```

This allows the object handler to call the default client library functions. On the other hand, the EXPORTS section contains the functions that client applications call. In this case, the function name contains the same root name, with the Dll prefix. Thus, when an OLE client application calls OleCreate(), the client library calls the object handler function, DllCreate(). If the object handler requires the assistance of the client library, it can call the default client library function, DefCreate(). Table 8.2 lists the exports required by the client library.

Table 8.2. Required exports for object handlers.

EXPORT Function Name

```
DllCreate()
DllCreateFromClip()
DllCreateFromFile()
DllCreateFromTemplate()
DllCreateLinkFromClip()
DllCreateLinkFromFile()
DllLoadFromStream()
```

Object Handler Function Management

The object handler object-creation functions (see Table 8.2) receive handles to OLEOBJECT structures. The OLEOBJECT structure points to an OLEOBJECTVTBL structure that contains pointers to object-management functions. The object handler can replace the object-management functions with its own customized version of the functions. To do this, the object handler simply replaces the function pointers in the OLEOBJECTVTBL structure with pointers to its own functions. At the same time, the object handler can save the pointers to client library object-management functions so that the object handler can call these functions directly.

You see the effect of this when an OLE client application calls a client library function. The client library uses the OLEOBJECTVTBL structure to call the function. If the object handler replaces a client library function with one of its own, the client library calls the object handler. Otherwise, the reference to the client library function should still exist. The typedef for the OLEOBJECTVTBL structure shows the functions available to object handlers to redefine. **Bold-faced** members indicate those used by POLYHAND.DLL.

```
typedef struct _OLEOBJECTVTBL{
 LPVOID (FAR PASCAL *QueryProtocol)(LPOLEOBJECT, LPSTR);
 OLESTATUS (FAR PASCAL *Release)(LPOLEOBJECT);
 OLESTATUS (FAR PASCAL *Show)(LPOLEOBJECT, BOOL);
```

```
OLESTATUS (FAR PASCAL *DoVerb)(LPOLEOBJECT, WORD, BOOL, BOOL);
OLESTATUS (FAR PASCAL *GetData)(LPOLEOBJECT, OLECLIPFORMAT,
                                LPHANDLE);
OLESTATUS (FAR PASCAL *SetData)(LPOLEOBJECT, OLECLIPFORMAT,
                                HANDLE);
OLESTATUS (FAR PASCAL *SetTargetDevice)(LPOLEOBJECT, HANDLE);
OLESTATUS (FAR PASCAL *SetBounds)(LPOLEOBJECT, LPRECT);
OLECLIPFORMAT(FAR PASCAL *EnumFormats)(LPOLEOBJECT,
                                       OLECLIPFORMAT);
OLESTATUS(FAR PASCAL *SetColorScheme)(LPOLEOBJECT, LPLOGPALETTE);


// Server has to implement only the above methods.

#ifndef SERVERONLY
    // Extra methods required for client.
OLESTATUS (FAR PASCAL *Delete)(LPOLEOBJECT);
OLESTATUS (FAR PASCAL *SetHostNames)(LPOLEOBJECT, LPSTR, LPSTR);
OLESTATUS (FAR PASCAL *SaveToStream)(LPOLEOBJECT, LPOLESTREAM);
OLESTATUS (FAR PASCAL *Clone)(LPOLEOBJECT, LPOLECLIENT,
     LHCLIENTDOC, LPSTR, LPOLEOBJECT FAR *);
OLESTATUS (FAR PASCAL *CopyFromLink)(LPOLEOBJECT, LPOLECLIENT,
     LHCLIENTDOC, LPSTR, LPOLEOBJECT FAR *);
OLESTATUS (FAR PASCAL *Equal)(LPOLEOBJECT, LPOLEOBJECT);
OLESTATUS (FAR PASCAL *CopyToClipboard)(LPOLEOBJECT);
OLESTATUS (FAR PASCAL *Draw)(LPOLEOBJECT, HDC, LPRECT, LPRECT,
                             HDC);
OLESTATUS (FAR PASCAL *Activate)(LPOLEOBJECT, WORD, BOOL, BOOL,
                                 HWND, LPRECT);
OLESTATUS (FAR PASCAL *Execute)(LPOLEOBJECT, HANDLE, WORD);
OLESTATUS (FAR PASCAL *Close)(LPOLEOBJECT);
OLESTATUS (FAR PASCAL *Update)(LPOLEOBJECT);
OLESTATUS (FAR PASCAL *Reconnect)(LPOLEOBJECT);
OLESTATUS (FAR PASCAL *ObjectConvert)(LPOLEOBJECT, LPSTR,
     LPOLECLIENT, LHCLIENTDOC, LPSTR, LPOLEOBJECT FAR *);
OLESTATUS (FAR PASCAL *GetLinkUpdateOptions)(LPOLEOBJECT,
                                       OLEOPT_UPDATE FAR *);
OLESTATUS (FAR PASCAL *SetLinkUpdateOptions)(LPOLEOBJECT,
                                       OLEOPT_UPDATE);
OLESTATUS (FAR PASCAL *Rename)(LPOLEOBJECT, LPSTR);
OLESTATUS (FAR PASCAL *QueryName)(LPOLEOBJECT, LPSTR,
                                  WORD FAR *);
OLESTATUS (FAR PASCAL *QueryType)(LPOLEOBJECT, LPLONG);
```

```
OLESTATUS (FAR PASCAL *QueryBounds)(LPOLEOBJECT, LPRECT);
OLESTATUS (FAR PASCAL *QuerySize)(LPOLEOBJECT, DWORD FAR *);
OLESTATUS (FAR PASCAL *QueryOpen)(LPOLEOBJECT);
OLESTATUS (FAR PASCAL *QueryOutOfDate)(LPOLEOBJECT);
OLESTATUS (FAR PASCAL *QueryReleaseStatus)(LPOLEOBJECT);
OLESTATUS (FAR PASCAL *QueryReleaseError)(LPOLEOBJECT);
OLE_RELEASE_METHOD (FAR PASCAL *QueryReleaseMethod)(LPOLEOBJECT);
OLESTATUS (FAR PASCAL *RequestData)(LPOLEOBJECT, OLECLIPFORMAT);
OLESTATUS (FAR PASCAL *ObjectLong)(LPOLEOBJECT, WORD, LPLONG);

// The following method is reserved for internal use only,
// do not use it
OLESTATUS (FAR PASCAL *ChangeData)(LPOLEOBJECT, HANDLE,
                                   LPOLECLIENT, BOOL);
#endif
} OLEOBJECTVTBL;
```

> **Note:** I should make a distinction between object-creation functions
> and object-management functions. Table 8.2 contains a list of object-
> creation functions. Each of these functions receives a pointer to an
> OLEOBJECT structure. The OLEOBJECT structure contains a pointer to
> an OLEOBJECTVTBL structure. The OLEOBJECTVTBL structure points to
> object-management functions.

Differences in Object-Creation Functions from the OLE API

The object handler's customized versions of the object-creation functions are
similar to the OLE API functions. In fact, only two functions are different:
DllCreateFromClip() and DllLoadFromStream(). DllCreateFromClip() and
DllLoadFromStream() contain additional parameters that the normal API
does not provide. The remaining object-creation functions have parameters
that match the OLE API.

The DllCreateFromClip() function has one additional parameter, objtype.
This parameter receives the value of OT_LINK or OT_EMBEDDED. If
DllCreateFromClip() calls DefCreateFromClip(), the objtype parameter
should be passed. The following prototypes show the difference between
DllCreateFromClip() and **OleCreateFromClip()**:

```
OLESTATUS FAR PASCAL DllCreateFromClip(LPSTR lpszProtocol,
     LPOLECLIENT lpclient, LHCLIENTDOC lhclientdoc,
     LPSTR lpszObjName, LPOLEOBJECT FAR * lplpObject,
     OLEOPT_RENDER renderopt, OLECLIPFORMAT cfFormat,
     LONG objtype);

OLESTATUS FAR PASCAL OleCreateFromClip(LPSTR lpszProtocol,
     LPOLECLIENT lpclient, LHCLIENTDOC lhclientdoc,
     LPSTR lpszObjName, LPOLEOBJECT FAR * lplpObject,
     OLEOPT_RENDER renderopt, OLECLIPFORMAT cfFormat);
```

The DllLoadFromStream() function has three additional parameters: objtype,
aClass, and cfFormat. The objtype parameter receives a value of OT_LINK or
OT_EMBEDDED. The aClass parameter is an atom that contains the class name
for the object. The cfFormat parameter specifies a clipboard format that the
object handler can use to render the object. If DllLoadFromStream() calls
DefLoadFromStream(), the three additional parameters should be passed to
DefLoadFromStream(). The following prototype shows the differences between DllLoadFromStream() and OleLoadFromStream():

```
OLESTATUS FAR PASCAL DllLoadFromStream(LPOLESTREAM lpstream,
     LPSTR lpszProtocol, LPOLECLIENT lpclient,
     LHCLIENTDOC lhclientdoc, LPSTR lpszObjname,
     LPOLEOBJECT FAR *lplpobject, LONG objtype, ATOM aClass,
     OLECLIPFORMAT cfFormat);

OLESTATUS FAR PASCAL OleLoadFromStream(LPOLESTREAM lpstream,
     LPSTR lpszProtocol, LPOLECLIENT lpclient,
     LHCLIENTDOC lhclientdoc, LPSTR lpszObjname,
     LPOLEOBJECT FAR *lplpobject);
```

Example Program

The example program for this chapter, POLYHAND.DLL, contains basic
object handler functionality. It has the normal dynamic-link library entry
point and exit functions, LibMain() and WEP(). The LibMain() function
initializes three global variables that contain clipboard formats. The WEP()
function just returns TRUE because POLYHAND.DLL does not have any
cleanup to perform.

POLYHAND.DLL contains the seven required object-creation functions with
the Dll prefix, which are listed in Table 8.2. The DllCreate() function checks

the `optRender` parameter to determine whether it contains the value `olerender_draw`. If so, the `DllCreate()` function calls `DefCreate()` with `olerender_none` for the `optRender` parameter. Otherwise, `DllCreate()` calls `DefCreate()` with the original value of `optRender`. This instructs the client library that the object handler will perform the drawing for native data.

After `DefCreate()` returns with a valid status, `DllCreate()` calls `CopyDefDll()`. The `CopyDefDll()` function fixes the object-management function pointers in the `OLEOBJECTVTBL` structure to point to POLYHAND's object-management functions. The `DllCreateFromFile()`, `DllCreateFromTemplate()`, and `DllCreateLinkFromFile()` functions follow the same format as `DllCreate()`.

The `DllCreateFromClip()` and `DllCreateFromLink()` functions are variations of `DllCreate()`. Because these functions pertain to the clipboard rather than the file, the clipboard is checked for the native data format. `DllCreateFromClip()` must check the object type before calling `DefCreateFromClip()` to ensure that the correct parameters are passed. If the object type is `OT_EMBEDDED`, if the native format is available in the clipboard, and if the `optRender` parameter is `olerender_draw`, `DllCreateFromClip()` calls `DefCreateFromClip()` with an `optRender` parameter of `olerender_none`. If the object type is `OT_LINK`, `DllCreateFromClip()` calls `DefCreateFromClip()` with an `optRender` parameter of `olerender_format` and a clipboard format of `cfNative`. `DllCreateFromLink()` assumes an object type of `OT_LINK`.

The `DllLoadFromStream()` function is similar also because it instructs the client library that the object handler will perform the drawing for native data. If the object type is `OT_LINK`, `DllLoadFromStream()` calls `DefLoadFromStream()` with a clipboard format of `cfNative`. Otherwise, `DllLoadFromStream()` calls `DefLoadFromStream()` and passes the original value of `cfFormat`.

The object-management functions are easy to implement. The `DllCopyToClipboard()` function calls `DefCopyToClipboard()`. If the call is successful, `DllCopyToClipboard()` retrieves the bitmap format of the object and sets the clipboard data.

The `DllDraw()` function retrieves the data for a polygon by calling `DefGetData()`. If the call to `DefGetData()` is not successful, `DllDraw()` instructs the client library to render the polygon by calling `DefDraw()`. Otherwise, `DllDraw()` locks down the data and calls `DrawPolygon()`, which is similar to the `DrawPolygon()` function in the objmgt.c source file for POLY.EXE. The `DrawPolygon()` function in POLYHAND changes the name of a polygon object to include `"Handler -"`. This indicates that the object handler rendered a polygon. The other object-management functions work essentially the same way. When an object-management function requires the aid of the client library, it calls the function with the `Def` prefix.

```
#include "windows.h"
#include "ole.h"
#include "resource.h"

#define MAXCLIENTS      30
#define MAXCOLORS       9
#define RED             0x000000ffl
#define GREEN           0x0000ff00l
#define BLUE            0x00ff0000l
#define WHITE           0x00ffffffl
#define GRAY            0x00808080l
#define CYAN            0x00ffff00l
#define MAGENTA         0x00ff00ffl
#define YELLOW          0x0000ffffl

typedef struct
    {
    int idmPoly;
    int idmColor;
    int nWidth;
    int nHeight;
    int nX;
    int nY;
    int nHiMetricWidth;
    int nHiMetricHeight;
    int version;
    char szName[32];
    } NATIVE, FAR *LPNATIVE;

/* Global Variables */
OLECLIPFORMAT cfObjectLink;
OLECLIPFORMAT cfOwnerLink;
OLECLIPFORMAT cfNative;
OLEOBJECTVTBL vtDLL;
HPEN hpen;
HBRUSH hbrush;
long rglColor[MAXCOLORS] =
    {RED, GREEN, BLUE, WHITE, GRAY, CYAN, MAGENTA, YELLOW};
```

<header>504</header>

```
/* Function Prototypes */
int CALLBACK LibMain(HINSTANCE, WORD, WORD, LPSTR);

extern OLESTATUS CALLBACK DefCreate(LPSTR, LPOLECLIENT, LPSTR,
    LHCLIENTDOC, LPSTR, LPOLEOBJECT FAR *, OLEOPT_RENDER,
    OLECLIPFORMAT);
extern OLESTATUS CALLBACK DefCreateFromClip(LPSTR, LPOLECLIENT,
    LHCLIENTDOC, LPSTR, LPOLEOBJECT FAR *, OLEOPT_RENDER,
    OLECLIPFORMAT, LONG);
extern OLESTATUS CALLBACK DefCreateFromFile(LPSTR, LPOLECLIENT,
    LPSTR, LPSTR, LHCLIENTDOC, LPSTR, LPOLEOBJECT FAR *,
    OLEOPT_RENDER, OLECLIPFORMAT);
extern OLESTATUS CALLBACK DefCreateFromTemplate(LPSTR, LPOLECLIENT,
    LPSTR, LHCLIENTDOC, LPSTR, LPOLEOBJECT FAR *, OLEOPT_RENDER,
    OLECLIPFORMAT);
extern OLESTATUS CALLBACK DefCreateLinkFromClip(LPSTR, LPOLECLIENT,
    LHCLIENTDOC, LPSTR, LPOLEOBJECT FAR *, OLEOPT_RENDER,
    OLECLIPFORMAT);
extern OLESTATUS CALLBACK DefCreateLinkFromFile(LPSTR, LPOLECLIENT,
    LPSTR, LPSTR, LPSTR, LHCLIENTDOC, LPSTR, LPOLEOBJECT FAR *,
    OLEOPT_RENDER, OLECLIPFORMAT);
extern OLESTATUS CALLBACK DefLoadFromStream(LPOLESTREAM, LPSTR,
    LPOLECLIENT, LHCLIENTDOC, LPSTR, LPOLEOBJECT FAR *, LONG,
    ATOM, OLECLIPFORMAT);

VOID PASCAL CopyDefDll(LPOLEOBJECT);

OLESTATUS CALLBACK _loadds DllCopyToClipboard (LPOLEOBJECT);
OLESTATUS CALLBACK _loadds DllDraw (LPOLEOBJECT, HDC, LPRECT,
                                    LPRECT, HDC);
OLESTATUS CALLBACK _loadds DllGetData (LPOLEOBJECT, OLECLIPFORMAT,
                                    HANDLE FAR *);
OLECLIPFORMAT CALLBACK _loadds DllEnumFormats (LPOLEOBJECT,
                                    OLECLIPFORMAT);
OLESTATUS CALLBACK _loadds DllQueryBounds (LPOLEOBJECT, LPRECT);

OLESTATUS (CALLBACK *DefCopyToClipboard)(LPOLEOBJECT);
OLESTATUS (CALLBACK *DefDraw)(LPOLEOBJECT, HDC, LPRECT, LPRECT,
                            HDC);
OLESTATUS (CALLBACK *DefGetData)(LPOLEOBJECT, OLECLIPFORMAT,
                            HANDLE FAR *);
```

continues

505

Listing 8.2. continued

```
OLECLIPFORMAT (CALLBACK *DefEnumFormats)(LPOLEOBJECT,
                 OLECLIPFORMAT);
OLESTATUS (CALLBACK *DefQueryBounds)(LPOLEOBJECT, LPRECT);

HBITMAP PASCAL GetBitmap(LPOLEOBJECT);
VOID PASCAL DrawPolygon(HDC, LPRECT, LPSTR);
HBRUSH PASCAL GetBrush(int);
```

Listing 8.3. The resource.h header file.

```
#define IDM_TRIANGLE      300
#define IDM_RECTANGLE     301
#define IDM_PENTAGON      302
#define IDM_HEXAGON       303
#define IDM_HEPTAGON      304
#define IDM_OCTAGON       305
#define IDM_STAR          306
#define IDM_RED           400
#define IDM_GREEN         401
#define IDM_BLUE          402
#define IDM_WHITE         403
#define IDM_GRAY          404
#define IDM_CYAN          405
#define IDM_MAGENTA       406
#define IDM_YELLOW        407
```

Listing 8.4. The polyhand.c source file.

```
#include "polyhand.h"

/*******************************************************************/
/* Function: LibMain                                               */
/* Purpose: Required by LibEntry()--registers clipboard formats.   */
/* Returns: TRUE                                                   */
/*******************************************************************/
int CALLBACK LibMain(HINSTANCE hInstance, WORD wDataSeg,
                 WORD wHeapSize, LPSTR lpszCmdLine)
```

```
    {
    cfObjectLink = RegisterClipboardFormat("ObjectLink");
    cfOwnerLink = RegisterClipboardFormat("OwnerLink");
    cfNative = RegisterClipboardFormat("Native");

    if(wHeapSize != 0)
        UnlockData(0);

    return TRUE;
    }

/*********************************************************************/
/* Function: WEP                                                     */
/* Purpose: Standard DLL exit.                                       */
/* Returns: TRUE                                                     */
/*********************************************************************/
int FAR PASCAL WEP(int Parm)
    {
    return TRUE;
    }


/*********************************************************************/
/* Function: DllCreate                                               */
/* Purpose: Replaces OleCreate.                                      */
/* Returns: OLESTATUS                                                */
/*********************************************************************/
OLESTATUS CALLBACK DllCreate(LPSTR lpprotocol,
    LPOLECLIENT lpclient,
    LPSTR lpclass, LHCLIENTDOC lhclientdoc, LPSTR lpobjname,
    LPOLEOBJECT FAR *lplpobj, OLEOPT_RENDER optRender,
    OLECLIPFORMAT cfFormat)
    {
    OLESTATUS   olestatus;

    if(optRender == olerender_draw)
        olestatus = DefCreate(lpprotocol, lpclient, lpclass,
                              lhclientdoc, lpobjname, lplpobj,
                              olerender_none, NULL);
    else
        olestatus = DefCreate(lpprotocol, lpclient, lpclass,
                              lhclientdoc, lpobjname, lplpobj,
                              optRender, cfFormat);
```

continues

507

Listing 8.4. continued

```
    if(olestatus <= OLE_WAIT_FOR_RELEASE)
        CopyDefDll(*lplpobj);

    return olestatus;
    }


/*********************************************************************/
/* Function: DllCreateFromClip                                     */
/* Purpose: Replaces OleCreateFromClip.                            */
/* Returns: OLESTATUS                                              */
/*********************************************************************/
OLESTATUS CALLBACK DllCreateFromClip(LPSTR lpprotocol,
    LPOLECLIENT lpclient, LHCLIENTDOC lhclientdoc, LPSTR lpobjname,
    LPOLEOBJECT FAR *lplpobj, OLEOPT_RENDER optRender,
    OLECLIPFORMAT cfFormat, LONG objType)
    {
    OLESTATUS olestatus;

    if((optRender == olerender_draw) &&
       (IsClipboardFormatAvailable(cfNative)))
         {
         if(objType == OT_EMBEDDED)
             olestatus = DefCreateFromClip(lpprotocol, lpclient,
                                   lhclientdoc, lpobjname, lplpobj,
                                   olerender_none, NULL, objType);

         else
             olestatus = DefCreateFromClip(lpprotocol, lpclient,
                                   lhclientdoc, lpobjname, lplpobj,
                                   olerender_format, cfNative,
                                   objType);

         }
    else
         olestatus = DefCreateFromClip(lpprotocol, lpclient,
                                   lhclientdoc, lpobjname, lplpobj,
                                   optRender, cfFormat, objType);

    if(olestatus <= OLE_WAIT_FOR_RELEASE)
        CopyDefDll(*lplpobj);

    return olestatus;
    }
```

```
/********************************************************************/
/* Function: DllCreateFromFile                                     */
/* Purpose: Replaces OleCreateFromFile.                            */
/* Returns: OLESTATUS                                              */
/********************************************************************/
OLESTATUS CALLBACK DllCreateFromFile(LPSTR lpprotocol,
    LPOLECLIENT lpclient, LPSTR lpclass, LPSTR lpfile,
    LHCLIENTDOC lhclientdoc, LPSTR lpobjname,
    LPOLEOBJECT FAR *lplpobj,
    OLEOPT_RENDER optRender, OLECLIPFORMAT cfFormat)
    {
    OLESTATUS olestatus;

    if(optRender == olerender_draw)
        olestatus = DefCreateFromFile(lpprotocol, lpclient,
                                      lpclass, lpfile, lhclientdoc,
                                      lpobjname, lplpobj,
                                      olerender_none, NULL);
    else
        olestatus = DefCreateFromFile(lpprotocol, lpclient,
                                      lpclass, lpfile, lhclientdoc,
                                      lpobjname, lplpobj,
                                      optRender, cfFormat);

    if(olestatus <= OLE_WAIT_FOR_RELEASE)
        CopyDefDll(*lplpobj);

    return olestatus;
    }


/********************************************************************/
/* Function: DllCreateFromTemplate                                 */
/* Purpose: Replaces OleCreateFromTemplate.                        */
/* Returns: OLESTATUS                                              */
/********************************************************************/
OLESTATUS CALLBACK DllCreateFromTemplate(LPSTR lpprotocol,
    LPOLECLIENT lpclient, LPSTR lptemplate,
        LHCLIENTDOC lhclientdoc,
    LPSTR lpobjname, LPOLEOBJECT FAR *lplpobj,
        OLEOPT_RENDER optRender,
```

continues

CHAPTER
8

Listing 8.4. continued

```
    OLECLIPFORMAT cfFormat)
    {
    OLESTATUS olestatus;

    if(optRender == olerender_draw)
        olestatus = DefCreateFromTemplate(lpprotocol, lpclient,
                                lptemplate, lhclientdoc, lpobjname,
                                lplpobj, olerender_none, NULL);
    else
        olestatus = DefCreateFromTemplate(lpprotocol, lpclient,
                                lptemplate, lhclientdoc, lpobjname,
                                lplpobj, optRender, cfFormat);

    if(olestatus <= OLE_WAIT_FOR_RELEASE)
        CopyDefDll(*lplpobj);

    return olestatus;
    }

/**********************************************************************/
/* Function: DllCreateLinkFromClip                                  */
/* Purpose: Replaces OleCreateLinkFromClip.                         */
/* Returns: OLESTATUS                                               */
/**********************************************************************/
OLESTATUS CALLBACK DllCreateLinkFromClip(LPSTR lpprotocol,
    LPOLECLIENT lpclient, LHCLIENTDOC lhclientdoc, LPSTR lpobjname,
    LPOLEOBJECT FAR *lplpobj, OLEOPT_RENDER optRender,
    OLECLIPFORMAT cfFormat)
    {
    OLESTATUS olestatus;

    if((optRender == olerender_draw) &&
       (IsClipboardFormatAvailable(cfNative)))
        olestatus =  DefCreateLinkFromClip(lpprotocol, lpclient,
                            lhclientdoc, lpobjname, lplpobj,
                            olerender_format, cfNative);
    else
        olestatus =  DefCreateLinkFromClip(lpprotocol, lpclient,
                            lhclientdoc, lpobjname, lplpobj,
                            optRender, cfFormat);
```

```
    if(olestatus <= OLE_WAIT_FOR_RELEASE)
        CopyDefDll(*lplpobj);

    return olestatus;
    }

/********************************************************************/
/* Function: DllCreateLinkFromFile                            */
/* Purpose: Replaces OleCreateLinkFromFile.                   */
/* Returns: OLESTATUS                                         */
/********************************************************************/
OLESTATUS CALLBACK DllCreateLinkFromFile(LPSTR lpprotocol,
    LPOLECLIENT lpclient, LPSTR lpclass, LPSTR lpfile,
        LPSTR lpitem,
    LHCLIENTDOC lhclientdoc, LPSTR lpobjname,
        LPOLEOBJECT FAR *lplpobj,
    OLEOPT_RENDER optRender, OLECLIPFORMAT cfFormat)
    {
    OLESTATUS olestatus;

    if(optRender == olerender_draw)
        olestatus = DefCreateLinkFromFile(lpprotocol, lpclient,
                            lpclass, lpfile, lpitem,
                            lhclientdoc, lpobjname, lplpobj,
                            olerender_format, cfNative);
    else
        olestatus = DefCreateLinkFromFile(lpprotocol, lpclient,
                            lpclass, lpfile, lpitem,
                            lhclientdoc, lpobjname, lplpobj,
                            optRender, cfFormat);

    if(olestatus <= OLE_WAIT_FOR_RELEASE)
        CopyDefDll(*lplpobj);

    return olestatus;
    }

/********************************************************************/
/* Function: DllLoadFromStream                                */
/* Purpose: Replaces OleLoadFromStream.                       */
/* Returns: olestatus                                         */
/********************************************************************/
```

continues

511

Listing 8.4. continued

```
OLESTATUS CALLBACK DllLoadFromStream(LPOLESTREAM lpstream,
    LPSTR lpprotocol, LPOLECLIENT lpclient, LHCLIENTDOC lhclientdoc,
    LPSTR lpobjname, LPOLEOBJECT FAR *lplpobj, LONG objType,
        ATOM aClass,
    OLECLIPFORMAT cfFormat)
    {
    OLESTATUS olestatus;

    if(objType == OT_LINK)
        olestatus = DefLoadFromStream(lpstream, lpprotocol,
                        lpclient,
                        lhclientdoc, lpobjname, lplpobj,
                        objType, aClass, cfNative);
    else
        olestatus = DefLoadFromStream(lpstream, lpprotocol,
                        lpclient,
                        lhclientdoc, lpobjname, lplpobj,
                        objType, aClass, cfFormat);

    if(olestatus <= OLE_WAIT_FOR_RELEASE)
        CopyDefDll(*lplpobj);

    return olestatus;
    }

/**********************************************************************/
/* Function: CopyDefDll                                             */
/* Purpose: Copies OLEOBJECTVTBL funcs to Def funcs and Dll Funcs */
/*          to OLEOBJECTVTBL funcs.                                 */
/**********************************************************************/
VOID PASCAL CopyDefDll(LPOLEOBJECT lpobj)
    {
    OLECLIPFORMAT cfFormat;
    BOOL fNative = FALSE;
    LONG lObjType;

    if((*lpobj->lpvtbl->QueryType)(lpobj, &lObjType) != OLE_OK)
        return;
```

```
        while(cfFormat = (*lpobj->lpvtbl->EnumFormats)(lpobj,
            cfFormat))
            {
            if(cfFormat == cfNative)
                {
                fNative = TRUE;
                break;
                }
            }
        if(!fNative && lObjType != OT_EMBEDDED)
            return;

        vtDLL = *lpobj->lpvtbl;
        lpobj->lpvtbl = (LPOLEOBJECTVTBL)&vtDLL;

        DefCopyToClipboard = lpobj->lpvtbl->CopyToClipboard;
        DefDraw = lpobj->lpvtbl->Draw;
        DefEnumFormats = lpobj->lpvtbl->EnumFormats;
        DefGetData = lpobj->lpvtbl->GetData;
        DefQueryBounds = lpobj->lpvtbl->QueryBounds;

        *lpobj->lpvtbl->CopyToClipboard = DllCopyToClipboard;
        *lpobj->lpvtbl->Draw = DllDraw;
        *lpobj->lpvtbl->EnumFormats = DllEnumFormats;
        *lpobj->lpvtbl->GetData = DllGetData;
        *lpobj->lpvtbl->QueryBounds = DllQueryBounds;
        }

/*********************************************************************/
/* Function: DllCopyToClipboard                                      */
/* Purpose: Copies to clipboard.                                     */
/* Returns: OLESTATUS                                                */
/*********************************************************************/
OLESTATUS CALLBACK _loadds DllCopyToClipboard(LPOLEOBJECT lpobj)
    {
    OLESTATUS olestatus;
    HBITMAP hBitmap;

    if((olestatus = (*DefCopyToClipboard)(lpobj)) == OLE_OK)
        if(hBitmap = GetBitmap(lpobj))
            SetClipboardData(CF_BITMAP, hBitmap);
```

continues

513

Listing 8.4. continued

```
    return olestatus;
    }


/*********************************************************************/
/* Function: DllDraw                                                 */
/* Purpose: Draws object.                                            */
/* Returns: OLE_OK if successful, OLE_ERROR_ if major problem        */
/*********************************************************************/
OLESTATUS CALLBACK _loadds DllDraw(LPOLEOBJECT lpobj, HDC hdc,
    LPRECT lprc, LPRECT lpWrc, HDC hdcTarget)
    {
    LPSTR       lpData = NULL;
    HANDLE      hData = NULL;

    if((*DefGetData)(lpobj, cfNative, &hData) != OLE_OK)
        return (*DefDraw)(lpobj, hdc, lprc, lpWrc, hdcTarget);

    if(!hData)
        return OLE_ERROR_BLANK;

    if(!(lpData = GlobalLock(hData)))
        return OLE_ERROR_MEMORY;

    SaveDC(hdc);
    IntersectClipRect(hdc, lprc->left, lprc->top, lprc->right,
                    lprc->bottom);
    DrawPolygon(hdc, lprc, lpData);
    RestoreDC(hdc, -1);
    GlobalUnlock(hData);
    return OLE_OK;
    }


/*********************************************************************/
/* Function: DllEnumFormats                                          */
/* Purpose: Enumerates clipboard formats.                            */
/* Returns: Clipboard format                                         */
/*********************************************************************/
OLECLIPFORMAT CALLBACK _loadds DllEnumFormats(LPOLEOBJECT lpobj,
    OLECLIPFORMAT cfFormat)
    {
    OLECLIPFORMAT rcfmt = NULL;
```

```
    if(cfFormat == CF_BITMAP)
        return rcfmt;

    if(!(rcfmt = (*DefEnumFormats)(lpobj, cfFormat)))
        return CF_BITMAP;

    return rcfmt;
    }

/******************************************************************/
/* Function: DllGetData                                           */
/* Purpose: Gets polygon data.                                    */
/* Returns: OLESTATUS                                             */
/******************************************************************/
OLESTATUS CALLBACK _loadds DllGetData(LPOLEOBJECT lpobj,
    OLECLIPFORMAT cfFormat, HANDLE FAR *lpHandle)
    {
    OLESTATUS olestatus;

    if(cfFormat == CF_BITMAP)
        if(*lpHandle = GetBitmap(lpobj))
            return OLE_WARN_DELETE_DATA;

    olestatus = (*DefGetData)(lpobj, cfFormat, lpHandle);

    if(olestatus == OLE_OK ¦¦ olestatus == OLE_ERROR_BLANK ¦¦
       olestatus == OLE_BUSY)
        return olestatus;

    if(cfFormat == CF_BITMAP)
        return OLE_ERROR_BLANK;

    return olestatus;
    }

/******************************************************************/
/* Function: DllQueryBounds                                       */
/* Purpose: Queries polygon window height and width.              */
/* Returns: OLESTATUS                                             */
/******************************************************************/
OLESTATUS CALLBACK _loadds DllQueryBounds(LPOLEOBJECT lpobj,
                                          LPRECT lprc)
```

continues

Listing 8.4. continued

```
    {
OLESTATUS olestatus;
HANDLE hData = NULL;
LPSTR lpData = NULL;

if((olestatus = (*DefQueryBounds)(lpobj, lprc)) == OLE_OK)
    if(lprc->top || lprc->bottom || lprc->right || lprc->left)
        return OLE_OK;

if((*DefGetData)(lpobj, cfNative, &hData) != OLE_OK)
    return olestatus;

if(!hData)
    return OLE_ERROR_BLANK;

if(!(lpData = GlobalLock(hData)))
    return OLE_ERROR_MEMORY;

lprc->left      = 0;
lprc->top       = 0;
lprc->right     = ((LPNATIVE) lpData)->nHiMetricWidth;
lprc->bottom    = -((LPNATIVE) lpData)->nHiMetricHeight;

GlobalUnlock(hData);
return OLE_OK;
    }

/********************************************************************/
/* Function: GetBitmap                                          */
/* Purpose: Gets bitmap format.                                 */
/* Returns: Handle to bitmap                                    */
/********************************************************************/
HBITMAP PASCAL GetBitmap(LPOLEOBJECT lpobj)
    {
    LPSTR       lpData = NULL;
    HANDLE      hData = NULL;
    HDC         hdc;
    HDC         hdcmem;
    RECT        rc = {0, 0, 0, 0};
    HBITMAP     hbitmap;
```

```
HBITMAP        holdbitmap;

if(((*lpobj->lpvtbl->GetData)(lpobj,
     cfNative, &hData) == OLE_OK)
        && (lpData = GlobalLock(hData)))
    {
    hdc = GetDC(NULL);
    hdcmem = CreateCompatibleDC(hdc);
    rc.right = ((LPNATIVE)lpData)->nWidth;
    rc.bottom = ((LPNATIVE)lpData)->nHeight;
    hbitmap = CreateCompatibleBitmap(hdc, rc.right, rc.bottom);
    holdbitmap = SelectObject(hdcmem, hbitmap);
    DrawPolygon(hdcmem, &rc, lpData);
    GlobalUnlock(hData);
    DeleteDC(hdcmem);
    ReleaseDC(NULL, hdc);
    return hbitmap;
    }

return NULL;
}

/********************************************************************/
/* Function: DrawPolygon                                          */
/* Purpose: Draws a polygon.                                      */
/********************************************************************/
VOID PASCAL DrawPolygon(HDC hdc, LPRECT lprc, LPSTR lpData)
    {
    char          buf[40];
    static  POINT tript[] =
    {-100, -100, 0, 100, 100, -100};
    static POINT rectpt[] =
    {-100, -80, -100, 80, 100, 80, 100, -80};
    static POINT pentpt[] =
    {-100, 0, -60, 100, 60, 100, 100, 0, 0, -100};
    static POINT hexpt[] =
    {-60, -100, -100, 0, -60, 100, 60, 100, 100, 0, 60, -100};
    static POINT heptpt[] =
    {-40, -100, -100, -40, -100, 40, 0, 100, 100, 40, 100, -40,
     40, -100};
```

continues

517

Listing 8.4. continued

```
static POINT octpt[] =
{ -40, -100, -100, -40, -100, 40, -40, 100, 40, 100, 100, 40,
 100, -40, 40, -100};
static POINT starpt[] =
{ -100, -100, -50, 10, -100, 50, -20, 50, 0, 100, 20, 50, 100,
 50, 50, 10, 100, -100, 0, -30, -100, -100};
HPEN      hpen;
hpen    = NULL;
hbrush  = NULL;

if(hbrush = GetBrush(((LPNATIVE)lpData)->idmColor - IDM_RED))
    SelectObject(hdc, hbrush);

hpen = CreatePen(PS_SOLID, (lprc->bottom-lprc->top) / 10,
                 0x00808080);

SelectObject(hdc, hpen);

SetMapMode(hdc, MM_ISOTROPIC);
SetWindowExt(hdc, 220, -220);
SetViewportExt(hdc, lprc->right, lprc->bottom);
SetWindowOrg(hdc, -110, 110);
SetPolyFillMode(hdc, ALTERNATE);

switch(((LPNATIVE)lpData)->idmPoly)
    {
    case IDM_TRIANGLE:
        Polygon(hdc, tript, sizeof(tript) / sizeof(POINT));
        break;

    case IDM_RECTANGLE:
        Polygon(hdc, rectpt, sizeof(rectpt) / sizeof(POINT));
        break;

    case IDM_PENTAGON:
        Polygon(hdc, pentpt, sizeof(pentpt) / sizeof(POINT));
        break;

    case IDM_HEXAGON:
        Polygon(hdc, hexpt, sizeof(hexpt) / sizeof(POINT));
        break;
```

```
        case IDM_HEPTAGON:
            Polygon(hdc, heptpt, sizeof(heptpt) / sizeof(POINT));
            break;

        case IDM_OCTAGON:
            Polygon(hdc, octpt, sizeof(octpt) / sizeof(POINT));
            break;

        case IDM_STAR:
            Polygon(hdc, starpt, sizeof(starpt) / sizeof(POINT));
            break;
        }

    lstrcpy(buf, "Handler-");
    lstrcat(buf, (LPSTR)((LPNATIVE)lpData)->szName);
    SetBkMode(hdc, TRANSPARENT);
    TextOut(hdc, lprc->left+5, (lprc->top+lprc->bottom)/2-10, buf,
            lstrlen(buf));

    SelectObject(hdc, GetStockObject(SYSTEM_FONT));
    DeleteObject(hpen);
    DeleteObject(hbrush);
    }

/******************************************************************/
/* Function: GetBrush                                           */
/* Purpose: Gets brush from table.                              */
/* Returns: Brush                                               */
/******************************************************************/
HBRUSH PASCAL GetBrush(int type)
    {
    if((type >= 0) && (type < MAXCOLORS))
        return CreateSolidBrush(rglColor[type]);
    else
        return NULL;
    }
```

Listing 8.5. The polyhand.def module definition file.

```
LIBRARY POLYHAND

DESCRIPTION "OLE Object Handler for Polygons Application"

EXETYPE WINDOWS

STUB 'WINSTUB.EXE'

CODE PRELOAD MOVABLE DISCARDABLE

DATA PRELOAD MOVABLE SINGLE

HEAPSIZE 0

EXPORTS
    WEP                     @1 RESIDENTNAME
    DllCreate               @2
    DllCreateFromClip       @3
    DllCreateFromFile       @4
    DllCreateFromTemplate   @5
    DllCreateLinkFromClip   @6
    DllCreateLinkFromFile   @7
    DllLoadFromStream       @8
    DllCopyToClipboard      @9
    DllDraw                 @10
    DllEnumFormats          @11
    DllGetData              @12
    DllQueryBounds          @13


IMPORTS
    DefCreate=olecli.DefCreate
    DefCreateFromClip=olecli.DefCreateFromClip
    DefCreateFromFile=olecli.DefCreateFromFile
    DefCreateFromTemplate=olecli.DefCreateFromTemplate
    DefCreateLinkFromClip=olecli.DefCreateLinkFromClip
    DefCreateLinkFromFile=olecli.DefCreateLinkFromFile
    DefLoadFromStream=olecli.DefLoadFromStream
```

Listing 8.6. The polyhand.rc resource file.

```
#include <ole.h>
```

Listing 8.7. The POLYHAND make file.

```
CC = cl -c -AS -Gsw -Od -W3 -Zpi -Fo$@

all: polyhand.dll

polyhand.h: resource.h

polyhand.res: polyhand.rc resource.h
  rc -r polyhand

polyhand.obj: polyhand.c polyhand.h
  $(CC) $*.c

polyhand.dll: polyhand.obj polyhand.def
    link /CO /MAP /NOD polyhand libentry, polyhand.dll,,\
    libw sdllcew, polyhand.def
    mapsym polyhand
    rc polyhand.res polyhand.dll
```

Summary

This chapter explored the basics of object handlers. You should now be able to develop object handlers to modify the default behavior of the client library for client applications interacting with your server applications. Although this may not be necessary for most server applications, you will have object handlers at your disposal. Keep in mind that you can access any of the methods found in the OLEOBJECTVTBL structure. Because these methods directly correspond to the OLE client API, your object handlers are limited only by the current OLE methods and your imagination.

A

OLE and
DDEML Usage

The object-linking and embedding API is based on the DDE protocol. It is possible to perform some DDE functions with the OLE API without using the DDEML or message-based DDE. It is also possible to implement OLE by using message-based DDE. This is not advisable, however, because the OLE standard will evolve and it will be much easier to change OLE applications that use the OLE API than to change an application that uses message-based DDE to provide OLE functionality.

In some instances an application may require extensive use of OLE and a somewhat limited use of DDE. In these instances, the OLE libraries can perform some of the basic DDE functions. The OLE libraries can initiate conversations based on application names and topic names. They can establish advise loops, request data, send data, and send commands. It is fairly easy to see what parts of the OLE API relate to DDE functions. For instance, `OleRequestData()` asks OLECLI to retrieve data from a server application in a specified format. The `OleExecute()` function sends DDE execute commands to a server for a specified object.

Because you can use the OLE libraries or the DDEML library to support DDE in applications, I have constructed a few guidelines for choosing the best method for implementation.

- If an application requires multiple simultaneous links that are updated regularly and frequently, the application should use the DDEML.

- If an application requires persistent embedding and linking of objects, activating embedded and linked objects, and creating objects and links from the clipboard, the application should use the OLE library.

- If an application requires the use of the OLE libraries as in the preceding item, and the application needs to perform only a minimal amount of DDE communications, the application should use the OLE library if it provides all the needed DDE features.

- When an application requires the use of the DDEML library and the OLE library as in the first two items, the application should use both the DDEML and OLE libraries.

There are special programming considerations when you use both the DDEML and the OLE libraries. Although the libraries can be used by the same application at the same time, the programmer must ensure that server applications which use both the DDEML and OLE libraries have different service names for OLE and DDE conversations.

This means that the server application must have a different application name for DDE conversations and a different service name for OLE conversations. If the application does not differentiate between the two, there is no way for the OLE libraries and the DDEML library to distinguish between the two types of conversations.

Index

D

M

Installing the Disk

Windows Programmer's Guide to OLE/DDE comes with a disk that includes all the code listings from the book. To install the disk, follow these steps:

1. Start Microsoft Windows.

2. Insert the disk in drive A.

3. From the File menu in the Program Manager, choose Run.

4. Type a:install and press Enter.

   (You can substitute another valid drive for drive A.)

If you want to install individual files, you can use the utility program EXPAND.EXE, which is found in the root directory of the install disk. The format for EXPAND.EXE is

```
EXPAND <sourcefile> <destinationfile>
```

Example:

```
EXPAND CLIENT.EX C:\OLEDDE\CLIENT.EXE
```

Licensing Agreement